The Basics of Sociology

**Recent titles in
Basics of the Social Sciences**

The Basics of Western Philosophy
Eugene Kelly

The Basics of Economics
David E. O'Connor

THE BASICS OF SOCIOLOGY

Kathy S. Stolley

Basics of the Social Sciences

GREENWOOD PRESS
Westport, Connecticut • London

Library of Congress Cataloging-in-Publication Data

Stolley, Kathy S.
   The basics of sociology / Kathy S. Stolley.
      p. cm.—(Basics of the social sciences)
   Includes bibliographical references and index.
   ISBN 0-313-32387-9 (alk. paper)
      1. Sociology. 2. Sociology—History. 3. Sociologists—Biography.
   4. Internet—Social aspects. 5. Sociology—Vocational guidance.
   I. Title. II. Series.
HM585.S77   2005
301—dc22   2004044863

British Library Cataloguing in Publication Data is available.

Library of Congress Catalog Card Number: 2004044863
ISBN: 0–313–32387–9

First published in 2005

Greenwood Press, 88 Post Road West, Westport, CT 06881
An imprint of Greenwood Publishing Group, Inc.
www.greenwood.com

Printed in the United States of America

The paper used in this book complies with the
Permanent Paper Standard issued by the National
Information Standards Organization (Z39.48–1984).

10   9   8   7   6   5   4   3   2   1

To Billy

and

To Mrs. Elkins, Grade 3,
who told our class,
"Someday we'll get to read a book that Kathy wrote."

Contents

Contents

Contents

Contents

Figures and Tables

FIGURES

TABLES

Figures and Tables

Sociology Timeline of Selected Events and Influential Publications

1200s   *Wen Hsien T'ung K'ao* (*General Study of the Literary Remains*), Chinese historian Ma Tuan-Lin

1300s   Ibn Khaldun conducts studies of Arab society

1790   First U.S. Census conducted

1798   *First Essay on Population,* Thomas Malthus

1800s   Scholars begin studying how society actually is and how society "works"

1838   Term *sociology* first used in *Positive Philosophy,* Auguste Comte

1846   *The Holy Family,* the first book marking the collaboration of Karl Marx and Friedrich Engels

1848   *The Manifesto of the Communist Party,* Karl Marx

1853   Harriet Martineau translates and edits Comte's *Positive Philosophy*

1855   Term *demographie* coined by Achille Guillard

1859   *On the Origin of Species,* Charles R. Darwin

1867   *Capital: A Critique of Political Economy,* Karl Marx

1876   *The Criminal Man,* Cesare Lombroso

1876   First course in the United States identified as "sociology" is taught by Yale University's William Graham Sumner

1887   *Community and Society (Gemeinschaft and Gesellschaft),* Ferdinand Toennies

1889   Emile Durkheim establishes and becomes editor of *L'Annee Sociologique*

1889   Hull House social settlement founded in Chicago by Jane Addams with Ellen Gates Starr

1892   The University of Chicago establishes the first graduate department of sociology in the United States

1892   Albion Small appointed the first professorship in sociology in the United States, at the University of Chicago

1894   First American textbook on sociology: *Introduction to the Study of Sociology,* Albion Small and George E. Vincent

1895   *The Rules of the Sociological Method,* Emile Durkheim

Sociology Timeline of Selected Events and Influential Publications

1896   *The Crowd: A Study of the Popular Mind*, Gustave Le Bon
1897   *Suicide: A Study in Sociology*, Emile Durkheim
1898   *The Principles of Sociology*, Herbert Spencer
1899   *The Philadelphia Negro: A Social Study*, W.E.B. Du Bois
1902   *Human Nature and the Social Order*, Charles Horton Cooley
1904–5 *The Protestant Ethic and the Spirit of Capitalism*, Max Weber
1905   American Sociological Society established, later becoming the American Sociological Association (ASA)
1906   *Folkways: A Study of the Sociological Importance of Usages, Manners, Customs, Mores, and Morals*, William Graham Sumner
1906   *The Protestant Ethic and the Spirit of Capitalism*, Max Weber
1910   Most colleges and universities offering sociology courses, although not in separate departments
1911   First Ph.D. in sociology awarded to a person of color, Richard Robert Wright, by the University of Pennsylvania
1911–12 First sociology classes taught in high schools
1914   *Economy and Society*, Max Weber
1923   *The Ego and the Id*, Sigmund Freud
1928   The Thomas Theorem is expressed in *The Child in America: Behavior Problems and Programs*, W. I. Thomas and Dorothy S. Thomas
1934   *Mind, Self, and Society*, George Herbert Mead
1936   Literary Digest sends out 10 million surveys and predicts presidential race incorrectly; Gallup uses better sampling and accurately predicts the race with a smaller sample
1937   Term *symbolic interactionism* introduced by Herbert Blumer
1943   *Street Corner Society*, William Foote Whyte
1944   *An American Dilemma*, Gunnar Myrdal
1951   *The Social System*, Talcott Parsons
1957   *Social Theory and Social Structure*, Robert K. Merton
1959   *The Sociological Imagination*, C. Wright Mills
1959   *Presentation of Self in Everyday Life*, Erving Goffman
1962   *The Structure of Scientific Revolutions*, Thomas Kuhn
1963   The Center for Culture and Technology (now the McLuhan Program in Culture and Technology) established at the University of Toronto and directed by Marshall McLuhan
1963   The first account of Stanley Milgram's obedience studies appears in the *Journal of Abnormal and Social Psychology*
1963   *The Outsiders: Studies in the Sociology of Deviance*, Howard S. Becker
1963   *Stigma: Notes on the Social Organization of Spoiled Identity*, Erving Goffman
1964   Napoleon Chagnon begins his fieldwork among the Yanomamo people
1964   *Exchange and Power in Social Life*, Peter M. Blau
1966   *The Social Construction of Reality*, Peter Berger and Thomas Luckmann
1967   *Studies in Ethnomethodology*, Harold Garfinkel
1967   *The Levittowners: Life and Politics in a New Suburban Community*, Herbert Gans
1967   *The American Occupational System*, Peter M. Blau and Otis Dudley Duncan
1968   Jessie Bernard attends her first feminist meeting

1969   *Causes of Delinquency,* Travis Hirschi
1970   *The Social Reality of Crime,* Richard Quinney
1971   First ASA Code of Ethics becomes effective
1971   Philip Zimbardo conducts the Stanford Prison Experiment
1974   National Research Act mandates Institutional Review Boards (IRBs)
1975   *Sociobiology: The New Synthesis,* Edward O. Wilson
1976   *The Modern World-System,* Immanuel Wallerstein
1977   *Man and Women of the Corporation,* Rosabeth Moss Kanter
1978   Clinical Sociology Association established (today the Sociological Practice Association)
1979   Society for Applied Sociology founded
1982   *Neofuntionalism,* Jeffrey Alexander
1984   Certified Clinical Sociologist Program for practicing sociologists established by the Clinical Sociology Association (today designated as Certified Sociological Practitioner)
1986   *The Constitution of Society: Outline of the Theory of Structuration,* Anthony Giddens
1987   *The Truly Disavantaged,* William Julius Wilson
1990   *Black Feminist Thought: Knowledge, Consciousness, and the Politics of Empowerment,* Patricia Hill Collins
1992   *The McDonaldization of Society,* George Ritzer
1998   *The Women Founders: Sociology and Social Theory, 1830–1930,* Patricia Madoo Lengermann and Jill Niebrugge-Brantly

CHAPTER 1

Introduction

The study of sociology starts from the basic premise that human life is social life (Rebach and Bruhn 2001, 5). Most of us are constantly involved in interactions with other human beings. From the families we are born into, through school, work, and play; retirements; and even the gatherings that memorialize our deaths, we spend our lives within a tapestry woven of interlocking social arrangements. Sociology focuses on these arrangements, including how they are created, how they change, and how they impact our lives, opportunities, and options (Rebach and Bruhn 2001, 5).

The word *sociology* itself actually derives from the Latin word *socius* (companion) and the Greek word *logos* (study of). Thus, sociology is most literally the study of companionship (Abercrombie, Hill, and Turner 2000, 333). A textbook definition often expands that literal definition of **sociology** to read something close to *the scientific study of the development, structure, interaction, and collective behavior of social relationships*. But so what? What does that definition actually mean? Why is sociology important? Why should anyone study sociology? What does sociology offer to us in our personal lives? And what does it offer to wider society?

This book answers those basic questions. It introduces core concepts in sociology and illustrates how the field is dynamic and relevant. Throughout, it explains how those who engage in the study of sociology understand the relationships and interactions that make up our social worlds, worlds that include "everything that constitutes the collective life of groups of people . . . their economics, their politics, their shared mental lives, their cultures, and more" (Lemert 2001, 5–6).

The study of sociology encompasses the diversity of these social worlds, ranging from intimate, one-to-one exchanges to impersonal gatherings of large numbers of people. The focus can be as small as couples, or it can be much larger. It can include families, communities, entire cities, and even nations, or relationships and interactions among nations. Additionally, "virtual" social worlds such as those existing on the Internet are also included in sociological studies.

People who practice sociology are called **sociologists.** In his classic work *Invitation to Sociology,* Peter Berger describes a sociologist as someone who is "intensively, endlessly, shamelessly interested" in the doings of humans (1963, 18). To the sociologist, the social world is "a living laboratory [and] a moving picture that never stops" (Rebach and Bruhn 2001, 7). Because any aspect of the social world is fair game for sociological study, the potential topics of study are limitless. Simply put, "being a sociologist means never having to be bored" (Kimmel 1998, 8).

A series of brief biographical profiles throughout the book introduces notable social scientists. These biographies provide some insight into the lives and work of many sociologists who have been, and continue to be, influential in shaping the field. However, many important contributions have been made by people who are not known as sociologists. Several of the biographies profile individuals who have made important contributions to the field of sociology but were trained in, or claim, other disciplines.

Additionally, each chapter contains a section that includes the types of jobs available for those interested in sociology. Training in sociology provides an excellent background for a variety of careers. Chapter 11 describes in more detail how to prepare for a career in sociology and career opportunities for sociologists. Each chapter concludes with a section that suggests additional resources (both print and online) for those interested in further information.

WHAT SOCIOLOGY OFFERS

A sociological look at the world provides a number of unique benefits and perspectives.

Sociology provides an understanding of social issues and patterns of behavior. It helps us identify the social rules that govern our lives. Sociologists study how these rules are created, maintained, changed, passed between generations, and shared between people living in various parts of the world. They also study what happens when these rules are broken.

Sociology helps us understand the workings of the social systems within which we live our lives. Sociologists put our interactions with others into a social context. This means they look not only at behaviors and relationships, but also how the larger world we live in influences these things. **Social structures** (*the way society is organized around the regulated ways people interrelate and organize social life*) and **social processes** (*the way society operates*) are at work shaping our lives in ways that often go unrecognized. Because of this perspective, sociologists will often say that, as individuals, we are *social products.*

Even though we recognize their existence, these structures and processes may "appear to people in the course of daily life as through a mysterious fog" (Lemert 2001, 6). Sociologists strive to bring these things out of the fog, to reveal and study them, and to examine and explain their interrelationships and their impacts on individuals and groups. By describing and explaining these social arrangements and how they shape our lives, sociologists help us to make sense of the world around us and better understand ourselves.

Sociology helps us understand why we perceive the world the way we do. We are inundated with messages in a variety of forms about how we, and the world around us, both are and should be. These messages come in forms as diverse as guidance from parents and teachers, laws handed down by religious and political entities, and advertisements ranging from pitches for athletic shoes to feeding hungry children. Sociology helps us examine the types of messages we are constantly receiving, their source, how and why they influence us, and our own roles in producing, perpetuating, and changing them.

Sociology helps us identify what we have in common within, and between, cultures and societies. Sociologists know that, although people in different parts of the city, country, or world dress differently, speak differently, and have many different beliefs and customs, many of the same types of social forces are at work shaping their lives. This is an especially important perspective in a world where media headlines are often accused of focusing on divisive issues. Sociologists look for what social structure and processes mean for various groups. They look at how various groups shape, and are impacted, by society. Sociologists can help groups find common concerns, understand other groups' perspectives, and find ways to work together rather than work at odds with each other.

Sociology helps us understand why and how society changes. Obviously, the social world is constantly changing. This change has been a major interest to sociologists from the beginning of the discipline. However, many sociologists believe that sociology should not stop with only explaining society and how and why the world changes. They argue that sociologists also have an obligation to act, using their unique skills and perspectives to work to improve the world. Sociology, they argue, is a "field of inquiry simultaneously concerned with understanding, explaining, criticizing, and *improving* (italics mine) the human condition" (Restivo 1991, 4). Armed with a sociological perspective, we can more effectively take action if we don't like what is happening. We can better participate in shaping the future for ourselves and for others.

Sociology provides us theoretical perspectives within which to frame these understandings and research methods that allow us to study social life scientifically. Sociology is a social science. That means sociologists work to understand society in very structured, disciplined ways. Like scientists who study the physical world, sociologists follow scientific guidelines that incorporate an assortment of theories and methods that provide for accuracy in gathering, processing, and making sense of information.

In the case of sociology, theories focus on how social relationships operate. They provide a way of explaining these relationships. Scientific methods provide ways of generating accurate research results. The major theoretical perspectives sociologists utilize are discussed in detail in chapter 2. The ways that sociologists conduct scientific research are discussed in chapter 10.

Sociology is not just common sense. Results of sociological research may be unexpected. They often show that things are not always, or even usually, what they initially seem. "People who like to avoid shocking discoveries, who prefer to believe that society is just what they were taught in Sunday School, who like the safety of the rules and maxims of what Alfred Schultz . . . has called 'the world-taken-for-granted', should stay away from sociology" (Berger 1963, 24).

This challenge means that sociological findings are often at odds with so-called common sense, or those things that "everybody knows." What we think of as common sense, or something that everybody knows, is actually based on our own experiences and the ideas and stereotypes we hold. This gives us a very limited view of how the larger world actually is. Taking a sociological perspective requires that we look beyond our individual experiences to better understand everyday life (Straus 1994). It allows us to look for the social forces that impact our lives and form those experiences. Once we have a solid understanding of these forces, we can better address them.

For example, a common perception is that suicide is an act of those with individual psychological problems. However, an early sociological study of suicide by Emile Durkheim (1858–1917) revealed the importance of social factors, including relationships within church and family, in suicide (Durkheim 1966). (Durkheim is profiled in chapter 10, and his research on suicide is covered in more detail there as well.) Another common perception is that crimes are always committed by some "criminal element," identifiable as troublemakers. In his textbook on social problems, Thomas Sullivan (1973, 296) introduces the chapter on crime by arguing that this is a far too simplistic view of criminality. He notes a study (Zimbardo 1973) in which researchers abandoned a car on a New York City street and watched from a hidden position to see if it was vandalized and by whom. The vandals discovered by the researchers included a family, a person with a toddler in a stroller, and many people who were well dressed and interacted with people who passed by during their activities.

HISTORY OF SOCIOLOGY

Sociology is rooted in the works of philosophers, including Plato (427–347 B.C.), Aristotle (384–322 B.C.), and Confucius (551–479 B.C.). Some other early scholars also took perspectives that were sociological. Chinese historian Ma Tuan-Lin developed, in the thirteenth century, a sociological history by looking at the social factors influencing history in his general-knowledge encyclopedia *Wen Hsien T'ung K'ao* (*General Study of the Literary Remains*). Ibn Khaldun (1332–1406), profiled below, conducted studies of Arab society (Restivo 1991, 18–19).

Enlightenment thinkers also helped set the stage for the sociologists that would follow. The Enlightenment "was the first time in history that thinkers tried to provide *general explanations* of the social world. They were able to detach themselves, at least in principle, from expounding some existing ideology and to attempt to lay down general principles that explained social life" (Collins 1994, 17). Writers of this period included a range of well-known philosophers, such as John Locke; David Hume; Voltaire (the pseudonym of François-Marie Arouet); Immanuel Kant; Charles-Louis de Secondat, Baron de La Brède et de Montesquieu; Thomas Hobbes; and Jean-Jacques Rousseau.

As Macionis (1995, 12) explains to introductory students, scholars have been interested in the nature of society throughout history. They typically focused on what the ideal society would be like. During the 1800s, however, scholars began studying how society actually is and how social arrangements actually operate (how society "works"). Armed with this knowledge, they felt they could better attack social problems and bring about social change (Collins 1994, 42). These scholars became the first sociologists.

The term *sociology* was coined by French philosopher Auguste Comte (1798–1857), who would become known as the "Father of Sociology." Comte is profiled below. He first publicly used the term in his work *Positive Philosophy* (1896, orig. 1838; Abercrombie, Hill, and Turner 2000, 67). Originally an engineering student, Comte became secretary and pupil to French social philosopher Claude Henri de Rouvroy Comte de Saint-Simon (1760–1825). Saint-Simon was an advocate for scientific and social reform. He advocated applying scientific principles to learn how society is organized. Armed with this knowledge, he believed he could ascertain how best to change, and govern, society to address social problems such as poverty.

Comte saw history as divided into three intellectual stages. The first, or *theological,* stage included the medieval period in which society was seen as reflecting the will of a deity. The second, or *metaphysical,* stage arose during the Enlightenment and focused on forces of "nature," rather than God, to explain social events. Comte considered his own time period the third stage, which he termed the *positivistic,* or *scientific,* stage.

During Comte's lifetime, scientists were learning more about the laws that govern the physical world. For example, in the area of physics, Sir Isaac Newton (1641–1727) had developed the law of gravity. Advances were also being made in other natural sciences, such as biology. Comte felt that science could also be used to study the social world. Just as there are testable facts regarding gravity and other natural laws, Comte thought that scientific analyses could also discover the laws governing our social lives. It was in this context that Comte introduced the concept of **positivism** to sociology—*a way to understand the social world based on scientific facts.* He believed that, with this new understanding, people could build a better future. He envisioned a process of social change in which sociologists played crucial roles in guiding society.

Other events of that time period also influenced the development of sociology. The nineteenth and twentieth centuries were times of many social upheavals and changes in the social order that interested the early sociologists. As George Ritzer (1988, 6–12) notes, the political revolutions sweeping Europe during the eighteenth and nineteenth centuries led to a focus on social change and the establishment of social order that still concerns sociologists today. Many early sociologists were also concerned with the Industrial Revolution and rise of capitalism and socialism. Additionally, the growth of cities and religious transformations were causing many changes in people's lives.

These "early founders of sociology all had a vision of using sociology" (Turner 1998, 250). Sharing Comte's belief, many early sociologists came from other disciplines and made significant efforts to call attention to social concerns and bring about social change. In Europe, for example, economist and philosopher Karl Marx (1818–83), profiled in chapter 2, teamed with wealthy industrialist Friedrich Engels (1820–95), profiled in chapter 7, to address class inequality. Writing during the Industrial Revolution, when many factory owners were lavishly wealthy and many factory workers despairingly poor, they attacked the rampant inequalities of the day and focused on the role of capitalist economic structures in perpetuating these inequalities. In Germany, Max Weber (1864–1920), profiled in chapter 2, was active in politics. In France, Emile Durkheim advocated for educational reforms.

In the United States, social worker and sociologist Jane Addams (1860–1935), profiled in chapter 11, became an activist on behalf of poor immigrants. Addams established Chicago's Hull House, a settlement house that provided community services such as kindergarten and day care, an employment bureau, and libraries. It also provided cultural activities, including an art gallery, music and art classes, and America's first Little Theater. Louis Wirth (1897–1952), profiled in chapter 8, built child-guidance clinics. He applied sociology to understand how social influences impacted children's behavioral problems and how children could be helped by using this knowledge. During World War II, sociologists worked to improve the lives of soldiers by studying soldiers' morale and attitudes as well as the effectiveness of training materials (Kallen 1995).

Sociologists are also responsible for some of the now familiar aspects of our everyday lives. For example, sociologist William Foote Whyte (1914–2000), profiled in chapter 11, improved restaurant service by developing the spindles that waitstaff in many diners use to submit food orders to the kitchen (Porter 1962). Robert K. Merton (1910–2003), profiled in chapter 2, developed the concept of what would become the focus group, now widely used in the business world. Sociological perspectives are also the basis of many concepts and terms we use on a daily basis. Lawyers plead "extenuating circumstances" on their clients' behalf, an acknowledgment of the sociological position that social forces influence human behavior; to talk about "fighting the system" acknowledges that social structures exist and influence our lives (Babbie 1996).

Sociologists have also been actively involved throughout the civil rights movement. Ida B. Wells-Barnett (1862–1931) who is profiled below, published and spoke out against lynching. W.E.B. Du Bois (1868–1963), profiled in chapter 7, was involved for most of a century in studying race and social activism. Gunnar Myrdal's *An American Dilemma* (1944) focused public attention on race. The voter-rights efforts of Charles G. Gomillion in the 1940s and 1950s were instrumental in the U.S. Supreme Court decision that defeated gerrymandering that had excluded almost all Macon County blacks from voting (Smith and Killian 1990, 113).

Although they have not traditionally received the recognition of their white male counterparts, women and sociologists of color have made significant contributions to the discipline since its founding. In recent years, efforts have been undertaken to reinvigorate the voices of these "lost" sociologists. What we know about their lives and works shows some truly outstanding accomplishments. For example, Comte's *Positive Philosophy* (1896, orig. 1838) was translated into English by Harriet Martineau (1802–76), who is profiled below. Comte was so pleased with the results of her translation that he had her abridgment retranslated back into French. Martineau was a prolific writer and bestselling author in her own right on a variety of social issues. Her work earned her recognition as the first female sociologist and "Mother of Sociology."

These early women and scholars of color were working in a social context in which women and blacks were often denied education and faced other types of discrimination. Most were trained outside the field. The first Ph.D. in sociology was not awarded to a person of color until 1911, when Richard Robert Wright received his doctorate at the University of Pennsylvania. Many of these early sociologists were active in fighting for a number of social causes. For example, many supported the suffragist movement. Also, black sociologists often "sought not simply to investigate and interpret social life, but to redress the conditions affecting the lives of African Americans" (Young and Deskins 2001, 447).

Today, women and persons of color continue to make important contributions to the discipline and beyond. Just among those individuals profiled in this book are Dorothy Smith (profiled in chapter 10) who has changed the way sociologists think about the world and the way they conduct research. Rosabeth Moss Kanter (profiled in chapter 5) has become an internationally renowned name in studying and improving organizations. Coramae Richey Mann (profiled in chapter 6) has challenged the criminal-justice system and its treatment of minorities, youth, and women. William Julius Wilson (profiled in chapter 7) has challenged thinking on class, race, and poverty. Patricia Hill Collins (profiled in chapter 2) has increased our understanding of how race, class, and gender together all have social consequences in our world.

SOCIOLOGISTS IN SOCIETY

Contemporary sociologists are continuing the early sociologists' tradition of using sociology to make differences in diverse areas of society. Many sociologists are, of course, teachers and researchers. However, sociologists are actively using their skills throughout society in ways that extend well beyond academics and the classroom. Some sociologists, called *applied* or *clinical* sociologists, use their skills to find answers to practical problems. For example, they apply their unique perspectives on conflict and social life to finding new ways to assist in mediation and dispute resolution (Diaz 2001; Rebach 2001), improving community services (e.g., finding ways to extend phone service to the speech-disabled [Segalman 1998]), improving help for victims of violence (Kilpatrick, Resick, and Williams 2001), or even in designing more effective social settings for human interactions from child-care centers to offices to night clubs (DuBois 2001). Some sociologists are also starting to work in high-tech fields (Guice 1999). Sociologists are even working with scholars in a variety of disciplines on future studies (Bell 1997; Masini 2000; Shostak 2003).

People trained in sociology are found across society, even though they are not always famous for being sociologists. Peter Dreier (2001) has put together a "Sociology All-Star Team" to demonstrate the widely varied activities of a number of well-known people who majored in sociology. His list includes entertainment personalities Regis Philbin, Robin Williams, Dan Aykroyd, and Debra Winger, and sex therapist Dr. Ruth Westheimer. Well-known sociology majors in the world of sports include NBA all-star Alonzo Mourning, NFL Hall of Fame quarterback Joe Theismann, and sportscaster Ahmad Rashad. Olympic track and field gold medalist Gail Devers also holds a sociology degree (Gail Devers).

Beyond their accomplishments in the entertainment and sports arenas, sociologists have made many world-changing contributions to society. Saul Bellow won the 1976 Nobel Prize in Literature, and Jane Addams and Emily Balch both won the Nobel Peace Prize. The civil rights leader Martin Luther King Jr. and the Reverend Jesse Jackson studied sociology. So did Frances Perkins, an industrial sociologist who fought to improve conditions in early-twentieth-century textile mills. Perkins became the first female member of a presidential cabinet, serving as secretary of labor under President Franklin Roosevelt. Ronald Reagan, 40th president of the United States, also had a sociology degree (Dreier 2001). A number of other notable politicians, including Shirley Chisolm and Maxine Waters, studied sociology. The range of careers for sociologists, the job skills sociologists have, and the training they receive is discussed in more detail in chapter 11.

THE SOCIOLOGICAL IMAGINATION

Sociologists talk about *the connection between learning to understand and then change society* as being the **sociological imagination.** C. Wright Mills (1916–62), a colorful and controversial professor at New York's Columbia University who is profiled below, coined this term. The sociological imagination is the ability to see the interrelationships between biography and history, or the connections between our individual lives and larger social forces at work shaping our lives (e.g., racism or political agendas). Mills urged us to understand that our own personal fortunes or troubles (e.g., gain/loss of a job, divorce) must be understood in terms of larger public issues (e.g., the health of the economy, societal changes in the institution of marriage). They cannot be fully understood outside of this social context.

Mills opens his well-known classic *The Sociological Imagination* by noting how intertwined social forces and personal lives are:

When a society is industrialized, a peasant becomes a worker; a feudal lord is liquidated or becomes a businessman. When classes rise or fall, a man is employed or unemployed; when the rate of investment goes up or down, a man takes a new heart or goes broke. When wars happen, an insurance salesman becomes a rocket launcher; a store clerk, a radar man; a wife lives alone; a child grows up without a father. *Neither the life of an individual nor the history of a society can be understood without understanding both.* (1959, 3; italics mine)

Without a sociological perspective, we might tend to think of these personal experiences primarily in individual terms. We might locate both the source of a problem and the solution to that problem as lying within individuals. Unemployment, for example, is an individual problem for the unemployed person that may be due to his or her characteristics such as work ethic, job skills, or opportunities. If this person is one of few unemployed in a city, then employment might be secured if these factors change at the individual level: the person decides to get up when the alarm rings and work hard enough to keep a job, gain job training, or move to a different town where there is a demand for their existing skills. However, when the unemployment rate soars and large numbers of people are unemployed, something is clearly amiss in the structure of the society that results in inadequate employment opportunities. Although there will certainly still be lazy or unskilled people among the unemployed, millions of cases of unemployment cannot be explained at these individual levels, and individual solutions will not solve the problem. Working harder, getting more training, or seeking different work venues will not produce jobs when the economy is poor and there are no jobs to be had. As Mills puts it, "The very structure of opportunities has collapsed" (1959, 9). Finding solutions to these large-scale problems requires examining the structure of society (Mills 1959).

Mills felt that developing a sociological imagination will help us to avoid becoming "victims" of social forces and better control our own lives. By understanding how social mechanisms operate, we can better work to bring about change and influence history.

SOCIOLOGY AS AN ACADEMIC DISCIPLINE

Economics was the first social science. It grew out of the practical application of gathering factual information for business and taxation during the 1700s. In the early 1800s, history developed as an academic discipline. Psychology then grew out of medicine, philosophy, and pedagogy. Anthropology developed from the European discoveries of the Americas, Africa, and Asia. Sociology is one of the youngest academic disciplines, established as a distinct field of study in Europe only during the 1800s. It was at first indistinguishable from political science, and most early sociologists wrote about political issues outside of academics (Collins 1994, 30–32).

The earliest sociologists discussed throughout this book came to sociology from a variety of disciplines. Emile Durkheim and Max Weber had studied law. Charles Horton Cooley (1864–1929), profiled in chapter 4, was an economist. Lester Ward (1841–1913), profiled in chapter 10, was a biologist. Georg Simmel (1858–1918), profiled in chapter 5, was a philosopher. Even today, sociologists come to the discipline from varying backgrounds, such as Andrew M. Greeley (1928–), a Catholic priest turned sociologist profiled in chapter 10.

The U.S. growth of academic sociology coincided with the establishment and upgrading of many universities that were including a new focus on graduate departments and curricula on "modern subjects" (Collins 1994, 41). In 1876, Yale University's William Graham Sumner (1840–1910), profiled in chapter 3, taught the first course identified as "sociology" in the United States. The University of Chicago established the first graduate department of sociology in the United States in 1892. By 1910, most colleges and universities were offering sociology courses, although not in separate departments. Thirty years later, most of these schools had established sociology departments (Bloom 2002, 25–37). Sociology was first taught in high schools in 1911–12 (Grier 1971; cited in DeCesare 2002, 303).

Sociology was also growing in Germany and France during this period. Britain was later in developing sociology as core academic area. However, the discipline in Europe suffered great setbacks as a result of World Wars I and II. The "Nazis hated sociology," and many sociologists were killed or fled Germany and France between 1933 and the end of World War II (Collins 1994, 46). As Erwin Scheuch notes, it is "easier to name sociologists who did not emigrate as the Nazi regime came to power than to list the émigrés" (2000, 1075). After World War II, sociologists returned to Germany influenced by their studies in America. The result was that American sociologists became the world leaders in theory and research for many years.

The 1970s saw a "vigorous expansion" in British and European academic circles (Collins 1994), as well as in sociology around the world. For example, most German universities now offer sociology degrees up to doctorate level, and there are a variety of institutes for academic, market, and social research (Scheuch 2000). Sociology in Japan was first taught in the late 1800s, largely as a German import. Since the 1960s, American sociology has been influential there (Sasaki 2000). Indian sociology derives from work of British civil servants and missionaries that were interested in understanding people to better conduct business and evangelization activities. Predating sociology, Thomas Robert Malthus (1766–1834), a clergyman and political economist profiled in chapter 8, was a professor at the East India Company's college. Formal teaching of sociology started in India in the early 1900s. Sociology is now a core subject at many colleges and universities there, and several Indian research institutes now exist (Shah 2000).

Sociology has grown into a diverse and dynamic discipline, experiencing a proliferation of specialty areas. The American Sociological Association (ASA) was formed as the American Sociological Society in 1905 with 115 members (Rhoades 1981). By the end of 2004, it had grown to almost 14,000 members and more than 40 "sections" covering specific areas of interest. Many other countries also have large national sociology organizations. The Interna-

Table 1.1
The Sociological Focus as Compared with Other Social Sciences

Social Science Discipline	Discipline Focus	Shared Interests with Sociology	Differential Focus Taken by Sociology
Economics	Structure of material goods, financial markets, and transactions	Social consequences of production and distribution	Focuses beyond a single structure
History	Context of past events/relationships	Establishing social contexts	Focuses on the present
Political Science	Group competition for power and scarce resources in the context of politics or government	Patterns and consequences of government	Focuses beyond a single structure
Anthropology	Variations between cultures	Patterns of culture; types and consequences of interactions and communication	Focuses on industrialized rather than pre-industrial societies
Psychology	Individualistic perspective	Adjustments to life situations	Influences external to the individual

Source: Henslin (2001c, 11–12).

tional Sociological Association (ISA) boasted more than 3,300 members in 2004 from 91 different countries. The ISA sponsored research committees covering more than 50 different areas of interest, covering topics as diverse as children, aging, families, law, emotions, sexuality, religion, mental health, peace and war, and work (see chapter 11). There is even a fast-growing subfield of sociology that focuses on the relationships between humans and other animals (e.g., Alger and Alger 2003, Arluke and Sanders, 1996, Irvine, 2004). Additionally, courses on animals and society are increasingly being included in college and university offerings.

Sociology grew out of, and overlaps with, many disciplines. However, it also extends the boundaries of many traditional disciplines. As shown in table 1.1, sociologist James M. Henslin (2001c: 11–12) contrasts sociology with the other social sciences.

Many concepts that originated in sociology have been adopted by other disciplines. Sociologists have, likewise, adopted concepts from other disciplines. For example, Herbert Spencer (1820–1903), one of the earliest sociologists, profiled in chapter 2, used the concept of *structure* that is now used in anthropology and political science (Dogan 2000). Sociologists also work with specialists in other disciplines. Sociology provides much of the theory and research applied by social workers in their practice. The field of social psychology has even developed that combines the individualistic perspective of psychology and the focus on interaction and social influence of sociology.

SOCIOLOGY IN A CHANGING WORLD

Changes in our social world have required sociologists to focus attention in new ways. Among these changes are the growth of internationally connected systems and the technologies that increasingly allow our interactions to be conducted in ways other than face to face (e.g., the Internet and e-mail). Although more than 6 billion people now live on Earth, many sociologists and others have argued that the advent of jet airliners, telephones, the Internet, and around-the-clock news services beamed by satellite around the world have made the world a smaller place, at least in a social sense.

They often argue that a process of globalization is at work. With **globalization,** *geographical constraints on social and cultural patterns are diminishing, and people are becoming increasingly aware of those changes* (M. Waters 2001). Globalization is demonstrated through events as diverse as the growing popularity of soccer in the United States—a sport largely imported from outside—the demand for American movies, blue jeans, and athletic shoes around the world, the North American Free Trade Agreement (NAFTA), and even the attacks of September 11, 2001. Other terms that refer to forms of globalization include the *world-economy, world-market,* and *world-system.* These terms are often used to refer to the economic aspects of globalization. Sociologists have been studying these networks at least since the early 1970s (Chase-Dunn and Grimes 1995, 387–88). The world-systems perspective is discussed in more detail in chapter 7.

Globalization is a controversial issue. The literature on the topic is steadily growing, and a range of diverse perspectives abound. Debates even surround when the process began. The dawn of history? Trade routes centuries ago? When Europeans traveled to the Americas? Colonialism? The post–World War II era? Whether the ultimate impact of globalization is positive, negative, or both is also a matter of contention (e.g., Barber 1996; Guillen 2001; Gros 2003). However, regardless of their position on these issues, globalization requires that sociologists expand their traditional purviews across societies, cultures, and national borders by examining these interrelationships that make the social world increasingly complex (e.g., Giddens 2000). Sociologist Anthony Giddens, well known for his work on globalization, is profiled below.

The ways in which technologies change social interaction has long been an interest for researchers. Communication and information technologies contribute to globalization and increase the complexity of our social lives. They also often lead to unanticipated effects. For example, the telephone started its "social life" as a business tool and only later became a tool for other types of social interaction (Fischer 1992).

In recent years, sociologists have given much attention to the innumerable implications of the Internet to society. From its initial use by a relatively small, computer-literate population of users, the Internet grew rapidly beginning in the 1990s (Abbate 1999; Castells 2001). It is now used for social interaction, business and commerce (legitimate and illegitimate), education, research, news, propaganda, entertainment, and more. There is widespread agreement among sociologists and others that the Internet and other communication technologies are vastly changing society. There is, however, less agreement about whether those changes are positive, negative, or a combination of both (DiMaggio et al. 2001, 308). Sociologists have now expanded their interests to include the myriad online social activities and behaviors to which these technologies have given rise. The following chapters give attention to these areas.

BIOGRAPHIES

Auguste Comte

Auguste Comte (1798–1857) was born in the French city of Montpellier. Comte, described as "small, delicate, and subject to many illnesses" (Coser 1977, 18) was an excellent student and exhibited an early proficiency in mathematics. He even planned to teach mathematics, but found that the income was unsatisfactory (Marvin 1965, 35).

Comte was considered a leader among his classmates. However, his usual behavior was "insubordinate and insolent behavior toward the school authorities," and he was constantly revolting against authority (Coser 1977, 15). Comte was also involved in revolutionary activities while a student, which ultimately resulted in his dismissal, and he never completed a university degree. He did, however, lecture for a period at the prestigious Ecole Polytechnique in Paris, eventually losing that position after criticizing the institution.

Comte's intellectual life can be divided into three periods (Marvin 1965, 43–46). The first period encompassed six years he spent with the much older Claude Henri de Rouvroy Comte de Saint-Simon. Starting as Saint-Simon's secretary and later his collaborator, Comte worked with Saint-Simon even during periods when the elder mentor could not pay him. Their collaboration ended in 1824 due to a quarrel over whose name would appear on a major publication and developing intellectual differences. The rift between the two men was never repaired (Coser 1977, 15).

It was during the second period that Comte produced most of his intellectual writings. It is also the period during which he became known for developing the scientific view of positivism. He thought sociology could draw on the same resources as the natural sciences, namely observation, experimentation, and comparison (Coser 1977, 5).

In the third period of Comte's intellectual life, he did not add to his scientific material. Rather, he became head of a new religious organization, which he foresaw as someday being led by sociologist-priests. He also practiced "cerebral hygiene," which "consisted in abstention from the reading of current literature, especially of periodicals, and the exclusive study of a few masterpieces of the past" (Marvin 1965, 45). The result was that he became increasingly out of touch with scientific and intellectual developments.

In 1826, in the midst of a lecture series, Comte suffered from a mental breakdown. He spent time in an asylum and was then treated at home. He continued to suffer from mental problems throughout his life. Comte died in 1857. He was 60 years old.

Anthony Giddens

Anthony Giddens (1938–), director of the London School of Economics from 1997–2003, names globalization and information technology as two of the key issues facing sociologists at the turn of the twenty-first century. He adds that a lessening of tradition in our everyday lives is a third important and consequential change that should interest sociologists (Giddens, "An Interview").

Giddens's early publications were largely based on his reinterpretation of "classical" European sociologists (Clark 1990, 21; Poggi 1990). He credits Max Weber, one of sociology's "founding fathers," who is profiled in chapter 2, with having the most "pervasive and enduring" impact on the nature of sociology today (Giddens, "An Interview"). When asked why he thinks people should study sociology, Giddens says, "Sociology is a genuinely enlightening subject. Most people who study sociology are changed by the experience. The reason is that sociology offers a different perspective on the world from that which most people have when they start out in the subject. Sociology helps us look beyond the immediate contexts of our lives and so helps us understand the causes of our own actions better. Sociology also can help us change the world for the better" ("An Interview").

Giddens's own theoretical work is largely a theory of "structuration." It aims to "provide a conceptual framework for analyzing how human beings make their own history, how society is produced, reproduced and changed (or, in his own shorthand, how it is 'constituted')" (Clark 1990, 23). A prolific writer, Giddens has authored more than 30 books and over 200 articles and reviews. His books have been translated into 30 languages. Giddens himself is the subject of a dozen more books and recipient of 15 honorary degrees and awards. As 1999 BBC Reith Lecturer, his lectures were published as *Runaway World: How Globalization Is Reshaping Our Lives* (2000).

Abu Zaid Abdal Rahman Ibn Khaldun

Abu Zaid Abdal Rahman Ibn Khaldun (1332–1406) was a historian, philosopher, and founder of Arab social science. Born in Tunis, North Africa, Ibn Khaldun worked for a variety of North African princes as an emissary and in administrative positions. He was active in politics during a period of intense rivalries among the leaders in the Arab world, and even spent time in prison for his activities. Ibn Khaldun lived the last years of his life in Egypt as a scholar, teacher, and magistrate.

He wrote a lengthy history of world that laid groundwork for sociology. In seven volumes, he covered the history of Arabs and Berbers, the nature of civilization, and the meaning of historical events (Baali 1988). He advocated empirical research and has been called an excellent deductive sociologist who was "*more* positivistic than Durkheim" (Gellner 1975, 203).

After the attacks on New York and the Pentagon on September 11, 2001, interest in Ibn Khaldun's work and his analysis of civilizations was revived (e.g., Ahmed 2002). Today, the Ibn Khaldun Center for Development (ICDS), an independent applied-social-science research institution in Egypt that applies social science perspectives to serve Egypt and Arab development, bears his name.

Harriet Martineau

British-born Harriet Martineau (1802–76) is sometimes called the "Mother of Sociology" and the first female sociologist. She is perhaps most remembered for translating Auguste Comte's *Positive Philosophy* (1896, orig. 1838) into English. However, Martineau was an important sociologist in her own right. She sought "to create a science of society that would be systematic, grounded in empirical observation, and accessible to a general readership, enabling people to make personal and political decisions guided by a scientific understanding of the principles governing social life" (Lengermann and Niebrugge-Brantley 1998, 31). William Graham Sumner, profiled in chapter 3, took on some of her ideas about rights (Healy 1972, 65).

Because her parents were Unitarians, Martineau received more education than most females of her day. She spent much of her time with books and writing after losing most of her hearing at age 12 (Pichanick 1980). Martineau was never, however, allowed to pursue a university education.

Always a prolific writer, Martineau began to sell her writing to help support her family after her father's death in 1826. She authored hundreds of books, articles, and editorials on topics including literature, children's literature, politics, history, religion, economics, and sociology. In 1830 alone, she wrote 52 articles for a Unitarian journal, one novel, a book-length manuscript on religious history, and three essays for writing contests. Martineau's 25-volume series on economics (written in 24 months) outsold numerous other popular authors of the time, including John Stuart Mill and even Charles Dickens (Lengermann and Niebrugge-Brantley 1998, 26).

Martineau saw her writing talent as a way she could educate the public on social issues. She spent two years in America (1834–36). *Society in America* (1836), *How to Observe Morals and Manners* (1838), and *Retrospect of Western Travel* (1838) were all results of that trip. In *Society in America,* she tackled a sociological analysis of the issues of slavery abolition, race, and women's rights. *How to Observe Morals and Manners* discussed the methods of fieldwork. Her other sociological works include *Eastern Life: Past and Present* (1848), a book about the social construction of religion she wrote after a trip to the Middle East, and *Household Education* (1849), a work on childhood socialization. Overall, her works laid the groundwork for both the interpretive and feminist paradigms of modern sociologists (Lengermann and Niebrugge-Brantley 1998, 239).

C. Wright Mills

C. Wright Mills (1916–62) was a colorful, contentious, and influential figure in American sociology. He was a tall man (6′2″), originally from Texas, described as speaking with a "thundering drawl" (Horowitz 1983, 4). Mills cultivated a renegade image with his motorcycle and leather jacket. After riding to work, he would deposit "his paratroop boots on the podium before lecturing to his enthralled students" (Tilman 1984, 9). He reportedly bragged about his prowess with women, married three times, and fathered a child during each marriage.

As a student at the University of Texas–Austin, Mills excelled in sociology and other subjects he liked with professors he respected. His work in other areas was only average. Yet several of his professors recognized his abilities even as an undergraduate and his talent for presenting interesting lectures (Horowitz 1983, 19–21; Tilman 1984, 6–7). Always one to do things his own way rather than bow to conformity, Mills received both a baccalaureate and master's degree from the University of Texas on the same date in 1939 (Horowitz 1983, 19). He went to the University of Wisconsin to obtain his doctorate.

By most accounts, Mills was a controversial figure, and not particularly well liked in academic circles. His career was marked with estrangement, friction, and acerbic relationships with many other academics. Even his oral dissertation defense proved contentious. As Horowitz reports in his biography of Mills, "Mills was unwilling to make the small changes asked of him and in turn had a dissertation committee unwilling to acknowledge his achievements. The defense became a standoff, and the dissertation was quietly accepted without ever being formally approved" (1983, 53).

Mills took a position at the University of Maryland and later moved to Columbia University, where he stayed until his death. He gained public notoriety at Columbia as a social critic. Unlike many academics, he was an excellent writer who addressed his topics in straightforward and readable language. As Elwell explains, Mills "writes about issues and problems that matter to people, not just to other sociologists, and he writes about them in a way to further our understanding" ("Sociology of C. Wright Mills").

Mills's topics included white-collar jobs, bureaucracy, power and authority, the social elite, rationalization, social problems, communism, the cold war, ideology, the social sciences, and sociology itself. During his time at Columbia, Mills published some of his most important works, including *The Power Elite* (1956), addressing the organization of power in the United States; *The Causes of World War III* (1958), decrying the U.S.-Russian arms race; *The Sociological Imagination* (1959), addressing social science itself; and *Listen, Yankee: The Revolution in Cuba* (1960), a comment on the Cuban Revolution and U.S.–Latin American relations. He died in his sleep of a heart attack, his fourth, when he was only 45 years old.

Albion Small

Albion Woodbury Small (1854–1926) was born in Buckfield, Maine. He received his bachelor's degree from Colby College in 1876. Small then continued his studies at the Newton Theological Seminary, and in Europe at the University of Berlin and the University of Leipzig. Upon his return to the United States, he took a position as professor of history and economics at Colby, later becoming president of the school.

Small was appointed professor of sociology at the University of Chicago in 1892. At that time, "the university was less than two years old and not yet open to students" (Bannister 1987, 37). Small's appointment was the first professorship in sociology in the United States. His annual salary was $7,000. That was not an extraordinary amount for Chicago professors. It was, however, high for even the most well-known professors elsewhere.

For three decades, Small chaired Chicago's sociology department and edited the prestigious *American Journal of Sociology.* He coauthored the first American textbook on sociology, *Introduction to the Study of Sociology,* in 1894 with his pupil George E. Vincent. Small served two terms as president of the American Sociological Society (the organization that would become today's American Sociological Association) and was elected a member of the International Institute of Sociology in 1913 (Bannister 1987, 33; Hayes 1927, 160).

"The characteristic thing about Small is that he was almost universally well-liked. As a scholar, he was creative and serious; as a teacher, devoted and helpful; for tedious administrative tasks, willing and industrious; as a colleague, friendly, warm, indulgent; as a person, ethical, spiritual" (Becker 1971, 3–4). Another biographer portrayed Small and his sociological perspective by describing Small as "a man of distinct personality. Of all his traits the most fundamental is that he is earnest about life" (Hayes 1927, 184). Small was also interested in "moral" society and social reform. As his biographer continues, "Sociology he regards as a study of life with a view to understanding it in order that its values may be realized by men. His interest is primarily ethical; that is, it is an interest in the values of human experience and the method of their realization. He became and remained a sociologist because he believed that this realization of values could be promoted by understanding."

Ida B. Wells-Barnett

Ida B. Wells-Barnett (1862–1931) was born the daughter of Mississippi slaves. It is her parents that Wells-Barnett says gave her "the interest in politics, the clear sense of justice, and the confidence for independent thought which are hallmarks of her sociology" (Lengermann and Niebrugge-Brantley 1998, 151). She attended Rust College until her parents' death from yellow fever in 1876 required that she go to work to support her five younger siblings.

Wells-Barnett took a job teaching school in Memphis. She also worked as a journalist and became and part-owner of the *Free Speech and Headlight of Memphis.* She gained quite a bit of notoriety among the black community by refusing to move to the segregated section of a railroad car and a subsequent lawsuit she brought against the railroad. Although her case was won in circuit court, it was lost on appeal.

Wells-Barnett worked nationally and internationally for a variety of civil rights causes. She was a founding member of the National Association for Advancement of Colored People (NAACP) and a number of other organizations, including a neighborhood center and the first kindergarten in a black neighborhood. She was also a suffragist.

It was lynching, however, that became Wells-Barnett's lifelong cause. She wrote of her crusade against lynching, "I felt that one had better die fighting against injustice than to die like a dog or a rat in a trap" (1970, 62). In *The Red Record: Tabulated Statistics and Alleged Causes of Lynching in the United States* (1895), Wells-Barnett used newspaper statistics from the white press to systematically analyze lynching. Her antilynching campaign would result in the offices of the *Free Speech* being burned to the ground, more extensive writing opportunities, a public-speaking career, an opportunity to take her cause internationally, and an eventual move to Chicago.

Wells-Barnett's contributions to sociology include the creation of social theory viewed through race relations, her part in the long-overlooked social analyses by African Americans, a focus on justice and morality, and a focus on the intersection of race, class, and gender that has been central to modern feminist theory (Lengermann and Niebrugge-Brantley 1998, 171–72). Among the numerous acknowledgments of her work across society, Wells-Barnett's likeness was placed on a 1990 U.S. postage stamp.

CAREERS IN SOCIOLOGY

For those interested in the social world, sociology provides career preparation for a variety of career opportunities, as noted throughout the following chapters. Those with an overall interest and training in the basics of sociological study have backgrounds that prepare them for careers including

- administrator
- advocate
- applied sociologist
- clinical sociologist
- consultant
- development officer
- executive director
- graduate work in sociology and other fields, such as medicine and law
- outreach coordinator
- professional periodicals staff
- professional sociologist
- researcher
- social historian
- social-research assistant

- social-science analyst
- teacher
- writer/publisher/editor

Additional Resources

Abercrombie, Nicholas, Stephen Hill, and Bryan S. Turner. 2000. *The Penguin Dictionary of Sociology.* 4th ed. London: Penguin Books. This dictionary is an excellent quick reference covering many of the important classical concepts and evolving, contemporary issues in sociology.

American Sociological Association (ASA). http://www.asanet.org/. The ASA is the largest professional organization representing sociology in the United States. Its site contains a wealth of information for anyone interested in the field, including professional sociologists, students, and the public.

Berger, Peter L. 1973. *Invitation to Sociology: A Humanistic Perspective.* Woodstock, N.Y.: Overlook Press. This classic work enthusiastically explains what sociology is, the sociological quest to understand society, and the unique contribution sociologists can make to shaping the world.

Collins, Randall. 1992. *Sociological Insight: An Introduction to Non-Obvious Sociology.* 2nd ed. New York: Oxford University Press. This textbook introduces many basic sociological concepts and explains what is unique about a sociological perspective.

Electronic Journal of Sociology. http://www.sociology.org/. This is a free international online refereed journal that publishes a broad range of sociological works.

International Sociological Association (ISA). http://www.ucm.es/info/isa/. This organization has members who are sociologists and social scientists from around the world.

Internet Scout Report. http://scout.cs.wisc.edu/report/sr/current/. A team of professional librarians and subject-matter experts compile high-quality Internet resources into an excellent resource for online information.

Kearl, Michael C. A Sociological Tour through Cyberspace. http://www.trinity.edu/~mkearl/index.html. Michael C. Kearl at Trinity University provides an interesting and informative online "tour" exercising the sociological imagination.

Mills, C. Wright. 1959. *The Sociological Imagination.* New York: Oxford University Press. This book critiques sociological thinking and shows the ways that our personal lives are inevitably linked with social issues.

SocioSite. http://www2.fmg.uva.nl/sociosite/index.html. Under chief editor Albert Benschop, this site provides an extensive set of links to topics of interest to social scientists internationally.

Steele, Stephen F., AnneMarie Scarisbrick-Hauser, and William J. Hauser. 1999. *Solution-Centered Sociology: Addressing Problems through Applied Sociology.* Thousand Oaks, Calif.: Sage. This book shows how to apply a range of sociological tools to solve real-life problems.

Stephan, Ed. A Sociology Timeline from 1600. http://www.ac.wwu.edu/~stephan/timeline.html. This extensive timeline contains a wealth of events including births, deaths, and publications of many influential sociologists (and others). There are also links to additional online information for some entries and a calendar that allows users to see what happened in sociological history, by date.

CHAPTER 2

Sociological Theory

Sociologists depend on theories to help them explain the social world and organize their ideas about how it operates. A **theory** is *the analysis and statement of how and why a set of facts relates to each other.* In sociology, theories help us understand how social phenomena relate to each other.

Theories help sociologists explain why and how society works. Through the use of theory, they work to answer such questions as "why are things as they are, what conditions produce them, and what conditions change them into something else? If we have such a theory, we will at last be in a position to know what we really *can* do about the shape of our society" (Collins 1988, 119). By understanding the real causes of how and why things operate as they do, we can find ways to address the things that need improvement.

Sociologists use scientific research methods to test these theories. Theories can then be refined or rejected after they are evaluated. Chapter 10 discusses how sociologists do research in more detail.

SOCIOLOGICAL PARADIGMS

Like scientists in all disciplines, sociologists develop theories based on **paradigms,** *broad assumptions about how the world works.* These paradigms guide the way social scientists develop theories, conduct research, and evaluate evidence. An important work in understanding paradigms is Thomas Kuhn's book *The Structure of Scientific Revolutions* (1970). Kuhn was able to show that scientific assumptions come in and out of favor at different times. Since these paradigms encompass assumptions about how various parts of the world are connected, they guide responses to perceived situations and solutions to any problems that are identified.

An example from the field of medicine illustrates this concept (Weiss and Lonnquist 1994, 19–40). Very early theories of disease causation were based on the supernatural. Ancient peoples believed diseases were caused by deities or magic. Based on this theory, their treatments often involved rituals designed to remove the evil spirits from the body such as bloodletting (draining blood from the body) or a procedure called *trephination* in which holes were made in the skull using sharp stones.

Hippocrates (460–377 B.C.) popularized the theoretical paradigm that disease was a natural process. He developed a humoral theory of disease that explained illness as an imbalance of four humors (hot, cold, dry, and wet) within the body. Based on his theory, treatments were designed to rebalance these humors (e.g., cool someone with a heat-related illness). This remained the dominant theory for centuries.

The germ theory of disease that guides today's medical paradigm was not developed until French chemist Louis Pasteur (1822–95) turned his attention to human diseases in the late 1800s. After his research, treatments began to focus on fighting bacteria. Sometimes all of these treatments worked, regardless of whether evil spirits were actually released, humors were rebalanced, germs were killed, or some other mechanism was the actual cause of the recovery. Results, however, tend to be interpreted according to the prevailing paradigm of the time.

In sociology, theoretical paradigms differ in how much of society or what aspects of society they focus on at one time. In other words, they differ on how "big" their look at society is. **Macro perspectives** are *"big" perspectives that look at social processes throughout society.* Social theorists who take macro perspectives examine the interrelationships of large-scale social structures and interrelationships (e.g., the economy, the government, and the health-care system). They look at how these facets of society fit together and any troubles or stress within these interrelationships. They are also interested in why and how society changes as a result of these relationships.

Conversely, **micro perspectives** *focus on patterns of individual interactions.* Social theorists who take a micro perspective focus on the daily interactions we have on an individual level. They are interested in why and how individuals relate to each other, how our day-to-day interactions with each other are shaped by larger society, and how these day-to-day interactions can, in turn, shape larger society.

MAJOR SOCIOLOGICAL PERSPECTIVES

There is no clearly identifiable date when sociological theory began. However, the mid-to-late 1800s marks the period when social thought turned to what we today call sociology (Ritzer 1988, 4).

There are currently three major theoretical paradigms in sociology: the structural-functionalist paradigm, the social-conflict paradigm, and the symbolic-interactionist paradigm (Babbie 1994). No one of these three perspectives is singularly "right" or "wrong." Each provides a different way to view and analyze society. They can reveal different issues and suggest different answers to tackling any problems they identify. Two of the major paradigms, the structural-functionalist and the social-conflict perspective, take a macro perspective on society. The third perspective, symbolic-interactionism, takes a micro perspective.

Structural-Functionalism

Structural-functionalism is the earliest sociological paradigm. It is rooted in the scientific advances of the physical sciences occurring in the nineteenth century. Based on these advances, Herbert Spencer (1820–1903) approached the study of social structures through an "organic analogy" that emphasized evolutionary laws (Spencer 1898). In this model, Spencer viewed society as being similar to a body. In the most simplistic terms, just as the various organs in the body work together to keep the entire system functioning and regulated, the various parts of society (the economy, the polity, health care, education, etc.) work together to keep the entire society functioning and regulated. Spencer also saw similarities in the way physical bodies and societies evolve. Spencer actually coined the term *survival of the fittest,* which is often incorrectly attributed to evolutionary biologist Charles Darwin.

Spencer influenced early French sociologist Emile Durkheim (1858–1917), who is profiled in chapter 10. Durkheim took this organic analogy and refined it into a perspective that would become **structural-functionalism.** The perspective is also called **functionalism,** or the *functionalist paradigm.* This paradigm *views society as a complex system of interrelated parts working together to maintain stability* (Parsons 1951; Turner and Maryanski 1979). According to this perspective; (1) a social system's parts are interdependent; (2) the system has a "normal" healthy state of equilibrium, analogous to a healthy body; and (3) when disturbed, the system parts reorganize and readjust to bring the system back to a state of equilibrium (Wallace and Wolf 1999, 18). Any changes in society occur in structured, evolutionary ways.

Durkheim realized that society influences our human actions but that society is also something that exists beyond individuals. He felt that society must be studied and understood in terms of what he called *social facts.* These **social facts** include *laws, morals, values, religious beliefs, customs, fashions, rituals, and the myriad cultural and social rules governing social life.* Durkheim (1964b) saw this system of social facts as making up the structure of society.

He was interested in how these social facts are related to each other. He was also interested in the function each of the parts of a social system fulfill as well as how societies manage to remain stable or change. In other words, how do social facts fit together? What needs do the various parts of society serve? What part does each segment of society play in keeping the system operating and balanced? How and why do systems change?

Functionalism has been very influential in sociology. It was especially popular in the United States when championed by Harvard sociologist Talcott Parsons (1902–79) during the 1940s and 1950s. Parsons, profiled below, is known for his **grand theory,** *an abstract level of theorizing that tried to explain the entire social structure at once and was difficult, if not impossible, to test through research.*

Robert K. Merton (1910–2003), Parsons's student, who is also profiled below, turned away from these grand theories in favor of what he called theories of the middle-range. These **middle-range theories** are *theories that are more limited and can be tested through research.* They explain, for example, deviant behavior (further discussed in chapter 6), public opinion, or how power is transmitted between generations.

He also showed that social patterns are complex, with the various parts of society fulfilling different types of functions. Some functions, which Merton called **manifest functions,** are *obvious and intended.* Other functions, called **latent functions,** are *less recognized and unintended.* These functions may be either beneficial or neutral. However, *some functions may be undesirable.* These are called social **dysfunctions.**

A simple illustration of these concepts is the widespread use of cars in America and many other countries (Macionis 1995, 17). Cars provide transportation and status. Both are manifest functions. Cars also provide personal autonomy, allowing drivers to come and go as they please, on their own schedules. This is a latent function of the vehicular transportation system as it currently exists. However, cars also pollute the environment. Thus, relying on cars as a major means of transportation is also dysfunctional in that regard.

Structural-functionalists also recognize that as one part of the system changes, other parts of the system have to readjust to accommodate the change that has taken place elsewhere. A change in one part of the system may have manifest, latent, and dysfunctional consequences. An example of a change that has had a number of consequences is the addition of lighting at Chicago's historic Wrigley Field. Built in 1914, Wrigley Field is the home stadium of the Chicago Cubs professional baseball team. All games at Wrigley Field traditionally had to be played during daylight hours because the field did not have lighting for nighttime games. In 1988, lights were added to the field as a result of a lengthy and contentious process aimed at generating income and reviving the economy in the immediate area of the field.

Examining the Lake View neighborhood around Wrigley Field as a social system allows application of a functionalist perspective to this situation. Nighttime games can now be played at the field. This one change resulted in a number of other complicated neighborhood effects (Spirou and Bennett 2002). The Cubs have a more flexible schedule and can take economic advantage of televised evening programming, thus achieving the manifest function of lighting the field. A number of other manifest and latent functions can also be noted. For example, the nighttime games have resulted in needed new investments in the surrounding area, population growth, and an acceleration of residential investments by affluent buyers. Sports-oriented businesses catering to a younger crowd, such as sports bars, have flourished. However, dysfunctions have also occurred. Some smaller businesses not catering to the baseball trade have suffered.

For example, pharmacies, bookstores, dry cleaners, and restaurants have seen business decline as bar business increased. Automobile traffic around the ballpark has also increased, and area residents and businesses have been faced with more elaborate parking restrictions.

According to its critics, the functionalist focus on social order cannot adequately explain social change. They also argue that this focus on order discounts the conflicts and tensions that exist within society and downplays the impact of factors such as race, class, and gender that impact our lives and social positions. Some critics feel that the perspective also ignores the importance of small-scale, micro-level interactions. Structural-functionalism is also criticized as being **tautological,** meaning that it *makes circular arguments.* This criticism says functionalists argue that, because something exists, it serves a function for the system, and thus it exists. Such a view fails to satisfactorily explain how social structures arise in the first place.

Functionalism lost favor in American sociology during the social upheavals of the 1960s. During the mid-1980s, there was resurgence in interest in Parsons's work. Theorists, including Jeffrey C. Alexander (1998) and Neil Smelser (e.g., 1985) (profiled in chapter 9) in the United States and Niklas Luhmann (1982) in Germany, who is profiled below, revisited Parson's perspectives on social systems. Their work became classified as *neofunctionalism.* This new twist on the old theory draws on Parsons's basic premises. **Neofunctionalism** expands the perspective by *trying to respond to critics in such ways as incorporating some of the ideas of conflict theorists and also recognizing the importance of the micro perspective.* Neofunctionalists argued that by rethinking some of the basics of functionalism and focusing on how it links with micro perspectives, much of this criticism can be overcome (e.g., Turner 2001). Structural-functionalism is also still widely used in sociological studies of the family (Mann et al. 1997, 340).

Social-Conflict Theory

The other major macro-sociological theoretical framework in sociological theory is the social-conflict paradigm, also referred to as the conflict perspective. **Social-conflict theory** *focuses on competition between groups.* Whereas functionalists focus on balance and stability within a social system, conflict theorists view society as comprised of social relations characterized by inequality and change.

According to conflict theorists, groups are constantly competing for unequally distributed resources, such as wealth and power, with each group seeking to benefit their own interests. In this scenario, one or a few groups control these resources at the expense of others. Thus, these theorists look at social structures and ask, "Who benefits?" This constant conflict between groups also results in social change.

Conflict theories did not arise with sociology. As Randall Collins points out, much of the history of the world is a history of conflict. This perspective has appeared repeatedly when social thinkers have written about what happened in society and the "whys" behind those events (Collins 1994, 48–49). In this tradition, conflict sociologists look at historical material and patterns of long-term change. They also now look at the world globally, for example, through the world-systems perspective discussed in chapter 7 on stratification.

The works of Karl Marx (1818–83) are often credited with providing the sociological roots of the conflict perspective. Marx (profiled below) was born in Prussia, now Germany, during the stormy period in which western Europe was transitioning from feudalism to capitalism. The Industrial Revolution was in full swing, and Marx observed inequality throughout the growing capitalist society. The economics of capitalism, he felt, resulted in social classes that were constantly in competition for society's limited resources. Marx saw rich factory owners who obtained their wealth from the labor of factory workers who were paid little, often toiled long hours in dangerous conditions, and frequently lived in crowded and unhealthy spaces. Society, as Marx saw it, was an ongoing struggle between the classes: the "haves" (illustrated by the factory owners) and the "have nots" (illustrated by the workers). The result was social conflict and change as those without resources challenged those holding the resources for a piece of the proverbial pie.

Later conflict theorists have extended and adapted this idea of continuous tension between groups. They have moved well beyond Marx's emphasis on class and economics, focusing on other areas such as inequality between races or sexes. This wider look at social inequalities has provided the basis for **feminist theory.** To be a feminist theory, "a theory must recognize gender as a system of inequality, assume that it is a mutable rather than constant or necessary feature of human societies, and [support] a commitment to a gender equitable system" (Chafetz 2001, 613). In other words, feminist theories *argue that social systems oppress women and that this oppression can and should be eliminated.*

Feminists, however, differ greatly in their views on why inequality occurs and how to overcome it (Andersen 1993). Drawing from Marx's emphasis on economics, **Marxist feminism** *argues that capitalist economic structures favor men*—for example, with higher paying jobs. Solutions rely on eliminating capitalism as the source of the problem. **Liberal feminism** *argues that inequality lies in a lack of opportunity and education for women as well as traditional views of gender that limit women's roles.* Liberal feminists feel that if women are allowed to compete equally with men in all areas of society, they will do so successfully (Lorber 1998). **Radical feminism** *argues that, regardless of economic system and other inequalities women face in their lives (e.g., racism), male domination is the most fundamental and violence is one key method of controlling women.* Solutions lie in eliminating all forms of sexual violence and enhancing women's culture and lives.

In the United States, feminism evolved as women sought the right to an education and joined the abolitionist movements of the 1800s. Many early female sociologists, including Jane Addams (profiled in chapter 11), Harriet Martineau (profiled in chapter 1), and Ida Wells-Barnett (also profiled in chapter 1) participated in this "first wave" of the women's movement, as did some male sociologists. The second wave of feminism was established amid the social movements of the 1960s, when conflict theory overall was gaining popularity. Many changes were occurring in women's lives (e.g., increasing women's labor-force participation, the development of the birth-control pill) during that decade with sociologists such as Jessie Bernard (profiled below) embracing the movement.

An additional dimension has also been added to feminist perspectives. Many feminists from the 1960s were educated, white, and middle class. Today, feminist writings have expanded to encompass women of diverse backgrounds (e.g., Collins 2000) as well as the concerns of globalization and the circumstances of women in less developed countries. A **multicultural global feminism** has developed that *recognizes the need to include the diversity of women's voices by other characteristics such as race, ethnicity, class, age, sexual orientation, and able-bodiedness.* Sociologists such as Patricia Hill Collins (profiled below) and Dorothy Smith (profiled in chapter 10) focus on what feminism brings to sociological theory and our understanding of society.

Critics have charged that the conflict perspective has become too politicized by its association with Marx and by its widespread use by advocates in numerous causes and movements. The women's movement and feminist theory provides one example of its co-optation for political use. Critics also argue that the conflict perspective downplays the unity that exists in society and takes a negative view of society by overemphasizing conflicts, tensions, and coercion.

At this writing, conflict theory is widely used in American sociology. It began to unseat functionalism as the dominant sociological paradigm with challenges C. Wright Mills (profiled in chapter 1) and others made to Parsons's theory in the late 1950s, and grew in popularity during the social turmoil of the 1960s. The social-conflict perspective is sometimes combined with elements of micro-level theories to offer a more robust view of social life.

Symbolic Interactionism

Symbolic interactionism is the prevailing micro-theoretical framework in sociological theory. As a micro-level perspective, **symbolic interactionism** *focuses on patterns of individual interactions.* Although sociologists working in this tradition recognize that larger social structures exist and are important in shaping our lives, they point out that society is actually created by people interacting together on a daily basis. It is these smaller interactions that actually make up the larger social structures that are of the focus of functionalists and conflict theorists.

According to this perspective, society and these larger social structures must be understood through studying social interactions that are based on shared understandings, languages, and symbols. A **symbol** is *something that stands for, represents, or signifies something else in a particular culture.* Symbols can be anything—gestures, words, objects, or events—and they can represent any number of others things, ideas, events, or emotions. (Symbols are discussed in chapter 3.) Symbolic interactionists argue that we are able to interact with others because we create symbols and learn to *interpret* what those symbols mean in our interactions. Thus, symbolic interactionism is sometimes referred to as *interpretive theory.* Social change occurs as people develop a shared understanding that a change needs to take place and interact to make that change happen.

Symbolic interactionism is based partly on the writings of German sociologist Max Weber (1864–1920), profiled below. Unlike other sociologists who had focused only on large structural relationships, Weber was also interested in how individuals interact. The aspect of his work that influenced the symbolic-interactionist perspective was his focus on how we interpret and understand the situations we encounter and the interactions in which we participate. To Weber, the concept of **verstehen,** or *subjective understanding,* was central to explaining human behavior. Weber felt that *we have to be able to take someone else's position mentally, to stand in their shoes, so to speak, to understand their actions.* From our own perspectives, we may not understand why a person acts in a certain way, what that behavior means to them, or the purposes it serves for them. For example, we may only be able to explain why an abused wife stays with her violent husband by understanding the totality of her situation from her perspective—her emotional attachment to him, her economic situation, her religious views, and so on.

Although it has German roots, symbolic interaction is a "distinctively American tradition . . . [and America's] most original contribution to sociological thought" (Collins 1994, 242). The perspective was developed during the 1920s by George Herbert Mead (1863–1931). Mead (profiled in chapter 4) was a philosopher and social psychologist who was interested in how our personalities are formed through social interaction. The term *symbolic interactionism* was, however, not actually coined until a decade later. Herbert Blumer (1900–1987), a student of Mead profiled in chapter 9, expanded on Mead's concepts and introduced the term in 1937. More contemporary theorists expanded symbolic interactionism in new directions. For example, labeling theory (discussed in chapter 6) analyzes how we define deviance. Other perspectives that incorporate interpretative approaches to understanding social behaviors include the concept of the *social construction of reality,* Erving Goffman's (1922–82) concept of dramaturgy, and Harold Garfinkel's (1917–) work in ethnomethodology (all discussed in chapter 4).

Sociologists have drawn from interpretative perspectives and even other disciplines to develop more complex theories. For example, **rational-choice theories** *examine how people make choices purposely, based on their preferences and evaluation of options and opportunities* (Voss and Abraham 2000). In simple terms, of all the options or courses of action a person sees as being available, they act based on a calculation of pros and cons. Related to rational choice theories, **exchange theories** *assume that people interact and trade the resources (money, affections, etc.) that they bring to interactions in ways that maximize benefits and reduce costs to themselves* (Homans 1974; Blau 1964; Cook 1987; Coleman and Fararo 1992). These theories can become complex as they examine how people weigh such factors as perceived costs and benefits, the personal resources they can rely on (money, prestige, personal connections, etc.) and other factors in making decisions and determining courses of action.

Critics of symbolic interactionism often argue that the perspective focuses on specific, small-scale situations while overlooking the effects of larger society (e.g., the impacts of class, racial or gender discrimination). The result, they say, is a disregard for the larger social forces at work shaping our lives. Critics also argue that symbolic interactionism focuses on rational and conscious interactions at the expense of considering irrational or unconscious behavior.

In American sociology, symbolic interactionism was popular in the early part of the twentieth century. It was widely developed and utilized by sociologists at the University of Chicago, the first American university to have a graduate department of sociology. Functionalism eclipsed the popularity of symbolic interactionism during the 1940s and 1950s. However, symbolic interactionism has continued to evolve and remains an important and vibrant sociological paradigm.

APPLYING THE PARADIGMS

A comparison of the three major theoretical paradigms in sociology is provided in table 2.1. Sociologists use these theoretical perspectives as the basic tools for analyzing social issues. The sociologist's perspective shows their assumptions about how the world works and how change occurs. It will guide the questions the researcher asks and, in many ways, solutions to any problems that are identified.

Table 2.1
Comparison of Major Sociological Paradigms

Theoretical Paradigm	Level of Analysis	Assumptions	Questions	How Change Occurs
Structural-Functionalist	Macro	Society functions as a system of interrelated parts working together to maintain stability	How does society operate? What functions do the different parts serve?	Evolutionary; Re-balancing of the system
Social-Conflict	Macro	Society is comprised of social relations characterized by inequality and struggle between groups	Who benefits? What is the source of conflicts between groups? How can it be resolved?	Revolutionary; Conflict between groups vying for resources
Symbolic Interaction	Micro	Society is created through daily interactions	How do individuals interact?	Re-defining the situation

Drawing on the example of changing medical paradigms noted early in this chapter, a look at how sociologists apply their perspectives to medicine illustrates the different questions and criticisms each of these three paradigms raises. Looking at how these perspectives apply to medicine also demonstrates the complexity of the social issues that sociologists address.

Structural-Functionalist Perspective on Health Care

From a functionalist perspective, medicine is one of the interdependent parts of the social system that helps to maintain the stability of the system as a whole. According to Talcott Parsons (1951), who contributed to many early sociological studies of medicine, the function of the health-care system is to enable people to be healthy enough to do all the things they need to do to keep society functioning (Shilling 2002). They can contribute to society by being healthy workers, parents, consumers, and all the other things that healthy people do. In this view, people should want to be well. When they become ill, they should seek care from medical professionals and follow their guidance to get well. Doctors should use the skill and power derived from their training and expertise to direct the behavior of patients and cure illness. "Good" patients seek medical care and follow doctor's orders. "Good" doctors direct and help their patients to follow their guidance. A sociologist studying health care from a functionalist perspective might be interested in how, for example, public health officials can increase rates of people getting flu shots. Solutions to any problems identified would likely focus on adjusting the workings of the system.

Critics argue that the functionalist perspective on medicine applies only to some conditions and some people. For example, it does apply to acute illness such as the measles or the common cold. However, it does not adequately address chronic illness. Current medical capabilities might slow the decline or stabilize the condition of people with diseases such as heart disease, arthritis, or Alzheimer's disease, without the current ability to cure them. Thus, the perspective does not fit reality. No matter how much people try to get well or how much their doctors try to make them well, that outcome will not occur.

Critics also charge that the health-care system does not function optimally because of the profit motive that is sometimes at odds with the function of providing health care. Some people want to get well but cannot afford the things that are most likely to make that happen. Expensive or experimental technologies are not available to all who might benefit from them. The functionalist view also encourages the medical professional to be in charge of treatment, leading some critics to argue that it does not adequately support the growing interest and knowledge of patients who want to take an active role with their physician in directing their own health care.

Social-Conflict Perspective on Health Care

A conflict perspective on health care focuses on issues involving inequality and tension within the health-care system. Conflict theorists would not deny that modern health care can help people in maintaining or restoring their health. However, a sociologist looking at medicine from this perspective would identify a number of inequities that exist within the system. In studying medicine, they would ask the common social-conflict question "Who benefits?," looking at such things as what groups hold power within the system and competing interests. For example, one issue on which conflict theorists have focused a great deal of attention is the role of capitalism in health care (e.g., Navarro 1993, 2000). They identify problems within the system that are related to these inequalities, such as the number of uninsured in America and the lack of physicians in poverty-ridden areas. The power relations within and among various countries also impacts health and life quality across the globe (patterns of poverty and disease, the high rate of AIDS in Africa and the relative unavailability of AIDS drugs there, etc.). Feminists might call attention to the frequent lack of inclusion of women in clinical trials for various treatments or the way that the largely male medical establishment took obstetrical care out of the hands of women (Oakley 1984). Solutions would likely focus on eliminating inequalities.

Critics of the conflict paradigm often argue that it takes a negative view of the system, citing, for example, works such as Ivan Illich's book *Medical Nemesis* (1976). Illich argued that the medical establishment is more interested in perpetuating its own self-interest than curing patients. Conflict theorists are also criticized for discounting the many important advances in improving levels of health and life expectancy in recent decades as well as the contributions that medical technologies have had on our quality of life. For example, technologies such magnetic resonance imaging (MRI), although expensive and not accessible to all who could benefit, have had major impacts of the health of many people.

Symbolic-Interactionist Perspective on Health Care

Symbolic interactionists take a micro look at health care. Rather than focusing on the structure of the larger system or its interrelationships with other parts of society, these sociologists look at how people experience the health-care system. For example, they study the experiences of people who have illnesses such as AIDS that are associated with negative perceptions of the sick person (e.g., Tewksbury and McGaughey 1997). They study issues such as self-image and personal interactions of the disabled (e.g., Zola 1982). They focus on relationships between patients and physicians such as how they interact, what they discuss, who leads that discussion, whether physicians address all of their patients' concerns or only select ones, and the outcomes of these interactions for the patient. Solutions to any problems identified would focus at these individual levels.

Critics sometimes argue that this approach gives too much attention to individual situations rather than situations that are generalizable to others. That means symbolic interactionists have to focus on how much the individual interactions they study really reflect interactions of other people, not just that one interaction. Critics also charge that symbolic interactionists studying health issues ignore the larger social forces at work shaping health (poverty, racism, politics, etc.).

As this example shows, no one perspective can fully explain all the social aspects of medicine. Each reveals important information and different questions and solutions. Applying these three perspectives to medicine allows the sociologist to look at the structure of medical care (functionalism), any issues of power or tension (conflict), and collective definitions of the situation (interpretive). Taking into account the many ways that sociologists study medicine allows a more comprehensive understanding of the complexities and issues involved.

BIOGRAPHIES

Jessie Bernard

Over the course of her long career, Jessie Bernard (1903–96) published "a staggering scholarly output with enormous influence on the generations of scholars following her" (Cantor 1988, 264). Her writings and influence on the field cover a number of areas. However, Bernard is perhaps best known for her feminist scholarship and contributions to the feminist movement that she joined in her 60s, after she had retired from an academic career spanning decades. One biographer says that Bernard had an "unpretentious style," yet her life and sociological contributions "emanate reasonable, but unyielding, defiance—defiance of family tradition, life styles, occupational trajectories, sociological paradigms, and popular myths, as well as age-related patterns" (Lipman-Blumen 1979, 49).

Bernard spent much of her academic career at Pennsylvania State University. She also taught at Princeton University in 1959–60, when she was billed as Princeton's "first woman professor" (Bannister 1991, 144). After retiring, Bernard served as a Visiting Fellow at the National Institute of Education and a Scholar in Residence at the United States Commission on Civil Rights, and as visiting professor at Mills College in Oakland, the University of California–Los Angeles, and the University of Delaware.

She attended her first feminist meeting in the spring of 1968. Her well-known works that followed include *The Future of Marriage* (1972), which laid out Bernard's famous concept of "his" and "hers" marriages. According to Bernard, every marriage is really two marriages, experienced differently by men and women. The partners accrue different effects from the union, with benefits falling primarily to the male. Among her points in *The Female World in Global Perspective* (1986), Bernard argued that concepts developed by a male-biased sociology were not adequate to explain women's worlds. *Women and the Public Interest* (1971), *The Sociology of Community* (1972), and *The Future of Motherhood* (1974) were also penned during this period.

Jessie Bernard was active in forming, or holding a major office in, the American Sociological Association (ASA), Eastern Sociology Society, Society for the Study of Social Problems, and Sociologists for Women in Society. She received honorary degrees from Washington University, Northwestern, Hood

College, and Radcliffe. She also received awards from the American Association of University Women, the Society for the Psychological Study of Social Issues, the Association of Women in Science, and the Association for Women in Psychology (Cantor 1988; Bannister 1991, 189). A 1988 edition of the journal *Gender and Society* honored Bernard. Awards have also been established in her name, including awards established by the District of Columbia Sociologists for Women in Society and the ASA's annual Jessie Bernard Award, which recognizes scholarship on the role of women in society (Lipman-Blumen 1979).

Patricia Hill Collins

Patricia Hill Collins (1948–) was born in Philadelphia, Pennsylvania. She is Charles Phelps Taft Professor of Sociology in the African American Studies Department at the University of Cincinnati. Collins holds a doctorate from Brandeis University. Her work on the intersections of race, social class, and gender has expanded sociological and feminist analysis to show how these systems have complex and interlocking effects. To Collins, oppression is experienced and resisted at three levels: personal biography, group or community (within the cultural context created by race, class, and gender), and social institutions (2000). Her work demonstrates how acknowledging the experiences of all people gives a fuller picture of society and ways all groups can work together for mutual benefit (Andersen and Collins 2003).

In addition to her numerous journal publications, Collins has published several books. *Black Feminist Thought: Knowledge, Consciousness, and the Politics of Empowerment* (1990; rev. ed., 2000) won both the American Sociological Association's Jessie Bernard Award and the Society for the Study of Social Problems C. Wright Mills Award. That work also brought her national attention. Collins has also published *Fighting Words: Black Women and the Search for Justice* (1998), *Black Sexual Politics* (2003), and a coedited anthology of works on various aspects of race, class, and gender. (See "Collins, Patricia Hill" 1997.)

Niklas Luhmann

Before becoming a sociologist, Niklas Luhmann (1927–98) had been drafted into the German army during World War II. He was captured and held for a period as a prisoner of war. Luhmann went to law school after the war and worked as a lawyer in public administration. He also studied on scholarship for a year at Harvard University with Talcott Parsons (Bechmann and Stehr 2002, 67), who is also profiled in this chapter.

Luhmann was appointed to the faculty at the University of Bielefeld, Germany, in 1968. At that time, his university colleagues reportedly questioned him regarding what research agenda he intended to pursue. Luhmann's response was that he intended to develop a " 'theory of society' . . . that would take him thirty years and not cost anything" (Lee 2000, 320). Well known in European sociology circles before becoming known in the United States, Luhmann did produce an ambitious grand theory of society over the next three decades. His theory develops the concept of social systems made up of extensive and intertwined networks of communication processes. In hundreds of publications, Luhmann developed his theory by searching for fundamental features shared by all systems, including science, art, the economy, law, sociology, love, and politics. "Not only do all social systems share similar structures, but they also operate through communication. Hence, Luhmann asserts, society *is* communication."

At his death from cancer at age 70, Luhmann was a professor emeritus at Bielefeld. His two-volume work *Die Gesellschaft der Gesellschaft (The Society of Society;* 1997) had just been published the year before. Among his accolades, he has been called "one of the most distinguished sociologists and scholars of our time" having achieved in his life's work "arguably the most radical departure for the sociological classics available today" (Fuchs 1999, 118).

Karl Marx

Karl Marx (1818–83) was born in Prussia, now part of Germany. At university, Marx briefly studied law and then turned his interests toward philosophy. He completed his doctoral dissertation in 1841, when he was only 23 years old. Marx had hoped for an academic appointment. However, because he held radical political views, he could not obtain such a position. Marx then turned to journalism. He penned articles on censorship, social issues, and commentary on governmental laws and policies for the *Rheinische Zeitung,* a journal that was soon banned by the Prussian government.

Marx married and moved to Paris, where he became deeply involved in socialism. He also became close friends with Friedrich Engels (1820–95), the son of a wealthy German industrialist, who is profiled in chapter 7. They began a lifelong friendship and intellectual collaboration with the publication of *The Holy Family* (1956, orig. 1846), a book that focused on the importance of the masses in driving social change (Appelbaum 1988, 25). Engels would even provide financial support for Marx's work throughout his life.

Marx's writings attracted repeated government attention. Government officials asked him to leave Paris in 1845. He moved to Belgium, where he became the president of the Brussels chapter of the International Communist League. *The Manifesto of the Communist Party* (1848) was written as this organization's principal statement. After being expelled from Brussels for his revolutionary activities, Marx returned to Paris for a short time at the invitation of a provisional government that had struggled against the monarchy, then shortly moved to Cologne in Prussia and took over editorship of his revived former journal. He was accused of inciting rebellion, the journal was shut down, and Marx was expelled from Prussia. In quick succession, he traveled in Germany and then back to Paris, finally settling in London in 1849, where he would spend the rest of his life.

Marx supported his family through publications of some of his writing that covered, among other social topics, economic theory, industrial society, religion, property, communism, and philosophy. For a decade, he was also a foreign correspondent for the *New York Daily Tribune,* published by Horace Greeley. He also became involved with the London chapter of the International Communist League, advocated for German workers in London, and spent long hours in the British Museum reading British trade statistics and economic theory (Appelbaum 1988, 27).

The Marx family was very poor, often relying on Engels for funds or from pawning their possessions. They frequently lacked money for basic necessities and experienced illnesses and evictions. Three of Marx's children died before reaching adulthood. Eventually, both Marx and his wife inherited some funds that somewhat relieved their financial distress. When Engels became a partner in his father's textile mill, he paid off the Marx's debts and, in 1869, set up a small pension for his friend.

Marx's health grew progressively worse over time. Among his ailments, he suffered from painful boils, headaches, eye problems, a liver complaint, digestive and respiratory problems, and perhaps depression that made him unable to work at times. Marx died in 1883, probably of tuberculosis or pleurisy, two years after losing his wife and a daughter to cancer. Several of Marx's works, including two volumes of *Capital* (1977a, orig. 1867), were completed or published posthumously by Engels (Appelbaum 1988; Feinberg 1985; Siegel 1978).

Robert K. Merton

Robert King Merton (1910–2003) was born in Philadelphia, Pennsylvania. His birth name was Meyer R. Schkolnick. His name change came about when, as a teen, he became an amateur magician. He first adopted the name Merlin, then changed it to Merton when told that Merlin was "hackneyed." "Robert" was adopted from French magician Robert Houdin, the magician from whom Harry Houdini borrowed his stage name. Upon winning a scholarship to Temple University, "he was content to let the new name become permanent" (Calhoun 2003, 1, 8).

Merton pursued his graduate studies at Harvard University, where he earned his doctorate in 1936. He taught at Harvard for the following three years. He then moved to Tulane, and later to Columbia. He became a full professor in 1947. He was later named Giddings Professor of Sociology, Special Service Professor, and University Professor Emeritus (Martin, Mutchnick, and Austin 1990).

Over the course of his long career, Merton's work spanned a broad range of additional areas to include research methods, deviance, medicine, anomie, bureaucracy, and organizations. He received over 20 honorary degrees and international awards and was the first person to receive the Who's Who in America Achievement Award in the Social Sciences and Social Policy (Martin, Mutchnick, and Austin 1990, 211). His numerous contributions in the area of theory include middle-range theories and the concepts of latent and manifest functions and dysfunctions. He coined a number of phrases that are now part of the sociological jargon, including *self-fulfilling prophesy, unanticipated consequences,* and *anticipatory socialization.* He also developed an interview technique that has now become the focus group, used throughout political and market research (Calhoun 2003, 8).

By many reports, Robert Merton was both an inspiring and demanding teacher (Coleman 1990). He spent much time and effort reading and commenting on other people's manuscripts. Merton himself estimated that he had read over 200 book-length manuscripts and over 2,000 article-length manuscripts between 1930 and 1985 (Sztompka 1986, 265). He continued to be engaged in learning and writing until his death in 2003 at age 92.

Talcott Parsons

Talcott Parsons (1902–79) was born in Colorado Springs, Colorado. He was the son of a congregational minister who was also an English teacher and, later, president of Marietta College in Ohio. His mother was a suffragist.

Parsons received his undergraduate degree from Amherst College, where he majored in biology. He had originally intended to study medicine, and his training in the biological sciences would impact his sociology throughout his career. After graduation, an uncle financed a year of study at the London School of Economics, where Parsons first encountered the social sciences. He was then off to Heidelberg, Germany, for an exchange fellowship and, later, a doctorate. At Heidelberg, Parsons was introduced to Max Weber's works, and was even taught by Alfred Weber (a scholar who was also Max's younger brother). He also became interested in the relationship between sociology and economics, an interest that, like medicine, would also occupy much of his career (Martel 1979).

Parsons took a faculty position in the economics department at Harvard University in 1927. He became increasingly drawn to sociology and translated Weber's *The Protestant Ethic and the Spirit of Capitalism* (1930) into English. This was an important contribution to disseminating Weber's work in American sociology. He also later looked at Weber in *The Structure of Social Action* (1937). Parsons moved to the Department of Sociology in 1930 and remained there until retiring in 1973.

Over the course of his career, Parsons and Harvard became the center of American sociology (Trevino 2001, xix). He held visiting appointments at a number of institutions and served as President of the American Sociological Association and the Eastern Sociological Society. In person and personal relationships, Parsons has been described as being "extremely modest, unassuming, uncritical of others, reluctant to mention himself in conversation, much less to talk about his accomplishments . . . [yet becoming] the opposite in his writings, claiming for himself many 'major breakthroughs' in the development not only of his own theory but also of sociological theory more generally . . . [even equating] his own theory with sociological theory itself" (xviii–xix).

Several of Parsons's students, including Robert K. Merton, Kingsley Davis, Harold Garfinkel, and Neil Smelser are profiled in this book. Many of those students originally went to Harvard to study with Pitirim A. Sorokin, profiled in chapter 9, but gravitated toward Parsons instead (Hamilton 1983, 133–34; Martel 1979). Over 150 of Parsons's former students came to his retirement, some even traveling internationally to do so.

After his retirement, Parsons continued to lecture as a visiting professor as well as publish and present his work to colleagues at professional meetings. He died in Germany, where he was attending celebrations and delivering lectures on the occasion of the 50th anniversary of his doctorate.

Herbert Spencer

Herbert Spencer (1820–1903) was born in Derby, England. He was the only one of his parent's nine children to survive into adulthood. Spencer himself was an unhealthy child, so he was educated at home by his father and, as a teen, by a clergyman uncle. This education was heavily oriented toward the sciences. In addition to sociology, Spencer influenced the development of disciplines including biology, psychology, and anthropology (Carneiro 1968, 121).

In 1837, Spencer became a railroad engineer and draftsman. He was also an inventor, but did not profit significantly from his work in that area. After his work with the railroad was completed, Spencer began to publish articles on the social and political issues of the day. Unable to make a living as a writer, he eventually returned to the railroad, continuing to invent, write, and travel. In 1848, he finally landed stable employment in an editorial position with the *Economist*. Spencer wrote his first book, *Social Statistics* (1851), while in that position. He also published a theory of evolution that predated Charles Darwin's famous *On the Origin of Species* (1996, orig. 1859) by several years (Coser 1977, 102–5).

Shortly after these publications, Spencer's uncle died and left him a sizable inheritance. His newfound wealth allowed him to quit his job and live as a private scholar. He also had a nervous breakdown and developed a nervous condition at age 35 that left him unable to work long hours for the rest of his life. It also severely impaired his social interactions (Peel 1971). However, Spencer was able to continue to write prolifically on topics including biology, philosophy, and sociology. He became a renowned scientist. His writings were published in England and the United States, used as textbooks, and translated into French, German, Spanish, Italian, and Russian by the turn of the century. Yet Herbert Spencer never held a university degree or university position (Coser 1977, 102–7; Peel 1971).

Max Weber

German sociologist Max Weber (1864–1920) was the oldest of seven children. He grew up with many intellectual influences. Politicians and academics were frequent houseguests (Coser 1977, 235). He was an avid reader. Even as a youngster, he studied a variety of areas on his own, especially the classics, history, religion, economics, and philosophy. The teenage Weber was already writing essays on such topics as the family tree of Constantine and the history of civilized nations and "the laws covering their development" (Weber 1975, 45–46).

Weber studied law. He published articles on many current events and was active in politics. He taught briefly at the universities of Freiburg and then Heidelberg. However, because of his health, he never held a permanent academic position (Bendix 1968, 494). Weber wore himself down with chronic overwork. In 1898, after the death of his father, Weber suffered a mental breakdown and was unable to work for several years. He and his wife traveled widely during this time, eventually touring America at the behest of a former colleague who invited him to present a paper on the social structure of Germany. The Webers' travels included a visit to Booker T. Washington's Tuskegee Institute (now Tuskegee University). Weber eventually returned to Heidelberg to write, but he did not teach again until much later in his life (Coser 1977, 240–41).

Weber also served in the German military as a young man. He voluntarily returned to the military as a reservist during World War I, where he was commissioned to establish and run several military hospitals. Several articles he wrote during that period that were critical of Germany's execution of the war led the government to consider criminal prosecution (Coser 1977, 240–41). After the war, Weber returned to politics and published prolifically on current events.

The topics of Weber's sociological works were wide-ranging. They included political development in Russia, the social psychology of industrial work and factory workers, and economics. He cofounded the German Sociological Society with Ferdinand Toennies (profiled in chapter 8) and Georg Simmel (profiled in chapter 5). He was also keenly interested in religion, studying and writing about Christianity, Judaism, Hinduism, and Buddhism. Arguably his most famous work was *The Protestant Ethic and the Spirit of Capitalism* (1904–5), which, among other emphases, tied capitalism to the tenets of Calvinist religious doctrine. Even during his war service, he found time for his studies in the sociology of religion.

As a research methodologist, Weber was concerned with the potential influences and biases that could impact research findings. He advocated *verstehen,* or value-free, objective research. As Marianne Weber says, he warned against "an unconscious interweaving of factual perception with value judgements" (1975, 317).

Weber's wife, Marianne, would become a well-known sociologist in her own right and an active feminist in the women's movement. Together, the Webers entertained young scholars at their home on Sunday afternoons. Their guests included Russian, Polish, and Jewish students shunned by other professors, as well as pacifists and political radicals. "Wherever he perceived an injustice, Weber entered the arena like a wrathful prophet castigating his fellows for their moral sloth, their lack of conviction, their sluggish sense of justice" (Coser 1977, 242). Max Weber died of pneumonia in 1920.

CAREERS IN SOCIOLOGY

Those with an interest and training in social theory have backgrounds that prepare them for careers including

- consultant
- counselor
- development officer
- director/staff of professional organizations
- director/staff of religious activities/organizations/education
- executive director
- fiscal analyst
- grant writer
- institutional historian/museum staff-member
- medical ethicist
- minister
- outreach coordinator
- policy analyst
- professional-organization director/staff
- professional sociologist
- program evaluator
- public archivist
- recruiter
- resource developer
- social historian
- social worker
- teacher
- writer/publisher/editor

Additional Resources

Appelbaum, Richard P. 1988. *Karl Marx.* Newbury Park, Calif.: Sage. This book offers a biography and in-depth analysis covering a range of Marx's thought.

Coser, Lewis A. 1977. *Masters of Sociological Thought: Ideas in Historical and Social Context.* 2nd ed. New York: Harcourt Brace Jovanovich. This work covers the lives, social context, and contributions of 15 influential sociological thinkers. Some of this material is also provided online at the Larry R. Ridener's Dead Sociologists' Society (see below).

Lengermann, Patricia Madoo, and Jill Niebrugge-Brantley. 1998. *The Women Founders: Sociology and Social Theory, 1830–1930.* Boston: McGraw-Hill. This source serves as a rediscovery of many of the "founding mothers of sociology," with biographies and discussions of their contributions to sociology.

Ridener, Larry R. Dead Sociologists' Society. http://www2.pfeiffer.edu/~lridener/DSS/DEADSOC.HTML. Ridener has put together this online resource of biographical information and summaries of the work of 16 major figures in sociology, with

Coser's book (see above) serving as some of the source material. More information on theory is also linked here.

Ritzer, George, and Douglas J. Goodman. 2003. *Sociological Theory.* 6th ed. Boston: McGraw-Hill. This textbook covers major classical theorists as well as contemporary theories, theorists, and debates in sociology.

Trevino, A. Javier, ed. 2001. *Talcott Parsons Today: His Theory and Legacy in Contemporary Sociology.* Lanham, Md.: Rowman and Littlefield. This series of essays from Parsons' scholars in several countries examines and extends Parsons' work.

Wallace, Ruth A., and Alison Wolf. 1999. *Contemporary Sociological Theory: Expanding the Classical Tradition.* 5th ed.Upper Saddle River, N.J.: Prentice Hall. This text concentrates on the major sociological theories, including feminist perspectives throughout its discussion of these theories.

Weber, Max. 1946. *From Max Weber: Essays in Sociology.* Ed. and trans. Hans Gerth and C. Wright Mills. New York: Oxford University Press. This collection includes many of Weber's influential essays and a useful summary and biography provided by the authors.

CHAPTER 3
Culture and Society

Two concepts that are basic to sociology are *culture* and *society*. These words are so central to sociology that this book has already used the terms in previous chapters. They are also readily used in everyday, nonsociological conversation. But exactly what do these terms mean when used by sociologists? Why are they so central to sociology?

CULTURE

Culture is an extremely broad concept. To sociologists, **culture** is made up of *all of the ideas, beliefs, behaviors, and products common to, and defining, a group's way of life.* Culture encompasses everything humans create and have as they interact together.

Culture shapes the way we see the world. It impacts how we think, how we act, what we value, how we talk, the organizations we create, the rituals we hold, the laws we make, how and what we worship, what we eat, what we wear, and what we think of as beautiful or ugly. Culture impacts things that seem to nonsociologists as "scientifically determined" as medical care (e.g. Payer 1988; Snow 1993) and things as "natural" as personality (Cooper and Denner 1994; Cross and Markus 1999; J. G. Miller 1999) and sex (Grailey 1987; Kimmel 2000). Even our emotions (Hochschild 1983; McCarthy 1989) and our choices of many of the foods we eat (Belasco and Scranton 2002) are "cultural acquisitions."

Cultures vary widely around the world. Readers of this book are familiar with Western industrialized cultures. Such ways of life often seem "normal" and often "better" to readers. However, other vastly different cultures exist around the world that also seem "normal" or "better" to their inhabitants. Encountering these different cultures can result in **culture shock,** *confusion that occurs when encountering unfamiliar situations and ways of life.* Often-cited research conducted by anthropologist Napoleon Chagnon (1997), profiled below, provides a good example of this concept. Starting in the early 1960s, Chagnon studied the Yanomamo people, who live in the rain forests of Brazil and Venezuela. When Chagnon first traveled to meet them, he encountered people who had been virtually isolated from other cultures. They were almost naked, had little privacy, did not have electricity, hunted with bows and arrows, and engaged in intervillage warfare. Many had wads of green tobacco stuck in their teeth and strands of green slime hanging from their nostrils from commonly using an inhaled hallucinogenic. Chagnon was initially horrified. He found them hideous and the odor of the area sickening. The Yanomamo found the clothing, look, and smell of Chagnon just as curious as he found them.

Chagnon's work is also informative for sociologists interested in globalization and the changes that occur as a result of evolving cultural contact. When he returned several decades later, Chagnon found that contact with the outside world in the form of missionaries and corporations seeking the rain forest's resources had vastly and tragically changed the Yanomamo's lives. Much of their traditional land had been taken and their people exploited.

Chagnon's own research has even become an example of the difficulties that can be involved in studying other cultures. A recent, extremely controversial book by Patrick Tierney charged that, among other things, Chagnon's research as an outsider to the Yanomamo had exposed them to dangerous diseases and the very sorts of negative consequences that Chagnon had documented (Tierney 2000). Chagnon and a number of other supporters dispute those accusations (e.g., Hagen, Price, and Tooby 2001; "Napoleon Chagnon Responds to Darkness in El Dorado").

Types of Culture

It is important to sociologists to look at the various facets of culture. Every culture is composed of both material and nonmaterial components. **Material culture** includes *all the tangible products created by human interaction.* Any physical objects created by humans are part of the material culture. This includes clothing, books, art, buildings, computer software, inventions, food, vehicles, tools, and so on. **Nonmaterial culture** consists of *the intangible creations of human interaction.* These exist as our ideas, languages, values, beliefs, behaviors, and social institutions.

Material culture, such as technology, may change faster than nonmaterial culture. The result may by a **cultural lag,** in which *a gap occurs as different aspects of culture change at different rates* (Ogburn 1964; Volti 2001). Cloning provides an example of this situation. Scientific advances make animal, and perhaps human, cloning a reality. However, the procedure is extremely controversial morally and ethically. Similarly, science has investigated ways to transplant human genes into animals or animal organs into humans. These procedures erode traditional boundaries and definitions between human and other animals and challenge traditional values of life (Birke and Michael 1998; Woods 1998).

Sociologists also emphasize the importance of not confusing the socio-logical use of the word *culture* with the popular usage of the term. In everyday usage, someone might be referred to as "having culture" or as being "cultured" or "uncultured." Sociologically speaking, however, everyone has a culture. The pop-ular usage of the term *culture* typically refers to what sociologists call *high culture*. **High culture** consists of *things that are generally associated with the social elite*. The opera, cotillions or debutante balls, classical music and literature, wine tast-ings, and the fine arts are all examples of high culture. These activities may not be available to everyone, for several reasons. They may be too expensive, or they may be located in exclusive locations that are largely inaccessible without special mem-bership or hefty financial resources. Additionally, special preparation or knowledge may be important in understanding or fully appreciating these activities.

Unlike high culture, **popular culture** consists of *activities that are wide-spread in a culture, with mass accessibility and appeal, and pursued by large num-bers of people across all social classes*. Examples of popular culture include fast-food restaurants, rock concerts, television situation comedies, and best-selling novels. Sociologists have devoted considerable attention to studying many facets of our popular culture. Works that examine the business of selling cars (Lawson 2000), high-school proms (Best 2000), formal weddings (Ingraham 1999), and John Wayne movies (Shivley 1992) illustrate some of the range of sociological re-search in this area to which many people can readily relate. To sociologists, high culture is not evaluated as being "better" than popular culture. They are simply dif-ferent aspects of the larger culture that sociologists find so interesting.

SOCIETY

Society is also a central component of sociological study and everyday lives. A **society** consists of *people who interact and share a common culture*. "Society is indispensable to the individual because it possesses at a given mo-ment an accumulation of values, of plans and materials which the child could never accumulate alone . . . But the individual is also indispensable to society because by his activity and ingenuity he creates all the material values, the whole fund of civilization" (Thomas and Thomas 1928, 233–34).

Some definitions of *society* (particularly older ones) specify that interac-tion occurs within some shared boundary. Increasing globalization and the rapid expansion of communication, information, and transportation technologies all make culture sharing and convergence possible across the globe. Dropping this geographic aspect of the definition of society allows a more accurate and complex understanding of all that a society is. For example, Palestinian society defies any strictly defined territorial boundaries (Abercrombie, Hill, and Turner 2000, 330).

SOCIAL STRUCTURE

Society includes our **social institutions,** *the major social organizations formed to meet our human needs.* The family, medical system, military, religious system, political system, economy, and educational system are all examples of social institutions. Many introductory sociology textbooks have chapters that discuss these institutions separately, explaining how sociologists apply their theoretical perspectives and research skills to each of these aspects of society.

All of these social institutions are interrelated. Together, they comprise a society's **social structure,** *the way a society is organized around the regulated ways people interrelate and organize social life.* What happens in the economy, for example, impacts all other institutions to some extent. If the economy takes a downturn, large numbers of people have might trouble supporting their families and paying for medical care or college. They might vote a new political candidate into office. Military recruitment and retention rates might increase because people are unable to find civilian-sector jobs. The interconnections go on and on.

Status

Status is central to social interaction and social structure. To sociologists, **statuses** are *established social positions.* Unlike popular usage of the term, having "status" in sociological terms does not equate to prestige. To sociologists, everyone has status, although some do have higher status than others as judged by society. The different statuses in a medical clinic, for example, include physician, nurse, lab technicians, janitorial staff, and patient. In this setting, the relationships between these positions are socially defined, with the doctor having the greatest power and prestige.

Statuses are obtained in different ways. They can be either achieved or ascribed. **Achieved statuses** are those *positions acquired through personal effort.* Being a law-school student, architect, parent, square dancer, or shoplifter are all achieved statuses. Individuals had to do something to become each of these things. **Ascribed statuses** are *positions involuntarily acquired through birth.* Being a female, a Caucasian, a toddler, a son, a brother, or a princess are all ascribed statuses. Some achieved statuses may depend at least to some extent on ascribed statuses. For example, because of their sex, women are not currently allowed to achieve positions as submariners in the U.S. navy.

Collectively, *all the statuses a person holds at once* comprise his or her **status set.** Each of the people in the clinic holds a number of different statuses at the same time. The doctor may also be a daughter, wife, mother, member of the garden club, and civic-league president. This status set changes frequently over a person's lifetime. Continuing with the doctor as an example, her status set changed when she moved from being a medical student to a doctor. It changed when she married and would change again if she were to divorce or be widowed. She could remove or add statuses from her set by resigning from the civic league or running for political office.

Some statuses in a status set are more socially important and influential than others. A very influential status may become a **master status,** *a status that becomes more socially important than all other statuses.* A master status may attach to either positive or negative statuses. The doctor in our example may be defined by her occupation. Whatever else she is, she is first a doctor to those she meets in social settings. Other people may respond to her with the prestige accorded that position. If the doctor were to be convicted of a serious crime such as insurance fraud or selling prescription narcotics, she might find that her master status becomes that of a criminal.

Roles

Roles, like statuses, are also central to social interaction and social structure. The two concepts of status and role go hand in hand. A **role** is a *behavior expected of someone in a particular status.* Using the status of the doctor from the examples above, a number of role expectations can be identified. Doctors should come to work. They should examine patients competently and discuss their concerns. They should prescribe medicine lawfully. All of these examples illustrate how we expect doctors to act. These roles together illustrate a **role set,** *all of the roles that go with a single status.*

The *roles for different statuses the person holds may conflict with each other.* This is known as **role conflict.** Our doctor, who is also a mother, may find it difficult to devote the long work hours required of her job and concurrently fulfill the expectations of being a parent. Long work hours may make attending her child's school plays or teacher conferences difficult. **Role strain** occurs when *two or more roles associated with a single status are in conflict.* This requires balancing expectations. For example, the doctor may find it difficult to give patients all the time she would like to during appointments while holding to her appointment schedule and seeing the number of patients she must see daily to meet the financial obligations of the clinic.

Aspects of Culture

Sociologists studying culture and society focus on several aspects of nonmaterial culture: cultural values, norms, symbols, and language. A look at each of these aspects contributes to our overall understanding of what culture is, how it is created and passed between generations, and how important culture is in everything we do.

Values

Values, *culturally defined ideas about what is important,* are central to culture. Values delineate how a culture should be. In the United States, sociologists have identified cultural values including success, hard work, freedom, equality, democracy, individualism, and progress (Bellah et al. 1985; Inkeles 1979; Williams 1970). Of course, not everyone in a culture shares identical values. They also do not share them equally. Some people or groups hold more tightly to certain values while rejecting others.

There may also be a mismatch between **ideal culture,** *the values and norms claimed by a society,* and **real culture,** *the values and norms that are actually practiced.* For example, in the United States, equality is a core value. Encompassed within this value is the ideal that all workers regardless of gender and race should have equal opportunity in the workplace. In reality, however, even women in high-status positions continue to earn less than men (Figart and Lapidus 1998) and experience discrimination in career promotions (Glass Ceiling Commission 1995; Rhode 2001), as do black males seeking high-level positions (Elliott and Smith 2004). These problems are even more pronounced for women of color (Collins 2000; St. Jean and Feagin 1998).

Norms

Norms are derived from our societal values. **Norms** constitute the *shared rules or expectations specifying appropriate behaviors in various situations.* We need norms to maintain a stable social order. They both direct and prohibit behavior (Hechter and Opp 2001). Norms tell us what we should do (wait our turn, pay bills on time, show respect for our elders, etc.); they also tell us what we should not do (hit our spouse, curse aloud at a church service, run red lights, etc.). Norms are enforced through a process of internalization. They become part of who we are as individuals and as a culture. However, external social enforcement in the form of both positive and negative sanctions is also critical (Horne 2001).

Norms vary over time. Women wearing trousers, especially in public areas or to work, is a relatively recent occurrence. Similarly, recent bans on smoking in many public places signifies shifting norms regarding smoking.

Norms, and the social reaction to breaches, vary in strength and intensity (Sumner 1906). **Folkways** are *weak norms that are often informally passed down from previous generations.* They often deal with everyday behaviors and manners. Most folkways are not written down and enumerated. They are the type of things that most of us learn from others to do or not to do. We learn from direct guidance and reinforcement. Parents teach children to share their toys and reward them with hugs and smiles. We also learn folkways through encountering others' reactions. People react perhaps with stares or avoidance when we act "inappropriately" by singing aloud on a bus or wearing a swimsuit while shopping in an expensive downtown boutique.

Violations of folkways are not considered severe breaches of great moral significance. Generally, no serious negative social sanctions (e.g., arrest) result when a folkway is broken. The reaction to a person who violates a folkway may be as minor as ignoring the behavior. Failing to say "thank you" may be considered rude, but will not result in some harsh penalty for norm violation.

We find folkways governing our behavior throughout our lives. They govern situations that are familiar to large segments of the population and smaller groups. For example, folkways govern Christmas gift-giving behavior, an event familiar to many. These norms are not written down anywhere, but they are "thoroughly familiar" to participants in the gift-exchange process. Among the folkways observed by Theodore Caplow (1984), gifts should be wrapped before they are given, distributed at gatherings involving reciprocal gift giving, and surprise the recipient. Additionally, gifts are scaled in economic value to the emotional value of the relationship. For example, a casual date would likely receive, and expect, a less expensive gift than a long-term date, fiancé, or spouse. Folkways also provide guidance in less widespread activities such as gathering mushrooms. Gary Alan Fine (2001) studied the Minnesota Mycological Society, the second-oldest continuously active mushroom society in the United States. He found that members are expected not to brag about the number of mushrooms they find, downplay big finds, offer to share, and not hoard a big find for themselves. They transfer these norms to new members through socialization (as discussed in chapter 4), talking, warnings of negative sanctions, and even moral messages indicating appropriate behaviors (Fine 2001, 157).

Mores (pronounced *more*-ays) are *strongly held norms.* They represent deeply held standards of what is right and wrong. Prohibitions on murder, robbery, and assault are all examples of mores across many cultures. Mores are considered morally significant breaches and are often formalized as laws. For this reason, punishment for violations of mores can be severe, involving sanctions such as arrest or imprisonment. Some mores are so strongly held they have been termed **taboos,** *norms that are so objectionable that they are strictly forbidden.* Taboos are often things considered unthinkable in a culture. Common examples include incest and cannibalism. Chapter 6 discusses violations of norms in much more detail.

Symbols

Symbols are central to our understanding and sharing of culture. A **symbol** is *something that stands for, represents, or signifies something else in a particular culture.* It can represent, for example, ideas, emotions, values, beliefs, attitudes, or events. A symbol can be anything. It can be a gesture, word, object, or even an event.

Sharing symbols can help build a sense of unity and commitment among people. A crucifix, cross, or Star of David are all symbols that have deep, shared meanings regarding Christianity or Judaism. National flags become rallying symbols for citizens and troops. The rush to buy American flags in the aftermath of the September 11, 2001, attacks in the United States is a good example of this effect in action.

The meaning of symbols derives from the way they are interpreted within a culture. The American flag may be interpreted as standing for individual freedom. However, some (e.g., American militia groups that think the federal government is too involved in their personal business) may see the flag as a symbol of a lack of freedom. People from other cultures see the flag as having various meanings filtered through their own cultural lenses (e.g., as a symbol of democracy, as a symbol of repression). To someone unfamiliar with the United

States, the American flag is not a symbol at all. It is simply a red, white, and blue pattern devoid of any such meanings.

Symbols may take on different meanings in different times or circumstances. White wedding gowns, originally intended to symbolize virginity, are now traditional in the United States even though many brides are not virgins. However, until Anne of Brittany wore white when she wed Louis XII of France in 1499, brides wore yellow or red. In China and Japan, brides wear white because that color symbolizes mourning and the symbolic death of the woman leaving her birth family to join her husband's family. Blue symbolized purity in biblical times, with both bride and groom wearing a blue band around the bottom of their wedding clothing. This old symbol is the origin of modern brides having "something blue" as part of their current wedding attire (Ackerman 1994, 271).

Some symbols are purposely given new meanings over time. During World War II, a pink triangle with the point facing downward was used by the Nazis to identify homosexual prisoners in concentration camps. Every group singled out for persecution in the camps was identified by similar symbols. Perhaps the best-known symbol was the yellow Star of David, composed of two triangles, one inverted on top of the other. In the 1980s, gay rights activists adopted the pink triangle as a symbol of pride and solidarity, a symbol of overcoming a history of oppression. Some groups, such as the activist group AIDS Coalition to Unleash Power (ACT-UP), have turned the triangle point up to further communicate activism and empowerment over oppression and passivity. (See chapter 9 for more discussion of people in action.)

Languages

Another major component of culture, and a special kind of symbol, is language. **Language** is *a system of symbols that allows communication among members of a culture.* These symbols can be verbal or written.

Language is central to the way we understand our world. According to the **linguistic-relativity hypothesis,** *languages reflect cultural perceptions.* This hypothesis is also known as the *Sapir-Whorf hypothesis* or the *Whorf hypothesis.* It is named after the anthropological linguists Edward Sapir (1884–1936) and his student Benjamin Lee Whorf (1897–1941), profiled below, who largely developed it. For example, because snow is so central to their lives, Eskimos have different words for falling snow, snow on the ground, drifting snow, and a snow drift (Boas 1911). The Canadian Aleuts have over 30 words for snow (Hiller 1933). Some other cultures in tropical climates have no word for snow, because they have no need for such a term. Yet, the Philippine Hanunoo people have almost 100 terms for rice (Thomson 2000).

Language also defines, at least to some extent, how we think about the world and how we act. Research has demonstrated that when people hear the pronoun *he* they think of a male, even if the pronoun was intended to encompass both males and females (Gastil 1990; Switzer 1990). Such findings are part of the impetus behind changing the grammatical convention away from use of male pronouns to represent everyone. Political spin doctors make careers of choosing words to influence the way we perceive issues. Additionally, the military carefully chooses euphemisms such as *collateral damage, friendly fire, shock and awe,* and *incident* to address such unpleasant realities as civilian deaths and troops mistakenly killed by allies (Deva 2003; Page 2003).

DIVERSITY

Sociologists are quite interested in the large amount of diversity that occurs even within particular cultures. Observers of culture in the United States would easily find many differences if they studied Hollywood's celebrity community, a neighborhood in Chicago largely populated by descendants of Eastern European immigrants, a Florida town that is home to many retirees, and a coal-mining town in southwestern Virginia. Although some sociologists have tried to find a common American culture and have often discussed middle-class culture as if that lifestyle applied to everyone, sociologists are increasingly recognizing the importance of studying, or even promoting, cultural differences.

As part of their interest in cultural diversity, sociologists study subcultures. A **subculture** is a *smaller culture within a dominant culture that has a way of life distinguished in some important way from that dominant culture.* Subcultures form around any number of distinguishing factors. They may form, for example, around hobbies (as with ham-radio operators, custom-car enthusiasts, bingo players, online-game players, hunters, stamp collectors, recreational-vehicle owners), shared interests such as music styles (jazz, hip-hop, rap), other behaviors or interests (cheerleaders, Bible study participants, skydivers, drug users, gamblers, outlaw bikers), occupations (car racing, pilots, police officers), or racial and ethnic backgrounds. Subcultures can also consist of even smaller divisions. For example, although the "teen subculture" may be discussed as if there is little diversity, teens are actually very diverse. They include jocks, hippies, preppies, ravers, skaters, and more. Each of these smaller subcultures has their own beliefs, interests, and means of interaction (Finnegan 1998). Yet members of a subculture share most of the values of the dominant culture. They earn money by having a job, pay bills, and see that their children get an education.

Not all smaller cultures within a dominant culture largely share the dominant culture's values. A *culture that opposes patterns of the dominant culture* is known as a **counterculture.** Countercultures are often youth-oriented (Spates 1976). In the 1960s, hippies advocated dropping out of the mainstream culture into a communal, peaceful, self-exploration lifestyle. Many hippies have today become, at least largely, part of the dominant culture. Militias and white supremacists are examples of modern-day countercultures.

A major issue in the United States, as well as in other cultures, is how much conformity to dominant cultural patterns will be required. America has long been called a melting pot into which others cultures meld into one new culture. The *process of a cultural group losing its identity and being absorbed into the dominant culture* is known as **assimilation.**

Many groups do claim shared cultural patterns. However, there is an increasing recognition and interest across the United States in **multiculturalism**— *a recognition of and respect for cultural differences.* Multiculturalism allows much of the dominant culture to be shared while valuing some traditions of various subgroups. Events such as Black History Month and courses such as Women's Studies acknowledge and embrace multiculturalism.

When studying cultures and cultural variations, sociologists must be aware of **ethnocentrism,** *judging other cultures by the standards of one's own culture.* Because we all live within a culture, we tend to see the way our culture does things as "normal" or "natural" and the ways that other cultures do things as "abnormal" or "unnatural." We also tend to judge our own familiar culture's ways of doing things as "better." This is the situation Napoleon Chagnon encountered with his study of the Yanomamo, discussed above.

Restaurant service provides a familiar and simple example. Americans often consider attentive restaurant waitstaff who check with diners several times during a meal as providing good service. Europeans visiting the United States might consider such service annoying. Good service in many places in Europe is defined by an almost invisible waitstaff that provides service without "hovering" around tables. Conversely, Americans visiting Europe might find such service lacking.

Things that are greatly different than our own cultures may evoke ethnocentric feelings. For example, learning that some cultures make meals of bugs or cats may seem especially unappealing to someone raised in the United States. Yet, these are seen as natural and readily accessible fare in the cultures where they are regularly eaten.

Rather than being ethnocentric, sociologists need to develop **cultural relativism.** This means they should be careful to *judge other cultures by those cultures' own standards.* In other words, sociologists try to understand other cultures and why they behave and believe as they do rather than judging them "unnatural" or "wrong."

A classic study by Marvin Harris (1974), who is profiled below, shows how ethnocentric views can result in major misunderstanding of other cultures. If these misguided views were used to enact social change, the consequences could be severe. Harris examined the Indian Hindu culture, in which cows are venerated as the mother of life. Thus, slaughtering cows for food is not an option. To someone from a wealthy Western country, an ethnocentric perspective on this reverence for cows would likely posit that cow worship is one factor in India's massive problems of poverty and hunger. Why not eat the cattle, they might ask?

Harris, examined the Indian ecosystem and studied the interplay between humans, culture, and their environment. His findings show how cultural relativism can give a new perspective to this issue. In India, cattle supply fertilizer, tractor power, and milk. Cattle dung provides fuel for cooking and flooring material. Children help their families and earn money by gathering and selling cow dung. Owning a cow provides one final hedge against creditors. The lower castes, that segment of society considered "untouchable" by the rest of society, are allowed to dispose of dead cattle. They are allowed to eat the meat and benefit from a huge leather-craft industry. Overall, Harris concludes that Indians would surely starve if they did eat cows.

SOCIOBIOLOGY

Sociologists focus on the importance of social influence in developing cultural patterns. Their emphasis is on how culture is created and perpetuated through social interaction. From this perspective, culture is a social creation and a product of social learning. It is not a product of biology.

However, a controversial area of study called **sociobiology** *ties together culture and biology.* The term *sociobiology* was coined in the 1970s by entomologist Edward O. Wilson, profiled below. Drawing from Charles Darwin's theory of evolution (1996, orig. 1859), research on evolutionary theory, and his own background in studying insect behavior, Wilson (1975, 1978) forwarded a perspective that argues that there are biological bases for some human behaviors.

According to Wilson, humans have certain genetically based instincts that influence behaviors and can be observed across cultures. From this perspective, "human beings inherit a propensity to acquire behavior and social structures, a propensity that is shared by enough people to be called human nature . . . Although people have free will and the choice to turn in many directions, the channels of their psychological development are nevertheless—however much we might wish otherwise—cut more deeply by the genes in certain directions than in others. So while cultures vary greatly, they inevitably converge toward these traits" (Wilson 1994, 332–33). These genetically based behaviors include a division of labor between sexes, parent-child bonding, incest avoidance, tribalism, establishing patterns of dominance between groups, and male dominance (332).

Critics argue that sociobiology is both unsupported by the preponderance of research and can be used to justify discrimination based on race or gender. If people of one race or gender are born with different skills, abilities, or predispositions than dominant groups, their qualities may be interpreted as inferior. Advocates argue that sociobiologists have conducted rigorous research. Although they acknowledge the potential for misuse, these advocates counter that there are important practical applications of sociobiology (e.g., counselors being able to help couples better understand sexual issues) that, if truly understood by the public, would not be misused (e.g., Alcock 2001).

GLOBALIZATION AND THE INTERNET

The structure of society has changed across time, largely due to various technological advances. These technologies range from the most basic (e.g., learning how to raise animals for food, cultivate crops, or use oxen to plow a field) to what we would consider today the most sophisticated (e.g., wiring financial transactions, knowledge sharing via the Internet). The spread of a common language (primarily English) is also central to the diffusion of culture and globalization (e.g., Smith 1990; Berger 2002). Some sociologists argue that these changes have led to increasing similarity across societies over time. Whether globalization and these technologies are leading to the rise of a global culture or society is, like many aspects of globalization, open to debate (McLuhan 1964; McLuhan and Fiore 1967). However, globalization and communications technologies will undoubtedly continue to change cultures and societies in new ways (Bell 1973, 1989; Lenski, Lenski, and Nolan 1991).

At a basic level, globalization facilitates business relationships and interactions that may seem deceptively simple. For example, in American culture, business cards are casually handed out to others and filed in wallets or folders for later reference. Such treatment of a business card would insult a Japanese businessperson. In that culture, to receive a business card and immediately place it in a wallet would be an insult. Cards should be handled graciously by the recipient and referred to during conversation with the owner. During a business dinner, diners may arrange the business cards of other diners around their place settings to reflect the seating of the card owners around the table. Doing so is not only a practical way for diners to recall names and affiliations, it also demonstrates respect for the card owners.

Culture is often adapted to fit the local area into which it is infused. The U.S. restaurant McDonald's has spread to many countries. In America, McDonald's is a fast-food restaurant: people buy an inexpensive meal, eat and leave, or get their order to go. They do not typically linger over the meal and make an evening out, as they might do at a more exclusive establishment. The McDonald's business model is designed around this fast-food idea. (See more about McDonald's and efficiency in chapter 5.) In east Asia, however, McDonald's patrons (especially housewives and children) linger over their food rather than eating and leaving. The establishments are clean and have restrooms, and the women are not hassled by men making unwanted advances. This patron behavior has required management strategies designed around fast food to adapt to the culture (Berger 2002, 10).

Existing culture is also being adapted to the virtual world of the Internet. Norms, for example, have also developed for online culture. According to online etiquette, typing in all capital letters is the equivalent of yelling. The Internet user who types messages in all capital letters might receive a range of sanctions by other users, including polite advice if they perceive the person to be an uninformed novice, "flaming" (written attacks aimed at the violator), or ignoring them. However, online venues may allow behaviors that would be considered unacceptable in offline interactions. For example, some multiuser domains commonly known as MUDs (online social worlds where the participants are able to interact and control various aspects of the program) create a violent virtual world in which characters are expected to fight, curse, rape, or kill other online characters (Dibbell 1999).

Subcultures also exist in cyberspace. For example, fans of such popular television series as *Star Trek, Xena: Warrior Princess,* and *The X-Files* have expanded a number of their subcultural activities online. There are over 1,200 *Star Trek* fan sites and over 200 *Xena: Warrior Princess* sites online (Bell 2001, 169).

Other subcultures exist because of, and relate closely to, the technology itself. These include MUDs, cyberpunks (those involved in writing that envisions a future of ever-present and ever-powerful computer technology), and hackers (programmers who engage in activities of breaching computer security systems or writing viruses) (Bell 2001). Additionally, largely through its global reach and acceleration of information exchange, the Internet has also contributed to the enlargement and reshaping of conspiracy subcultures and what Bell labels "fringe" beliefs (e.g., Ufology) (170–73).

BIOGRAPHIES

Napoleon Chagnon

Napoleon A. Chagnon (1938–) was born in Port Austin, Michigan, a small tourist town of only 500 people. Chagnon was the second child in a poor family of 12 children. He received his undergraduate and graduate degrees from the University of Michigan, completing his Ph.D. in 1966. After graduation, he joined the University of Michigan faculty, where he held joint appointments in the Department of Anthropology and in the Department of Human Genetics at the University's medical school. Chagnon held several subsequent positions and then moved to the University of California–Santa Barbara in 1984, until his retirement (Chagnon, 1997).

Starting when he was at Michigan, Chagnon has made several trips to South America to study the Yanomamo people. He says of those studies, "I wanted to get a job in anthropology and the best way to get a job was to do something different . . . If I was going to make a name for myself, I would have to do it by going to the most difficult, least desirable point in the world" (quoted in Bortnick 1999). Chagnon's book that chronicles his studies, *Yanomamo* (1997) is in its 5th edition and has sold over 800,000 copies. Chagnon is also involved in the authorship and production of documentary films.

The conclusions Chagnon drew have proven to be controversial among his colleagues (e.g., Bortnick 1999; Tierney 2000) and others. He even reports death threats (Bortnick 1999). However, Chagnon also has supporters. One colleague calls him "an inspiration . . . Some people don't like his results, but no one else in the world can match his data gathering" (quoted in Bortnick 1999). Among Chagnon's professional recognitions, he is a Fellow of the American Association for the Advancement of Science, the American Anthropological Association, and Current Anthropology. He also founded the Yanomamo Survival Fund in 1988 to support the Yanomamo people (Chagnon 1997; "Chagnon, Napoleon A." 1990).

Marvin Harris

Marvin Harris (1927–2001) was born in Brooklyn, New York. He earned his undergraduate and graduate degrees from Columbia University. After receiving his doctorate in 1953, Harris taught at Columbia for 27 years. In 1980, he took a position as Graduate Research Professor of Anthropology at the University of Florida–Gainesville. He remained there, often summering on the Maine coast, until his retirement in 2000 (Margolis 2002).

In *The Rise of Anthropological Theory* (1968) and *Cultural Materialism: The Struggle for the Science of Culture* (1979), Harris originated and developed the paradigm of cultural materialism, for which he is best known. According to Harris's paradigm, social and cultural patterns develop as people find ways to solve the practical problems of existence and best use available resources. Although a controversial paradigm, as many as half of U.S. anthropologists now claim to be cultural materialists to some extent (Margolis 2002, 9). Indeed, in 1986, *Smithsonian* magazine called Harris "one of the most controversial anthropologists alive" (quoted in Martin 2001).

Harris's research topics included finding explanations for a variety of "riddles of culture" involving race, evolution, food preferences (which he termed *human foodways*), and warfare, among others. By looking for the reasons behind such questions as why Hindus do not eat cows but Muslims, Jews, and Christians do, Harris felt that by "bring[ing] some light to bear on problems like that . . . people will be enlightened not only on the question but also on a way of approaching such questions" (Harris 2001).

Over the course of his career, Harris conducted research in such diverse locations as the United States, India, Mozambique, and Brazil. He also addressed American culture in *Why Nothing Works: The Anthropology of Daily Life* (1981). He wrote 17 books that were translated into 14 languages. His work included textbooks as well as books written for a popular audience. Harris also served as the president of the General Anthropology Division of the American Anthropological Association (Margolis 2002, 9).

Marshall McLuhan

Herbert Marshall McLuhan (1911–80) was born in Edmonton, Alberta, Canada. He earned his doctorate from Cambridge in 1943. Three years later, McLuhan joined the faculty of St. Michael's College, University of Toronto, where he stayed for the remainder of his career. He became a full professor in 1952. Beginning in 1963, he also served as the director of the Center for Culture and Technology, a center created to keep McLuhan at Toronto when other schools attempted to hire him away (Federmann, "Marshall McLuhan").

McLuhan addressed many aspects of culture, communication, and the media. His work is complex and not written in linear arguments. As one McLuhan scholar says, "How does one understand Marshall McLuhan? The answer is a quintessentially McLuhanesque paradox: To understand McLuhan, you must read McLuhan, but to read McLuhan, you must first understand McLuhan"

(Federman, "On Reading McLuhan," 1). McLuhan's books include *The Gutenberg Galaxy: The Making of Typographic Man* (1962), *Understanding Media: The Extensions of Man* (1964), and *War and Peace in the Global Village* (1967). He loved wordplay, titling one book *The Medium Is the Massage* (1967), and is credited with adding such terms as *global village* to our vernacular.

McLuhan was recognized around the world for his work. He was a Fellow of the Royal Society of Canada. He received an appointment as a Champion of the Order of Canada and a Vatican appointment as consultor of the Pontifical Commission for Social Communications. His awards include the President's Cabinet Award from the University of Detroit, Great Britain's Institute of Public Relations President's Award, the Christian Culture Award from Assumption University, and a Gold Medal Award from the President of the Italian Republic at Rimini, Italy. He also held honorary degrees from several universities.

Marshall McLuhan died in his sleep on New Year's Eve, 1980. After his death, the University of Toronto closed the Center for Culture and Technology. However, continued demand resulted in the creation of the McLuhan Program in Culture and Technology. In 1994, that program became a distinct segment of Information Studies at the University (Federman, "Marshall McLuhan"; McLuhan Program in Culture and Technology, "History and Mandate").

William Graham Sumner

William Graham Sumner (1840–1910) was born in Paterson, New Jersey. He obtained an undergraduate degree from Yale University in 1863. He then traveled to Europe for graduate studies in Britain, Switzerland, and Germany, after which he returned to Yale as a tutor. Sumner left Yale three years later and became an Episcopal pastor. In 1872, he returned once again to Yale as the chair of the Political and Social Science Department, where he would stay for 37 years.

In addition to being a pioneering sociologist, Sumner was a pastor, professor, economist, political scientist, historian, educator, and public servant (Curtis 1981). Intellectually, he was "vividly alive and insatiably curious," once writing to his father that he intended to "learn all I can about everything I can" (Starr 1925, 519).

Sumner offered his first sociology course in 1875. He became a popular lecturer, although he often did not know students by name (Curtis 1981, 47–48). He also became an educational reformer and a member of the Connecticut State Board of Education, and was elected for a term as alderman. Sumner was honored with an honorary doctorate of laws after his retirement in 1909, and he was elected president of the American Sociological Society (now the American Sociological Association) in the same year.

Although less known and influential among contemporary sociologists, Sumner was a well-known and influential sociologist during his lifetime. He "wrote with ease" (Starr 1925, 306), producing material on economic history, biographies, essays, political economy, and political science that included a dozen research-based books. His one major sociological work, *Folkways: A*

Study of the Sociological Importance of Usages, Manners, Customs, Mores, and Morals (1906), has been called one of "the few enduring monuments of American sociological theory," and his "concepts of folkways, of in-groups and out-groups, and of ethnocentricism" continue to be important in sociological thought (Curtis 1981, 154).

During his later years, Sumner was studying the customs and mores of a number of different cultures for a work on the "science of society." Albert Galloway Keller, Sumner's successor at Yale, estimated that for this single project Sumner had "collected and filed—without graduate student assistants—more than 150,000 notes from sources in the dozen languages that he read. His cross-referenced note system filled fifty-two file cabinet drawers" (Curtis 1981, 49). After suffering a stroke, Sumner died in 1910 before his final work was completed. Keller completed the work and published it as a coauthored four-volume series titled *The Science of Society* in 1927 (Curtis 1981; Starr 1925).

Benjamin Lee Whorf

Famous for reformulating the ideas of his teacher Edward Sapir into a view of language and culture known as the Sapir-Whorf hypothesis, Benjamin Lee Whorf (1897–1941) began his linguistic studies in his late 20s by learning Hebrew. His "personal struggle to resolve the competing claims of science and religion led him to focus on the study of language as a likely source of insight" (Schultz 1990, 7). His interest progressed to studies of Mexican people and language, correspondence with scholars in those areas, the presentation of his first scholarly paper in 1929, and a Social Science Research Council fellowship to study the Mayan language. He would also later study other languages (Carroll 1956; Schultz 1990).

Through his studies and interactions with Sapir and other Yale University faculty, Whorf refined his powerful concept of the connection between language and culture. To Whorf, "the way man talks about the universe is his only way of knowing anything about it . . . an Aztec had Aztec ideas about the world, an ancient Hebrew had Hebrew ideas . . . They all talk about reality, but to each, reality is what he can talk about in his own language" (Trager 1968, 537).

This may seem a successful, albeit unremarkable, career. However, until 1931, when he enrolled in a Yale course under Sapir, Whorf had been self-taught. He also held dual careers. Whorf was not an academic and held a job outside of the area of linguistics and anthropology throughout his life. He was a chemical engineer with a degree from the Massachusetts Institute of Technology and worked in fire-prevention engineering at the Hartford Fire Insurance Company. Economically, he did not feel he could leave that position to become an academic (Trager 1968). Whorf died at age 44.

Edward O. Wilson

Edward O. Wilson (1929–) was fascinated by and studied insects and sea life as a child. In addition to his interest in these creatures, he was also a self-described workaholic by the age of 13, delivering 420 newspapers each morning. Wilson had his first experience in teaching at age 14 as a nature counselor at a Boy Scout summer camp (Wilson 1994).

Wilson attended the University of Alabama, graduating in 1949. He earned a doctorate from Harvard University five years later. At age 26, he became an assistant professor at Harvard on a five-year contract. He was initially tasked to create a new biology course for non-science majors. Harvard offered him a tenured position only when he was recruited by Stanford University. As Pellegrino University Professor at Harvard four decades later, Wilson was still teaching his course on biology to non-science majors.

In 1975, Wilson authored *Sociobiology: The New Synthesis.* That work was followed in 1978 by *On Human Nature.* Both books were highly controversial, even among Wilson's colleagues at Harvard. They led to public attention, various groups distributing opposition leaflets, anti-sociobiology teach-ins, and small protests. An August 1, 1977, cover feature on sociobiology in *Time* magazine also generated strong reaction. Wilson recalls attending the annual meeting of the American Association for the Advancement of Science two months after that feature appeared. Before he could present his scheduled lecture, demonstrators took the stage, dumped a pitcher of ice water over his head, and chanted, "Wilson, you're all wet" (Wilson 1994, 307).

Among his many notable accomplishments, Wilson is curator in entomology at Harvard's Museum of Comparative Zoology. He has written 21 books, almost 400 articles, won two Pulitzer Prizes, and received 27 honorary doctoral degrees. Wilson's lengthy list of additional awards includes the National Medal of Science, presented at a White House dinner by President Jimmy Carter in 1977. He has also been awarded the 1990 Crafoord Prize of the Royal Swedish Academy of Sciences (an award that recognizes scientific fields not covered by the Nobel Prize), the 1993 International Prize for Biology, Saudi Arabia's King Faisal International Prize for Science (2000), the Franklin Medal of the American Philosophical Society (1999), and the Audubon Medal of the National Audubon Society (Wilson, "Dr. Edward O. Wilson Biography").

CAREERS IN SOCIOLOGY

Those with an interest and training in sociological perspectives on culture and society have backgrounds that prepare them for careers including

- advertising agent
- advocate for special-interest organization
- alumni-relations director/staff
- athletic/recreation coordinator
- college-recruitment/placement/admissions personnel
- communication director
- community specialist

- foreign-service worker
- human-resources management/staff-member
- industrial-relations specialist
- international-aid agency worker
- international-business researcher
- international-relations analyst
- journalist
- liaison for international organizations
- marketing/consumer researcher
- meeting/convention planner
- organizational trainer/facilitator
- outreach coordinator
- protocol officer
- public-relations specialist
- recruiter
- relocation coordinator
- resource developer
- seminar/workshop consultant
- special-events coordinator

Additional Resources

Alcock, John. 2001. *The Triumph of Sociobiology.* Oxford: Oxford University Press. This book tackles and defends many of the criticisms of sociobiology. It champions the perspective, but provides food for thought for both sides of the sociobiology debate.

Bell, David. 2001. *An Introduction to Cybercultures.* London: Routledge. This book covers a range of topics in cyberculture, including technology and research in cyberspace.

Berger, Peter L., and Samuel P. Huntington, eds. 2002. *Many Globalizations: Cultural Diversity in the Contemporary World.* New York: Oxford University Press. This series of essays look at the many cultural and societal impacts of globalization.

Chagnon, Napoleon. 1997. *Yanomamo.* 5th ed. Fort Worth, Tex.: Harcourt Brace. Follow Chagnon's famous research on the Yanomamo people and the changes that contact with the outside world has brought to the Yanomamo people.

Harris, Marvin. 1974. *Cows, Pigs, Wars, and Witches.* New York: Random House. Harris applies his concept of cultural materialism to explain the roots of human behaviors ranging from religious dietary prohibitions to beliefs in witches.

National Geographic Society. http://www.nationalgeographic.com/. This site covers a wealth of information on world cultures.

Peace Corps. *Culture Matters.* http://www.peacecorps.gov/wws/culturematters/. The Peace Corps has designed this cross-cultural training workbook to help new volunteers develop the skills they will need to work in other cultures.

University of Toronto, McLuhan Program in Culture and Technology. http://mcluhan. utoronto.ca/. Visit the Web site of this program, now a distinct research and teaching unit within the Faculty of Information Studies at the University of Toronto, to learn more about ongoing work in the McLuhan tradition.

U.S. Department of State. http://www.state.gov/. Search this page for information on country facts, travel advisories, cultural issues, and more for countries around the world.

CHAPTER 4
Socialization and Social Interaction

As humans, we are social beings who spend our lives interacting with others. Most of us have contact with other humans to some extent every day. Indeed, research shows that isolation from human interaction can be quite damaging. Sociologists and others have studied cases of children who spent their early childhood virtually isolated from all human contact, some literally locked away from human contact by abusive adults. These children lacked basic human responsiveness. Only after focused efforts to teach them social skills did these children begin to develop the social behaviors that are required to interact and live as a social being (e.g., Curtiss 1977; Davis 1940, 1947; Rymer 1993).

Sociologists study how we learn to live in society and interact with others—in other words, how the world is socially organized. They want to know how we learn social expectations, how we learn that these expectations apply to us, and how these expectations become part of us as individuals. They also want to know how these expectations are developed and perpetuated.

Socialization is a key to this social organization. **Socialization** is *a lifelong social process of learning cultural patterns, behaviors, and expectations.* Through socialization, we learn cultural values, norms, and roles. We develop a **personality,** *our unique sense of who we are.* We also pass along culture and social patterns to our children through socialization.

THEORIES OF SOCIALIZATION

An ongoing debate is whether human behavior is inborn and instinctual (resulting from "nature") or produced through socialization and social experience (resulting from "nurture"). In the nineteenth and early twentieth centuries, a widely held belief supported biologically based "human nature." Today, sociologists position themselves on the "nurture" side of this debate. Rather than talking in terms of behavior based on "human nature," sociologists talk in terms of human behavior based on socialization.

Research on how humans behave while drinking alcoholic beverages provides support for the influence of socialization. A common perception is that alcoholic beverages have a chemical impact on the brain, impacting sensorimotor skills, loosening inhibitions, and breaking the power that social norms typically hold on us. The resulting behavior is called a *drunken comportment.* If drunken comportment is entirely due to biology, then all people should exhibit the same behaviors as a result of drinking alcoholic beverages, regardless of their culture. If socialization is at play, then drunken comportment can be expected to vary according to cultural expectations.

To test this concept, Craig MacAndrew and Robert Edgerton (1969) explored accounts of drinking behavior among various cultures. They found that drunken comportment does indeed vary based on cultural expectations of how people act when under the influence of alcohol. Drunks among the Camba in Eastern Bolivia do not exhibit the heightened aggression, sexual activity, clowning, or boasting that are stereotypical drunken behaviors in the United States. Drinkers in Oaxaca, Mexico, are also not aggressive. Conversely, the Kaingang Indians in Brazil are very violent when drinking. All of these behaviors fit the expectations for drunken comportment in those particular cultures.

How and why do the members of each of these cultures know how to act drunk? How do they learn social expectations for various situations? And what is the impact of these expectations? Sociologists and others have developed and debated several theories to explain the socialization process and its implications.

The Looking-Glass Self

Charles Horton Cooley (1864–1929), profiled below, developed the concept of the **looking-glass self.** According to Cooley, *society provides a sort of mirror, or "looking-glass," that reflects to us who we are. We form our self image on the basis of how we think others see us.* This concept consists of three major parts: "the imagination of our appearance to the other person; the imagination of [the] judgment of that appearance; and some sort of self-feeling, such as pride or mortification" (Cooley 1964, 184). We come to think of ourselves in terms of how we imagine others see us. If we think that others see us as beautiful or humorous, for example, we come to see ourselves in those terms. If we think they see us negatively, our self-image is likewise negative.

Our self-image also impacts how we interact with others. For example, if a person perceives that others think they are humorous, that person forms a self-image of themselves as someone who can make others laugh. Acting on this self-image, they may routinely joke with others in social situations or become the "class clown." If a person forms a self-image of themselves as dumb, they will act accordingly by hesitating to speak up in class. However, our perceptions are not always correct. We may incorrectly interpret what others think of us. The person who thinks others see him as an amusing jokester may actually annoy or embarrass people.

Cooley also recognized that everyone's view of us is not equally important. Those people who are more important to us have greater impact on our self-image than do others. A spouse's compliment or derogatory statement may have a greater effect on someone's self-perception than the same comment made by a stranger passing on the sidewalk.

Those whose views are most important to us are those in our primary group. **Primary groups** are those *small groups in which all the members have enduring, intimate face-to-face interaction and cooperation.* Cooley coined the term *primary* for these groups because they include the family, our first social group, and these groups provide much of our early and important socialization and social linkages. Close friends, children's play groups, and perhaps even some neighbors and some work groups also constitute primary groups. As Cooley explains, primary groups are "fundamental in forming the social nature and ideals of individuals. The result of intimate association . . . is a certain fusion of individualities in a common whole . . . [T]he simplest way of describing this wholeness is by saying that it is a 'we' " (1963, 23).

In primary groups, members value each other as individuals and achieve some personal fulfillment. They do things that will benefit the group, without expectation of payment or self-serving benefit. One member of a family might wash laundry or perform housework that benefits all family members. A few close friends might spend several unpaid days working to repair the roof on another friend's house.

Other groups in our lives are **secondary groups,** *larger groups in which all members do not interact directly and have relationships that are not permanent.* Members do not share the intimate bonds characteristic of primary groups and, thus, are somewhat interchangeable. They join the group because it benefits them in some way. They may leave the group or join other groups as it behooves them to do so. However, these groups may still have some shared norms and sense of group identity. Examples of secondary groups include office workers, students in an exercise class, neighborhood civic leagues, and professional organizations. These groups are also important to our views of ourselves, but less so than primary groups. (See chapter 5 for a more extensive discussion of groups.)

The I and Me

George Herbert Mead (1863–1931), profiled below, developed a concept of the self that was central to our understanding of the socialization process and the development of symbolic interactionism (as discussed in more detail in chapter 2.) To Mead (1934), we are not born with a "self." We develop a self through social experience and interaction.

There are two phases to this self that we form: the *I* and the *Me.* The *I* is a spontaneous, impulsive, creative actor. The *Me* is the part of us that conforms, reflecting and acting on the reactions of others. We have a mental conversation with ourselves that guides our behaviors that goes like this: When *I* do something, it will reflect on *Me,* and others will appraise that behavior. *I* can then fashion new actions and reactions in response to my perception of how others have appraised *Me.*

The core of socialization in Mead's concept is **role taking,** or *the ability to take the role of others in social interaction, enabling us to see ourselves as we perceive society sees us.* In other words, we learn to assess and adjust our behavior based on the anticipated and perceived reactions of others. We develop this role-taking ability through a series of four stages. As we move through each of these stages, we become increasingly able to take the role of others and further develop our self. In the *preplay stage,* babies do not have the ability to take the role of others. They only respond to their environment. As children develop, they grow into the *play stage.* They play at being some particular person, such as Mommy or Daddy, or a teacher, and they play with imaginary playmates. This, according to Mead, is the stage during which the self begins to form. In the organized *game stage,* children learn to take the role of multiple other players and understand the relationship these roles have to each other. A child playing kickball must understand the roles of each player on the field to play his own role. Upon reaching the *adult stage,* the person becomes able to take on a role Mead calls the *generalized other.* In this stage, they learn to take the attitude of the whole community. They learn to think about how the community perceives their behavior. The self is finally formed as the person comes to understand and respond to societal values. They can then fashion their behavior by having the complete *I/Me* mental conversation.

More recent research by sociologists has considered whether the concepts of Cooley and Mead can be applied to animals. Mead said that animals could not engage in these types of interactions because they lacked the cognitive skills (e.g., memory and language) to do so. However, Cooley did not see language as critical for such interaction. In their study of a cat shelter, sociologists Janet and Steven Alger found that "although the caretakers did not believe that the cats had conversations with themselves in human language, they gave examples of cats appearing to make mental calculations based on memory, taking the role of the other, and accessing future consequences. These mental calculations allowed the cats to define the situation, choose a course of action, and change that course when necessary" (2003, 16). Other researchers (e.g., Arluke and Sanders 1996) are also examining the interactions in the social world of animals.

Personality and Social Development

Sociologists have also looked to the field of psychology for insights that help inform their understanding of the socialization process. Much of the work of Sigmund Freud (1856–1939), profiled below, is both complex and controversial. However, Freud made important contributions to our understanding of socialization. He argued that early socialization is critically important to personality development and to managing natural desires that promote self-interest rather than social interests. He also addressed the importance of internalizing norms and values. Additionally, Freud (1950) moved beyond Cooley's and Mead's focus on conscious perceptions, identifying the importance of the unconscious mind.

Freud (1950) saw personality as divided into three parts: the id, the ego, and the superego. The **id** is made up of *our basic biological drives and needs.* These are our sexual drives and fundamental needs, including food. They are self-centered rather than socially centered, and they crave immediate gratification.

The **ego** is *our "self," our personality, which balances the urges of the id with the requirements of a civil society.* The desires of the id have to be tempered. Chaos would result if everyone was constantly seeking to gratify all of their own desires. Society would not be able to exist as we know it. Through socialization, which Freud saw as primarily the responsibility of parents, we learn to repress our id and develop the ego.

The **superego** consists of *our internalized social controls, culture, values, and norms.* It is our conscience. The id and the superego are engaged in a constant struggle, mediated by the ego in a largely unconscious process. If the ego mediates properly, the person will be well socialized and well adjusted. Otherwise, the result will be a personality problem.

Freud focused largely on the importance of early childhood (the preschool-age years) in our socialization and later development. Other psychologists have developed theories that, while often focusing on the importance of childhood, elaborate on other age-based life stages and social experiences.

German psychologist Erik Erikson's (1985) cross-cultural studies have led him to conclude that we pass through eight stages of age-based development, from early infancy through our late adult years. According to his perspective, developmental tasks must be accomplished each stage before the person can move on to the next stage to grow up and live in a psychologically healthy way.

Jean Piaget (1896–1980), a Swiss psychologist, developed a theory of **cognitive development** that examined *how children develop the ability to learn, understand, and engage in logical thought.* Piaget felt that humans develop through four stages as they learn to use language, understand reality, discover how and why things work as they do, and then think abstractly. They learn to make causal connections and reason out alternatives. A corresponding theory of **moral development** examined *how people progress from the self-centeredness of a small child, through learning, to understand others' standpoints and develop an abstract sense of fairness.* Social experience is a vital role throughout this development (Piaget 1926, 1928, 1930, 1932).

This theory of moral development was further expanded by Lawrence Kohlberg. According to Kohlberg (1984), moral development also occurs in stages. Children do what meets their needs to stay out of trouble. As young teens, people are socialized into meeting socially accepted norms and values. Some adults are then able to engage in abstract ethical reasoning, considering not only "right" and "wrong" but the reasons for these positions.

How socialization impacts this moral reasoning has been the subject of further research by psychologist Carol Gilligan (1982; Gilligan, Ward, and Taylor 1989). Considering gender, she argues that boys and girls use different principles in moral reasoning. These principles reflect **gender-role socialization,** *the process of learning to take on socially approved roles for males and females.* Boys tend to focus on justice, whereas girls tend to focus on caring and responsibility. Gender-role socialization impacts us throughout our lives. It influences the way we approach social relationships, leisure activities, even our jobs. For example, Lawson (2000) demonstrates that gender even impacts how men and women sell cars. Male salespeople focus more on aggressive sales tactics, while women are more likely to use their interaction skills.

These psychological theories have been targets of various criticisms. Critics argue that they are largely based on studies of males (excluding Gilligan) and the middle class and tend to generalize findings from Western cultures to other cultures. However, they are important in pointing out that socialization is a process of development.

THE SOCIALIZATION PROCESS

Sociologists recognize that the experience of socialization is a lifelong process. It occurs from childhood through adulthood and even into old age. It occurs across our entire life span and, to some extent, across all of our social interactions. People move into, and out of, roles throughout their lives from "getting a driver's license, high school graduation, marriage, divorce, the first full-time job, retirement, [through] widowhood. In general, each major transition initiates a new socialization experience or situation that has implications for the individual's self-concept" (Gecas 2000, 2861). At the end of life, socialization processes even help people prepare for death (Kubler-Ross 1969).

Across all societies, the *family* is the first and most important location for socialization (an *agent* of socialization). The family into which we are born provides us social characteristics such as social class, race and ethnicity, and religious background. Our families are our initial teachers of behaviors, language, cultural knowledge, values, and social skills. They are also central to gender role socialization (Fenstermaker Berk 1985). In other words, they provide our primary socialization.

Older research focused almost exclusively on parents as agents of socialization for children. Newer research examines how children influence parents as well (Gecas 2000, 2858). Researchers are also looking at how changing family structures, such as the increasing number of single-parent families, impact child socialization (McLanahan and Sandefur 1994).

In schools, students are exposed to a variety of different experiences. They interact with people of different races, ethnicities, religions, social classes, and value systems, perhaps for the first time. These secondary-group interactions with schoolmates and staff are different than the primary-group interactions they have had with their families. When children enter school, they enter a bureaucracy where they are expected to learn how to be a student (Gracey 2001). They will be educated not only in academic skills, but also in a **hidden curriculum** that encourages *conformity to the norms, values, and beliefs held by wider society.* Students learn to speak with proper grammar, stand in line, wait their turn, and in some schools, say the Pledge of Allegiance to the U.S. flag. In addition to families, schools also contribute to gender-role socialization. Formal and informal institutional activities such as recess periods and games socialize children into culturally approved gender roles (e.g., Best 1983; Block 1983; Thorne and Luria 1986).

Socialization also occurs among **peer groups,** *those of similar age, social class, and interests.* Peer settings allow children to engage in activities outside of parental control and other adult supervision. Peers become especially important in adolescence. They influence students' study habits (Bogler and Somech 2002), music, and clothing choices, and views of self (Eder 1995). Theories that address peer socialization are often used to explain adolescent deviance (see chapter 6). Friends are a major source of information about sexuality for adolescents, and they have a greater influence on dating choices than do adults (Wood et al. 2002). Pressure from peers encourages teens to engage in sexual intercourse, with boys in particular pressing each other to talk about sexual prowess and "scoring" (Sprecher and McKinney 1993). Parents, however, have influence over many of the "big" areas in adolescents' lives, such as their long-term goals (Davies and Kandel 1981).

Mass media, *impersonal communications that are directed in a one-way flow to a large audience,* are also important in the socialization process. These media are pervasive throughout society. They include newspapers, magazines, movies, radio, and television. We are exposed to a variety of behaviors, ideas, beliefs, and values through the media. We also obtain many of our views about society and how things are or should be through the mass media. For example, whether or not we have ever met a team of emergency room physicians or observed surgery, we develop expectations about these people and situations based on media portrayals (e.g., televised medical dramas and documentaries about medical procedures). A number of studies have found that the mass media in various forms including children's books (e.g., Davis 1984; Peterson and Lach 1990), television programming (e.g., Thompson and Zerbinos 1995), and advertising (Kilbourne 2000) perpetuate gender stereotypes and gender role socialization.

The socialization process continues in a variety of settings, including religious organizations, political organizations, recreational settings, and voluntary associations such as clubs (Gecas 2000, 2860). The workplace is also a major location for socialization. Workplace socialization requires that we learn to fulfill the role of worker, demonstrating the requisite job skills and norms associated with the position (Moreland and Levine 2002). Nurses, for example, must learn how to transfer the skills and values acquired during training to the work setting (Lurie 1981). That includes fitting the norms of how nurses interact with physicians, colleagues, and patients, how they dress, and how they present themselves as a "nurse."

While in nursing school, student nurses are also influenced by **anticipatory socialization.** They *learn and adopt the behavior and attitudes of the group they desire or expect to join.* This occurs as they interact with their peers and attempt to fit in with their mentors and established colleagues. Anticipatory socialization occurs in many settings across society. It's not specific to the workplace. It occurs in any group we wish to join or use as a reference group. For example, we anticipate how to fit in with classmates, a potential spouse's family, or members of a sports team we join (see Chapter 5).

Retirement from paid work also continues the socialization process. Many workers look forward to being able to leave their jobs and move on to another position or leisurely activities. What they find may be unexpected, at least to some degree. Social expectations for retirees are not as clearly defined as for other stages in the life course. This leaves some retirees in a "roleless" role. However, loss of the worker role is less of a problem to retirees than other issues such as health or income (e.g., Solomon and Szwabo 1994), and most retirees experience their retirement years positively (Atchley 2000; Palmore et al. 1985; Crowley 1985).

Overall, as the population ages, sociologists and other researchers are devoting more attention to socialization in adulthood and later life. They are even questioning whether we are expanding later life stages (e.g., post-retirement and widowhood) or creating new ones (e.g., "nursing home stage") (Gecas 2000, 2861).

TOTAL INSTITUTIONS AND RESOCIALIZATION

A specific type of socialization occurs when people are in places such as prisons, mental hospitals, and military boot camps. These settings are total institutions. According to Erving Goffman, a **total institution** is *"a place of residence and work where a large number of like-situated individuals, cut off from wider society for an appreciable period of time, together lead an enclosed, formally administered round of life"* (1961, xiii; italics mine). Staff separate "inmates" from the outside world and enforce a routinized lifestyle within the institution. Mealtimes, work periods, recreation periods, and bedtimes may be tightly scheduled, and uniforms are often required.

A major goal of enforcing these routines is to achieve **resocialization,** *altering the person's personality by controlling the environment.* This resocialization reshapes the inmate's personality to fit the needs of the institution. It takes place in two steps. First, the existing sense of self must be broken down. The inmate is systematically separated from the old self and outside life. Second, a new self must be built with new behaviors and attitudes. This is often accomplished through staff manipulation of rewards and punishments.

Louis A. Zurcher (1967) drew from his own experience and other data to explain resocialization in navy boot camp. In that setting, all aspects of a recruit's life are controlled by the central authority (i.e., the U.S. navy). There is a single plan for all recruits that challenges their civilian selves and reorients them to a military standard. The recruits' personal autonomy is challenged by requiring them to adhere to strict schedules and rules for care and storage of gear. Their sense of personal privacy is removed by staff access to their personnel folders and by requirements to disrobe for medical lineups. Their physical self-concepts are challenged by requiring that they wear naval attire and get haircuts. Their bodies are even controlled by requiring them to stand at attention and march in formation everywhere they go as a group. As a result of the resocialization process, recruits replace their former identities with the new role of sailor.

SOCIALIZATION AND SOCIAL INTERACTION

To interact effectively with each other, people must have some shared sense of the world. They must interact within some social "reality" that defines how to interact and what those interactions mean. To sociologists, this "reality" is not objective. Rather, it is subjectively understood and built through our day-to-day contacts with each other. This concept is central to the symbolic-interactionist perspective, discussed in chapter 2.

The **social construction of reality** is *the process by which people interact and shape reality* (Berger and Luckmann 1966). According to this concept, society is not some objective entity that evolves in a predetermined and unchangeable way. Humans create it through social interactions. As we interact with others, we constantly talk, listen, observe, evaluate, and judge situations based on the ways we have been socialized to understand and react to them. Through this ongoing process of perceiving and defining events, we "interpret" reality and "negotiate" meaning. For example, a worker who has been repeatedly disciplined by management might perceive a supervisor striking up a conversation as harassment, intimidation, or management checking up on them. A worker with no disciplinary actions on their record might perceive the same conversation as friendly chat.

Central to this idea is the **Thomas Theorem,** *the understanding that if we define situations as real, they are real in their consequences* (Thomas and Thomas 1928). This means that we respond to the subjective meanings that a situation has for each of us. We then behave based on that interpretation. As Lewis Coser summarizes, "If people believe in witches, such beliefs have tangible consequences—they may, for example, kill those persons named to be witches . . . It stands to reason, of course, that there are benevolent as well as malevolent consequences of such definitions of the situation; peasant girls can become saints and politicians high-minded statesmen. In any case, and regardless of the consequences, definitions always organize experience" (1977, 521–22). In Coser's example, it does not matter whether witches actually exist. What matters is whether people believe they exist. They act on the basis of that belief in ways that have very real consequences. Peter Berger and William I. Thomas, two of the sociologists first articulating these important concepts, are both profiled below.

Dramaturgy

How this shared sense of realty develops and plays out is basic to sociologists' understanding of society and social organization. Erving Goffman (1959, 1963a, 1967), profiled below, developed a **dramaturgical analysis** in which he *compared our everyday social interactions to theatrical performances.* According to Goffman, we interact as if we are actors performing roles on a stage. We *use these performances to direct and control the impressions we make in others' minds.* This is called **impression management.** Through a "presentation of self," we consciously attempt to influence how other people see us. The campaign literature published by political candidates is an excellent example of this concept in action (King 2002).

Developing the theater analogy, Goffman divides social interaction into *front-stage* and *back-stage* regions. Just like in a play, **front-stage behavior** is *action that occurs for an audience.* We use appearances, mannerisms, and props in this front stage to facilitate our act and better manage the impression we seek to make. Consider, for example, behaviors on a first date. Clothing, conversation topics, and location are selected to convey the way the daters wish to present themselves. During a job interview for an office position, the interviewee might wear a conservative business suit, carry a résumé in a nice folder, and lean forward when answering questions in an attempt to create a positive image in the interviewer's mind.

Back-stage behavior *occurs out of sight of any audience.* That is where the props and performances are prepared. It is also where we can truly be ourselves. Preparing for the date or interview in the privacy of home occurred back stage, as clothing and appearances were selected. During a front-stage event, a person might go back stage into a restroom to check or readjust his appearance. After the date or the interview, the person can go home, put on comfortable clothes, and "be himself."

Our social performances are complex interactions. They consist not only of actively presenting information but also often include concealing information as well. Daters may not reveal, for example, that they have a child or that they smoke cigarettes in an attempt to convey certain images to their date. Job candidates might conceal a police record or lack of computer skills. Regina Kenen found people in a public laundromat engaged in impression management even among strangers. She observed people as they tried to conceal "padded bras, torn underwear, stained garments, or even designer bedsheets . . . [as items that may reveal too much personal information] and may contradict the intended presentation of self" (1982, 178).

Goffman also notes that in our social interactions we are both actor and audience at the same time. On the first date, both parties are concerned with managing their own performances as well as interpreting their dates' performance. Throughout the date, they are evaluating performances by asking, "How am I coming across? What does that person think of me?" as well as "What do I think of this person? Do I want another date?" In the interview situation, the interviewer as well as the person being interviewed are both engaged in a performance, an act of attempting to convey information to the other person. The office in which the interview is conducted, the way the office furniture is set up, the types of decor used, the way the interviewer is dressed, and the interviewer's tone and mannerisms all convey an image about the company and the interviewer.

We are constantly reevaluating our performances in light of feedback we perceive we are getting from others. This does not mean that we always perceive feedback correctly, only that we adjust our own acts in response to whether we think we are making the desired impression on others. We may feel we need to appear more sincere, more hardworking, more free-spirited, less anxious, and so on and try to adjust our "performance" to convey these desired impressions.

Ethnomethodology and Conversation Analysis

Ethnomethodology is based on work Harold Garfinkel (1967, 2002) started in the 1940s. Garfinkel is one of the sociologists profiled below. Literally meaning the "people's methods," **ethnomethodology** is defined as *people making sense of their everyday social activities.* This perspective examines our patterns of everyday life and how people construct their social worlds. To this end, ethnomethodologists study the routine and small interactions that we engage in on a daily basis.

Ethnomethodology starts from the idea that our everyday interactions with each other produce an orderly world. However, we live by social rules that we are only vaguely aware of, if we are aware of them at all. These are not the mores or laws discussed in chapter 3 or the criminal deviance discussed in chapter 6. Rather, the rules that interest Garfinkel are the norms and folkways that guide routine interactions and behaviors. His premise argues that even as we interact and follow these rules, we still take much of our world for granted.

Ethnomethodologists often seek to demonstrate the existence of these rules by breaking them. Garfinkel conducted a series of "breaching experiments" in which he asked his students to break, or breach, the rules of social order. This would allow them to expose that order and how it is constructed and taken for granted. In one of these now classic experiments, Garfinkel asked students to act as boarders in their own homes. For 15 minutes to one hour, they were to be polite and use formal addresses (e.g., Mr., Mrs.), not make personal conversation, and speak only when spoken to by others.

Students reported that family members' reactions covered a range of emotions. They were variously irritated, astonished, bewildered, anxious, or embarrassed. Students were accused of being selfish, impolite, mean, superior, and inconsiderate. They were asked what was wrong and whether they were ill, working too hard, or angry. They were then often isolated with statements such as "Don't bother with him, he's in one of his moods again." Family members often demonstrated emotional reactions as they tried to understand behaviors that did not fit their constructions of typical family behavior (Garfinkel 1967, 47).

Conversation analysis is an offshoot of ethnomethodology that *focuses on the importance of conversation in creating social order.* The everyday inquiry of "How are you?" that is commonly used as a polite greeting provides an example. A common response to this question is something such as "Fine" or "I'm well, thank you." The common understanding between the parties to the conversation is that the question is generally a social greeting, not a literal inquiry into the state of one's health. If the respondent were to reply with what may be a truthful answer, such as "I'm feeling awful—I have a pain in my back, the children are wearing me out, my spouse is constantly nagging me about money, and my supervisor is asking for a report I haven't had time to start yet," the social interaction would change considerably.

To expose these types of taken-for-granted understandings that guide our conversations, Garfinkel recounts the following exchange. It occurred during an assignment in which his students were directed to ask for clarification of statements that would otherwise be understood through these taken-for-granted assumptions:

The victim waved his hand cheerily.

(S) How are you?
(E) How am I in regard to what? My health, my finances, my school work, my peace of mind, my . . . ?
(S) (Red in the face and suddenly out of control.) Look! I was just trying to be polite. Frankly, I don't give a damn how you are. (1967, 44)

Critics of ethnomethodology argue that these details are too trivial to be important. They argue that the approach focuses too much on orderliness in society and does not adequately take the larger social structure into account. Ethnomethodologists respond that there is much to be learned from the assumptions they challenge and the rules they expose. "It is possible that detailed study of small phenomena may give an enormous understanding of the way humans do things" (Sacks 1984, 24).

GLOBALIZATION AND THE INTERNET

As the complexity of society grows, so does the complexity of the issues involved in socialization. The larger world provided by globalization and information technologies are changing the processes and outcomes of socialization. Researchers interested in socialization are increasingly extending beyond the mainstream American perspectives that have long typified socialization research. Increasing numbers of cross-cultural comparisons, such as the similarities and differences in socialization experiences in varying cultures, are being undertaken.

Different cultures have varying concepts of life-stages such as "childhood," "adulthood," and "old age," and associated social roles (Aries 1962). Globalization is challenging these concepts as well as concepts of ethnicity and identity. Researchers are seeking ways to make children more active participants in their own socialization in this changing world (e.g., Ackroyd and Pilkington

1999; Bellamy 2002). They are also focusing on how families can better prepare their children for a globalized world (Rapoport 1997).

Much less attention has been given to how such technologies as the Internet are changing how socialization happens and the results of the socialization process (Gecas 2000, 2862). However, globalization and the Internet together are combining to impact how socialization occurs. For example, the Internet appears to be helpful in resocializing Chinese students and scholars in the United States to American behaviors (Melkote and Liu 2000).

Sociologists have identified several other impacts on socialization brought about by the Internet. Computing changes such as networked school classrooms and increasing bandwidth have been a factor in changing curriculums that include new ways of learning and more emphasis on social issues. The potential result could ultimately be a reconsideration of the role and purposes of schools (Russell 2000).

Sociologists interested in the impact of the Internet on socialization processes have also been able to study how a shared sense of reality develops in virtual interactions. For example, Goffman's concepts are not found only in face-to-face interactions. They are also a part of online interactions. Presentation of self occurs on the Internet via the personal home page (Bell 2001, 117–18). People pick and choose various facets of their personalities and lives to present online, or they can present themselves any way they choose to do so. Cyberspace allows participants to play with their identity and create multiple selves online. They present themselves and basic characteristics of race, class, gender identities in various ways (Kendall 2002).

People may also act differently on the Internet than when interacting face to face (Joinson 1998). Online norms may accept behaviors that would be considered unacceptable in offline interactions. For example, some multiuser domains (MUDs) create a violent virtual world in which characters are expected to fight, curse, rape, or kill other online characters (Dibbell 1999). However, other research suggests that the Internet may actually facilitate building social bonds among physically separated people who can share perspectives and connections aside from the familiarity of face-to-face interactions (Chayko 2002). Further research into social interactions on the Internet is a rich field for research and will help us better understand how we relate in the virtual world and how these interactions will impact other aspects of our lives.

BIOGRAPHIES

Peter Berger

Peter Berger (1929–) was born in Vienna, Austria. He became a naturalized U.S. citizen in 1952 ("Berger, Peter Ludwig" 1981). Berger is currently University Professor of Sociology and Theology at Boston University. He holds a doctorate earned from the New School for Social Research in 1954. He has also studied at the University of Michigan, the Yale Divinity School, and

Philadelphia's Lutheran Theological Seminary. Berger has received honorary degrees from Loyola University, Wagner College, the University of Notre Dame, the University of Geneva in Switzerland, and the University of Munich in Germany. He is also a novelist.

Berger is a prolific, widely read, and widely cited sociologist. His work *The Social Construction of Reality* (1966), coauthored with Thomas Luckmann, is one of the most important works in interpretive sociology. *Invitation to Sociology* (1963) is also an influential work that is widely assigned to students in introductory sociology courses. Berger's work includes writings on social theory and the sociology of knowledge, the sociology of religion, and work on modernization and social change that incorporates his theological and political concerns (Hunter and Ainlay 1986). Berger has also held the presidency of the Society for the Scientific Study of Religion. Of his career, Berger says, "You might say that I became a sociologist by accident. I took some courses in sociology and liked them. I have always been curious about what makes people tick, and that is what sociology is all about" (quoted in Henslin 2001a, xx).

For almost two decades, Berger has been Director of the Institute for the Study of Economic Culture. He is coeditor of *Many Globalizations: Cultural Diversity in the Contemporary World* (2002), a collection that addresses social change across the globe. His work in the area of global culture was recognized in 1992 when he received the Mannes Sperber Prize from the Austrian government (Berger, "Peter Berger").

Charles Horton Cooley

Charles Horton Cooley (1864–1929) was born the fourth of six children to a well-known Ann Arbor, Michigan, family. His father was "hard-driving and success-oriented," (Coser 1977, 314) serving as the first dean of the University of Michigan Law School, the first chair of the Interstate Commerce Commission, a Michigan Supreme Court justice, and legal author. The younger Cooley has been described as being "overawed" and alienated from his father and as having a "withdrawn, passive, and retiring character." He was somewhat shy and insecure with a slight speech impediment and variety of health problems. As an adult, Cooley and his family led a simple, quiet life summering at their lake cabin in Northern Michigan. He was an amateur botanist and bird watcher (Coser 1977).

To Cooley, sociology was "a means of interpreting life-situations" (Healy 1972, 95). His own self-examination and observation of his children aided him in forming his concepts of the *looking-glass self* and *primary groups* (Coser 1977). A journal he began at age 18 provided as the source for his 1927 book *Life and the Student* (Angell 1968).

Cooley did not turn to sociology until he was in his late 20s. He earned an undergraduate degree in engineering, worked as a draftsman and as a statistical researcher in Washington, D.C., and studied political economy as a graduate student at University of Michigan. He earned his Ph.D. in 1894. His dissertation, "The Theory of Transportation," was an early work in the area of human ecology (a perspective discussed in chapter 8).

Cooley took a teaching position in economics and sociology at Michigan before he completed his degree and remained there for his entire career. Although he was not as popular with undergraduates, he had a powerful influence on many of his graduate students. "The lectures that this slight, nervous, and somewhat sickly looking professor delivered with a high-pitched voice lacking resonance often would not go over well with the undergraduates. Yet he appealed to a number of graduate students who were inspired by his probing and searching intellect. Many of the graduate students felt that it was a privilege to sit in his seminars . . . [A]s many of his students have testified, those who managed to gain privileged access in his seminars and classes to the workings of his complicated mind were influenced by his approach throughout their lives" (Coser 1977, 316).

Cooley, himself a voracious reader, wrote only a few journal articles and books, including *Human Nature and Social Order* (1902), *Social Organization* (1909), and *Social Process* (1918). He was a founding member of the American Sociological Society (the organization that would become the American Sociological Association) and served as its president in 1918.

Sigmund Freud

Sigmund Freud (1856–1939) was born in Freiberg, Monrovia. His family moved to Vienna, where he spent almost his entire life. Freud entered the University of Vienna in 1873, earning his medical degree in 1881. He took a position as a resident at Vienna General Hospital and joined the hospital's Department of Nervous Diseases two years later. He studied in Paris, then returned to Vienna, married, and established his private practice in 1886.

Among Freud's many accomplishments are his discovery of the unconscious mind, his use of hypnosis as a treatment for hysteria, and his development of psychoanalysis. The latter depended on his recognition of the relief that talking could bring to some patients. He saw his "talking cure" as a catharsis, or purging, of intense emotions.

Freud's writing included a number of influential books. *Civilization and Its Discontents* (1929) was a theoretical piece examining social relations. He laid out his concept of the id, ego, and superego in *The Ego and the Id* (1923). Freud conducted his own self-analysis and developed his theory of the unconscious in *The Interpretation of Dreams* (1950, orig. 1900), a book that has been called by some his most important work.

Among his awards, Freud received an honorary degree from Clark University in Worcester, Massachusetts, and the Goethe Prize for literary achievement. He was elected a Corresponding Member of the Royal Society. He also founded an international publishing firm.

In pre–World War II Germany, Freud's books were among those publicly burned by the Nazis. Shortly after Germany's 1938 invasion of Austria, Freud fled to London. In 1939, he died of mouth cancer, which he had fought for the last 16 years of his life. Treatments had required the removal of much of his right jaw and palate in a series of 33 painful surgeries. He had also had to use a metal prosthesis as an artificial roof of his mouth. Freud continued to conduct psychoanalyses of a few patients until several weeks before his death (condensed from Clark 1980; B. Mann 1993).

Harold Garfinkel

Harold Garfinkel (1917–), originally from Newark, New Jersey, started his college education by taking business and accounting courses at the University of Newark. The original plan was that he would take courses by day, work in his father's furniture business at night, and then go into his father's business after graduation. However, even at that stage in his education, Garfinkel was already viewing his lessons in sociological terms. In accounting class, for example, he realized that "choosing . . . whether to place an item in the debit or the assets column was already a social construction" (Rawls 2002, 10).

Garfinkel studied sociology at the University of North Carolina–Chapel Hill. He completed his master's thesis and then joined the air force after the United States entered World War II. Garfinkel was tasked to teach strategies for small arms warfare against tanks. However, he had no tanks, only photos of tanks. All real tanks were committed to combat. His troops were required to train by attacking, and avoiding being seen by, imaginary tanks (Rawls 2002, 15). This military assignment was "ironically appropriate" for the "father of ethnomethodology" (Rawls 2002, 15). Ethnomethodology is a perspective that "has its origins" in Parsons's *The Structure of Social Action* (Garfinkel 1988, 104). It looks for "what more" there is to formal analyses (Garfinkel 1996, 107).

After the war, Garfinkel returned to graduate school at Harvard University. He taught at Princeton while a student and completed his doctorate in 1952. After short-term positions at Ohio State University and Wichita, Garfinkel accepted a position at the University of California–Los Angeles in 1954. He remained there until his retirement in 1987. At this writing, he is still an active professor emeritus. In 1995, he received the Cooley-Mead Award for his lifetime contributions to social psychology. When introducing Garfinkel for that award, Douglas W. Maynard stated, "When scholars of the twenty-first century write the history of twentieth century sociology, Harold Garfinkel will stand out as one of the towering figures" (1996, 2).

Erving Goffman

Erving Goffman (1922–82) was born in Manville, Alberta, Canada. During his first year of university work, Goffman studied chemistry before dropping out to work for the National Film Board in Ottawa. When he returned to school, Goffman completed an undergraduate degree in sociology. He then went to graduate school at the University of Chicago, where he studied both sociology and social anthropology.

Goffman's dissertation research was conducted in the Shetland Islands. There, he became interested in means of communication between islanders, how his hotel staff interacted with outsiders (including other islanders and tourists), and how they interacted among themselves. His observations formed the basis for his famous dramaturgical concepts of *front-stage* and *back-stage* behavior, how people try to control their situations, and their successes and failures in doing so (Burns 1992, 11).

After completing his doctorate in 1953, Goffman took a job as "visiting scientist" at the National Institute of Mental Health (NIMH). In 1957, he joined the Department of Sociology at Berkeley, becoming full professor by 1962. Goffman moved to the University of Pennsylvania in 1968, where he remained until his death from cancer, which occurred the year he was president of the American Sociological Association (Collins 1986, 112).

Goffman has been described as being "difficult to get close to" and having an "acerbic wit" (Martin, Mutchnick, and Austin 1990, 323). Unlike many academics, Goffman's writing style was easy to read. Most of his work has been published in 11 books. Several of these books received attention beyond the academic community, such as *Presentation of Self in Everyday Life* (1959), *Stigma* (1963b), and *Forms of Talk* (1981). During the course of his academic career, Goffman focused on themes including social interaction (ranging from talking to oneself to radio and TV broadcasts), the self, and social order (Burns 1992, 8). His unique microsociology "made clear what was previously unknown, pointed to the significance of things which had been regarded as of little or no consequence, and disentangled what was previously an indiscriminate muddle" (Burns 1992, 6).

George Herbert Mead

George Herbert Mead (1863–1931) was a philosopher rather than a sociologist. Mead was an excellent and popular lecturer, but he did not publish often or seek prestigious journals. Mead found expressing his thoughts in the written word to be a difficult effort, even to the point of frustration. His first major paper was not published until he was 40 years old (Coser 1977, 354). He had published only some 30 or so articles and no books at the time of his death (Baldwin 1986, 12). Mead also never completed his Ph.D. However, his influence on sociology, particularly symbolic interactionism, can hardly be overstated.

Mead was born in South Hadley, Massachusetts. His father, a minister, took a position at Oberlin College's theological seminary. Mead grew up at Oberlin and attended college there. Oberlin was one of the first colleges in the United States that admitted blacks and granted degrees to women. It was also a stop on the Underground Railroad and later a home of the temperance movement (Coser 1977, 341–42).

Mead taught grade school briefly, losing his job amid a controversy surrounding his dismissal of a number of disruptive students. He then worked as a surveyor for the railroad, where he gained an appreciation for the scientific method (Baldwin 1986, 7). He later studied philosophy at Harvard and in Germany (Cook 1993, 1–36).

Mead eventually accepted a position as instructor of philosophy and psychology at the University of Chicago, where he became active in a number of educational advocacy efforts. He was also involved with Jane Addams's Hull House. In addition, Mead worked with various civic organizations and causes, including labor issues and women's suffrage.

Mead was interested in a broad range of issues, including philosophy; the physical, biological, and social sciences; mathematics; music; and poetry (Coser 1977, 347). He even "worked on integrating Einstein's theory of relativity with his own thinking, attempting to bring unity to the entire scientific and pragmatic worldview" (Baldwin 1986, 10). On a personal level, Mead has been described as "kind, cheerful, mild mannered, soft spoken, and with no affection or pretense . . . [someone] respected and held in high esteem by his colleagues and his students" (Baldwin 1986, 12). He died in 1931 at age 68.

William I. Thomas

William Isaac Thomas (1863–1947) was born in Russell County, Virginia, but moved to Knoxville, Tennessee, as a child. He attended the University of Tennessee, excelling socially and doing well enough academically to remain at the university as an instructor after his 1884 graduation. After interim work and travel, Thomas enrolled in the University of Chicago when the school opened its sociology department. He started teaching for Chicago while still a student. He received a faculty appointment after earning his doctorate in 1896 and was a full professor by 1910.

Thomas focused on ethnographic and comparative studies, teaching courses that would now be called cultural and physical anthropology (Coser 1977, 532). Although he published seven books and 38 articles (Volkart 1968, 2), his renowned work was a sociological look at the lives of Polish immigrants in Chicago, *The Polish Peasant in Europe and America* (1918–20), which he authored with Florian Znaniecki. During the course of his research, he learned Polish, made several trips to Europe, and produced a final work over 2,000 pages long.

Thomas developed a life-history analysis for which he is now well known. Walking in an alley, he had to step around a bag of garbage being thrown out of a window. The bag spilled open and a letter fell out in front of Thomas. He read it and discovered that it was from a Polish girl who was recounting various family events and concerns. This inspired Thomas to buy letters from Poland and to search Polish newspapers, parish histories, records from immigrant organizations and charities, and Polish diaries as a major part of his research (Coser 1977, 533).

In addition to his academic activities, Thomas was a social activist known for progressive and sometimes unpopular ideas. He was dismissed from the University of Chicago after the *Chicago Tribune* reported a scandalous story involving Thomas and a woman. He lost a publishing contract for additional volumes of *The Polish Peasant,* and his name was removed from a work that had been commissioned by the Carnegie Foundation. He taught at the New School for Social Research and then at Harvard, but was unable to ever find another permanent university position. Thomas was, however, able to continue to conduct research through Chicago philanthropist Mrs. W. F. Drummer, grants, and associations with research organizations. He also served as president of the American Sociological Association in 1927 (Coser 1977, 534–36; Volkart 1968). He died in Berkeley, California, when he was 84 years old.

CAREERS IN SOCIOLOGY

Those with an interest and training in socialization have backgrounds that prepare them for careers including

- activity coordinator
- adoption/foster-agency director/staff
- athletic/recreation coordinator
- child-care-agency director/staff
- child-welfare advocate
- community specialist
- director/staff of religious activities/organizations/education
- education coordinator
- educational administrator
- family counselor
- family life director
- gerontologist
- group-home director/staff-member
- human resources specialist
- mental-health service staff
- minister
- occupational-rehabilitation staff
- personnel/training specialist
- public relations specialist
- recreation worker

- rehabilitation counselor
- school counselor
- seminar/workshop consultant
- social worker
- special-events coordinator
- teacher
- vocational counselor
- youth counselor

Additional Resources

Berger, Peter, and Thomas Luckmann. 1966. *The Social Construction of Reality.* New York: Doubleday. Berger and Luckmann's classic work lays out one of the most important concepts in sociology.

Goffman, Erving. 1959. *Presentation of Self in Everyday Life.* Garden City, N.Y.: Anchor. This book lays out Goffman's dramaturgical framework of social interaction and the "art" of impression management.

Goffman, Erving. 1961. Asylum. New York-Doubleday. Goffman's classic offers an analysis of life in total institutions.

Kearl, Michael C. "Self Types and Their Differences across Generations and the Life-Cycle." http://www.trinity.edu/mkearl/socpsy-6.html. This stop on the Sociological Tour through Cyberspace from Michael C. Kearl (Trinity University) covers socialization and formation of the self from birth to death.

Kendall, Lori. 2002. *Hanging Out in the Virtual Pub.* Berkeley: University of California Press. Among the topics explored in this study are virtual relationships and identities and their interconnections with physical relationships.

Kilbourne, Jean. 2000. *Killing Us Softly 3: Advertising's Image of Women.* Northampton, Mass.: Media Education Foundation. Video. Using over 150 ads and commercials, this video from an award-winning lecturer focuses on advertising's views of women and the social implications of those images.

Kubler-Ross, Elizabeth. 1969. *On Death and Dying.* New York: Macmillan. The stages of death and the impact of pending death of the dying, their families, and those who care for them are outlined in this important work.

Lawson, Helene M. 2000. *Ladies on the Lot: Women, Car Sales, and the Pursuit of the American Dream.* Lanham, Md: Rowman and Littlefield. This ethnography of women who sell cars provides is an easy-to-read example of how gender socialization and social structure impact our entire lives. Lawson demonstrates how even selling cars is a reflection of these influences at work.

The Mead Project. This site provides an extensive web-based repository of information by and about George Herbert Mead. Department of Sociology, Brock University St. Catharines, Canada. http://spartan.ac.brocku.ca/%7ELward/

New York Psychoanalytic Institute and Society. Freud Archives. http://www.psycho analysis.org/lib_freu.htm. This site links to a variety of online information by and works about Sigmund Freud.

Tannen, Deborah. 1990. *You Just Don't Understand: Men and Women in Conversation.* New York: William Morrow. A former best-seller, this book analyzes gender-based differences in communication that are largely based on socialization patterns.

United Nations Children's Fund (UNICEF). http://www.unicef.org/index.html. This international organization focuses on the rights of children around the world, addressing many situations such as war and poverty that impact their socialization and life-chances. The publications page (http://www.unicef.org/publications/index.html) includes links to several online reports, including UNICEF's annual report, "The State of the World's Children."

CHAPTER 5
Social Groups and Organizations

The study and understanding of social groups is central to sociology. We live most of our lives within social settings, so sociology is actually a study of our experiences within groups. Sociologists devote much attention to groups of all sizes and characteristics. Much sociological study investigates "how individuals are shaped by their social groups, from families to nations, and how groups are created and maintained by the individuals who compose them" (Kimmel 1998, 7).

SOCIAL GROUPS

The term *group* has a specific definition in sociology that differs from everyday usage. In everyday language, almost any collection of people might be called a group. However, two or more people being in close physical proximity does not constitute a group in the sociological meaning of the word. Sociologically speaking, a **group** is *a collection of people who interact regularly based on some shared interest and who develop some sense of belonging that sets them apart from other gatherings of people.* They form a social relationship. This is sometimes referred to as developing a sense of "we-ness." All groups share this factor of interdependence (Lewin 1948).

People who just happen to be in the same place at the same time are not a group. Rather, they are an **aggregate.** Individuals riding the bus or walking their dogs in a park are examples of aggregates. If these people interact and develop some sort of shared interests or sense of themselves as a group, then they become a group by definition. For example, the individual dog walkers might begin to talk with each other about their pets, start to walk their dogs on the same schedule, and even plan events together, such as an obedience class. Through these shared interests and interactions, the dog walkers may begin to identify themselves as members of a group. They might even adopt some sort of name to identify themselves. Another, albeit tragic, example of an aggregate developing very quickly into a group was on September 11, 2001, when hijackers flew airplanes into the World Trade Center and Pentagon. The passengers on United Airlines Flight 93 that crashed in Pennsylvania started as an aggregate and became a group when they joined together to fight the hijackers.

Another term that is often confused with group is category. A **category** refers to *people who share some common characteristic or status.* Categories are often used by sociologists and other researchers interested in studying social life. Age, race, gender, income level, religious affiliation, being a musician, owning a pet, or living in a apartment are all categories. People in a category do not necessarily interact or share any sense of belonging, and may not even know each other.

Researchers have also pointed out that sometimes categorizations are as basic in our minds as *those groups with which we identify and feel a sense of belonging and loyalty,* **in-groups,** and *those with which we do not identify or toward which we may even feel animosity,* **out-groups.** We also tend to develop a bias in which we favor our in-groups, perceiving them in a better light than those "others" (Sumner 1906). We often prefer our fraternity or sorority, our church, or people from our ethnic group, for example, over others for this reason.

This in-group/out-group distinction works to build group identity and solidarity. Groups use a variety of means to distinguish who is "in" and who is "out." Rituals such as secret handshakes (Collins 1989) or symbols such as team uniforms, gang colors, or awards honoring member's accomplishments are all ways to exhibit group identity and reinforce membership.

Conflict with another group (or groups) can also strengthen group solidarity (Coser 1956). The members of one group draw together to challenge a common enemy—the age-old idea of "us" against "them." Thus, having an out-group to focus on can strengthen that sense of belonging and support the development of a sense of group identity as members tend to focus on differences between groups rather than any similarities (Coser 1956; Sherif 1966; Quattrane 1986). Street gangs or racist groups such as skinheads or the Ku Klux Klan illustrate this concept in action.

This group identity can even overpower and eliminate any previously existing relationships members held with those of the "other" group. Well-known research conducted by Sherif and associates demonstrate this process in their Robbers Cave Experiment. A number of boys participated in a camping trip during which they were closely observed by the researchers. The research team set up and manipulated various situations involving group membership and competition. After the boys had participated in camp activities and formed friendships for a week, researchers divided the boys into two competitive groups, purposely putting best friends into different groups. The resulting in-group/out-group conflict became stronger than the previous friendship ties (Sherif and Sherif 1953). A more recent example of this dynamic occurred in the former Yugoslavia, where an emphasis on in-group/out-group conflict led to horrible bloodshed between Serbs and Muslims, some of whom had individually been friends previously.

Reference Groups

Sociologists are also interested in how we use groups to judge ourselves and our attitudes, beliefs, behaviors, and actions (Hyman 1942; Hyman and Singer 1968; Singer 1981). The groups we use for this purpose are reference groups. **Reference groups** are *those with which we compare ourselves.* Any group can become a reference group if we use them to judge something about ourselves. Considering what best friends will think about your new boyfriend or girlfriend or how to dress to fit in with your new colleagues on your first day of work are both ways of using reference groups.

We can also have negative reference groups that we do not want to be like. Dressing in hip-hop, punk, or goth styles sets children apart from their parents and a conservative establishment. Reference groups do not even have to be real. Girls and women who judge their bodies against the apparently flawless, thin, air-brushed models shown on the cover of women's magazines or advertisements are measuring themselves against a fictional, and unattainable, reference group (Kilbourne 2000). Children who compare their parents to parents on television sitcoms are making a similar fictional reference-group comparison.

Group Size

Group size influences the interactions that take place within the group. Sociologist Georg Simmel (profiled below) addressed the importance of this concept. Simmel notes that the smallest possible group is composed of two persons. This *group of two* is called a **dyad.** These are often our strongest, most intimate relationships, such as a marriage. The existence of the dyad depends on both people. If one leaves, the group ceases to exist. As Simmel says, "for its life, [the dyad] needs *both,* but for its death, only one" (1964, 124). Each person holds full responsibility for group accomplishment or failure, since there are no additional members to which to shift the blame or effort. Because of the importance of marriage to society and the instability of the dyad as a group, cultural, religious, and legal guidance are often provided to support marriages and enhance the dyad's stability.

A *three-person group* is a **triad.** The addition of the third person changes the group dynamics considerably. The addition of just this one person also makes the group more stable. Simmel noted that this third person adds the possibility of mediator when two members disagree. If one person takes some attention away from maintaining group relationships, the group continues to exist with the effort of the other two members. However, the addition of the third person also adds the possibility of a coalition forming against one person. Another possibility is that this third person might instigate trouble between the other two for personal benefit.

Simmel also noted that as groups become larger in size, they generally become more stable and less intimate, with less required of each member. Larger groups can lose members and still exist. For example, owners regularly trade members of sports teams, and a military unit can lose members in battle but still exist. Although the relationships between individuals in the unit may have been somewhat intense, the lost members are replaced by new arrivals, and the unit continues to function. Interaction with members outside the group may also increase as the group gets larger (Blau 1977; Carley 1991). As groups become larger, they also tend to develop formal structures such as bureaucracies that are discussed later in this chapter.

NETWORKS

Sociologists have also demonstrated the importance of our relationships that occur outside of defined groups in **networks,** *the patterned relationships that connect us with those outside of our established groups.* Network relationships are ever changing as people come and go from our lives. Sociologist Barry Wellman (profiled in chapter 8) offers a good illustration of networks when explaining that it would have been impossible to make a membership list of New York City gangs when he was growing up there during the 1950s: "My New York consisted of unbounded networks of friends and of friends of friends. When a fight was coming up, groups of friends would call each other and come together to be a gang for that night. On another night, when other friends would call, some of the same teens would become members of another gang" (1999a, 94). Although these network ties are weaker than those within our defined groups, they are nonetheless very important in our everyday lives (Granovetter 1973, 1982).

Social networks exist across society. They are important aspects of kinship ties (Lai 2001), providing advice (Cross, Borgatti, and Parker 2001), organized crime (Chambliss 1988), drug use and prevention of HIV/AIDS (Friedman 1999), finding a job (Lin, Ensel, and Vaughn 1981), and the deal making between business and politicians that takes place at social events (Domhoff 1974). Networks also form among Internet users in cyberspace (Wellman 1999b; Kendall 2002). Sociological research on how networks link people in diverse places (Milgram 1967; White 1970) was even the basis for the popular Hollywood movie *Six Degrees of Separation.*

GROUP DYNAMICS

An entire field of study known as **group dynamics** has developed around *the scientific study of groups and group processes.* Drawing from both sociology and psychology, group dynamics includes studying the influences groups have on our behavior (Johnson and Johnson 2000, 37–44; Forsyth 1990). Areas of interest include how groups form and develop, the socialization that takes place within groups, power structures, conformity to group ideas, conflict, leadership, and decision making. Kurt Lewin, profiled below, is generally considered the founder of group dynamics as a field of study.

Group Formation

Many groups are formed to accomplish some task. This requires that the members work together somewhat as a team. Groups coming together to design a military action, plan a golf tournament, or decide on annual fund-raising activities for the local school Parent-Teacher Association (PTA) all go through some group-formation process. Researchers have identified over 100 various models of group development (Forsyth 1990, 77).

Following on the work of Bruce Tuckman (1965), perhaps the best-known model depicts four stages of group development that are often termed *forming, storming, norming,* and *performing.* As groups come together and try to accomplish goals as a team, they evolve through each of these four stages. They come together, work out differences, get to work on the task at hand, and then get the task done. Some models of team development also add a fifth stage, called *adjourning* or *mourning,* during which the group disbands. These stages of team building apply to all types of groups.

When individuals are first together as a group, they enter the *forming* (or orientation) stage. They learn about the other members, explore the group goal, and share their backgrounds and expertise. As issues become contentious, the group moves into the *storming* (or conflict) stage. Members may express dissatisfaction, criticism, hostility, or even drop out of the group. Most groups do experience conflict at some point. Although it may at first appear destructive, this storming stage can actually be constructive if differences are presented and resolved openly. When members start to resolve their issues and work together, they are *norming* (or building cohesion). They begin to form a cohesive unit, establish rules and roles to get their job done, and start to think of the group as "we." Then the group *performs* by "getting down to business" and working toward their goals. There may also be a dissolution stage, in which the group wraps up their tasks and terminates their roles. This stage can be planned, such as when the group accomplishes its goal (e.g., completing a fund-raising event), or spontaneous (e.g., a budget cut ends a project before its completion).

Donelson Forsyth (1990) uses the Beatles as an example to illustrate the applicability of this model to a familiar real-life group. When the musicians who would achieve world fame during the 1960s as the Beatles first came together as a band, they formed by getting to know each other and explore each other's strengths and weaknesses. They experienced conflict as John and Paul argued over talent, the drummer changed, and tempers flared. The members began to settle their differences and norm by writing songs and working together. They performed, literally and figuratively; then, finally, they dissolved as a team amid controversies and rumors (as discussed in chapter 9).

Leadership

Sociologists recognize the important distinction in groups that not all members have equal influence. Some members emerge as **leaders,** *those who are able to influence others toward some future direction, event, goal, or purpose.* However, all leaders do not lead in the same way or focus on the same goals. Some leaders take an **instrumental** approach, *focusing on getting specific jobs done,* while others take an **expressive** approach, *concerning themselves with the emotional well-being of the group* (Bales and Strodtbeck 1951). Groups actually have a need for both types of approaches. In meetings, for example, groups have to accomplish whatever task is at hand (e.g., deciding on next year's marketing strategies) and also negotiate relationships between group members (e.g., people who may disagree or dislike each other have to remain civil enough with those others to make a decision).

Leaders also differ in regard to how they motivate others and what they seek to achieve. **Transactional leaders** are *task-oriented and focus on getting group members to achieve goals* (Jung and Avolio 1999). These type of leaders reward accomplishing routine goals but do not especially inspire performance beyond the routine. In other words, their group members accomplish their tasks but generally do not make extra efforts beyond those required. In an accounting department, for example, the billers would get the monthly invoices out as required but not do more (e.g., meet to develop ways to improve the invoicing process).

Another type of leader is **transformational.** These leaders *encourage others to go beyond the routine by building a different type of organization that focuses on future possibilities* (Kanter 1983). Transformational leaders use enthusiasm and optimism to inspire others. They encourage innovation and creativity. They exhibit characteristics that others can identify with, trust, and follow. Transformational leaders also focus on mentoring others as leaders (Hellriegel, Slocum, and Woodman 2001, 362–68). In an accounting department headed by a transformational leader, the staff might regularly meet to discuss more efficient ways to work or how to improve customer satisfaction, or devote time to testing new software that would help the department improve its efficiency.

Power

Leaders have differential levels of **power,** *the ability to influence others, even if those others resist* (Weber 1947). Greater power also allows a person or group to better resist when others try to control them. *Power* is a relative term. It is measured in relation to another person or group.

French and Raven (1959) have shown that power can be rooted on one or more of five bases. First, when someone or some group controls the distribution of valued rewards or negative reinforcements, they hold *reward power.* A manager who has the ability to give pay raises holds reward power. Second, when someone or some group can punish others for noncompliance with their wishes, they hold *coercive power.* A school principal exercises coercive power when expelling a student for rule breaking. Third, those with whom someone wishes to identify or be like (in other words, their reference group), hold *referent power.* An example of referent power is a rock star whose dress, demeanor, and singing style is copied by an aspiring young singer. Fourth, those who have, or are perceived as having, some special expertise hold *expert power.* An engineer who has overseen the building of several bridges has expert power over a team of inexperienced junior engineers working on a similar project. Fifth, when someone or some group is recognized as having a valid claim to require compliance to their wishes, they hold *legitimate power.* This may also be referred to as *authority.* A police office holds legitimate power or authority.

An entire school of theory is based in how sociologists understand power. As noted in chapter 2, **exchange theory** *focuses on the alternatives people have, or think they have, in various situations* (e.g., Blau 1964; Homans 1974). This perspective is sometimes discussed as a variant of symbolic interactionism. Other theorists discuss it separately. Although there are several complex variations, a main idea is that a person does something they would rather not do because that is the best available choice they see. For example, a worker may put us with criticism from a supervisor because that option is seen as preferable to quitting or being unemployed. The worker recognizes the supervisor's power. Peter Blau (1918–2002) and George Caspar Homans (1910–89) are two influential sociologists who have done much groundbreaking work on exchange theory. Both are profiled below.

Conformity

Sociologists and their colleagues in fields such as social psychology have demonstrated that groups can shape members' behavior in powerful ways. Groups may require members to **conform,** *sharing certain norms, values, behaviors, and sometimes even opinions.* Peer pressure to smoke (or not) or to dress a certain way to "fit in" are examples of this process. Enforcing conformity is the means through which groups survive.

Some classic experiments illustrate the power groups have in producing conformity. Solomon Asch (1952, 1955) was able to demonstrate that groups have such a strong influence on their members that individuals can be influenced to agree with group perceptions even when it is obvious that the other members are wrong. He used a simple series of cards, presented two by two, for his experiment. One card had a single vertical line drawn in the center. The second card had three vertical lines of varying lengths drawn on it. One of these three lines was exactly the same length as the single line on the first card. The members of the Asch's experimental group were asked to identify aloud which of the three lines was the same length as the single line on the other card. Asch made the correct answer apparent to anyone without vision problems and found that most people could answer correctly when responding in individual settings.

In a group setting however, answers were frequently influenced by the responses of other group members. One at a time, members identified the correct line aloud. There were a series of cards presented so members had several opportunities to answer. Everyone in the group except the last person to answer was a collaborator with Asch on the experiment. These collaborators were instructed to answer incorrectly on several responses.

Asch's results showed that, on average, over one-third of all the research subjects who were not collaborators conformed to the group opinion, giving the same incorrect responses as the rest of the group. He explains the results of his experiment: "Among the extremely yielding persons we found a group who quickly reached the conclusion: 'I am wrong, they are right.' Others yielded in order 'not to spoil your results.' Many of the individuals who went along suspected that the majority were 'sheep' following the first responder, or that the majority were victims of an optical illusion; nevertheless, these suspicions failed to free them at the moment of decision" (Asch 1955, 33).

Obedience

Social psychologist Stanley Milgram (1933–84), a student of Asch profiled in chapter 10, performed a controversial set of experiments at Yale University during the early 1960s that have also become classics. Rather than focus on a benign question such as the length of lines, Milgram (1963, 1974) developed a series of experiments in which conformity could have real and potentially serious consequences.

Milgram told his participants that his experiment was a study of the impact of negative reinforcement on learning. Two research subjects were to participate: one "learner" and one "teacher." The teacher would read a series of simple word pairs to the learner, who was supposed to learn the lesson and repeat it correctly at the teacher's prompting. The teacher was instructed to administer increasingly severe shocks (the negative reinforcement) to the learner each time he answered incorrectly.

To conduct the experiment, the learner was hooked up to an elaborate "shock machine" that had a series of 30 switches marked from 15 volts (labeled "Slight Shock") to 450 volts (labeled "Danger: Severe Shock" and "XXX"). The machine, however, did not actually administer shocks. The learner, who was Milgram's accomplice, only pretended to be receiving jolts of electricity when the teacher engaged the switch. At predetermined points in the experiment, the learner complained of pain, protested, or refused to answer any further questions. If the teacher resisted administering any further shocks, a researcher wearing a white lab-coat would state that although the shocks could be painful, they were not actually dangerous and that the experiment must continue.

In Milgram's initial experiment, over half of the teachers continued to administer shocks when told to do so by the researcher until the end of the experiment (i.e., when they reached the 450-volt level). Surprised at these findings, Milgram repeated his experiment with a number of variations to see what variables influenced the teacher's willingness to conform to the directions of the researcher. In some versions, the learner complained of heart trouble or even feigned unconsciousness, yet some teachers still continued to administer shocks. Sometimes the teacher could confer with other "teachers" (all Milgram's accomplices), who encouraged an increase in voltage levels. When conferring with others, many teachers administered shocks at higher voltages than those administered by lone teachers who had to decide on their own whether to continue participating.

Why did these ordinary people conform to orders by authority figures (i.e., the experimenters) and to group consensus (i.e., the other teachers)? Clearly they were not sadistically enjoying administering the shocks. Many were highly nervous, anxious, agitated, or angry; they verbally protested, sweated, trembled, stuttered, bit their lips, groaned, or dug their fingernails into their flesh. They also exhibited obvious relief when the experiment was over. Milgram explained their behavior as an *agentic state.* The teachers became "agents" acting on the orders of a more powerful authority. Through following the orders of the authority figure, they were relieved of responsibility for their actions. Their behavior became the responsibility of the authority. Because an agentic state is easier than being disobedient, disobedience occurred only when personal beliefs managed to overcome pressure to conform and obey.

Researchers have applied Milgram's studies to a number of situations, including the Holocaust (Saltzman 2000; Blass 2002) and doctors' orders to nurses (Krackow and Blass 1995). Kelman and Hamilton (1989) applied Milgram's findings to an infamous event of the Vietnam War—the 1968 My Lai massacre. In that event, American soldiers found a village filled with noncombatants (old men, women, and children) where they had been told they would find Viet Cong fighters. As many as 500 of these villagers were killed by the soldiers. A subsequent trial depicted massacres that had taken place, generally organized and ordered by Lt. William Calley. Some of the men who followed Calley's orders in the massacre did so under protest and even in tears. Calley himself used the defense that he was only following superior orders.

Milgram's findings have even been applied to airplane crashes. According to Eugen Tarnow, "the role of the experimenter is taken by the captain, the teacher's role belongs to the first officer, and the harm to the learner is the airplane crashing" (2000, 115). The authoritarian relationship that exists between the captain and first officer establishes a cockpit dynamic in which captains are either not questioned or hard to convince of mistakes being made. This situation leads to errors that may account for as many as 25 percent of all airplane accidents.

Group Decision Making

Irving Janis (1983, 1989, 1991) has shown that pressure to conform is also at work in group decision-making situations. By studying a number of military events and policymaking groups, Janis identified a phenomenon he calls *groupthink.* In **groupthink,** *group members faced with making a decision focus so much on getting along, being seen as a "good" group member, and agreeing* *that they may not adequately evaluate the option they are considering.* As one idea becomes the focus of group consensus, other ideas may be eliminated without careful consideration. Anyone who supports something other than the group consensus may be seen as a foe. This is especially a problem in groups with members who are close-knit, like and respect each other, and want to stay in good standing with other group members. Since group members do not want to start an argument or be seen as an outsider, they do not readily voice objections or criticize each other's ideas.

Janis found that groupthink was a major factor in several historical events, including the European powers' engagement in WWI, the British government attempting to appease Germany before WWII, the United States being unprepared for the bombing of Pearl Harbor, the U.S. participation in the Korean War, the escalation of the Vietnam War, and the 1961 Bay of Pigs invasion. In the latter event, the U.S. government under President John F. Kennedy sent a group of Cuban exiles into Cuba on a poorly planned mission to overthrow Fidel Castro. The mission failed, the exiles were captured or killed, Castro remained in power, and the United States was publicly embarrassed.

Griffin (1996: 235-37) and others describe the 1986 explosion of the space shuttle *Challenger* as an example of groupthink. The shuttle exploded less than two minutes after launch killing all the astronauts aboard and Christa McAuliffe, the first "teacher in space." The explosion was caused by the failure of a rubber O-ring seal that allowed rocket fuel to spew out. Engineers had raised safety concerns about the integrity of the O-rings in the very cold weather during a teleconference the day before the launch. However, their concerns had been discounted by NASA personnel who ultimately pressured the engineers to change their "no-go" recommendation. Others (e.g., Schwartz and Wald 2003) also connect the 2003 *Columbia* shuttle loss with groupthink as well.

Many organizational leaders and corporate chief executive officers (CEOs) are concerned about groupthink in their organizations (Hambrick 1995). To avoid being caught up in groupthink, group members should actively work to develop group norms that encourage critical evaluation, input from outside experts, and careful attention to any signs that groupthink is developing. Janis showed this effort to overcome groupthink in another Kennedy administration event, the 1962 Cuban Missile Crisis. When the United States discovered the Russians were moving offensive missiles into Cuba, President Kennedy and his advisors paid attention to their past groupthink mistakes. Almost the same group of men that had designed the disastrous Bay of Pigs invasion shortly before were able to handle this situation successfully using well-thought-out policies and contingency plans. The crisis was resolved in a matter of weeks without war or a nuclear exchange.

Institutions and Conformity

Another classic experiment demonstrated how social institutions impose conformity. In 1971, social psychologist Philip Zimbardo (1972, 2000; Haney,

Banks, and Zimbardo 1973) conducted what has come to be called the Stanford Prison Experiment. Zimbardo set up a mock prison in the basement of a Stanford University building. He selected volunteers from among Stanford University students to participate, assigning them to the roles of guard or prisoner by the flip of a coin. The study began when prisoners were picked up by Palo Alto police, "booked" for their crimes, and taken to the Stanford University "prison."

Zimbardo's guards controlled the prison, setting rules for the prisoners and punishing those who violated those rules. The original plan was to study the groups' interactions for two weeks. However, the experiment had to be called off after only six days.

During that short period, the students had so completely adapted to their roles that they seemed to have difficulty remembering they were only volunteers in an experiment and could have left the situation at any time. Several of the guards had become tyrannical and abusive. Prisoners were exhibiting depression and trauma. Even the researchers themselves had so conformed to their roles as prison warden and administration that they did not see that the experiment had become unnecessarily dangerous to the students involved. They only came to this realization when an outside researcher came into the "prison," observed the situation, and pressed for an end to the experiment (Zimbardo 2000). The Stanford Prison Experiment is a powerful illustration of how institutions like prisons can enforce conformity and even alter our perceptions of who we are as individuals outside of that institutional setting. (Chapter 4 discusses socialization in total institutions.)

FORMAL ORGANIZATIONS

Sociologists are also interested in social **organizations,** those *identifiable groups that have a specific purpose* (Aldrich and Marsden 1988). Many of the social collectivities discussed earlier in this chapter take the form of **informal organizations,** because they *do not involve formalized or rigorous rules, roles, and responsibilities.* They may occur spontaneously and involve personal relationships. They are not especially designed for efficiency, but they work well in informal settings.

This informal organizational structure, however, does not work well in many areas of our lives. Governmental or corporate organizations require a different form. These entities are **formal organizations,** *large, secondary social collectivities that are organized and regulated for purposes of efficiency by structured procedures.* Formal organizations take a variety of forms, with people joining or participating for a variety of reasons. There are **normative organizations,** such as civic causes (political campaigns, religious organizations, Rotary Clubs, etc.), that *people join voluntarily and without financial compensation because they believe the cause is worthy.* Prisons constitute a form of **coercive formal organization** that *people join involuntarily.* Another form of formal organization, **utilitarian organizations,** are those *people join to gain some material benefit.* Taking a job at a bank or hospital constitutes joining a utilitarian organization (Etzioni 1975).

Bureaucracy

A specific kind of formal organization is a **bureaucracy,** defined by Randall Collins as *"organizational control achieved by explicit rules and regulations and by specifying responsibilities for action in written records"* (1999, 33; italics mine). Bureaucracies are a large part of our modern lives. School, work, and services such as banks, medical clinics, and day-care centers are all examples of the types of bureaucratic structures most of us deal with on a daily basis.

Max Weber, profiled in chapter 2, was the first sociologist to examine bureaucracies (1946). His interests included the structure and operation of large-scale enterprises such as governments, religions, and economies. As part of his analysis of capitalism, he developed a concept of rationalization. To Weber, **rationalization** meant *an ongoing search for increasing efficiency, or looking for the most efficient means of doing things.* In capitalism, increasing efficiency could lead to increasing profits. Since increased efficiency, or rationalization, is the reason behind bureaucracies, Weber used bureaucracy as a major case in his analysis.

Weber developed an ideal type of bureaucracy composed of several elements that typify bureaucracies.

- *Hierarchy.* A hierarchical structure exists with clear lines of authority. When depicted in organizational charts, this hierarchy takes a pyramid shape, with a smaller number of people at the top of the pyramid having authority over an increasingly larger number of people lower in the structure.

- *Formal rules and regulations governing the organization.* Written rules and regulations govern administration and conduct. These rules and regulations ensure consistency, standardization, and that people within the bureaucracy do not make up rules as they go along.

- *Written documentation.* This documentation (the "files") encompasses the policies that are to be followed in the organization.

- *Specialization.* A formal division of labor is set forth in bureaucracies, with positions organized on the basis of the duties assigned to each position. Every member of an organization has certain functions to perform, meaning that members may be required to be experts in their areas.

- *Technical knowledge.* Members of a bureaucracy should meet all the required qualifications to competently fulfill the duties of their position. By fitting skill sets to positions, rather than designing positions to fit the skills of individual workers, bureaucracies create a situation in which members who leave a position can be replaced by someone with the same qualifications and the organization can continue to operate.

- *Impersonality.* Organizational members are required to follow procedures and deal with all clients on the basis of policy rather than personal relationships or opinions.

- *Career employment.* Career advancement is through achievement-based promotion. Promotions should be determined by such prescribed factors as seniority, job performance, or increased training, not on factors such as being the supervisor's relative.

- *Salaried positions.* Compensation for work performed is assigned on the basis of the position. It is not determined by personal factors (for example, how physically attractive a worker is or how much the supervisor enjoys his or her jokes).
- *Separation of "official" and "private" income and duties.* The "office" is separate from the sphere of private life. Official monies and property of the organization are not intermingled with members' private funds or interests.

Although he felt they were inevitable, Weber saw enormous difficulties with the establishment of bureaucracies. Bureaucracies can suffer from inefficiencies and problems. The bureaucratic emphasis on following the rules can lead to inflexibility and something called *bureaucratic ritualism* (Merton 1968) and *trained incapacity* (Veblen 1967). In other words, bureaucrats get so involved in following the rules that they are unable to respond creatively when a unique situation arises that is not in their written guidelines. Cases that do not fit within established guidelines can be problematic because the process (i.e., the "ritual") that bureaucrats are directed to follow is not designed to accommodate them. The workers themselves are not trained or allowed the latitude (the "capacity") to respond in other than established ways. Elderly people whose birth was not recorded on any formal government record have faced this problem when applying for social services that require a birth certificate for age or citizenship documentation. Problems arise when their documents (e.g., perhaps a notation in a worn family Bible) do not meet written bureaucracy requirements (e.g., a government-issued birth certificate).

This emphasis on treating everyone as a "case" based on specific rules rather than as an individual can also be dehumanizing to both the bureaucrat and the customer. However, in many instances, an informal bureaucracy arises in which individuals learn to circumvent rules (Crozier 1964). Informal guidelines also develop that may circumvent bureaucracy guidance. In production jobs where productivity is measured and management's expectations are based on existing productivity, employees may deal informally with "rate busters" to keep their production in line with established rates (Ackroyd and Thompson 1999). Taken together, these problems can lead to waste and incompetence.

An additional problem with bureaucracies is a loss of personal privacy. Think of all the people who have access to your medical record after an annual medical checkup: receptionists, nurses, doctors, lab technicians, billing clerks, transcriptionists, and insurance-company personnel. You may even be asked in a public waiting room to state why you are there.

Rationalization, or efficiency itself, can also raise new problems (Weber 1946). It can lead to goal displacement meaning that the emphasis becomes the survival of the bureaucracy rather than any service that the organization was designed to provide. Frank Elwell (1999) illustrates this problem with the example of the Chevrolet Corvair. The Corvair came on the American market in 1960. It was marketed as a sports car even though Chevrolet's own premarket tests had demonstrated an engineering design problem that could result in vehicle rollover. When accidents occurred and the problem was exposed, General Motors attempted to cover up prior knowledge of the problem rather than face the facts head-on. Although none of the executives involved would have individually set out to build a car that would hurt people, the bureaucratic structure that embraced sales and profits enabled this to happen (Elwell 1999, 63). Ford Motor Company made a similar decision resulting in as many as 500 burn deaths when evidence showed that the gas tanks on Ford Pintos were prone to rupture when the cars were hit from the rear (Dowie 1977). Unfortunately, news stories continue to appear in the press routinely that suggest similar problems in other organizations.

Oligarchy

Robert Michels (1876–1936), a contemporary of Weber profiled below, also took a pessimistic view of bureaucracies. Michels's conclusions were drawn primarily from his study of the socialist parties of Europe and, in particular, the prewar German socialist party. Michels is perhaps most famous for the **Iron Law of Oligarchy,** or *rule by a few.* According to Michels (1962), every bureaucracy would invariably turn into an oligarchy. This is an "iron law." Michels gave three reasons. First, he felt human nature involves an innate tendency to seek power. Second, the nature of political struggles leads to oligarchy as groups struggle for position. Third, the structure of large-scale organizations gives rise to oligarchies because they need people with special skills. Leaders tend to be educated and have expertise; thus, they tend to be oligarchs. Michels felt that the masses were apathetic and incompetent, and in need of strong leaders. He concluded that, since leadership is necessary for organizational survival and organizations cannot check the power of leaders, organizational structure (including the search for efficiency and the division of labor) leads to a ruling elite, even in Democratic organizations.

Whether powerful bureaucracies in democracies do become oligarchies is a matter of debate. Michels's ideas have influenced research on trade unions and political parties. Some observers point out corporate scandals and abuses as examples of Michels's fear. Others argue that bureaucracies are held accountable in democratic societies. Another argument against the inevitability of oligarchy comes from the trend toward democratization in the eastern European countries formerly in the Soviet orbit.

THE MCDONALDIZATION OF SOCIETY

Sociologist George Ritzer, profiled below, has coined the term **McDonaldization** to refer to *how the principles used in fast-food restaurants to achieve maximum efficiency "are coming to dominate more and more sectors of American society as well as the rest of the world"* (2000b, 1; italics mine). Restaurants have long existed, but the search for efficiency led to new types of restaurants, including diners, cafeterias, and drive-ups. By looking at the hamburger as an assembly-line product comprised of a number of component parts,

Ray Kroc (the founder of McDonald's) and his associates were able to optimize the efficiency with which each part could be prepared. They separated and presliced buns. They changed the shipping materials and packaging for buns and meat, even designing the wax paper between the frozen patties to make the patties quicker to separate and get onto the grill. The later addition of the drive-through window added a new dimension to this concept of efficiency.

This quest for rationalization has spread far beyond fast food. As Ritzer (2000b) points out, we now routinely seek quicker, more efficient options throughout society. Microwave ovens are commonplace and resulted in the associated development of microwave foods. Large freezers were a development that allowed the introduction of the ever-efficient TV dinner. Diet plans offer prepackaged diet meals as part of an entire quick weight-loss system including books, centers, and counselors. Health clubs with various exercise machines designed to maximize workout time also often provide radios and televisions to maximize entertainment or news gathering. Shopping malls bring many stores, food, and entertainment options together in one location. Further efficiencies in shopping are provided by catalogs, television shopping networks, and e-commerce. Video rentals, pay-per-view cable options, and picture-in-picture television sets all make movie watching more efficient. Package tours in which large numbers of people are bused between sites to see as much as possible in the allotted time maximize travel time. Computer-graded tests allow faster exam grading. We can achieve efficiencies in studying or recreational "reading" by listening to books-on-tape (many of which are abridged to reduce "wasted" time listening to "insignificant" parts). Even religion is designed for efficiency when offered on television.

The outcomes of these processes are not only efficiencies. Human contact becomes minimized and impersonal. High employee turnover means customers and staff do not get to know each other well, and interactions are often short, through a window, or not even face to face (as in Internet shopping). Staff training often focuses on efficiency and key phrases rather than making conversation. These processes may also result in a dehumanization of the worker and the customer (as in the case of fast-food restaurants where workers are required to have or use minimal job skills and customers move through lines to buy food waiting in a bin). Although Ritzer, like Weber before him, hopes that we will resist this rationalization, he sees it instead growing.

Another concern that Ritzer shares with Weber is about the possibility of escaping the press of bureaucracies in our lives. Weber feared that the future would be an "iron cage" of vast, impersonal bureaucratic structures. Ritzer also talks about the "iron cage of McDonaldization," a situation in which McDonaldization comes to dominate ever more sectors of society, making it increasingly impossible to avoid (2000b, 143). He acknowledges, however, that many see the future as a "velvet cage," because they are comfortable with McDonaldization. Others may see it as a "rubber cage" in which they bounce from disliking some aspects of McDonaldization and finding others appealing (e.g., predictability, impersonality, speed, efficiency).

GLOBALIZATION AND THE INTERNET

In the area of organizations, globalization includes academic networks, foundations, nongovernmental organizations (NGOs), and some governmental and intergovernmental agencies that often promote ideologies and lifestyles including human rights, feminism, and environmentalism (Berger 2002, 4). Even the large humanitarian relief organizations that provide international refugee relief find themselves mired in bureaucratic structures and requirements. They are also faced with the need to attract resources for their cause. This distracts from their efficiency in delivering their service, because it forces them to devote considerable time and attention to fund raising and soliciting donations. In a tense world with many demands on these organizations, they are increasingly forced to try to find even more ways to improve rationality and efficiency (T. Waters 2001).

Globalization can be a threatening concept to those around the world that fear it means American economic, political, and cultural dominance, as well as to American organizations that fear lost profits and jobs to worldwide corporations (Berger 2002, 2). Rosabeth Moss Kanter (profiled below) focuses on how business and community leaders can use globalization to their own advantages. Although a business professor, Kanter's concepts incorporate many sociological tenets, such as examining and teaching how global, corporate, national, community, and individual interests are intertwined. In *World Class: Thriving Locally in the Global Economy* (1995b), she argues that American organizations must embrace globalization, address negative attitudes and prejudices, and expand their multicultural understanding to compete. She cites three areas (Boston; Spartanburg-Greenville, South Carolina; and Miami) as examples of areas that provide models that other areas can follow.

Information and collaborative technologies that *make information sharing easier, more convenient, faster, and often real-time* are changing organizations in a number of ways and contributing to globalization. These types of technologies include the Internet and intranets, video conferences, desktop computer cameras, computer whiteboards, and special software packages. They are used to complement traditional face-to-face ways of communicating and working. One of these changes is the creation and existence of virtual teams. **Virtual teams** *allow members to work on a project from more than one location* (Lipnack and Stamps 1997; Townsend, DeMarie, and Hendrickson 1998). They also extend globalization by allowing people to work together from anywhere in the world if they have compatible technology. The use of these technologies is changing the dynamics of business operations and decision making (Sproull and Kiesler 1991; Wellman et al. 1996; Konicki 2002) and allowing new ways to bring diverse and widely dispersed parties together to tackle social issues such as teen violence and terrorism (Hasson 2002).

These technologies can also help information flow and cut down on bureaucratic red tape. Increasingly, internal organizational functions are computerized for efficiency—for example, by implementing Internet-based time cards, reports, and evaluations. These technologies, however, can also make bureaucratization even stronger. Computer programs that monitor e-mail or Internet activity allow surveillance of employee activities by previously unavailable means. Telecommuting allows workers to work longer hours at home via the Internet. Although organizations implement specific technology strategies to achieve certain goals, they are generally applied to pursue strategies and directions that managers have already selected (DiMaggio et al. 2001).

Recognizing the complexities and challenges presented by globalization and these technologies, Kanter expands her perspectives on organizational globalization by studying hundreds of companies around the world to better understand how the Internet will alter future business practices. Her findings (2001) suggest that human attitudes, rather than technology, are the greatest impediments to finding ways to work in the new digital culture.

BIOGRAPHIES

Peter M. Blau

Peter M. Blau (1918–2002) was born in Vienna, Austria. By his own account (1995), Blau's life took a "circuitous path" to, and through, his career. As a teen, he attracted police attention by publishing articles in opposition to the government. He was convicted of treason when he was 17 years old and sentenced to 10 years in prison. Blau was released after an agreement between Austria and Germany freed a number of political prisoners. He was captured, imprisoned again, and tortured when attempting an escape across the Czechoslovakian border.

Blau ultimately did get to Prague, leaving when Hitler invaded the country on the last train before the borders were closed. He then spent time in a French labor camp before making his way to the United States. He arrived at a Elmhurst College through a chance meeting with graduates of the school who were in Europe offering a scholarship to a Jewish refugee. Blau lost touch with his parents after arriving in America. He learned years later that they had died in the Auschwitz concentration camp the month he received his bachelor's degree (Blau 2002). Blau served in the U.S. army and won a Bronze Star ("Blau, Peter Michael" 1981, 55).

Blau completed his doctorate at Columbia University in 1952. His academic career included positions at Wayne University (now Wayne State University), Cornell, the University of Chicago, and Columbia University, where he remained a professor emeritus after his retirement while also holding a distinguished professorship at the University of North Carolina–Chapel Hill. Blau's professional accomplishments include being named Fellow of the National Academy of Sciences, Fellow of the American Philosophical Society, and Fellow of the American Academy of Arts and Sciences. He was editor of the *American Journal of Sociology* from 1961 to 1967 and president of the American Sociological Association in 1973 (Blau 2002; "Blau, Peter Michael" 1981).

Blau authored hundreds of articles and 11 books. His first book, *The Dynamics of Bureaucracy: A Study of Interpersonal Relations in Two Government Agencies* (1955), began as his dissertation. In a quarter-century, it had been cited over 6,500 times in other scholarly work (Merton 1990, 56). *Bureaucracy in Modern Society* (1956) was translated into Japanese, Korean, Arabic, Spanish, Italian, and Danish in just over a decade. *Formal Organizations: A Comparative Approach* (1962) began as coauthor W. Richard Scott's dissertation and was also soon translated into several other languages. Other books by Blau include *Exchange and Power in Social Life* (1964), called "one of the most important books in sociology" (Cook 2002); *The American Occupational Structure* (1967), coauthored with Otis Dudley Duncan, winner of the American Sociological Association's Sorokin Award; and *Inequality and Heterogeneity: A Primitive Theory of Social Structure* (1977), winner of the American Sociological Association's Distinguished Scholarship Award.

George Caspar Homans

George Caspar Homans (1910–89) was born in Boston, Massachusetts, and grew up in the prestigious Beacon Hill and Back Bay areas of the city. His ancestors on both sides were prestigious and well-known New Englanders. Homans attended Harvard, as had his maternal and paternal ancestors since the 1700s. He spent his entire academic career there.

Homans entered in Harvard in 1928, the year Pitirim Sorokin went to Harvard to found the Sociology Department. He became involved in the hierarchy of Harvard social clubs that, in many ways, determined a student's status and networking opportunities. Homans was eventually elected as a member of the Spee Club, the same club that John F. Kennedy would be elected to during his undergraduate years. He credits his family background, Boston's many different ethnic and class groups, and the hierarchy of the Harvard club structure as important factors in his development of a sociological class consciousness (Homans 1984).

As an undergraduate, Homans studied English rather than sociology. When an anticipated newspaper job evaporated as a result of the Depression, he became coauthor with Charles Curtis of a book about sociologist Vilfredo Pareto (*An Introduction to Pareto,* 1934). Homans was subsequently elected to the Harvard Society of Fellows as a sociologist.

During World War II, Homans was a naval reserve officer called for active duty. His service included minesweeping, antisubmarine escort, and submarine chasing variously in the Caribbean and the Pacific theaters (Homans 1984).

After the war, Homans returned to Harvard as an associate professor. Two of his major publications were *The Human Group* (1950) and *Social Behavior: Its Elementary Forms* (1974). His theoretical orientation emphasized small-group behavior. This perspective also led him to oppose theorist Talcott Parsons's concept of functionalism. In his autobiography, Homans reports that when Parsons asked him to read and criticize the manuscript later published as *The Structure of Social Action,* "I conscientiously read it, but did not criticize it, I hated it so much . . . Rarely did it make contact with actual human behavior. In such a book it is easy to claim one has demonstrated whatever one wants to demonstrate. Social science bulges with books of this sort" (1984, 323). His critique added that, although Parsons would hail new "breakthroughs" in his own work, "the more breakthroughs he made, the more his theory remained essentially the same" (324).

Homans never earned a doctorate. However, he became a well-known and important figure in sociology. He saw himself as "far more the observer than the experimenter" (Homans 1969, 21). Of his life's work he wrote, "My great interest and pleasure in life is bringing order out of chaos . . . I see this trait in the long weekends I have spent on my fifty-four acres of land at Medfield, Massachusetts . . . For years I have tried to organize this abandoned farm, now grown up to blueberry pasture and second-growth trees, on soil thin and full of rocks at best, into what I call a walking woods, clear enough of dead branches and fallen timber so that I can stroll about . . . This effort has been characteristic of my work in sociology from the beginning" (13).

At Harvard, he chaired the Committee for Undergraduate Education. He also served as the president of the American Sociological Association, using his presidential address to criticize functionalism (Homans 1964), and earned that Association's Distinguished Scholarship Award.

Rosabeth Moss Kanter

Rosabeth Moss Kanter (1943–) is currently the Ernest L. Arbuckle Professor of Business Administration at Harvard Business School. She became a member of the Harvard Business School faculty in 1986. Kanter is also a strategy consultant for business and government interests in the United States and internationally, engaged in projects such as her work with IBM's Reinventing Education initiative, which targets elementary and secondary schools. Her current focus involves leadership of turnarounds (when business fortunes change for the better or worse) and leadership in the digital age. Of the United States' competitiveness in the global marketplace, Kanter says, "Cheap labor is not going to be the way we compete in the United States. It's going to be brainpower" (1995a).

Among Kantor's numerous accomplishments, she served several years as editor of the *Harvard Business Review*. She is a Fellow of the World Economic Forum and serves on the U.S. Secretary of Labor's Committee on Skills Gap of the 21st Century Work Force Council. Among her numerous awards, she received the 2001 Academy of Management's Distinguished Career Award and the 2002 World Teleport Association's Intelligent Community Visionary of the Year Award. She is also the recipient of 21 honorary doctoral degrees and over a dozen leadership awards. Kanter has also been named on lists of the 50 most influential business thinkers in the world, 100 most important women in America, and the 50 most powerful women in the world.

She has authored or coauthored over 200 articles and 15 books. Kanter's insights have informed many disciplines. Sociologists have found some of her work to be particularly useful. For example, *Men and Women of the Corporation* (1977) examines gender issues in the workplace, and the spin-off *A Tale of "O"* (1980) simply and effectively explains the impact of tokenism in the workplace and beyond (Kanter, "Business: The Ultimate Resource"; "Kanter, Rosabeth Moss" 2002).

Kurt Lewin

Kurt Lewin (1890–1947) was one of the "founding fathers" of social psychology. Lewin earned a Ph.D. in philosophy from the University of Berlin in 1914. He taught there for 12 years after completing his degree. Originally from Prussia, he immigrated to the United States in 1933 and became an American citizen in 1940.

In the United States, he taught at Stanford, Cornell, and Iowa, as well as being a visiting professor at the University of California–Berkeley and Harvard. In 1944, he established the Research Center on Group Dynamics at the Massachusetts Institute of Technology (MIT) and the Commission on Community Interrelations (CCI) of the American Jewish Congress (Marrow 1969).

Among his many notable achievements and contributions to our understanding of the social psychology of group dynamics, Lewin authored several works, including *A Dynamic Theory of Personality* (1935), *Principles of Topological Psychology* (1936), and *Frontiers in Group Dynamics* (1946). He also served a term as president of the Society for the Psychological Study of Social Issues. Today, one legacy of Lewin's work is the Kurt Lewin Institute (KLI). This center for graduate training and research has members from six Dutch universities. The center's activities are focused on stimulating interest in the field of social psychology, analyzing the psychological factors contributing to social behavior, and the applications of the perspective.

Robert Michels

German sociologist Robert Michels (1876–1936) was born in Cologne. After serving in the army and studying in England and at the Sorbonne, he obtained his Ph.D. in history from the University of Halle. Michels joined the Italian Socialist Party (ISP) in the early 1900s. He resigned his membership a few years later, but continued his studies of socialist organizations and politics.

Michels is widely known for his work *Political Parties: A Sociological Study of the Oligarchical Tendencies of Modern Democracy* (1962, orig. 1911). In it, he discusses the Iron Law of Oligarchy that is associated with his name. However, Michels's interests extended well beyond this issue. He gave more attention to politics of the working class than did many of his contemporaries. Additionally, he wrote about topics they were largely uninterested in, including eugenics, feminism, sex, and morality (Kandal 2001).

In a far lesser-known work, *Sexual Ethics: A Study of Borderland Questions,* Michels focused on gender issues, describing power and conflict in gender politics. His discussion included ties between sex-role inequality and unhappiness, advocacy for family planning (although not abortion), and an argument that feminists "must not cease to protest against all those external forms of public life which imply a depreciation of woman, or a lower estimation than man" (quoted in Kandal 2001, 64).

George Ritzer

George Ritzer (1940–) was born in New York. He earned a Ph.D. from Cornell University in 1968. Ritzer is Distinguished University Professor of Sociology at the University of Maryland. In Ritzer's own words, he "became a sociologist because sociology offers me a variety of intellectual tools that allow me to better understand the wonderful complexity of social life" (quoted in Henslin 2001a, xxvii). As evidence that he passes on his enjoyment of sociology to his students, Ritzer has been named Distinguished Scholar-Teacher and won a Teaching Excellence Award from the University of Maryland. Ritzer received a Fulbright-Hayes fellowship. He also received the American Sociological Association's (ASA) Distinguished Contributions to Teaching Award in 2000. Ritzer has chaired the ASA section on Theoretical Sociology and the section on Organizations and Occupations.

Ritzer has authored a number of books, several of which focus on sociological theory. He is also editor of *The Blackwell Companion to Major Social Theorists* (2000a). Ritzer has published well-known and influential work on consumerism and rationalization. These books include *Expressing America: A Critique of the Global Credit Card Society* (1995) and *Enchanting a Disenchanting World: Revolutionizing the Means of Consumption* (1999). Ritzer's *The McDonaldization of Society* (2000b) has already been translated into more than a dozen languages. He is also a co-founding editor of the *Journal of Consumer Culture* (Ritzer, "George Ritzer"; "Ritzer, George" 1987).

Georg Simmel

Georg Simmel (1858–1918) was born in Berlin, Germany. He studied philosophy at the University of Berlin, receiving his doctorate in 1881. Four years later he became a *privatdozent* there (an unpaid lecturer dependent on student fees) and remained in that position for 15 years. He was then granted the honorary title of Ausserordentlicher Professor. Simmel was a popular lecturer, teaching courses on a range of topics, including logic, ethics, social psychology, and sociology. He may have been the first to teach sociology in a German university (Frisby 1984, 13).

Simmel was friends with many notable academics and intellectuals of his day. He was well published, with several books and numerous articles translated into English, French, Italian, Polish, and Russian. However, prewar anti-Semitism, his eclectic interests that defied disciplinary boundaries, and his originality and intellect, which some academics found threatening, led to poor treatment by some universities (Coser 1977, 195–96). Simmel did not achieve a full professorship until 1914, when he moved to the University of Strasbourg. He remained there until his death of liver cancer in 1918.

Simmel was an outstanding essayist and prolific writer on a wide range of themes. Over the course of his lifetime, he authored over 200 articles and 15 major works (Coser 1977, 198). Nine of his pieces were translated and appeared in the *American Journal of Sociology* between 1896 and 1910. The inaugural issue of Emile Durkheim's journal *L'Annee Sociologique* had a piece by Simmel as its second article. Together with Ferdinand Toennies (profiled in chapter 8) and Max Weber (profiled in chapter 2), he was one of the three original executive members of the German Sociological Association, formed in 1909 (Frisby 1984, 14–15).

As Simmel scholar David Frisby summarizes, Georg Simmel was "one of the first sociologists in Germany to establish sociology as a circumscribed, independent discipline . . . [offering a] wealth of insights into social life . . . general theory of modernity and a sociology of modern life (especially metropolitan life) . . . everyday life (mealtimes, writing a letter) . . . social types (the stranger, the adventurer) . . . [and a] master of the analysis of psychological states (pessimism, the blasé attitude, etc.)" (1984, 18). This richness of intellectual work has led Peter Hamilton to summarize succinctly that Simmel was "the thinker who first developed so many concepts we now take for granted" (1984, 9).

Philip G. Zimbardo

Social psychologist Philip G. Zimbardo (1933–) is largely known to sociologists as the creator of the Stanford Prison Experiment. His body of work is, however, expansive and covers a range of diverse areas including shyness, madness, violence/evil, persuasion, hypnosis, and teaching. His body of work also addresses terrorism. He has been a professor at Stanford University since 1968, where he is currently professor emeritus. Zimbardo offers large and popular lecture courses in introductory psychology with an average course size of 300 students (Zimbardo, home page).

He has leveraged the media to educate students and the public with his PBS-TV series *Discovering Psychology* and a video documentary on the Stanford Prison Experiment. Zimbardo has also collaborated on using scenarios from the classic television show *Candid Camera* to design a video and accompanying teaching materials that illustrate basic psychological themes and principles. (*Candid Camera* was a television show that set up unusual and unanticipated situations and filmed people's reactions with a hidden camera. These scenarios were edited into a series of short, often humorous clips.)

Zimbardo has authored or coauthored over 300 publications. These works include scholarly articles, publications, reports, scholarly books, trade books, edited readers, almost two dozen textbooks, and a similar number of workbooks and manuals. He has also served as the president of the American

Psychological Association. Work that began in Zimbardo's laboratory in the mid-1970s has now grown into The Shyness Clinic that promotes shyness research and the treatment of adult and adolescent shyness (Zimbardo, home page).

CAREERS IN SOCIOLOGY

Those with an interest and training in the sociology of groups and organizations have backgrounds that prepare them for careers including

- activity director
- adoption/foster-agency director/staff
- advocacy-group director/staff
- athletic/recreation coordinator
- business-process engineer
- client services representative
- communications director
- community specialist
- compliance coordinator
- consultant
- consumer researcher
- development officer
- employment counselor
- executive director
- group home director/staff member
- human resources specialist
- industrial-relations specialist
- industrial sociologist
- labor-relations researcher
- lobbyist
- market-research data analyst
- mediator
- organizational planner
- organizational trainer/facilitator
- outreach coordinator
- personnel/human-relations manager
- program evaluator
- program manager
- program/project coordinator
- public-relations specialist
- quality enhancement/control specialist

- sales manager
- seminar/workshop consultant
- special-events coordinator
- strategic planner
- vocational counselor
- volunteer coordinator

Additional Resources

Alfino, Mark, John S. Caputo, and Robin Wynyard, eds. 1998. *McDonaldization Revisited: Critical Essays on Consumer Culture.* Westport, Conn.: Praeger. This multidisciplinary selection of essays examines the McDonaldization concept from different perspectives, such as feminism.

American Sociological Association. The Sociology Major: As Preparation for Careers in Business and Organizations. http://www.asanet.org/pubs/brochures/businesshome.html. The American Sociological Association explains the importance of a sociological perspective for those interested in careers in the world of business.

Blass, Thomas, ed. 2001. *Obedience to Authority: Current Perspectives on the Milgram Paradigm.* Mahwah, N.J: Lawrence Erlbaum. This selection provides biographical chapters on Milgram and several applications of his findings.

Communication and Information Technologies. American Sociological Association. http://www.citasa.org/. The areas of interest covered by this organization include the social aspects of computing, the Internet, new media, computer networks, the digital divide plus the design and use of the technology itself.

Ferguson, Kathy E. 1984. *The Feminist Case against Bureaucracy.* Philadelphia: Temple University Press. This book reexamines Weber's concept of bureaucracy through a feminist lens.

Forsyth, Donelson R. 1998. *Group Dynamics.* 3rd ed. Belmont, Calif.: Wadsworth. This textbook provides a comprehensive look at the field of group dynamics.

Immelman, Aubrey. Group Dynamics Text. http://www.users.csbsju.edu/~aimmelma/. This site from provides an online group-dynamics text covering a variety of material in the field.

Kanter, Rosabeth Moss. 2001. *Evolve! Succeeding in the Digital Culture of Tomorrow.* Boston: Harvard Business School Press. Kanter looks at "e-culture," examining the importance of the human-technology interface in the increasingly global and digital culture.

Kearl, Michael C. Social Psychology. http://www.trinity.edu/~mkearl/socpsy.html. The Sociological Tour through Cyberspace includes this examination of issues in social psychology, the field of several of those researchers profiled in this chapter.

Milgram, Stanley. 1974. *Obedience to Authority.* New York: Harper and Row. Milgram's original descriptions of his research remain an informative and fascinating read.

Ritzer, George. 2000. *The McDonaldization of Society.* Rev. ed. Thousand Oaks, Calif.: Pine Forge Press. Ritzer discusses the social implications for our search for ever-increasing efficiency and provides his thoughts about coping in a McDonaldized world.

Waters, Tony. 2001. *Bureaucratizing the Good Samaritan: The Limitations of Humanitarian Relief Operations.* Boulder, Colo.: Westview Press. This book examines the organization of large refugee relief programs, showing how humanitarian relief is delivered by rationalized bureaucracies working within institutionalized frameworks.

Wellman, Barry. 1999. *Networks in the Global Village.* Boulder, Colo.: Westview Press. This book compares the personal communities and social networks (e.g., friends, relatives, neighbors, and workmates) of people around the world and how they use those networks to get resources.

Zimbardo, Philip G. Home page. http://www.zimbardo.com/zimbardo.html. Dr. Zimbardo's Web site provides a slideshow and further information about the classic Stanford Prison Experiment.

CHAPTER 6
Deviance and Social Control

Much of sociology focuses on social order and conformity. But what about those who do not conform to society's norms and values? Why does this happen? And what are the implications and consequences? To answer these questions, some sociologists turn their attention to the study of **deviance,** *the violation of some cultural norm or value.*

Some forms of deviance are serious violations of our mores. They are considered severe enough breaches of cultural norms and values to be classified as crimes. **Crimes** are *acts defined as so unacceptable they are prohibited by a code of laws.* Some sociologists focus their interests specifically on issues involving criminal behavior. These *sociologists or other social scientists who study the criminal justice system, criminal law, and social order* are called **criminologists.**

However, *deviance* also refers to many things that are not criminal in nature. Anything that is considered nonconformist or unusual is, by definition, deviant. Sociologists do not use the term *deviance* to refer specifically to things that are immoral or "bad," only to address things outside of the boundaries of cultural norms or values.

To sociologists, deviance is relative. "It is not the act itself that is deviant; rather it is people's interpretation of it or judgment about it that makes it deviant" (Sullivan 2003, 301). Behavior that is considered inappropriate (deviant) in one situation may be considered appropriate (nondeviant) in another situation. A graphic example of this concept comes from an event that grabbed world headlines in 1972. An airplane carrying an amateur rugby team, their family, and friends crashed high in the Andes mountains. Because the plane was off-course when it crashed and painted white against the snow-covered terrain, rescuers were unable to locate the plane until a few survivors made their way to help 70 days later. The only food on the plane, a bit of chocolate and wine, had been quickly consumed. Those who survived the ordeal did so by eating the bodies of the dead passengers. In their dire situation, old definitions of deviance were socially reconstructed. Cannibalism, considered taboo in most cultures, was redefined by the group, and later by much of the world and the Roman Catholic Church, as acceptable under the circumstances (Henslin 2001b; Read 1975).

Behavior may also be seen as deviant because it is outside the limits of expected behavior for particular categories of people. Children engaging in "adult" behaviors illustrate this idea (e.g., drinking alcoholic beverages, little girls wearing heavy makeup and high heels). Conversely, an elderly person who uses a skateboard as a mode of transportation or mimics the clothing styles worn by a young rock star would be seen as deviating from the expected norms for elderly behavior.

Social reactions toward deviant behavior are tempered by how strongly held expectations are for certain situations or groups. For example, feminists often argue that women are held to more stringent limits of "acceptable" behaviors than men and are also more strongly criticized than men when they deviate from those norms. Rowe (2001) examines how the comedian Roseanne built a career by acting outside the social limits established for women, behavior that Rowe calls being an "unruly woman." Among her behaviors, Roseanne has been known for tattooing her buttocks, mooning fans, flatulence, and her heavy weight. Although this behavior set her apart from other women comics and led to great popularity, it also led to much criticism. This criticism hit an apex after she was invited to open a professional baseball game by singing the national anthem. Rather than a traditional rendition, Roseanne "screeched out the song, grabbed her crotch, spit on the ground, and made an obscene gesture to the booing crowd" (274). Her intention to parody baseball rituals resulted in outraged phone calls, massive negative media response, and even death threats. Rowe argues that a number of male singers, including Jose Feliciano, Bobby McFerrin, Marvin Gaye, and Willie Nelson, have been criticized for their artistic treatment of the national anthem. However, these male performances have not provoked the harsh reactions aimed at Roseanne's female "unruliness."

Definitions of deviance can also change over time. As cultural norms and values change, activities that were once considered deviant can be redefined as nondeviant. They become an accepted part of society. One example of deviance going mainstream is the use of contraceptives in the United States. In the early twentieth century, the transport of contraception by public mail was illegal in the U.S. In 1914, based on the Comstock Law that banned "obscene" and "immoral" literature, activist Margaret Sanger (1879–1966) was indicted for violating postal obscenity laws for distributing informational literature advocating contraceptive use (Chesler 1992). However, by the mid-1990s, 39 million American women of childbearing age reported using contraceptives (Piccinino and Mosher 1998). By 2004, Planned Parenthood, an organization founded by Sanger, had well over 800 health centers providing services in 49 states and the District of Columbia to almost 5 million people annually (Planned Parenthood Federation of America, "Planned Parenthood Health Centers" 2003).

This example involved a change of laws. Some deviance becomes part of mainstream society simply by a change in the culture. For example, in the 1950s, Becker (1963) conducted a study on "outsiders." He looked at how certain groups defined as deviant lived. Becker's study included research on jazz musicians. Today, jazz festivals are popular draws for large mainstream audiences. Similarly, rock music was considered deviant and even dangerous when Elvis Presley began to perform and gyrate his hips on stage. Rock eventually became accepted as mainstream music earning billions of dollars, spawning television networks (e.g., MTV, VH1), and popular competitions naming a singer as the "American Idol."

THEORIES OF DEVIANCE

Sociologists use a variety of different theoretical perspectives to explain deviance. These theories provide the core perspectives that sociologists apply in a variety of criminal-justice and deviance-related careers. These perspectives include biological theories of deviance as well as applications of the functionalist, conflict, and interactionist perspectives discussed in chapter 2.

Biological Perspectives

Writing in the wake of Charles Darwin's publication of *On the Origin of Species* (1996, orig. 1859) and *The Descent of Man* (1981, orig. 1871), Italian army psychiatrist Cesare Lombroso (1835–1909), profiled below, argued that he could distinguish "born criminals." They were identifiable, he contended, by physical characteristics common to criminals but not shared by the wider population. Lombroso's research consisted of recording anatomical and physiological measurements from thousands of living and dead Italian soldiers and prisoners. His data included the length of arms and fingers, facial features, amount of body hair, distance between the eyes, and even measurements of brains, bones, and internal organs.

Lombroso (1876) concluded that the "criminal man" was atavistic, or less evolved and closer to apes or Neanderthals, than were noncriminals, and shared five or more physical characteristics on a list of "stigmata" he developed. His list included large jaws, high cheekbones, handle-shaped ears, insensitivity to pain (physical and moral), and good eyesight, as well as characteristics such as excessive laziness, sexual drive, and craving for evil. Lombroso used his data to argue that criminality was instinctual. A subsequent study of women resulted in similar conclusions about female criminality. Female "born criminals" were, however, fewer in number and more difficult to detect (Lombroso 1980).

In Lombroso's later work, he did move beyond atavism as the only explanation for crime. Thus, his list of potential causes of criminality grew significantly. It eventually included, among other factors, degenerative processes, extremes in weather, the soil, physical illness, race and ethnicity, population congestion and density, famines, insurrections, the price of bread, alcoholism, illiteracy, wealth and poverty, religion, age, and employment status (Lombroso 1968; Jones 1986).

Other researchers continued to search for connections linking physique with criminality. Using similar methods, Charles Goring (1972) demonstrated that both criminals and noncriminals shared the physical features (stigmata) identified by Lombroso. He did, however, argue that criminals were inferior physically and mentally. Earnest Hooton (1939a, 1939b) used physical measurements from thousands of criminals and non-criminals to conclude that criminals were "organically inferior" and that genetic "criminal stock" surfaced occasionally. Comparing photographs of known criminals and noncriminals, William Sheldon (1949) concluded that muscular bodies (which he associated with aggression) indicated a criminal type. Sheldon and Eleanor Glueck (1950, 1956) expanded on Sheldon's work, adding more factors to consider. Although they agreed that more deviants had muscular builds, they also argued that additional factors were at work in criminality.

More recent biological approaches to crime have considered a range of variables. Researchers have consistently found criminals to have lower IQs than noncriminals. However, the reasons for this finding generate a great deal of debate, with researchers variously blaming official records and research biases, brain dysfunction, genetics, an associated lack of moral reasoning, and educational and social factors (Paternoster and Bachman 2001, 51–52). Other research, much of which has involved comparisons of behaviors of twins or adopted siblings, has looked for genetic links to deviant behaviors. Research that makes uses of sociobiology (discussed in chapter 3) involves comparing criminal records of individual twins and those of fraternal twins. Research findings in this area tend to be controversial. While some researchers have argued in support of a genetic connection to crime, social factors such as poverty and parenting skills are also necessary to consider (Christiansen 1977; Wilson and Herrnstein 1985; Raine 1993).

Other biological factors studied in relation to deviance include chromosomal abnormality, biochemical substances, cognitive deficits, and birth complications. Researchers have even drawn from the field of **psychophysiology** (*the science that deals with the interplay between psychological and physiological processes*) in considering variables such as the electrical activity of the skin and heart rate (Yaralian and Raine 2001). A review of this research leads Paternoster and Bachman to conclude that "some biological factors have been related to criminal and other antisocial behaviors [but] these biological factors are not the sole cause of crime. Rather, biological causes work in concert with other, social factors. We think this is a conclusion with which most biologically and sociologically-oriented crime scholars would agree" (2001, 55).

Structural-Functionalist Perspectives

For structural-functionalists, as explained in chapter 2, various aspects of society contribute to the operation of the entire system. Although it may seem unlikely to some observers that deviance contributes to society as a whole, Emile Durkheim, profiled in chapter 10, felt that deviance does indeed serve social functions. To Durkheim (1964a, 1964b), deviance strengthens social bonds by defining **moral boundaries,** *a shared sense of acceptable behavior that establishes right and wrong as well as sanctions for behaviors that fall outside permissible bounds.* In other words, identifying and punishing deviance also identifies what is considered okay. People draw together to respond to deviance. After the September 11, 2001, attacks on the World Trade Center, New Yorkers and many other Americans worked together to recover bodies, clean up the rubble, and support police officers, firefighters, and emergency workers. Many Americans' allegiance to each other, their nation, and their professed national values of freedom were strengthened. The attacks even generated gestures of support from around the world.

Social Bonds

Durkheim argued that social bonds were stronger in preindustrial societies than in industrial societies. In his view, preindustrial societies were more conducive to strong social bonds because people had to work together for the good of society. Industrial societies encourage people to focus on individual wants and desires, resulting in an increasing plurality of values and loss of social constraints. Thus, for Durkheim, "crime is one of the costs that we pay to live in the type of society that we do" (Sullivan 2003, 297).

This weakening of bonds in modern societies can result in **anomie,** *an uncomfortable and unfamiliar state of normlessness that results when shared norms or guidelines break down.* "Anomie does not refer to a state of mind, but to a property of the social structure. It characterizes a condition in which individual desires are no longer regulated by common norms and where, as a consequence, individuals are left without moral guidance in pursuit of their goals" (Coser 1977, 133). In his famous study *Suicide* (1966), discussed in chapter 10, Durkheim found that people experiencing a sense of anomie were more likely than those with strong social bonds to commit suicide.

Kai Erickson (1978) observed the problem of anomie among survivors after the entire community of Buffalo Creek, West Virginia, was washed away in a flood. Another often-cited work by Erikson (1966) argued that the witch trials of Puritan New England resulted from the social changes and breakdown of norms occurring during that period. As the strict religious codes of society began to change, the discovery of "witches" actually served to draw members of the community together by reaffirming the moral order. Witches provided the community a common enemy that threatened their very existence unless they all pulled together. Other researchers have argued that witch trials were actually targeted primarily against women who dared to challenge male authority (Chambliss and Seidman 1982; Chambliss and Zatz 1994).

Structural Strain

Robert K. Merton, profiled in chapter 2, expanded Durkheim's concept into a general theory of deviant behavior. According to Merton's (1968) **structural-strain theory,** *anomie results from inconsistencies between the culturally approved means to achieve goals and those actual goals.* There are goals in a society that most people pursue (e.g., financial and material wealth, power, status). There are also socially acceptable means to achieve these goals (e.g., hard work, honesty). Most people conform to the acceptable means to achieve goals. While some people are able to buy a nice home, designer clothing, and expensive vehicles through legally derived funds, others do not have legitimate means to obtain these things. Deviance results from a "strain" between means and goals—for example, when there is a contrast between wants and economic realities.

On the basis of this concept, Merton identified four deviant adaptations to strain (see table 6.1). The most common type of deviance is *innovation.* People accept culturally approved goals but pursue them in ways that are not socially approved. A person who steals property or money to pay rent or purchase a car is innovating, as is a drug dealer or embezzler.

Other forms of deviance involve a rejection of these culturally approved goals. *Ritualism* occurs when someone is unsuccessful at achieving these goals, yet continues to adhere to social expectations for their achievement. Merton identified lower-level bureaucrats as examples of this circumstance. They may adhere so strictly to rules that they may even overconform by focusing exclusively on following rules rather than other goals.

Retreatism occurs when both culturally approved goals and means are rejected. Retreatists are social "dropouts." They include alcoholics, drug addicts, the homeless, and the hopeless.

When both culturally approved goals and means are rejected and replaced by other goals and means, the response is a *rebellion* to those goals and means. Rebels substitute unconventional goals and means in their place. They may even form a counterculture (see chapter 3). Hippies, some religious groups, and revolutionaries would be characterized as fitting this category.

In support of strain theory, gender discrimination has been found to be a predictor of crime and substance abuse. Lack of opportunity (e.g., being denied a job, being discouraged by a teacher) was seen as leading to pressures that resulted in deviance in some cases (Eitle 2002). Research has also found property crime to be greater in areas of inequality and relative deprivation, where the acceptable means to achieve goals are blocked (Simons and Gray 1989).

Opportunity Structures

Richard Cloward and Lloyd Ohlin (1960) argued that deviance is more complex than Merton had explained. In addition to limited means to achieve legitimate goals, a person also has to have access to illegitimate opportunities. However much a person would like to embezzle "what they deserve for their

Table 6.1
Merton's Strain Theory of Deviance

Response	Culturally - Accepted Goals	Culturally - Accepted Means
Conformity	Accepted	Accepted
Innovation	Accepted	Rejected
Ritualism	Rejected	Accepted
Retreatism	Rejected	Rejected
Rebellion	Replaced	Replaced

Source: Merton (1968, 230–36).

hard work" from their employer, they will not be able to do so without access to the corporate funds.

According to Albert Cohen (1971), deviant subcultures (see chapter 3) arise to support criminal behavior. Blocked opportunities lead to subcultures that value other attributes (e.g., stealing rather than buying). These subcultures provide a way of life that supports criminal behavior. In his study of gangs, Cohen found teens stealing for "kicks" and committing vandalism. Gang values (e.g., achieving instant gratification rather than long-term thinking, an emphasis on the importance of the gang over others) replaced those of the larger culture. A more recent ethnography of life in a South London neighborhood also looked at streetwise teens (Foster 1990). Criminality, and the expectation of participation in delinquent activities, become part of the culture of the neighborhood itself. Streetwise teens graduated from petty crimes to involvement in a black-market economy as adults.

Social Control

Other theorists note that opportunities to deviate are all around us. Deviance can be fun, and it can be easier than conforming. With that in mind, social-control theories have been developed that focus our attention in another direction. **Social-control theories** *ask not why people deviate, but rather why they conform.* The answer, according to this perspective, is that people conform because of social bonds (Hirschi 1969). When those bonds are weak or broken, they are more likely to commit deviant acts.

Social control arises from several elements: *attachment* to others through strong, caring relationships; *commitment* to legitimate social goals, such as a college education or prestigious jobs, and consideration of the costs of deviance; *involvement* in legitimate activities, such as academic activities, sports teams, a religious body, or a job; and *belief* in a common value system that says conformity is right and deviance is wrong. The more vested a person is within the society and the more they have to lose, the less likely they are to become involved in deviance.

Some research from this perspective has focused on curbing juvenile delinquency by keeping teens involved in, and feeling attached to, socially approved activities and goals (Agnew 1991; Hirschi 1969). Other research adds that since many people have the opportunity to deviate, those who do so are more in tune with short-term benefits. They are more likely to be impulsive, short-sighted, insensitive, and risk takers than those who conform (Gottfredson and Hirschi 1990). Additionally, a study of over 450 people convicted of insider trading found that these offenders were lacking in overall self-control (Szockyj and Geis 2002).

Social-Conflict Perspectives

The conflict perspective on deviance is based on early observations of crime in capitalist society made by Karl Marx's friend and coauthor Friedrich Engels (1964, 1981). Marx is profiled in chapter 2. Engels is profiled in chapter 7. Engels argued that the inequalities inherent in capitalism set up a system in which the poor had little and would try to obtain more. Meanwhile, the rich had a vested interest in controlling the poor.

Conflict theory became a major criminological perspective during the 1970s and 1980s, in a stage set by the political activism of the 1960s (Moyer 2001, 190–241). Theorists working in this tradition continue to focus on the inequalities across capitalist society (Chambliss 1975; Spitzer 1980; Headley 1991). They see the legal and criminal justice systems as being established such that powerful groups benefit (Kennedy 1990; Quinney 1970, 1974, 1980). They argue that these systems focus the vast majority of attention and resources on the less powerful in society while largely overlooking the activities of the powerful. The powerful construct and apply definitions of crime that fit their own interests and impact less powerful factions. Vagrancy, loitering, and drug laws, for example, are all typically written such that they target the lower classes (Chambliss 1964; Lynch and Stretesky 2001; Brownstein 2000).

Conflict theorists also argue that the cost of corporate crimes (e.g., workplace deaths and injuries due to unsafe working conditions, consumers harmed by dangerous products) far outstrips the costs of street crime (Chambliss 1988; Reiman 1998; Frank and Lynch 1992). As Paternoster and Bachman summarize: "Those with economic and political power use it to their advantage by criminalizing the behaviors of the powerless. As a result, 'crime in the street' is met with the power of the criminal law, the police, courts, and penal system, while 'crimes in the suite' (organizational, white-collar, corporate, and political crimes) are defined either as shrewd business practices or as mere civil violations" (2001, 254).

Meanwhile, characteristics valued in corporate America are seen as problematic when exhibited by the "wrong" groups. Entrepreneurialism, competitiveness, and ambition for material success and status are all valued in the corporate world. Business executives are often hailed in these terms. However, these same characteristics are often cast in negative terms when they help some members of teen gangs assume leadership roles in the gang or help drug dealers gain wealth and status on the "street" where they conduct their business (e.g., Jankowski 1991; Williams 1989).

The result of elite control of the criminal justice system, according to conflict theorists, is that "crime control is, in reality, class control" (Moyer 2001, 210). The powerful use the resources at their disposal, such as the news media, to ensure that public attention stays focused on these "street crimes" rather than activities of the upper classes (Chambliss 1994). As a result, the wary public wants to be protected from these criminals, siphoning valuable resources away from other, beneficial areas, such as social services. An entire "crime industry" has arisen in which extensive amounts of assets, including time and attention of enforcement personnel, financial resources, court resources, space in penal institutions, and probation and parole services (to name a few of the major costs), are allotted to efforts by the powerful to control the lower classes (Christie 1993).

Conflict theorists also focus on the influence of inequality beyond class. They have turned their attention to the environment and "green" issues (Lynch and Stretesky 2001, 279–81). They have also begun to devote significant research attention to the issue of hate crimes (e.g., Perry 2001). Although the exact legal definition varies from location to location, **hate crimes** are crimes that are committed *based on the victims' characteristics such as race, ethnicity, gender, sexual orientation, disability, or religion.* These crimes can be committed against the person or property, or they can be considered crimes against society.

Race is the focus for many conflict studies of deviance. This work has a long history. Dutch Marxist criminologist Willem Bonger's (1876–1940) book *Race and Crime* argued against Lombroso's atavistic theories. He also attacked the Nazi emphasis on race and "was among the first to point out" (Moyer 2001, 195) that selective law enforcement patterns may play a role in the official statistics, with blacks being more frequently prosecuted than whites and less advantaged when dealing with the criminal-justice system. Early American sociologist W.E.B. Du Bois, profiled in chapter 7, included data on crime in his study of a black community in Philadelphia (see Moyer 2001). In more recent and controversial work, feminist scholar Coramae Richey Mann (1987, 1993), profiled below, argues that the interplay of historical patterns of racism and discrimination, and long-established stereotypes, have resulted in a racist legal system.

Conflict scholars working in a feminist framework have looked at a range of deviance issues. (Feminism is discussed in more detail in chapter 2.) Their interests are as wide ranging as the treatment of women within the legal system, violence against women and children, female criminal behavior and delinquency, and even wives of criminals (e.g., Daly and Chesney-Lind 1988; Chesney-Lind and Faith 2001). Many argue, however, that women have largely been overlooked in the literature on deviance. Simpson and Elis (1996), for example, draw this conclusion regarding women's experiences with white-collar crime (e.g., large corporations marketing dangerous silicone-gel breast implants and intrauterine devices).

Examining deviance issues from a feminist perspective also reveals previously unidentified complexities. For example, the majority of female inmates are also mothers. How these women try to fulfill the role of "mother" and prove their fitness to regain custody of their children, and the many implications for their children, their caregivers, and wider society, are all issues examined by recent feminist research but largely ignored by other scholars (Enos 2001).

Symbolic-Interactionist Perspectives

Symbolic-interactionist theories of deviance draw from the importance this perspective places on our daily interactions. These theories focus on our definitions of situations and the argument that our self-concepts are based on other's perceptions. In doing so, they provide a micro look at deviance that can be compared with the macro perspectives.

Labeling

The focus of **labeling theory** is not the behavior itself; rather, it is *the response of others than defines (labels) the behavior as deviant and impacts further deviance.* According to this theory, any number of behaviors might be considered normal or deviant. The crucial factor is the behavior being labeled deviant by others (Becker 1963; Cavender 1991). Labeling theory cannot explain the original causes of deviant behavior. The focus and value are in explaining reactions to deviance when it does occur.

According to Charles Lemert (1951), *violations of social norms that go undiscovered or are considered excusable by others* constitute **primary deviance.** Although a norm violation occurs, no label is attached to the behavior. When someone with the power to make the label "stick" notices the behavior and labels it deviant, however, the label can impact the way others see the person who committed the behavior as well as the labeled person's behaviors and self-perceptions. The result of a label can be **secondary deviance,** *deviance committed as a result of the reactions of others to previous deviant behavior.* When labeled deviant, a person might conclude that that is the behavior other people expect of them and respond by engaging in additional deviance. This reaction might occur even if the label was not an accurate reflection of their behavior.

When the labeled person comes to see themselves in terms of the label, the label becomes a **self-fulfilling prophecy.** The person *develops a self-concept based on the label and acts based upon that self-concept* (Heimer and Matsueda 1994). For example, an art student who is told repeatedly that her work is excellent is likely to form a different self-concept than another student who is labeled by her teachers as having no talent. The student who is labeled as talented may aspire to continue her art education, show and sell her work, or seek funding from arts organizations. The student told she has no talent might come to see herself in those terms, quit art school, and choose another course of study.

As this example shows, labels can focus on positive or negative attributes. Negative labels can become a **stigma,** *a powerful negative label that changes a person's social identity and how they see themselves* (Goffman 1963b). A stigma often becomes a master status (see chapter 3). The person is seen first in terms of the stigmatizing label, regardless of whatever other statuses he may hold. The concept of stigma has drawn increasing research attention in recent years, demonstrating that stigmas likely have "dramatic bearing" on the distribution of life chances and impact earnings, housing, health, criminal involvement, and even life itself (Link and Phelan 2001).

People who are voluntarily child-free are often seen as stigmatized in our pronatalist society (Lisle 1999; Orenstein 2000). Although increasing numbers of people are choosing to remain child-free, Kristin Park (2002) found that child-free women and men still feel so stigmatized that they regularly devise strategies to manage that stigma. Some use a "passing" strategy (i.e., younger people not acknowledging they have decided to remain child-free by saying things like "I'm not ready for that responsibility yet"). Some offer justifications (e.g., when told that remaining child-free is "selfish," they argue that having children is really the selfish act) or excuses (e.g., saying they have no biological drive to have children). They also redefine the situation (e.g., asserting that a person does not have to be a parent to be socially valuable). Another strategy is identity substitution, trading one stigma for a less stigmatized identity (e.g., making people back off questions by answering that they cannot have children). This latter tactic involves "trading down" to a "lesser" available stigma, so to speak.

William Chambliss (1973), who is profiled below, demonstrated just how powerful labeling can be in his classic study on teen deviance. Chambliss studied delinquency among two groups of teenage boys he referred to as the "Saints" and the "Roughnecks." These names referred to the ways the community viewed and labeled the boys, and the outcomes these labels had for members of each group. They had nothing to do with to the actual number of delinquent acts committed by each group.

Both groups engaged in about the same amount of delinquency, including truancy, drinking, speeding, theft, and vandalism. However, the Saints were middle-class boys from "good homes" who were well dressed and well mannered with authority figures and many of whom had cars enabling them to get away from the eyes of the community when doing these things. They were labeled as good, college-bound boys whose actions, when caught, tended to be excused as pranks. The Roughnecks were from working-class families with rough dress and demeanor and few automobiles. Labeled as troublemakers, these boys' actions tended to be defined as "more of the same" from bad kids. Over the two years of the study, not one Saint was officially arrested, but several of the Roughnecks were arrested more than once.

Both the Saints and the Roughnecks came to accept their labels. The Saints continued to college; the Roughnecks became increasingly deviant, even choosing new friends from among other "troublemakers." Chambliss concluded that how the community had labeled these boys had lasting impacts on their adult lives.

The Medicalization of Deviance

Sociologists have identified even further implications of labeling. They have observed a **medicalization of deviance** in recent decades. This means that *issues that were formerly defined in moral or legal terms have become redefined as medical issues.* In the parlance of labeling theory, these issues are relabeled as appropriate for medical intervention. Social reactions and understandings adjust accordingly when this relabeling occurs.

Alcoholism provides an example of medicalization (Conrad and Schneider 1980). During the colonial period, drunkenness was disapproved of but not rare. Churches and drinking houses were both considered social centers. Being drunk was seen as free choice and a method of avoiding some of life's unpleasantness. Alcohol use became deviant only if someone was repeatedly drunk. At the end of the eighteenth century, however, this view changed to a medical perspective, largely through the efforts of Dr. Benjamin Rush, a well-known physician active in numerous causes. Excessive use of alcohol is now labeled "alcoholism" and largely seen as a disease.

A major impact of medicalizing issues is their depoliticization. Specifically considering alcohol use and the issue of drinking and driving, if alcohol use is a problem because of individual alcoholics, and alcoholics are "ill" by medical definition, the individual behavior becomes the problem. Other potential problems located in larger institutions and social structures (e.g., the alcohol industry, governmental policies, taxation) can be ignored and excused of responsibility. The result is an "enormous emphasis on drinking and the drinker as causal elements while such institutional aspects as lack of alternate means of transportation are ignored both as causal agents and as possible considerations in providing avenues of solutions" (Gusfield 1980, viii).

Mental illness is a highly debated and highly stigmatized disorder that some argue is improperly medicalized, at least to some extent. A controversial argument by psychiatrist Thomas Szasz (1970) says that mental illness, rather than bring a real "sickness," is a label applied to those who are different to make them conform. Research by social psychologist D. L. Rosenhan (1973) demonstrated how powerfully these labels of mental illness stick.

He sent eight volunteer "pseudopatients" for evaluation by staff at a mental hospital. None of his volunteers had any history of mental illness. Each complained only of hearing voices that alluded to the emptiness of life, by saying things such as "hollow," "empty," and "thud." Each pseudo-student was diagnosed as schizophrenic and admitted to a mental hospital. After admission, all stopped complaining of any symptoms and behaved as they would normally outside of the hospital.

No staff ever recognized any of these pseudopatients as frauds. Their normal behaviors (e.g., note taking for their research, walking the halls out of boredom, or gathering for lunch early) were reinterpreted in medical terms to fit the schizophrenic label. Other patients, however, did suspect them of being "not crazy," journalists, professors, or someone investigating the hospital. When released, the pseudopatients were not considered "cured" by the medical staff. Rather, they were relabeled as having schizophrenia "in remission," leaving open the possibility, and even an expectation, that the illness would reappear in the future.

More recently, Nancy Herman (1993) interviewed almost 300 former mental patients and found that the mentally ill label remained after their treatment was completed. Many patients tried to conceal their past. However, some others openly acknowledged their illness or even became political advocates for the mentally ill.

Cultural Transmission

The basis of **cultural-transmission theories** is that *deviance is learned and shared through interaction with others.* It is transferred through the process of socialization. Albert Cohen's work on subcultures discussed above could easily be addressed under this heading. A widely tested theory drawing from this perspective is the theory of **differential association.** According to this theory, *deviance results from interacting with deviant associates* (Sutherland 1947; Sutherland and Cressey 1978; Sutherland, Cressey, and Luckenbill 1992). The greater the frequency, duration, importance, and intensity of that interaction, the greater the likelihood that deviance will be shared.

This is a widely tested theory. It has been applied to a range of behaviors, including embezzlement (Cressey 1953), white-collar crimes (Sutherland 1985), drug and alcohol use (Lindesmith 1968; Akers et al. 1979), and "professional" criminals (King and Chambliss 1984). One study finds more than 80 articles on differential association published just since 1990 (Hochstetler, Copes, and DeLisi 2002, 558).

Critics of differential association note that the theory is unable to explain how deviance arises in the first place and why some acts or groups are defined as deviant. However, when combined with Hirschi's control theory, discussed above, the result is an integrated theory that argues that children having weak bonds to their parents are those most likely to engage in deviance, associate with delinquents, and be influenced by them. At least one reviewer calls this integrated theory the "single best empirically-substantiated theory of crime that can be offered by modern criminology" (Warr 2001, 189).

GLOBALIZATION AND THE INTERNET

Globalization and the Internet have become important areas of research in the sociological study of deviance. Aspects of culture, including things that are considered deviant as well as those that are considered normal, are shared. Deviance often has different definitions in different cultures. This may cause social stress as people decide what aspects of various cultures they want to embrace, allow, or reject. In the Middle East, many countries are currently struggling with this issue. What aspects of Western culture will become part of their culture? And what will be shunned as deviant? Western-style dress for women? American movies and music? More democratic forms of government?

In addition to aspects of culture, globalization also involves immigration and rules regarding where and when people can physically move. These rules may even define crossing a border to find work, food, or a higher income as a crime. Immigration and other aspects of globalization also increase contact between different racial and ethnic groups. The result can be more violence between varying groups.

Some observers have also commented that globalization makes the world rich for other crime. Electronic financial systems that transcend national boundaries are difficult to control. Other concerns result from government upheavals and economic difficulties of many poorer nations or those undergoing major change. To some, the "so-called failed or collapsed state is the principal actor in criminalization of the world economy, while globalization itself is an unwitting but pre-eminent member of the supporting cast" (Gros 2003, 63). In periods of upheaval in poorer countries, the rich or well connected may acquire state resources and use them for their own profit. These upheavals may also ultimately result in a reduction in safety forces, low salaries, and smuggling conducted in the name of free trade. Solutions to making globalization less vulnerable to criminality are complex. They may involve a complicated monitoring of capital flows involving various financial and legal systems. They may also be aimed at reducing corruption and smuggling, or increasing workers' wages (Gros 2003).

Globalization supports other types of criminality as well—for example, the drug trade. Opiates grown in Afghanistan or coca leaves grown in Columbia are processed in surrounding areas, travel across numerous international boundaries, and are sold on the streets of American or western European countries. At each step in the trafficking process, the profits accrued increase. Chambliss (1989) argues that smuggling drugs and other goods may even be a state-organized crime. He cites as examples the CIA's involvement in moving opium in Southeast Asia during the Vietnam War and the so-called Iran-Contra Affair, in which an arms deal with Iran funded support for Nicaraguan fighters known as contras.

The Internet, which also transcends international boundaries, has provided a new venue for deviant and criminal activity. Online deviance ranges from breaches of etiquette (*netiquette*) to the enactment of violent crimes including rape and murder. Viruses and computer *hacking* and *cracking* are types of deviance that exist only because the Internet itself exists. The Internet provides a new venue for intellectual crimes such as plagiarism and economic crimes (embezzlement, fraud, etc.). Research has shown that deviant information spreads quickly over the Internet (Mann and Sutton 1998). It also has shown that complaints of Internet crime are on the rise, with the Internet providing new criminal arenas (National White Collar Crime Center and the Federal Bureau of Investigation 2003; Williams 2001).

The anonymity afforded by the Internet may be a major factor supporting deviance in cyberspace. Previous research has shown that those who believe their identities are unknown are more likely to behave aggressively in behaviors as diverse as driving (Ellison et al. 1995) and stealing Halloween candy (Diener et al. 1976). Research by Christina Demetriou and Andrew Silke (2003) was designed to test this concept online. For their study, the researchers established a Web site set purportedly for accessing legal games, shareware, and freeware. Once at the site, visitors were presented with links to what they thought were hacked programs (illegally obtained commercial software programs), pornography, and stolen passwords to paid-only pornography sites. Thus, site visitors came to the site for legitimate reasons and then were presented with the anonymous opportunity to engage in deviance. The researchers found that a large percentage of visitors who had originally visited the site for the legal information also visited sections they thought provided the deviant material. When presented with the anonymity and opportunity, many did not resist temptation.

BIOGRAPHIES

Howard Becker

Howard Saul Becker (1928–) was born in Chicago. Becker completed his bachelor's, master's, and doctorate degrees at the University of Chicago. He earned his Ph.D. in 1951, when he was only 23 years old ("Becker, Howard Saul" 1992).

Becker's work has included a famous coauthored study of medical students, *Boys in White: Student Culture in Medical School* (1961). He is also well known for his book *The Outsiders: Studies in the Sociology of Deviance* (1963). That manuscript was initially too short for a book. Becker only published it after being urged to do so by another sociologist who "read the manuscript and said it should be in print, so Becker decided to include his empirical studies on musicians and marijuana use"; a friend at a publishing house decided the book was "worth a gamble" (Martin, Mutchnick, and Austin 1990, 352). His 1986 book *Writing for Social Scientists: How to Start and Finish Your Thesis, Book, or Article* was hailed by reviewers as "charming and very personal" (Biggart 1987, 809) and "humane, wry, reflective, gentle, wise" (Erikson 1986). He has also authored, coauthored, or edited books and articles on topics including social problems, research methods, and art.

Becker has received a number of professional awards and has been credited with founding the labeling theory of deviance. He served as editor of *Social Problems*. He was also president of the Society for the Study of Social Problems and the Society for the Study of Symbolic Interaction.

Aside from his academics, Becker enjoys art and music. He studied photography at the San Francisco Art Institute. Becker is also a pianist who joined the Musician's Union in his teens, continuing to play professionally in jazz clubs until the 1970s, even supporting himself for a period with his music after earning his doctorate. When asked by a biographer who had influenced him, Becker's first response was a former jazz-piano teacher (Martin, Mutchnick, and Austin 1990, 349).

William Chambliss

William Joseph Chambliss (1933–) was born in Buffalo, New York. He completed his undergraduate degree in psychology at the University of California–Los Angeles in 1955. He was drafted during the Korean War, serving in the Counter Intelligence Corps. After completing his service, he received a master's and doctorate in sociology from Indiana University.

Chambliss had become interested in criminology while working in the fields with penitentiary inmates to earn money on a cross-country trip. He became further interested in crime when he saw soldiers committing crimes during his time in the military (Chambliss 1987). Chambliss reports that he became a sociologist out of his interest in "doing something about crime" (quoted in Henslin 2001a, xxi). He calls sociology "a beautiful discipline that affords an opportunity to investigate just about anything connected with human behavior and still claim an identity with a discipline. This is its strength, its promise, and why I find it thoroughly engaging, enjoyable, and fulfilling."

Chambliss has taught and conducted research in several countries. He has authored over 15 books. His professional recognitions include the Lifetime Achievement Award from the American Society of Criminology Crime and Deviance Division and the Bruce Smith Award from the Academy of Criminal Justice Sciences. He is also a past president of the American Society of Criminology. Chambliss is currently a professor of sociology at George Washington University in Washington, D.C. (Chambliss, "William Chambliss").

Peter Conrad

Peter Conrad (1945–) was born in New York. He earned his doctorate from Boston University in 1976. Conrad is currently the Harry Coplan Professor of Social Sciences and departmental chair in the Sociology Department at Brandeis University. Conrad joined that department in 1979.

Conrad's combining of his interests in deviance and medical sociology has led to his work in the medicalization of deviance and the medicalization of wider society. Together with coauthor Joseph Schneider, Conrad published his work in this arena in his book *Deviance and Medicalization: From Badness to Sickness* (1980). Conrad and Schneider also teamed to consider issues including stigma in *Having Epilepsy: The Experience and Control of Illness* (1993). The Society for the Study of Symbolic Interaction honored Conrad with the 1981 Charles Horton Cooley Award for that book. He has also published several other books and more than 60 other pieces on topics including epilepsy, hyperactive children, health care in developing countries, workplace health, and the rapidly evolving social issues involving genetics. Conrad's coedited collections *The Sociology of Health and Illness: Critical Perspectives* (2001) and *The Handbook of Medical Sociology* (2000) are in their sixth and fifth editions, respectively.

Conrad's professional activities include serving as past chair of the Psychiatric Sociology Division in the Society for the Study of Social Problems and the Medical Sociology Section of the American Sociological Association. Conrad has also been honored as a Distinguished Fulbright Scholar at Queen's University of Belfast in Northern Ireland (Conrad, "Peter Conrad"; "Conrad, Peter" 2000).

Travis Hirschi

Travis Hirschi (1935–) was born in Rockville, Utah. He earned his undergraduate and master's degrees from the University of Utah. After two years in the military, Hirschi earned his doctorate from the University of California–Berkeley in 1968.

He is currently a professor emeritus in the Department of Management and Policy as well as the Department of Sociology at the University of Arizona. Hirschi has served as the president of the American Society of Criminology. His book *Delinquency Research* (1967), written with Hanan Selvin, won the C. Wright Mills Award from the Society for the Study of Social Problems ("Hirschi, Travis" 1984).

Hirschi is well known among deviance scholars for his social-bond theory. In *Causes of Delinquency* (1969), he laid out four elements that create a bond between individuals and society. A number of researchers have tested this theory, including studies with females and different age groups, and it has "fared very well in empirical tests" (Brown, Esbensen, and Geis 1991, 373). Hirschi has also teamed with Michael T. Gottfredson for the more recent work *A General Theory of Crime* (1990).

Cesare Lombroso

Italian criminologist Cesare Lombroso (1835–1909) was born in Verona, which was under Austrian rule at the time. He earned a medical degree from the University of Pavia in 1858. The following year he earned a second degree in surgery from the University of Genoa. For several years, Lombroso was an army physician. He oversaw mental wards for almost a decade. He also held positions as professor of legal medicine and public hygiene, psychiatry and clinical psychiatry, and criminal anthropology. Lombroso's publications covered a range of topics, including the impact of cretinism and pellagra on mental and physical development, the nervous system, and genius. He became famous, however, for his work on "the born criminal," a term that actually came from his student Enrico Ferri (1856–1929) (Wolfgang 1973).

Although his biological theories of crime have been refuted, Lombroso is still widely hailed as the "father of modern criminology." Volumes have been written about his controversial work and influence. As one of Lombroso's biographers says, "In the history of criminology probably no name has been eulogized or attacked so much as that of Cesare Lombroso" (Wolfgang 1973, 232). Among his recognitions, Lombroso received the French Government's Legion of Honor Medal. He was also offered an appointment at Northwestern University for the 1909–10 academic year, but was physically unable to accept the position (Martin, Mutchnick, and Austin 1990, 23).

Aside from his flawed findings, Lombroso is credited with focusing on scientific studies of the criminal and the conditions under which criminality occurs. His physiological studies have inspired interest in criminal identification to include fingerprinting and classifying body fluids (Paternoster and Bachman 2001, 86; Jones 1986, 11). "Research anywhere that continues to examine differences between a delinquent and non-delinquent population, or that seeks to analyze differences within the criminal group can find its framework antedated by Lombroso" (Wolfgang 1973, 286). His work also helped set the stage for modern psychiatric analyses and interest in psychological differences among criminals.

Coramae Richey Mann

Coramae Richey Mann (1931–) excelled as a student. She loved school, often earning among the highest grades in her class. During high school and college, Mann had a brief modeling career and appeared on the cover of *Ebony* and other magazines. She later studied at Howard University for three years that she calls "clearly the most important in my educational life" (Mann 1995, 278). Mann received B.A. and M.A. degrees in clinical psychology from Roosevelt University. She earned her doctorate in sociology and criminology from the University of Illinois–Chicago in 1976.

Mann has held positions with the Chicago Welfare Department, the Chicago Psychiatric Institute, the Chicago Board of Health, Planned Parenthood, the Chicago Board of Education, and Northeastern University. For over a decade, she was also a practicing, licensed clinical psychologist (Martin, Mutchnick, and Austin 1990, 266–79; Mann 1995). Mann spent over a decade in the School of Criminology at Florida State University, where she says there were "seventeen white men and me" on the faculty there (1995, 281). She is currently a professor emeritus in the Criminal Justice Department at Indiana University–Bloomington.

The issues she tackles are controversial. Her work has addressed race and ethnicity; the power of stereotypes, discrimination, and racism; minority crime; women; juvenile justice; career criminals; domestic homicide; and unequal justice. Mann is a winner of the Academy of Criminal Justice Sciences' Bruce Smith Sr. Award. Her publications include more than 30 articles and book chapters. She has also written *Female Crime and Delinquency* (1984), *Unequal Justice: A Question of Color* (1989), and *When Women Kill* (1996). She is coeditor with Marjorie Sue Zatz of a collection of readings entitled *Images of Color: Images of Crime* (2002) (Mann, "Coramae Richey Mann").

Richard Quinney

Earl Richard Quinney (1934–) grew up on his family's farm in Wisconsin. Until the eighth grade, he attended a one-room schoolhouse. He saved money for college by raising breeding hogs on the farm. Quinney entered college intending to become a forest ranger. Before choosing a graduate program in sociology, Quinney even prepared to enter a graduate program in hospital administration. He finally settled on a doctoral program at the University of Wisconsin–Madison, graduating in 1962.

After completing his dissertation, Quinney accepted a position teaching sociology at the University of Kentucky and then moved to New York University. A later sabbatical leave at the University of North Carolina–Chapel Hill allowed him several years to concentrate on publishing and to begin, write for, and distribute a socialist newspaper (Martin, Mutchnick, and Austin 1990, 384). After several visiting professorships, Quinney joined the Department of Sociology at Northern Illinois University, where he became professor emeritus in 1998.

Quinney has authored, coauthored, or edited more than 20 books and 70 articles. He has presented guest lectures across the United States and internationally. His numerous awards include a Canterbury Visiting Fellowship at the University of Canterbury in New Zealand and the Major Achievement Award from the Critical Criminology Division of the American Society of Criminology. Quinney and coauthor Kevin Anderson were awarded the 2000 International Erich Fromm Prize for their book *Erich Fromm and Critical Criminology: Beyond the Punitive Society* (2000).

Quinney has written three books about facets of his own life, also reflecting his lifelong interest in photography. *Borderland: A Midwest Journal* (2001) is a memoir and photo journal of the Midwestern U.S. areas that have always been important to him. He offers a personal, existential view in *For the Time Being: Ethnography of Everyday Life* (1998). *Journey to a Far Place: Autobiographical Reflections* (1990) is an autobiography with photographs of his travels (see Martin, Mutchnick, and Austin 1990, 379–407; Quinney, "Richard Quinney").

Edwin H. Sutherland

Edwin Hardin Sutherland (1883–1950) was born in Gibbon, Nebraska. He earned his Ph.D. magna cum laude in sociology and political economy from the University of Chicago in 1913. Sutherland worked for several different schools over the course of his career: Sioux Falls, Grand Island, and William Jewell colleges, and the universities of Illinois, Minnesota, and Chicago. He spent the final 15 years of his life as chair of the Sociology Department at Indiana University. His "greatest strength" as a teacher has been reported as "his willingness to take his students seriously as scholars" (Martin, Mutchnick, and Austin 1990, 143).

While teaching at the University of Illinois, Sutherland was invited to write a textbook on criminology. *Criminology* (1924), retitled in 1934 as *Prin-*

ciples of Criminology, "was to become the most influential textbook in the history of criminology" (Wright, "Sample Entry"). Other authors continued the text after Sutherland's death through its 11th edition in 1992.

Sutherland developed a life-history approach to research that involved biographical accounts of subjects. He used it to write *The Professional Thief* (1937) in collaboration with con man Broadway Jones (Gaylord and Galliher 1988, 109–20). As a result of his conversations with Jones, Sutherland developed his differential-association theory. The book itself would become a source for writers of the screenplay for the 1973 movie *The Sting,* starring Robert Redford. Sutherland's work *White Collar Crime* (1985), a term he coined, applied the theory in a study of the behavior of young executives in the 70 largest corporations in the United States. Because the publisher feared lawsuits, the names of corporations that had been accused but not convicted of crimes had been removed. An edition published in the 1980s finally included that information (Wright, "Sample Entry").

While walking to work on October 11, 1950, Sutherland suffered a fatal stroke (Martin, Mutchnick, and Austin 1990, 143). By the time of his death, Sutherland had held the presidencies of the American Sociological Association, the Sociological Research Association, and the Ohio Valley Sociological Society. Although Sutherland had taken only one criminology course, taught limited numbers of criminology courses, and "did not begin his organized work in criminology until 1921" (139), he had also earned the titles "premiere criminologist" and "dean of American criminology."

CAREERS IN SOCIOLOGY

Those with an interest and training in the sociology of deviance and social control have backgrounds that prepare them for careers including

- advocate for prisoner's rights or victim's rights
- client services representative
- correctional administrator
- correctional officer
- correctional-treatment specialist
- court clerk
- court coordinator
- crime prevention specialist
- criminal justice analyst
- criminologist
- crisis-intervention coordinator
- detective/investigator
- dispute mediator
- executive director

- family-violence counselor
- group home director/staff member
- high-risk intervention specialist
- jury consultant
- magistrate
- mental-health service staff
- outreach coordinator
- paralegal
- police officer
- pre-law student
- probation/parole officer
- program evaluator
- program manager/director
- program/project coordinator
- rehabilitation counselor
- restitution program coordinator
- shelter supervisor
- substance-abuse/addiction counselor
- vocational counselor

Additional Resources

Conrad, Peter, and Joseph W. Schneider. 1992. *Deviance and Medicalization: From Badness to Sickness.* Philadelphia: Temple University Press. This reissued classic includes several cases to discuss the origins, consequences, and larger implications of the medicalization of deviance.

Enos, Sandra. 2001. *Mothering from the Inside.* New York: State University of New York Press. This book looks at how incarcerated women (the majority of whom are mothers of children less than 18 years old) try to fulfill the "mother" role.

Federal Bureau of Investigation. http://www.fbi.gov/. This Web site provides publications on a range of crime-related topics and the Uniform Crime Reports, frequently cited statistics on crime across the United States.

Goffman, Erving. 1963. *Stigma: Notes on the Social Organization of Spoiled Identity.* New York: Free Press. Goffman's classic work is an important examination of the lives and self-images of those who are unable to meet societal standards of "normal."

Kearl, Michael C. The Medicalization of Old Age. http://www.trinity.edu/mkearl/ger-med.html. Michael C. Kearl's (Trinity University) stop on the Sociological Tour through Cyberspace that focuses on the social aspects of medicalizing problems of the elderly.

Mann, Coramae Richey. 1993. *Unequal Justice: A Question of Color.* Bloomington: Indiana University Press. Mann's controversial book examines inequities based on skin color in the criminal justice system.

Martin, Randy, Robert J. Mutchnick, and W. Timothy Austin. 1990. *Criminological Thought: Pioneers Past and Present.* New York: Macmillan. This in-depth series of profiles includes many sociologists who focused on the area of deviance as well as the contributions of many sociologists who are often associated with other areas of sociology.

Moyer, Imogene L. 2001. *Criminological Theories: Traditional and Nontraditional Voices and Themes.* Thousand Oaks, Calif.: Sage. This textbook provides historical and contemporary coverage of criminological theories, including people of color as well as feminist and peacemaking theories.

National Center for State Courts. http://www.ncsconline.org/index.html. This organization provides services to help courts better serve the public, including original research, consulting, and educational programs.

Paternoster, Raymond, and Ronet Bachman, eds. 2001. *Explaining Criminals and Crime.* Los Angeles: Roxbury. A comprehensive review of criminological theories and associated research are provided in the essays in this text.

Perry, Barbara. 2001. *In the Name of Hate.* New York: Routledge. Perry examines hate crimes in the larger context of social inequality.

Williams, Terry. 1989. *The Cocaine Kids: The Inside Story of a Teenage Drug Ring.* Reading, Mass.: Addison-Wesley. The author spent five years conducting this ethnographic study of teenage drug dealers in New York City. It provides an inside look at the drug trade, their lives, and their values.

CHAPTER 7

Stratification

Sociologists use a geological metaphor to explain how groups of people are divided into social rankings similar to the layers, or strata, in the Earth's surface. The term that sociologists use to describe this division of people into layers is **social stratification,** *the structured hierarchy, or social strata, that exist in a society.* Social stratification is one of the most basic concepts in sociology.

Stratification is systemic; it is actually part of our social system, not something that occurs haphazardly. Stratification is a "social arrangement patterned socially and historically, which is rooted in an ideological framework that legitimates and justifies the subordination of particular groups of people" (Aguirre and Baker 2000, 4). This means that stratification is an enduring facet of society, supported by social values and belief systems.

It results in inequalities of valued resources (wealth, social opportunities, power, etc.) between groups or categories of people. **Inequality** is *the degree of disparity of this distribution within society.* Although the term is sometimes used interchangeably with social stratification, inequality is actually more specific. It is one of the oldest concepts in sociology, dating at least as far back as the Hebrew prophets (Sernau, 2001) and Plato (427–347 B.C.). Like stratification, inequality is one of the most basic concepts in sociology and "is relevant for the study of social systems that range in size from the dyad [see chapter 5] . . . to the modern world-system," discussed below (O'Rand 1992, 795).

Some of the most important questions for sociologists studying stratification involve understanding the impacts of this inequality on our lives. To Charles Lemert, "these are questions of social *structures,* of the individual *subjects* who must live with them, and of the social *differences* these structures create" (2001, 3–4; italics in original). Stratification and inequality impact every facet of our lives. Stratification results in great variations in lifestyles representing systemic differences in opportunities (Bottomore 1965).

Stratification impacts our lives in ways that we might not immediately recognize, both materially and nonmaterially. It impacts our health through such factors as differential access to nutrition, health care, treatment quality, the resources people have available to cope with stress in their lives, and living conditions, with the poor being more likely to live in unhealthy locations (e.g., Crawford 1986; Pearlin 1989; Ross and Wu 1995; Knox and Gilman 1997; Stretesky and Lynch 1999). Stratification impacts our access to quality education (DiMaggio 1982), which will, in turn, impact other areas such as income. It impacts our toleration of controversial behaviors, our political affiliations, and our voting patterns (Erikson, Luttbeg, and Tedin 2000). In our family lives, it even impacts how we divide responsibilities (Bott 1971) and our child-care arrangements (Capizzano, Tout, and Adams 2000). Stratification impacts what we want for our children (Kohn 1977), the type of activities we feel comfortable participating in (Bourdieu 1984), and our life chances (Frank and Cook 1995). It impacts our likelihood of arrest, conviction, and imprisonment (Reiman 1998). Stratification can even impact whether we live or die. A famous example is provided by the *Titanic*. When that ship sank, over 60% of first-class passengers with more expensive tickets on the upper decks survived, while only a quarter of those holding third-class passage survived (Hall 1986).

FORMS OF STRATIFICATION

A variety of social-stratification systems with varying opportunities to move between strata have existed throughout history (Lenski 1984). The earliest types of societies were hunting and gathering societies stratified along tribal systems into groups of chiefs, shamans, and others. Other preindustrial societies were stratified by feudal systems (consisting of kings, nobles, and serfs) and slave systems. Feudal systems were justified by tradition and religion; slavery was justified by those in power as a matter of natural selection.

A type of stratification system widely associated with agrarian societies is a caste society. In **caste societies,** *a person's location in the social strata is ascribed by birth rather than based on individual accomplishments.* Movement between strata, or castes, is prohibited or severely limited. The system is maintained through **endogamous marriages,** *cultural rules requiring that people marry only within their own group.* Other strict restrictions on interactions between the castes are also important in maintaining the system.

Traditional Indian society was a caste system. Some rural areas in that country still remain largely caste systems (Human Rights Watch 1999). South African society under **apartheid** (laws that formalized strict racial segregation) was a caste system based on race. That system of legally sanctioned segregation was officially eliminated in 1992. Some scholars have also classified feudal medieval Europe and the southern United States under slavery as caste societies.

Industrial society gave rise to class-based systems of stratification. In **class societies,** *social stratification is based on a combination of ascribed and achieved statuses.* Strata are largely established along economic lines but are not as clearly delineated as in a caste system. Class societies allow movement between classes based on individual accomplishments. This movement, however, can still be limited by factors such as unequal treatment based on ascribed statuses, as discussed below.

The United Kingdom is a class society with remaining vestiges of a caste-based past. This past is seen in the monarchy and the British Parliament's House of Lords, a legislative body that was traditionally made up of individuals of noble birth. Some of these seats now, however, are occupied by "commoners." The other legislative body, the House of Commons, is made up of elected members.

Sociologists and others studying the United States do not agree on exactly how many classes characterize the American class structure or the exact boundaries between these classes. Some support a multidimensional view that precludes distinct labels (Blau and Duncan 1967). Others divide the population into as few as two or as many as seven classes.

Sometimes distinctions are based on more than income. For example, the highest class is sometimes divided into "old money" and "new money." Those with old money have wealth primarily due to birth. These elite have exclusive lifestyles and extensive networking opportunities. Even activities such as supporting charitable organizations often provide networking opportunities with other elites (Domhoff 1974; Ostrander 1984). In his autobiography, sociologist George Homans (1984), profiled in chapter 5, writes about his time at Harvard University. There, students sought membership in a hierarchy of social clubs that determined many of the networking connections the student would have for a lifetime.

Those with new money are people whose wealth is earned. This group includes sports stars, entertainers, and entrepreneurs, such as billionaire Microsoft founder Bill Gates. In 2004, Bill Gates led the list of the richest people in America (*Forbes* 2004). Forbes.com reported his worth at $48 billion. Following Gates on that list were investor Warren Buffett, having a reported worth of $41 billion, and Paul Allen Gardner, another Microsoft executive, worth $20 billion. Several members of the Walton family, whose wealth came from the Wal-Mart department store, tied for fourth. Their personal worths were recorded as $18 billion each. Michael Dell of Dell Computers, worth $14.2 billion. Oracle software executive Lawrence Joseph Ellison completed the top 10 with a worth of $13.7 billion.

On the other end of the stratification scale, some sociologists argue that those on the very bottom of the hierarchy are effectively treated like an outcaste—hence the term *underclass.* This term, they argue, depicts those trapped beneath the class structure largely by structural factors beyond their control (e.g., Wilson 1987). To others, *underclass* is a degrading term that implies personal deficiencies or values, rather than structural realities (Gans 1990a, 1995).

Classless societies *have no economic strata.* Although hunting and gathering societies may have been classless, no industrial society has ever been truly classless. The Soviets claimed to have created a classless society. However, that society was classless in name only. In practice, it was actually a system stratified by managers and workers with benefits for certain members of society (e.g., Kelly 1981; Lenski 1992).

STRATIFICATION IN THE UNITED STATES

One central factor in stratification is economic inequality. An examination of the structure of economic inequality in the United States shows that it has been increasing over past decades (Bernstein, Mishel, and Brocht, "Any Way You Cut It"; Perlow 1988; Frank and Cook 1995; Wolff 1995). The Census Bureau provides information on how income is distributed that shows this change. One method of examining this data is to divide all households into equal-size quintiles (fifths) and then look at how all the income earned in the country is distributed among these five categories.

Table 7.1 shows that in 2003, 49.8 percent of all income in the United States was earned by one-fifth of all households. These were the highest-earning one-fifth of all households. This percentage has increased since 1967, when this highest-income fifth of all households earned just less than 44 percent of household income. Across all other categories, the share of income received by households has decreased since 1967.

Income disparity becomes even more striking when breaking out the income share of the top five percent of all households—in 2003, those with incomes of $154,120 or more. In 2003, this small percentage of households earned 21.4 percent of the income earned in the United States. The other 95 percent of households shared less than 80 percent of the U.S. aggregate income (see table 7.2).

Poverty

Discussions of income inequality are often conducted in concert with discussions of poverty. But what is poverty, and who is poor? In a stratified system in which resources are unequally distributed, those having the least are the "poor." But exactly how *poor* is defined is not as straightforward as it may seem. Poverty can be defined in absolute or relative terms.

In the United States, the Office of Management and Budget sets an **absolute definition of poverty** with a "poverty threshold" that is used to officially define who is poor. Those *people living in families with an income below this poverty threshold are considered "poor" by the government definition.* These thresholds vary by family size and composition. However, they are not adjusted for variations in the cost of living across the nation. A snapshot of these poverty

Table 7.1

Share of Aggregate Income among Households, Selected Years 1967–2003

	Share of Aggregate Income				
Year	Lowest Fifth	Second Fifth	Third Fifth	Fourth Fifth	Highest Fifth
2003	3.4%	8.7%	14.8%	23.4%	49.8%
2000	3.6%	8.9%	14.8%	23.0%	49.8%
1990	3.9%	9.6%	15.9%	24.0%	46.6%
1980	4.3%	10.3%	16.9%	24.9%	43.7%
1970	4.1%	10.8%	17.4%	24.5%	43.3%
1967	4.0%	10.8%	17.3%	24.2%	43.8%

Source: U.S. Census Bureau (2004d).

Table 7.2

Share of Aggregate Income Earned by Top Five Percent of Households, Selected Years 1967–2003

Year	Percentages of Aggregate Income
2003	21.4%
2000	22.1%
1990	18.6%
1980	15.8%
1970	16.6%
1967	17.5%

Source: U.S. Census Bureau (2004d).

thresholds is shown in table 7.3. (The actual government table of poverty thresholds contains many more categories than shown here.) In 2003, the poverty threshold for a family of four (consisting of two adults and two children) was $18,660. By these official definitions, 35.8 million Americans (or 12.5 percent) lived in poverty in 2003 (U.S. Census Bureau 2004b).

Most people define poverty in nonnumerical terms based on their personal circumstances. They are using a **relative definition of poverty,** measuring it on the basis of *whether their basic needs and wants are met.* They are poor by

Table 7.3
Poverty Thresholds by Family Size, 2003

Family Size/Characteristics	Threshold Amount
One Person *(Under Age 65)*	$9,573
Two Adults *(Householder under Age 65)*	$12,321
One Parent, Two Children	$14,824
Two Parents, Two Children	$18,660

Source: U.S. Census Bureau (2004e).

Table 7.4
Median Household Income by Race, 2003

Race	Median Income
Asian	$55,699
Black	$29,645
Hispanic	$32,997
White	$45,631

Source: U.S. Census Bureau (2004c).

their own understanding of the term as subjectively determined by such things as whether they have enough food to eat, clothes to wear, or money to buy necessities (e.g., baby diapers).

Research has documented a number of hidden costs of being poor. The poor pay more for many items. Among these costs, rent-to-own arrangements are often available to the poor when other stores will not extend credit. These rent-to-own stores may charge lower payments for items, but they have longer contracts. They may also be able to avoid legal problems from charging high interest rates by replacing them with other fees and charges. Additionally, defaults and repossessions are common, and money invested by the poor is forfeited (Breyer 1996; Hudson 1993).

Costs are also more than financial. The poor face a bigger time squeeze than the affluent. They face trade-offs in demands between work and family life. This dilemma includes time to monitor their children's educational needs (e.g., supervised study time), which can have long-term consequences for children, especially in the context of increasing emphasis on standardized academic testing in schools (Heymann 2000; Newman and Chin 2003).

Income and poverty are unequally distributed by such factors as race and sex. Not all groups have an equivalent chance of being poor. As shown in table 7.4, the median household income varies by race and ethnic background.

Table 7.5
Poverty Rates by Race, 2003

Race	Percentage below Poverty Level
Asian	11.8%
Black	24.4%
Hispanic	22.5%
White	10.5%

Source: U.S. Census Bureau (2004b).

The median income for black and Hispanic households is lower than the median income for white and Asian households. Racial and ethnic minorities are also disproportionately poor. Table 7.5 provides poverty rate by race/ethnicity. The poverty rates for blacks and Hispanics is more than double the rate for whites and Asians. However, the economic success of Asians in the aggregate (due in part to cultural values emphasizing educational achievement and family and community support) can obscure the situation of those who have limited economic resources and face discrimination (as discussed below).

Income and poverty are also unequally distributed between males and females. In 2003, women in the United States earned 80 cents for every dollar earned by men. That was a record earning ratio (BLS 2004a). Even women in high-status positions earn less than their male counterparts (Figart and Lapidus 1998).

Recent decades have seen a **feminization of poverty,** *an increase in the proportion of the poor who are women.* Increasing divorce rates and single-parent families headed by women trying to care for children and support them on lower incomes than men have contributed to this trend. These female-headed households are also disproportionately poor, a situation that is compounded by race and ethnicity (see figure 7.1).

SOURCES OF STRATIFICATION

Two of the major questions sociologists studying stratification have tried to answer is why stratification exists and if it is inevitable. Sociologists working from the two major macro-theoretical perspectives discussed in chapter 2 provide varying responses.

Structural-Functionalist Perspectives

True to Emile Durkheim's (profiled in chapter 10) perspective that inequality serves a social function, sociologists working in the structural-

Figure 7.1

Percentage of Families with Children under Age 18 Living in Poverty, by Family Type and Race 2003

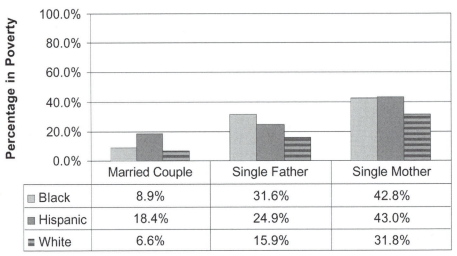

Family Type by Race	Married Couple	Single Father	Single Mother
Black	8.9%	31.6%	42.8%
Hispanic	18.4%	24.9%	43.0%
White	6.6%	15.9%	31.8%

Source: U.S. Census Bureau (2004a).

functionalist tradition (discussed in chapter 2) have examined how stratification contributes to the operation of society as a whole. Kingsley Davis, profiled below, and Wilbert Moore (1945) offered an early and controversial, but still influential, functionalist analysis of stratification.

They argue that some form of stratification is universal across all societies. To operate smoothly, societies face a "motivational problem" in ensuring that the best, most qualified people fill the most important roles in society. By offering the greatest rewards to people who fill the most important positions, stratification is an "unconsciously evolved device by which societies insure that the important positions are conscientiously filled by the most qualified persons" (Davis and Moore 1945, 243).

This perspective has been widely criticized (e.g., Tumin 1953, 1985). Critics have charged that the Davis-Moore thesis implies that individual attributes determine how people are located in society, and that the most talented earn their positions through their hard work and merits. This idea disregards the impact of social factors such as discrimination that are outside of individual control. It does not give appropriate attention to the tensions and divisiveness that can arise as a result of inequality. For example, hard feeling may result among those who work hard yet are treated unfairly or feel they are not properly rewarded for their efforts.

Davis and Moore have also been criticized for disregarding those who inherit their wealth or position. Someone born into privilege has not "earned" that position through her own efforts. Another factor that the perspective disregards is the ability of those with higher status to use their position and contacts to secure and further improve their own positions and resources (Wrong 1959). This includes politicians and corporate executives, who can often enact their own pay raises.

Critics also argue that the most highly rewarded positions (e.g., entertainers and sports figures that earn millions annually) do not always fill the most important roles in society. Additionally, critics argue that this perspective does not adequately account for the wide disparity between the rich and poor. They ask, if stratification is, indeed, a requirement for society to function, how much inequality is actually necessary?

Sociologist Herbert Gans (2001), profiled in chapter 8, analyzed the functions of poverty. He described 13 functions the poor play in society. Among these functions, the poor ensure that society's "dirty work" gets done, their existence creates jobs that serve the poor (e.g., social-service workers, shelter providers), and the poor buy goods others do not want (e.g., day-old bread, used clothing and vehicles). The existence of the poor also guarantees the status of those who are not poor (i.e., others are able to say that they themselves are not poor and are higher in the social strata). The poor also absorb the costs of social change (e.g., they are uprooted during urban-renewal projects).

Gans says that his analysis does not mean that poverty must, or should, exist, and he offers several more expensive alternatives for fulfilling these functions. He argues that a "functional analysis must conclude that poverty persists not only because it fulfills a number of positive functions but also because many of the functional alternatives to poverty would be quite dysfunctional for the affluent members of society" (Gans 2001, 328). He also uses his analysis to show that functionalism, accused by critics of being inherently conservative, can be used in more liberal and radical analyses.

Social-Conflict Perspectives

The social-conflict perspective on stratification focuses on the tensions in society that result from social inequalities (see chapter 2). Sociologists working from a conflict perspective argue that across society, groups are in a constant struggle for valued resources, vying for wealth, status, and power. Some groups will be successful; others will not. Social stratification is the outcome of this ongoing struggle.

Conflict theorists base their work on the writings of Karl Marx (profiled in chapter 2). Marx often collaborated with his friend and coauthor Friedrich Engels, who is profiled below. According to Marx (1983), capitalist society is comprised of two major social classes. These **social classes** are *positions based on the unequal locations of people within economic groups.* The smaller of these two classes is the **bourgeoisie,** or the capitalists, who *own the factories, industrial machinery, and banks.* As business owners, the bourgeoisie seek to maximize their profits by keeping production costs low and selling their product for as much as they can.

Most people fit into the other major class Marx identified. They are members of the **proletariat,** *the factory workers who actually work to produce these products.* Their desire for higher wages is at odds with the capitalists' desire for high profits. To survive in an industrial economy, the proletariats have no choice but to work for the bourgeoisie. By their ownership of the factories, the bourgeoisie control the work and wages available to the proletariat. This situation leads to exploitation of the workers by the owners.

Class conflict results as each segment of society looks out for its own interests. Marx felt that this conflict was the driving force for social change, writing that "the history of all hitherto existing society is the history of class struggles" (1983, 203).

Marx also felt that the capitalist system would eventually lead to its own demise. He predicted that through their class struggles workers would eventually develop a **class consciousness,** *a recognition of themselves as a social class with interests opposed to the bourgeoisie.* They would learn how to overcome their oppression, revolt against the capitalists, and establish a classless society.

Sociologists have intensively studied Marx's views and widely critiqued his prediction of class revolt. Although Marx did acknowledge some minor social classes, he predicted that class struggle would drive people into one major class or the other. The system of social stratification has not developed as Marx thought. He did not predict the rise of the middle class or the system of stockholders that spreads corporate ownership beyond a few capitalists. Additionally, some aspects of class conflict have resulted in improved conditions and pay for workers and helped to preclude the development of a class consciousness largely based on exploitation (Dahrendorf 1959). Additionally, critics of Marx and the conflict perspective argue that unequal rewards may indeed be useful and necessary. However, there is still much inequality in the United States and globally, as discussed below, and that inequality is increasing in many instances.

Multidimensional Perspectives

Max Weber, profiled in chapter 2, developed a more complex view of social stratification than Marx's view of economically based classes. Weber developed three separate but interrelated dimensions of stratification: class, status, and power. Class, to Weber, was also based on economic position, but, unlike Marx, he did not dichotomize class. Rather, he saw **class** as *a continuum of economic locations that leads to differences in lifestyle or life chances.* Weber's dimension of **status** referred to *established social positions based on social honor or social prestige* (see chapter 3). This dimension is often related to occupation (Blau and Duncan 1967). For example, one study found Supreme Court judge, physician, and college professor among the most prestigious occupations. Shoe shiner, street sweeper, and garbage collector rated among the least prestigious occupations, scoring even lower than those who live on public aid. Sociologists were rated between clergy and accountants on occupational prestige (Treiman 1977). Weber's third dimension of **power,** *the ability to influence others, even if* *those others resist* (see chapter 5), includes political connections and influence. Power is sometimes termed *party* in discussions of Weber's concept to capture this implication.

Sociologists combine all three of these dimensions together into a measure of **socioeconomic status (SES),** *a ranking derived from combining multiple dimensions of stratification.* Although all three dimensions are often consistent, that is not always the case. Mother Teresa, for example, commanded little wealth or political power, yet high status around the world for her humanitarian works. Former Iraqi president Saddam Hussein was extremely rich and powerful, but held low status internationally. The geographic metaphor that sociologists often use when addressing stratification fails to capture some of this complexity.

MAINTAINING STRATIFICATION

Stratification is influenced by ascribed statuses (see chapter 3), such as race, ethnic background, gender, and age. We are born with these statuses, and, despite our personal efforts and achievements, they impact our lifestyle and life chances. Prejudices and discrimination based on these ascribed statuses serve to justify and maintain systems of stratification.

Although the terms are often used interchangeably in everyday conversations, *prejudice* and *discrimination* are different. **Prejudice** is *a preconceived and irrational attitude toward people based on their group membership.* Just as the term suggests, this is a pre-judgment. It is inflexible and not based on direct evidence or contact. Prejudices can take the form of positive or negative attitudes toward a group, but the term is often used with a negative connotation. Socialization (see chapter 4) contributes to prejudice and people who hold prejudicial attitudes toward one group tend to be prejudice toward others as well. Eugene Hartley (1946) asked people to express their reactions to various minority groups. He found that people who expressed prejudice against actual racial and ethnic groups also expressed prejudicial attitudes against fictitious groups he had made up for his research.

Common and damaging forms of prejudice are found in the "isms" that exist throughout society (e.g., racism, sexism, ageism). All of these "isms" take the form of a *belief that one group is naturally inferior or superior, thus justifying unequal treatment of the group on the basis of their assumed characteristics.* In **racism,** that belief is based on racial or ethnic group membership. The early sociologist W.E.B. Du Bois (1868–1963), who is profiled below, spent almost a century studying race and racism. **Sexism** is *the belief that one sex is naturally inferior or superior, thereby justifying unequal treatment.* Feminist sociologists (see chapter 2) focus on sexism. **Ageism** takes the form of *prejudice against the elderly. Sociologists and others who study aging and ageism* are called **gerontologists.** Other "isms" include **ableism** (*prejudice against the disabled*) and **heterosexism** (*prejudice toward homosexuals*). Examples of each of these "isms" abound across society.

These "isms" reinforce, and are reinforced by, another common and potentially destructive form of prejudice, stereotypes. **Stereotypes** are *beliefs that generalize certain exaggerated traits to an entire category of people.* These common images can assign either positive or negative traits to various groups. They may arise out of observations of behaviors or traits that the observer applied to all people in the actor's category (sex, ethnicity, club membership, hair color, etc.). Like the "isms," stereotypical beliefs are used to justify unequal treatment of groups. If stereotypes are accepted by the people to which they refer, they can also become self-fulfilling prophecies (see chapter 6).

Stereotypes abound across society. For example, black professionals have reported troubles hailing cabs (Cose 1993). Research has shown that children's picture books tend to depict women in more traditional roles, working inside the home rather than in an occupation (e.g., Peterson and Lach 1990; Williams et al. 1987). Women are even depicted more negatively than men in college sociology textbooks (Ferree and Hall 1990). The elderly are frequently stereotyped as senile and less capable and competent in many areas of life than younger people (Butler 1975). Images of elderly women may be especially negative (Bazzini et al. 1997). Research on college textbooks used for courses covering issues in marriage and family courses has shown that the elderly tend to be included primarily under "elderly" subjects such as widowhood and retirement. They are not often mentioned in chapters on race/ethnicity, sexuality, and gender (Stolley and Hill 1996). Regarding poverty specifically, many of those who are not poor, including policymakers, stereotype the poor as being irresponsible or without ambition when, in reality, most poor do want to work (e.g., Dunbar 1988).

Prejudices may also result in **scapegoating,** *focusing blame on another person or category of people for one's own problems.* Hitler blamed Jews and other "enemies of the state" for Germany's troubles before World War II (Scheff 1994). Modern-day white-supremacist groups blame other races for economic problems.

Discrimination, *unequal treatment of people based on their group membership,* also perpetuates stratification. Discrimination differs from prejudice. Prejudice is an attitude; discrimination is a behavior. Although the two may, and often do, occur together, they can also exist separately (Merton 1976). When *discrimination becomes part of the operation of social institutions,* it is known as **institutional discrimination.** It perpetuates stratification patterns by systematically disadvantaging certain groups. According to Joe Feagin and Melvin Sikes (1994), racism is still alive and well, although less overt than in the past. However, institutional racism is rampant. It manifests in patterns of residential and educational segregation. The result is a social structure that adversely impacts the chances of those subjected to prejudice and discrimination.

These ascribed factors require a multidimensional approach to stratification. They can have multiple, interrelated effects. Stratification also applies to many more social factors than race, ethnicity, gender, and age. We are also ranked to varying degrees by other factors such as religious affiliation and sexual preference. People are even socially ranked by their physical appearance. These rankings have identifiable outcomes for their lives. The popular 1979 movie *10,* starring former model Bo Derek, was built around the idea of rating women on a 1–10 scale of physical attractiveness. Research has shown that highly attractive people receive better grades, jobs, promotions, salaries, and nursing home and medical care. They may fare better when charged in criminal cases. Having a beautiful wife can even improve how men are perceived (see the summary in Katz 2001). There is also a "halo effect" of physical attractiveness. Physically attractive people are perceived as having more positive characteristics, such as better classroom behavior, credibility, kindness, and sociability (Dion, Berscheid, and Walster 1972; Katz 2001).

Some sociologists are also starting to explore stratification and oppression regarding animals, just as they have long studied the impact of stratification and oppression of the poor, women, and minorities. They have added another "ism" to the sociological vocabulary with the term **speciesism,** *a belief in the superiority of humans over other species of animals.* They cite examples such as food industries that rely on animals bred and raised under poor conditions, experimentation on animals, and the use of animals in circuses, rodeos, and shows to argue that "animals are severely oppressed in modern, industrialized cultures" (Alger and Alger 2003, 209).

SOCIAL MOBILITY

Sociologists interested in stratification also focus on **social mobility,** *movement within the stratification system from one position, or strata, to another.* This movement can be upward or downward. It can be studied at the collective level using characteristics such as ascribed status (e.g., the upward mobility of African Americans in the United States since the end of slavery, the status of women) or even at the level of entire nations (e.g., ranking by economic factors such as gross domestic product). However, social mobility is usually addressed at the micro level by examining individual or family level movement within the social structure. Interestingly, these micro-level patterns of mobility are "considered a core characteristic of a society's social structure," even though structure which is typically considered a macro-level area of study (Riain and Evans 2000). (Chapter 2 provides a discussion of micro and macro perspectives.)

Mobility can be examined by how much time it takes to occur. **Intragenerational mobility** is *movement that occurs within the lifetime of an individual.* Individuals that change their social position over the course of their lifetime achieve this type of mobility (e.g., an employee that starts in the mail room and becomes corporate vice president). **Intergenerational mobility** is *movement that occurs from generation to generation* (e.g., the mail-room clerk's son becomes the corporate officer).

Mobility can also be examined by the factors behind the change. *Mobility that occurs as a result of changes in the occupational structure of a society* is **structural mobility.** A strong economy can create new options for upward mobility. The so-called dot-com businesses that arose with the growth of the Internet provided new, often high-paying employment opportunities during the late 1990s. When the dot-com bust came at the end of the decade, the occupational structure once again changed, and many workers lost their jobs. **Positional mobility** is *movement that occurs due to individual effort* (e.g., hard work, winning the lottery). This type of mobility does not depend on structural changes.

Because stratification persists over the long term, it results in limited social mobility. People generally remain in the social class in which they are born (Frank and Cook 1995). Movements within the social structure tend to be incremental as opposed to large leaps. Although cases do occur in which people go from rags to riches and make big moves across several strata, this is an exception rather than the rule.

In the United States, when mobility does occur, upward mobility has traditionally been more common than downward mobility (Featherman and Hauser 1978). It has been especially pronounced for minorities in white-collar occupations (Cose 1993). Additionally, the decades of the 1980s and 1990s saw an increase in the capitalist class (Stanley 1996). However, upward mobility is not always the pattern. For example, women tend to experience downward mobility after divorce (Weitzman 1985, 1996). Women divorcing powerful or well-connected men lose their husband's income as well as his status.

Research has shown that the structure of society can limit those who try to get ahead in spite of educational and occupational aspirations (MacLeod 1995; Solorzano 1991). Jonathan Kozol (1991) examined wealthy schools and poorly funded schools. He found that these schools provided different elements of success to their students, ranging from differences in physical structure and educational resources (e.g., computers, sports equipment) to the messages they sent students about their self-worth and value to society.

Rosabeth Moss Kanter (1977), profiled in chapter 5, studied how organizational structures limit women's mobility. She found that women in largely male-dominated organizations were highly visible and readily criticized. They became "tokens" representing all women. The power structures in these organizations devalued women's styles of leadership and largely placed women in jobs with no opportunity for advancement. These structural factors limited positional mobility and made moving up the corporate structure difficult for women regardless of their individual talents and abilities.

The factors behind lack of mobility are not always clear-cut. An ongoing debate about the influence of race and class provides an illustration. To some sociologists and others, racism is a factor that has a huge, limiting impact on mobility and achievements (e.g., Feagin and Sykes 1994). Another controversial argument by William Julius Wilson (1987, 1996), profiled below, offered the position that class is a more important factor than race in limiting social mobility. He argued that inner-city black poverty increased since 1970 largely as a result of urban changes. Although racism and discrimination do exist from Wilson's perspective, factors such as poor job training, limited job skills among inner-city youth, and little opportunity to obtain education and job skills perpetuate poverty. Other structural factors, such as the relocation of industries, the changing job market, and the relocation of African Americans who could afford to follow whites to the suburbs or more upscale urban areas, were important factors in this situation.

Although there is general agreement among researchers about the increasing concentration of urban poverty, they debate the reasons behind this change (Small and Newman 2001). They note that a number of structural factors may be at work, such as poorly enforced fair-housing laws that keep blacks in poor neighborhoods or the exodus of manufacturing jobs leaving the inner city. An examination of factors including demographic patterns (e.g., looking at the cities that are growing and increasing numbers of immigrants, birthrates of various racial/ethnic groups), changing urban housing markets, and the **digital divide** (*the gap between those who have access to, and can effectively use, information and collaborative technologies such as the Internet and those who are unable to do so*) that exist in the United States is necessary to better understand the processes at work.

GLOBALIZATION AND THE INTERNET

The digital divide also plays a role in patterns of global stratification. Sociologist Paul DiMaggio and his colleagues cite several studies that show that a digital divide exists globally (DiMaggio et al. 2001, 312–14). Less developed countries have less physical access to Internet connections and less diffusion of the economic development and skills needed for people to benefit from such technologies than more developed countries have.

These researchers point out that sociologists also need to examine the unequal attention given to Internet users. They argue that simply assessing access, although important, does not give a complete picture of the digital divide. A fuller picture is "not just whether or not one has 'access', but inequality in location of access (home, work, public facilities); the quality of hardware, software, and connections; skill in using the technology; and access to social support networks" are also factors to consider (DiMaggio et al. 2001, 314). Additionally, they urge researchers to show how such structural factors as government programs and pricing policies impact access.

This digital divide is but one, albeit important, aspect of global stratification. Just as for the United States, looking at income inequality globally shows that world income is distributed unequally, and this inequality is growing. By one calculation, in 1993 the richest 1 percent of people received as much income as the entire bottom 57 percent did; or, "in other words, less than 50 million income-richest people receive as much as 2.7 billion poor." Additionally, the top 10 percent of the U.S. population, approximately 25 million people, had aggregate incomes roughly equal to the poorest 43 percent of the world population, or almost 2 billion people (Milanovic 2002, 88–89). Another report finds that three-quarters of the world is poor, and the middle class is very small—8–11 percent of the world's population, depending on the calculation used (Milanovic and Yitzhaki 2002).

Sociologists turn to their basic theoretical perspectives to address global stratification and inequality. Functionalist ideas gave rise to modernization theory. Emerging in the 1950s, **modernization theory** *argued that countries breaking with tradition and embracing capitalist industrialization would lead to economic, social, cultural, political, and technological development.* Poor nations could improve their conditions by following Western examples. This is one of a school of market-oriented theories that support the idea that capitalist processes and institutions will lead poorer countries to embrace modernization.

A well-known proponent of this perspective was W. W. Rostow, an advisor to President John F. Kennedy. Using an airplane analogy, Rostow (1960) offered a model of modernization for poor countries that had four stages: a focus on traditional patterns of life; a takeoff stage when society starts to move away from traditionalism; the airplane becoming airborne during a drive to technological maturity as the economy begins to diversify, technology develops, and reinvestment occurs; and high mass consumption as standards of living improve and people buy more goods. In this fourth stage, the airplane levels out and continues cruising along. Rich nations help these poorer countries throughout the process in ways such as providing aid, technology, and guidance.

To critics, modernization theory is ethnocentric. It expects the entire world to conform to Western standards. It also does not account for the uneven development that has occurred around the world, with some countries remaining quite poor. It roots the causes of poverty within the poor countries themselves (Bradshaw and Wallace 1996). This perspective also fails to recognize that rich countries may have their own interests that are at odds with the full development of poorer countries. This final point, in particular, provides the starting point for the opposing perspectives of dependency theory.

Rooted in conflict theory, **dependency theory** *focuses on the reliance of poor nations on the wealthy.* This dependence arises from exploitation of the poor countries by the richer, more powerful countries. Colonialism was a crucial factor in shaping this situation.

World-systems theory emerged in the 1970s. It was developed by Immanuel Wallerstein (1974), who is profiled below, and rooted in classical sociology. **World-systems theory** *focuses on the capitalist world economy in which countries are linked by economic and political ties.* Development of this system began in Europe in the fifteenth and sixteenth centuries and grew with capitalism. The theory divides the world into three types of regions: *core, periphery,* and *semiperiphery.* **Core countries** are the *powerful industrial countries that dominate the global capitalist system.* **Peripheral countries** are *poor countries that are exploited for their raw materials and inexpensive labor by core countries.* This is largely a result of colonialism. Because these peripheral countries do not trade with other poor countries, they have to buy from rich nations. **Semiperipheral countries** are those countries that are *somewhat industrialized. They are able to exploit peripheral countries but are, in turn, exploited by core countries.*

The result of this world system is unequal trading patterns in which poor nations depend on rich nations. As summarized by Christopher Chase-Dunn, the whole process is a "stratification system composed of economically and politically dominant core societies (themselves in competition with one another) and dependent peripheral and semiperipheral regions, some of which have been successful in improving their positions in the larger core-periphery hierarchy, while most have simply maintained their relative positions" (2001, 590). Critics of world-systems theory argue that, while it has been successful in modeling "the long-term dynamics of capitalism," its weakness lies in "its attempt to derive all long-run state processes from economic processes" (Collins 1999, 41).

The concept of globalization is now replacing world-systems theory. The concern now is with shaping "the emerging world society into a global democratic commonwealth based on collective rationality, liberty, and equality" (Chase-Dunn 2001, 610). Feminist scholars also urge consideration of the impact of globalization processes on women. The inequalities in the global economy impact women especially hard. However, women are becoming empowered and learning to organize into networks that can improve their own positions and the positions of other labor in the globalized economy (Moghadam 1999). Indeed, the United Nations' *Human Development Report* for 2003 finds that, although discrimination against women persists, some poorer countries are actually doing better than some richer countries in terms of women's political and economic participation.

BIOGRAPHIES

Kingsley Davis

Kingsley Davis (1908–97) was born in Tuxedo, Texas. He held degrees in English and philosophy from the University of Texas when he went to Harvard to study sociology in the early 1930s. He earned his doctorate there in 1936.

Like many of the social scientists profiled in this book, Davis's accomplishments could be profiled under several different chapters. His research ranged across such diverse topics as sexuality, the family, and cities, and it included extensive work in the field of demography. Additionally, his article with Wilbert Moore (1945) offering a functionalist analysis of stratification caused a sociological uproar and "seemingly endless debate" over the "authors' irreverent dismissal of the dogma of equality" (Petersen 1979, 141).

Over the course of his career, Davis held positions at several universities, including Smith College, Clark University, Pennsylvania State University, Princeton, Columbia, the University of California–Berkeley, and the University of Southern California in Los Angeles. While affiliated with Princeton's Office of Population Research (OPR), he founded the university's department of sociology. At Berkeley, he founded a program in international population and urban research and helped found the Department of Demography. In 1981, in his 70s, Davis was appointed a part-time senior research fellow at Stanford University's Hoover Institution (Coale 1999; Peterson 1979).

Davis was the first sociologist elected to the National Academy of Sciences. He chaired the National Research Council's Division of Behavioral Sciences. He also served as president of the American Sociological Association and the Population Association of America (Coale 1999; Petersen 1979).

William Edward Burghardt Du Bois

William Edward Burghardt Du Bois (1868–1963), commonly referred to as W.E.B. Du Bois, was one of America's earliest sociologists. Dubois was both a scholar and an activist who founded or edited a number of publications and published more than 20 books and 100 scholarly articles of his own. In 1896, he received the first Harvard doctorate granted to a person of color. His dissertation, "The Suppression of the African Slave Trade in America," became the first volume in Harvard's *Historical Series.*

Sociology, to Du Bois, was a means to address contemporary social problems. His research in the slums of Philadelphia's Seventh Ward, a black ghetto, led to the publication of one of his most famous works, *The Philadelphia Negro* (1996, orig. 1899). That work provides an example of early empirical sociology and the study of race relations in the United States, and has been credited by some as initiating the field of urban sociology.

It was Du Bois's interest in race, however, that became his lifelong work and passion. It also led him into numerous public controversies. One of the most well known of these controversies was a bitter debate with Booker T. Washington, the well-known and influential African American founder and president of Tuskegee University (then known as Tuskegee Normal and Industrial Institute). Washington supported blacks generally working within the system and building up the African American community as means to gaining civil rights. Du Bois, however, accused Washington of accommodating what he termed the "color line," and advocated actively demanding equality and fighting for civil and voting rights.

Du Bois's activism included civil rights in the United States, women's suffrage, and the cold war. He was a founding member and leader in a variety of national and international organizations, including the National Association for the Advancement of Colored People (NAACP). At age 82, he even ran for the Senate in New York. His activism extended internationally to issues such as colonialism, capitalism, poverty, Africa, and the interconnections between those issues and race. Over the course of his long career, he traveled, studied, and lectured in numerous countries around the globe. Eventually he settled in Ghana, where he died on the eve of the 1963 March on Washington. Dr. Martin Luther King Jr. eulogized Du Bois as the march began (Lewis 2000).

Friedrich Engels

Friedrich Engels (1820–95) was born in Barmen, Germany, the oldest of eight children. Engels's family owned a textile business. He studied aspects of business and economics, as well as serving in the military, before writing an essay on socialism that attracted the attention of Karl Marx (profiled in chapter 2). After corresponding, the two men met in person in 1844. Engels and Marx became collaborators and close friends. Engels introduced Marx to economics, supported him financially for many years, and even claimed paternity for Marx's illegitimate child (Hunley 1991; Ramm 1968).

Engels's contributions are sometimes overshadowed by, or even credited to, Marx. However, it was Engels's command of economics that made him the "leading partner" early in their partnership. According to Engels, when he and Marx met, they were in "complete agreement in all theoretical areas." He also deferred much of the credit for their work to Marx, writing, "I could never have achieved what Marx did. Marx stood higher, saw farther, and had a broader and quicker grasp of a situation than all the rest of us. Marx was a genius; we others were at best talented" (quoted in Ramm 1968, 65).

Together, Marx and Engels coauthored *The Holy Family* (1956, orig. 1845), *The German Ideology* (1845), and the *Communist Manifesto* (1848). Engels continued to write after Marx's death, completing and publishing the second and third volumes of *Capital* (Marx 1977a, orig. 1867). He also authored a number of works on his own, including numerous articles on the war and military (Hunley 1991), *The Condition of the Working Class in England* (1845), *The Peasant War in Germany* (1850), and *The Origin of the Family, Private Property, and the State* (1884).

Immanuel Wallerstein

Immanuel Wallerstein (1930–) was born in New York to a politically conscious family. He served in the army from 1951 to 1953, between completing his undergraduate degree and entering graduate school. When he returned to his studies, he wrote his thesis on McCarthyism and his dissertation on the nationalist movements in the Gold Coast (Ghana) and the Ivory Coast. He earned his bachelor's, master's, and doctorate degrees all from Columbia University, completing his Ph.D. in 1959.

Although Wallerstein is most widely known for his world-systems perspective, he became an Africa scholar, traveling widely throughout the African continent and writing several books on his studies. In 1973 he became president of the U.S. African Studies Association. He credits his "African studies with opening [his] eyes both to the burning political issues of the contemporary world and to the scholarly issues of how to analyze the history of the modern world-system" (Wallerstein 2000, xvii).

Wallerstein is currently a Senior Research Scholar at Yale University. For more than two decades prior to that appointment, he was a sociology professor at Binghamton University, State University of New York (SUNY), where he also directed the Fernand Braudel Center for the Study of Economies, Historical Systems, and Civilizations. Wallerstein has also been a visiting professor in schools around the around the globe.

He has authored or coauthored hundreds of articles and dozens of books. His works have been translated into more than 15 languages. Wallerstein has been involved in numerous professional activities. He served as president of the International Sociological Association and chaired the Gulbenkian Commission on the Restructuring of the Social Sciences. He is a charter member of the Society for Comparative Research, and holds or has held memberships in the World Association for International Relations, the Sociological Research Association, and the Board of Directors of the Social Science Research Council (Wallerstein, "Immanuel Wallerstein Curriculum Vita," 2000).

William Julius Wilson

William Julius Wilson (1935–) was born in Derry Township, Pennsylvania. He is the Lewis P. and Linda L. Geyser University Professor at Harvard University, where he has the distinction of being one of only 17 professors who hold a University Professorship. Wilson also directs Harvard's Joblessness and Urban Poverty Research Program.

Among Wilson's professional achievements are over 20 honorary degrees. He was selected by *Time* magazine in 1996 as one of America's 25 Most Influential People, and received the 1998 National Medal of Science. Wilson was also the 80th president of the American Sociological Association. His work is controversial but also prize-winning. His fellow sociologists recognized *The Declining Significance of Race* (1978) with the American Sociological Association's Sydney Spivack Award. They also recognized *The Truly Disadvantaged* (1987) with the C. Wright Mills Award from the Society for the Study of Social Problems (Wilson, "William Julius Wilson Biography"; "Wilson, William J." 1981).

Regarding his perspectives on race and class, Wilson argues that "a system of racial discrimination over a long period of time can create racial inequality . . . That is because the most disadvantaged blacks victimized by decades and centuries of racial oppression do not have resources that allow them to compete effectively with other people. They are at a disadvantage . . . But our discussion of race was so myopic that we had a tendency to not pay attention to some of these non-racial factors that impacted significantly on the black community" (1997). Although he argues that race is "certainly implicit" in some of the issues he addresses, Wilson also argues for deracializing some policy issues and solutions. He argues that "there is so much emphasis on racial differences, especially in our society, that we lose sight of the things we have in common: common problems, common aspirations, common goals. And we have a vision of American society that emphasizes racial differences, and makes it difficult for the average person to see the need or appreciate the potential for mutual political support across racial lines" (2000).

CAREERS IN SOCIOLOGY

Those with an interest and training in stratification and inequality have backgrounds that prepare them for careers including

- administrator
- advocacy-organization director/staff
- case manager
- client services representative
- community-services manager
- compliance coordinator
- eligibility worker
- evaluation researcher
- fiscal analyst
- government-service worker
- graduate student in law
- grant writer
- lobbyist
- policy analyst
- political staffer
- political strategist
- politician
- program planner
- public-assistance-agency director/staff
- resource developer
- shelter supervisor
- social activist
- social-service-agency administrator/staff
- social worker
- strategic planner

Additional Resources

Bureau of Labor Statistics. http://www.bls.gov/. The U.S. Department of Labor provides this site that covers a wealth of information on labor economics and statistics.

Ehrenreich, Barbara. 2001. *Nickel and Dimed: On (Not) Getting by in America.* New York: Metropolitan Books. The author took a variety of low-paying jobs to write this account of the lives of the working class.

Ehrenreich, Barbara, and Arlie Russell Hochschild, eds. 2003. *Global Woman: Nannies, Maids, and Sex Workers in the New Economy.* New York: Metropolitan Books. This collection of essays addresses women who are often lost in the rhetoric of globalization.

Forbes. 2004. Forbes 400 Richest in America 2004. Forbes.com. http://www.forbes.com/richlist. Forbes.com's annual tracking of the 400 richest Americans includes profiles, tools to track their activities, and other information regarding this elite group.

Galbraith, James K., and Maureen Berner, eds. 2001. *Inequality and Industrial Change: A Global View.* New York: Cambridge University Press. This collection provides analyses of income inequality in the United States and other countries.

Kanter, Rosabeth Moss. 1977. *Men and Women of the Corporation.* New York: Basic Books. Kanter's classic look at organizations shows how organizational structure and tokenism impacts employees' careers.

Kearl, Michael C. Explorations in Social Inequality. http://www.trinity.edu/~mkearl/strat.html. This stop on the Sociological Tour through Cyberspace provides a wide range of online information introducing concepts in stratification and inequality.

Marx, Karl. 1977. *Capital: A Critique of Political Economy.* 3 vols. 1867. Reprint, New York: Random House. Marx's lengthy classic critique of capitalism helped set the stage for the conflict perspective in sociology.

Norris, Pippa. 2001. *Digital Divide: Civic Engagement, Information Poverty, and the Internet Worldwide.* New York: Cambridge University Press. This book examines Internet use and access in countries around the world and concludes there are divides both between nations and between classes within nations.

Sernau, Scott. 2001. *Worlds Apart: Social Inequalities in a New Century.* Thousand Oaks, Calif.: Pine Forge Press. This book covers the core concepts in the sociological study of stratification and inequality.

Wilson, William Julius. 1996. *When Work Disappears: The World of the New Urban Poor.* New York: Knopf. This controversial analysis looks at the impact of the global economy and movement of jobs from cities, racism, and class on African American urban youth.

World Bank Group. http://www.worldbank.org/. The World Bank, owned by almost 200 countries around the globe, has funded billions of dollars in development assistance for poor countries, including funding for improving education, health, and biodiversity.

CHAPTER 8

Population Structure, Movements, and Concentration

Some sociologists specialize in studying population structure, movements, and concentrations. Their focus is **demography,** *the study of human populations involving statistical description and analyses of population size and structure. People who practice demography* are called **demographers.** Demography is variously referred to as a subfield of sociology, a close cousin, an interdisciplinary field, or even as a separate area of study. Any way it is classified, the information that interests demographers is important in helping us develop a more complete picture of our social lives (Wrong, 1977).

Demographers look at the basic structure and characteristics of human populations and population trends. They use statistical techniques to make predictions about a population's future. Demographers produce familiar statistics such as those in the U.S. Census and actuarial life-tables for insurance companies. Demographers also address some vital social issues that arise as a result of demographic forces, for example, what happens when cities become overcrowded, large refugee populations are created by war or other catastrophes, or the environment is damaged by such situations.

POPULATION CHANGE

Population concerns are frequently in the press. To help predict and plan for social needs, demographers give much attention to population change. They study three sources of population change: births, deaths, and migration rates. Together, these figures help demographers estimate how populations will grow and change.

The first source of population change that interests demographers is **fertility,** *reproductive performance indicated by the incidence of childbearing in a population*—or, in other words, the birthrate of a population. To estimate population growth patterns and change, demographers calculate a figure called the **crude birthrate.** This calculation tells them *the number of live births in a year per 1,000 people in a population.* The crude birthrate is used as a rough measure of overall fertility and may be figured for specific populations (by race, religion, etc.). However, it allows only rough estimates of population growth because it does not include age or sex data. A much more accurate picture of a society's population growth can be derived from **age-specific fertility rates,** *the number of births to women in certain age groups in a population,* and age-sex pyramids, as discussed below.

The number of children women have varies widely based on a number of factors. It tends to be higher in less developed countries and agriculturally based economies than in industrialized nations. Children's farm labor is an asset in traditional agriculture, and cultural values often support large families. Effective birth control may not be readily available for those who do want it. Where health conditions are poor, large families are necessary to ensure that some children live until adulthood. In many places, adult children will provide the only care parents receive in their old age.

The second source of population change demographers consider when estimating population patterns is **mortality,** *incidence of deaths.* Calculating *the number of deaths in a year per 1,000 people in a population* provides a **crude death rate.** Like the crude birthrate, **age-specific mortality rates,** *the number of deaths per age groups in a population,* allow a more accurate measure when predicting population change.

Events such as war or genocide obviously impact death rates. So do changes designed to improve public health (e.g., digging a well for clean water) or raising the economic status of an area (e.g., more people can afford food and medicine for their children).

The third source of population change that interests demographers is **migration,** *the movement of people into and out of a specific area.* Migration includes both **immigration,** *the movement of people into the area,* and **emigration,** *the movement of people out of an area.* Immigration minus emigration yields a figure called the net **migration rate,** expressed as *the change per 1,000 people in the population of an area in a given year.* In addition to population size, migration impacts the demographic characteristics of areas. For example, migration of retirees to the warm sunbelt states in the U.S. means those areas have large aging populations. Thus, those areas have greater needs for retirement housing, health care facilities, and other services for the elderly.

The social factors that lead people to migrate and the social impacts of this movement are important to understand. Some migration is voluntary, meaning the people who move choose to do so of their own accord. Homesteaders, gold miners moving toward what is now the western United States, and retirees moving to warm climates from the northern states are voluntary migrants. However, much migration is involuntary. The Trail of Tears, in which the Cherokee people were marched from choice settlement land in the eastern United States to Oklahoma; slavery; the transfer of Jews during World War II; refugees fleeing disaster areas; and Muslim Croats being expelled from Serbian villages are all examples of involuntary migration. As these examples suggest, mass migration, when large numbers of people move at one time, is more often involuntary than voluntary. This forced migration has increased significantly since the end of the cold war, becoming a "central aspect of social transformation in the contemporary world" (Castles 2003, 30). Sociologists even study migration as a form of collective action (see chapter 9), looking at such things as the social conditions that lead to migration, the actions of authority figures and migrants, the actual journey, and living conditions (Miller 2000, 231–47).

Population Structures

Using these three concepts, demographers build graphs called **population pyramids,** which *depict a country's population composition.* These population pyramids may also be referred to as **age-sex pyramids,** because *they show the population not only by age but also by the relative proportion of men and women in each age group.* In general, there are three basic types of population pyramids: those showing rapid population growth, those showing slow growth, and those that show near-zero growth or population decline. All population pyramids are arranged with the oldest members of a population at the top and the youngest at the bottom. However, each type of pyramid has a distinctive shape based on the population's characteristics.

Fast Population Growth

Population pyramids for fast-growing countries actually do take the shape of a pyramid. Because each generation is larger than the preceding generation, the graphs are wide at the bottom and narrow toward the top.

Nigeria provides a good example of a country with a rapid population growth rate (see figure 8.1). The annual growth rate in 2000 was 2.7 percent. Nigerian birthrates far exceed death rates. The total fertility rate in 2000 was over five children per woman; the median age for females was 17.6 years old. That means half of all Nigerian women were older than 17.6 and half were younger. Thus, a large proportion of women in Nigeria still have many years of potential childbearing ahead. Although the total fertility rate per woman is expected to drop to 3.6 by 2025, other factors, such as anticipated decreases in infant mortality and death rates due to increasing access to health care, are projected to keep the annual rate of population growth in Nigeria high for the coming decades.

Slow Population Growth

With an annual rate of growth of only 0.9 percent in 2000, the United States provides an example of a slow-growth population (see figure 8.2). Birthrates were slightly higher than death rates, but not as imbalanced as Nige-

Figure 8.1
Nigerian Population Pyramid, 2000, 2050

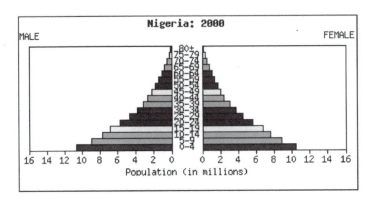

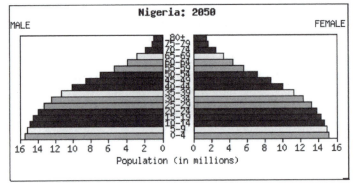

Source: U.S. Census Bureau (2003).

ria. The total fertility rate per woman was 2.1 children, the replacement rate for a population. This fertility rate provides two children to replace parents. The extra 0.1 allows for all those born who will not have children for various reasons (e.g., infertility, choice, or dying before becoming a parent) and the fact that slightly more males are born than females. The median age for females in the United States was 36.8 years old, meaning that many American women were nearing the end of, or were already beyond, their childbearing years.

Several events have caused this pattern—the low birthrates during the Great Depression (1930s), the post–World War II baby boom (people born after the war through the early 1960s), a mid-1970s "baby-bust," followed by a "baby boomlet" of the 1980s and early 1990s (McFalls 1998). As the so-called baby boomers have aged, fertility rates have remained low, and average life expectancy has increased. The result is that the U.S. population is getting older and the shape of the population pyramid is changing. Almost eight percent of all Americans will be in the 80-and-over age category by 2050. Because women tend to outlive men, the number of women in this age group will far exceed the

Figure 8.2
U.S. Population Pyramid, 2000, 2050

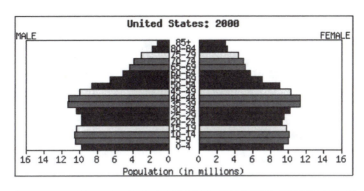

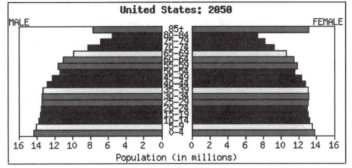

Source: U.S. Census Bureau (2003).

number of men. The top bar of the pyramid takes on an especially interesting shape for that year.

Declining Populations

Ukraine provides an example of a country with a declining population (see figure 8.3). The population pyramid for Ukraine takes on the distinctive shape of a declining population, as shown by its narrowing base. In the year 2000, the country had a negative annual growth rate of − 0.6 percent. The death rate was higher than the birthrate. The fertility rate per woman was only 1.3, well below the replacement level of 2.1 children as noted above. Half of all Ukrainian women were 39 years old or older.

Theories of Demographic Change

Demographers are also interested in why population changes as it does. Two of the major theories in this area are Malthusian theory and the demographic-transition theory.

Figure 8.3
Ukrainian Population Pyramid, 2000, 2050

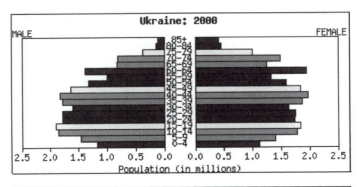

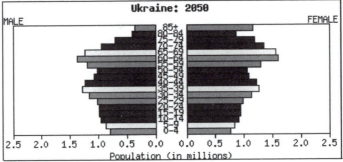

Source: U.S. Census Bureau (2003).

Malthusian Theory

English clergyman Thomas Robert Malthus (1766–1834), profiled below, is sometimes called the "father of demography." In 1798, he forwarded a dire prediction of overpopulation. Malthus began with two main assumptions—that food is necessary for human existence, and that the human sex drive, or "passion between the sexes," is strong and will not abate in the future. The thrust of his argument was that population growth would outpace Earth's ability to produce enough food. He predicted that human population would increase geometrically, doubling in a given period of time (1, 2, 4, 8, 16, 32, etc.). Food supplies would increase much more slowly (1, 2, 3, 4, 5, etc.). The depressing result of such unchecked population growth would be mass starvation.

Malthus argued that this inevitable situation might be delayed through what he called *preventative checks* and *positive checks*. **Preventative checks** *aim at reducing the birthrate.* They include marrying at later ages, abstinence, and birth control. **Positive checks** *increase the death rate.* Cases of war, disease, and famine are in this category.

Fortunately, Malthus's predictions have not yet come true. Critics point out that Malthus was writing during a period of high population growth. The burgeoning Industrial Revolution would ultimately result in smaller family size. Also, Malthus focused on available productive farmland in making his predictions. He did not predict the technological advances that would later be applied to agriculture. He also did not foresee the advances in contraception that have occurred in recent decades. However, some demographers and others argue that Malthus's work remains important because he calls our attention to overpopulation problems that the world still faces if we do not curb population growth. Malthus's work also provides the basis for evolutionary-ecological theories that examine ties between population and production (Elwell 2001).

Demographic-Transition Theory

The **demographic-transition theory** takes a different approach to world population growth. According to this theory, *specific patterns of population change are brought about by industrialization.* In preindustrial societies, where both birthrates and death rates are high, population growth is slow (Simon 1996). As industrialization begins, traditionally high birthrates remain high. However, death rates drop due to improvements in food supply, sanitation, and health. The result is a so-called demographic gap during which the population grows quickly (Brown 1987). When a society is fully industrialized, children are no longer an economic asset, as they are in agricultural societies. Cultural preferences change to smaller families. The society's birthrate drops, coming more in line with death rates. This leads to slowing population growth. Eventually, the population may stabilize or even begin to decline. Nations with mature industrial economies, such as those in western Europe, Japan, and the United States, have completed this demographic transition and are experiencing slowly growing, or even slightly declining, populations (van de Kaa 1987).

Critics question whether this theory paints an accurate picture beyond the industrialized countries on which it was based. A variety of factors will ultimately influence population trends in countries that do not fit this theory. Due to advances in public health (e.g., sanitation, vaccines), other countries are experiencing improved health without a corresponding period of industrialization. In those countries, fertility rates stay high, death rates fall, and the population grows. This is especially the case when religious beliefs are maintained that disallow or discourage birth control and encourage large families. Controlling the birth rate becomes a crucial factor in controlling population growth (Wrong 1977; Ching 1994).

Some observers argue that technology will actually divide the world, with some countries being able to industrialize while others cannot. The countries that do not industrialize will continue to experience high poverty rates. Problems of poverty are often exacerbated in these countries as the population grows. The role of poverty combined with man-made famines, such as those caused or worsened by genocide, war, or ineffective food-distribution methods, can also impact population changes (Independent Commissions on International Humanitarian Issues 1985; Kates 1993; Sen 1981).

MEASURING POPULATION

Demographers use data from a variety of sources including censuses, birth and death records and other vital registration data (e.g., marriage, divorce), migration data, and surveys (Steele and Price 2004, 87). Censuses are demographic counts that are familiar to many people. In the United States, the Census Bureau is the largest statistical agency of the federal government. In addition to conducting a census of the U.S. population every 10 years, the Census Bureau conducts over a hundred other demographic and economic surveys every year. When the first U.S. Census was taken in 1790, the population of the United States was less than 4 million people. By 2000, the U.S. population had grown to more than 281 million (see table 8.1).

Although many people may be unaware of how widely used census data are, these figures are important in many areas of our social lives. In the political arena, they are used for **apportionment,** *a process of determining how many of the 435 seats in the U.S. House of Representatives are allotted to each state.* (Because the Constitution provides two senators for each state, the distribution of members in the Senate is not affected by census results.) States also use the census results in **redistricting,** *a process of redrawing political districts after apportionment.*

Census data are used for market and advertising research, disease prevention, community advocacy, and resource allocation (e.g., where to locate hospitals and social services), and by genealogists tracing family trees. It is even used in disaster relief. For example, after Hurricane Andrew hit southern Florida in 1992, census information provided estimates of the number of people missing in each block as well as detailed maps of destroyed neighborhoods (U.S. Census Bureau 1999).

Because census data are used in so many ways and billions of dollars in federal funding are awarded based on the outcome, the accuracy of the count is important and politically charged. Ideally, censuses would count every individual in the population and not miss anyone. However, censuses do miss people in their counts, especially hard-to-reach populations, including the homeless (HUD 2004), minorities, low-income families, the homeless, recent migrants, and the unemployed (Simpson and Middleton 1997). For the 2000 census, the U.S. Census Bureau was aware of this problem and tried to take corrective measures to make up for this historical undercounting (US Census Bureau 2001b).

POPULATION AND URBANIZATION

In examining how population patterns influence social life, much attention focuses on the impact of **urbanization,** *the increasing percentage of a population living in urbanized areas.* **Urbanized areas** are *densely settled central places and adjacent territories with residential populations of 50,000 or more people.* Urbanized areas are contrasted with **rural areas,** *areas with sparse population densities that do not fit the definition of urban.* Urban lifestyles are generally considered more "modern" and faster paced than non-urban lifestyles.

Table 8.1
Total U.S. Population and Percentage Urban, Selected Years 1790–2000

Year	U.S. Population	Percent Urban
2000	281,421,906	80.3
1990	248,709,873	75.2
1980	226,542,199	73.7
1970	203,302,031	73.6
1960	179,323,175	69.9
1950	151,325,798	64.0
1940	132,164,569	56.5
1930	123,202,624	56.1
1920	106,021,537	51.2
1910	92,228,496	45.6
1900	76,212,168	39.6
1890	62,979,766	35.1
1880	50,189,209	28.2
1870	38,558,371	25.7
1860	31,443,321	19.8
1850	23,191,876	15.4
1840	17,063,353	10.8
1830	12,860,702	8.8
1820	9,638,453	7.2
1810	7,239,881	7.3
1800	5,308,483	6.1
1790	3,929,214	5.1

Sources: U.S. Census Bureau "Population: 1790 to 1990" and U.S. Census Bureau 2001a.

Rural areas are typically considered to have a more traditional and slower-paced lifestyle.

More Americans than ever are living in urbanized areas. When the first U.S. Census was conducted in 1790, only five percent of the population was considered urban. By the time the 2000 census was taken, 80 percent of all Americans were urban dwellers, living in cities and closely surrounding areas (see table 8.1). A look at cities gives a more complete picture of urbanization in the United States. **Cities** are *types of incorporated places with defined geo-*

graphic boundaries. New York City has been the largest city in the United States since the first census was conducted. In 1790, New York's population was just over 33,000 residents. By 2000, that city's population had topped 8 million people. The 10 largest cities are now spread across the United States (see table 8.2).

Across the globe, cities in poorer societies are also growing at a fast rate. Most of the world's population growth for the next quarter-century is expected to occur in cities in developing countries (Montgomery et al. 2003). In 2000, 2.9 billion people worldwide lived in urban areas. This number is expected to reach 5 billion by 2030. Fully one-half of all people in the world are expected to live in urban areas by 2007, and 60 percent of world population will be urban by 2030 (United Nations Population Division 2002).

This is quite a change in population patterns considering that, as recently as 1950, less than 30 percent of the world's population lived in urban areas (Palen 1986). Cities attract migrants looking for work and other opportunity such as education as well as those pushed out of their homes by political events (London 1987). However, as these cities grow, so do urban problems. The cities are often poorly equipped with even basic facilities, such as sewage treatment and garbage removal, to handle the increasing numbers of often very poor migrants. These cities also face increasing environmental problems (Livernash and Rodenburg 1998). Even city dumps may serve as homes for those with no other options.

The population in less developed countries is growing faster than the population in more developed countries. A look at the world's most populated countries shows that since 1950, the top 10 countries in that regard has increasingly included less developed countries. During the last half of the twentieth century, less developed countries have comprised an increasing share of world population. This trend is expected to continue (see table 8.3). Population growth in the less developed countries of the world is growing at six times the rate of population growth in more developed countries. The poorest of these less developed countries have growth rates that are even higher. For example, the populations in Burkina Faso, Mali, Niger, Somalia, Uganda, and Yemen are expected to quadruple in the next half-century (United Nations Population Division 2003). This growth pattern is likely to lead growing problems of poverty and unrest as people compete for increasingly limited resources both inside and between nations.

History of Urban Sociology

Early sociologists in both the United States and Britain were very much concerned with urban issues (Savage and Warde 1993). In the United States, an early study in urban sociology was conducted by W.E.B. Du Bois (1868–1963), profiled in chapter 7. His study *The Philadelphia Negro* (1996, orig. 1899) has been credited by some as initiating the field of American urban sociology. Du

Table 8.2
Ten Largest U.S. Cities and Other Urban Places, Selected Years 1790–2000

1790		1850		1900		1950		2000	
City	Population	City	Population	City	Population	City	Population	City	Population
New York City, NY	33,131	New York City, NY	515,547	New York City, NY	3,437,202	New York City, NY	7,891,957	New York City, NY	8,008,278
Philadelphia City, PA	28,522	Baltimore City, MD	169,054	Chicago City, IL	1,698,575	Chicago City, IL	3,620,962	Los Angeles City, CA	3,694,820
Boston Town, MA	18,320	Boston Town, MA	136,881	Philadelphia City, PA	1,293,697	Philadelphia City, PA	2,071,605	Chicago City, IL	2,896,016
Charleston City, SC	16,359	Philadelphia City, PA	121,376	St. Louis City, MO	575,238	Los Angeles City, CA	1,970,358	Houston City, TX	1,953,631
Baltimore Town, MD	13,503	New Orleans City, LA	116,375	Boston City, MA	560,892	Detroit City, MI	1,849,568	Philadelphia City, PA	1,517,550
Northern Liberties Township, PA	9,913	Cincinnati City, OH	115,435	Baltimore City, MD	508,957	Baltimore City, MD	949,708	Phoenix City, AZ	1,321,045
Salem Town, MA	7,921	Brooklyn City, NY	96,838	Cleveland City, OH	381,768	Cleveland City, OH	914,808	San Diego City, CA	1,223,400
Newport Town, RI	6,716	St. Louis City, MO	77,860	Buffalo City, NY	352,387	St. Louis City, MO	856,796	Dallas City, TX	1,188,580
Providence Town, RI	6,380	Spring Garden District, PA	58,894	San Francisco City, CA	342,782	Washington City, DC	802,178	San Antonio City, TX	1,144,646
Marblehead Town, MA; Southwark District, PA*	5,661	Albany City, NY	50,763	Cincinnati City, OH	325,902	Boston City, MA	801,444	Detroit City, MI	951,270

* Tied for 10th largest.
Source: Gibson (1998); Perry and Mackun (2001).

Table 8.3
Ten Largest Countries in the World, 1950, 2000, and 2050

Rank	1950		2000		2050	
	Country	Population	Country	Population	Country	Population
1	China	562,579,779	China	1,262,474,301	China	1,601,004,572
2	India	369,880,000	India	1,002,708,291	India	1,417,630,630
3	United States	152,271,000	United States	282,338,631	United States	420,080,587
4	Russia	101,936,816	Indonesia	224,138,438	Indonesia	336,247,428
5	Japan	83,805,000	Brazil	175,552,771	Nigeria	307,420,055
6	Indonesia	82,978,392	Russia	146,001,176	Bangladesh	279,955,405
7	Germany	68,374,572	Pakistan	141,553,775	Pakistan	267,813,495
8	Brazil	53,443,075	Bangladesh	130,406,594	Brazil	228,426,737
9	United Kingdom	50,127,000	Japan	126,699,784	Congo (Kinshasa)	181,260,098
10	Italy	47,105,000	Nigeria	123,749,589	Mexico	153,162,145

Source: U.S. Census Bureau (2003).

Bois conducted his study while living among residents of Philadelphia, Pennsylvania's Seventh Ward, where 20 percent of the city's black population lived.

In addition to his observations, Du Bois used a questionnaire to learn about the social life of the ward. His research included northern migration, the effects of slavery, families, and class and race issues. He even gathered or created blueprints and diagrams of buildings. Although Du Bois has been criticized for taking a moralistic and elitist tone toward lower-class blacks in the book, he used his research to argue sociologically that the ghetto resulted from, rather than caused, other problems of the black residents' lives.

Other black scholars would study blacks and the urban-rural transition. This work on urban issues predated the same community-centered sociology that would become the hallmark of the University of Chicago, where the faculty conducted much of the early research on urban sociology (Young and Deskins 2001, 453–54).

The University of Chicago established the first graduate department of sociology in the United States (see chapter 1). That allowed the school to attract and train many of the preeminent early sociologists in the country. Several Chicago-school sociologists are profiled throughout this book, including Jane Addams (chapter 11), Charles Horton Cooley (chapter 4), George Herbert Mead (chapter 4), and W. I. Thomas (chapter 4). Robert Park and Louis Wirth are profiled below. During the early decades of the twentieth century, the Chicago sociologists turned much of their attention to urban issues (Savage and Warde

1993). Their work set the stage for American sociologists for many years and remains influential today.

The Chicago-school sociologists produced several ethnographies of the urban life of Chicago residents, including studies of gangs, transients, and immigrants (Savage and Warde 1993). A 1938 piece by Louis Wirth (1897–1952) describing an urban lifestyle has been called "one of the most influential sociological articles ever written" (Savage and Warde 1993, 97). It is also reputed to be the article "most widely cited in sociology" (Abercrombie, Hill, and Turner 2000, 370). In his article, Wirth discussed differences between social interaction and life in cities and rural areas, focusing on isolation and loss of individuality. His argument was that cities change social relationships for the worse. Whether this is actually the case has been examined in a variety of subsequent studies.

Urban Ecology

An early effort connecting humans and their urban environments was urban ecology developed by the Chicago school. **Urban ecology** focuses on *the interaction between human population and the environment, including both material and nonmaterial aspects of human culture.* The perspective grows out of the organic analogy of the early sociologists (Gottdiener 1985, 25–27).

From the early 1900s through the 1930s, Chicago sociologists attempted to map "natural areas" of social segregation occurring in cities. They developed a series of models that segregated both land use and social groups. Ernest Burgess (1925) explained changing land-use patterns in terms of a **concentric-zone model** that saw *city growth as a series of five widening circles, or zones.* These zones arise as a result of a search for choice business and residence locations. The center circle, zone 1, is the central business district. This area in the middle of the city contains businesses, shops, and banks. As this district needs more space to expand, it pushes outward, forming a "zone of transition." This second circle, zone 2, becomes a run-down area of cheap housing, as some holdings remain undeveloped and residences are too close to industry to be preferable or maintain a high value. Beyond this is the third circle, zone 3, an area of working-class homes. Still further out, in zone 4, is the residential area, consisting of single-family homes or more expensive apartments. Zone 5 is beyond the city limits. This is the commuter zone.

The **sector model** of urban land use was promoted by Homer Hoyt (1939). According to this theory, *zones are not circular. They are wedge-shaped areas extending outward from the central business district of the city.* These sectors are based on economic activities. For example, manufacturing may grow outward along railroad tracks. Residential neighborhoods may follow new construction of shopping areas.

Another model, the **multiple-nuclei model,** sees *city development as occurring in irregular patterns* (Harris and Ullman 1945). Cities develop with not only one, but several "centers" or nuclei. For example, higher-class residential areas would be located away from industrial areas, perhaps closer to outlying business districts. Any residential areas near heavy manufacturing would be lower-class housing. Shopping districts may grow up adjacent to residential areas to accommodate the residents.

A later ecological analysis by Amos Hawley (1950) viewed the city in terms of an interdependent system. He focused on the importance of transportation and communication technologies in influencing the way cities develop. Critics of Hawley and similar approaches argue that they have a conservative bent. Their models are accused of ignoring such factors as class, status, and political power that shape cities and leaving out other important factors such as competing interests and government programs and policies (Gottdiener 1985, 40–41). More recent urban sociologists have turned to models influenced by the conflict perspective that accounts for these factors.

Urban Sociology Today

For the first century of urban sociology, sociologists largely influenced by Chicago perspectives focused on urban social organization. Their interests included community integration, organization and disorganization, urban growth and differentiation, how migrants adapted to their new cities, and social mobility. Current urban sociology has expanded well beyond these roots. It has become multidisciplinary, with important input from other fields, including political science, economics, and geography (Walton, 2000).

Starting in the late 1960s, the focus of urban sociology shifted to issues of inequality and social unrest (Walton 2000). As Zukin explains, the emphasis shifted to "tying together urbanization, the quest for profit and domination, and the state's attempts to moderate domestic conflict between social classes" (1980, 579). This new perspective is sometimes referred to as **political economy.** As the name suggests, the new focus is on *the interrelationships between political and economic forces and the way they propel urban events.* It draws from the conflict perspective of Karl Marx and Friedrich Engels (profiled in chapters 2 and 7, respectively), viewing urban problems as related to capitalism.

According to this perspective, in a capitalist system, urban areas develop largely as a result of competition for resources. Harvey (1985a, 1985b) argues that urban areas are "built environments" that serve the processes of capital production, accumulation, circulation, and consumption. Banking, shopping, manufacturing, and even roadways are constructed to facilitate capitalism. When they no longer serve this purpose satisfactorily, these areas are destroyed or rebuilt in an almost cyclical process to better accommodate capitalistic processes.

According to Logan and Molotch (1987), real-estate developers, owners, and agents; entrepreneurs; media; politicians; and professionals such as attorneys and architects comprise central positions in cities as part of a powerful elite. As such, they play a prominent role in an urban "growth machine" that seeks to maximize the growth and development of urban space and the economic value of the land. Competing political, economic, cultural, and geographic interests and factors conflict over growth and market resources, such as industry and retail centers.

Another view of urban development is provided by a **sociospatial model,** which *"views local areas as comprised of various, often competing, growth networks rather than a single coalition,* even though all urban areas in the United States remain dominated by business interests" (Gottdiener, Collins, and Dickens 1999, 7; italics mine). A study of the development of Las Vegas, Nevada, was conducted by Mark Gottdiener, profiled below, and colleagues. They argue that the city is run by elites composed of the most successful business interests at the time. These elites and their interests have changed over time as investment opportunities and government policies change.

In Las Vegas, the first elite were Mormon rulers. Business interests then began to serve gold prospectors, followed by railroad development, and later real estate speculators. The need to develop a means to travel across the continent and the gold rush of the 1800s provided external influences to this development. Later, federal funding spurred development through the Boulder Dam building project. Tourism grew with the dam. Other influential government policies included the legalization of gambling as a business proposition and federal spending on the World War II effort that boosted the local economy. During the 1970s and 1980s, the city leaders worked to enhance Las Vegas's image, re-creating the city as a family vacation destination. It is now an area of megaresorts and multinational corporate ownership (Gottdiener, Collins, and Dickens 1999).

Suburbs

Starting largely after World War II, urban-population patterns began to shift (Fishman 1987). The results of the 1950 census showed that patterns of urban residence were changing due to **suburbanization,** *the process of population moving out of central cities to surrounding areas.* First the upper classes, then the middle classes, and then the working classes were able to move out of the central city to the **suburbs,** *urban areas outside of city boundaries.* In many areas, this coincided with the advent of public transportation (e.g., railways, trams, cars) that made commuting into the city to work possible.

In 1946, Abraham Levitt and his sons bought 4,000 acres of potato fields in the town of Hempstead, New York, where "they planned the biggest private housing project in American history" (Jackson 1985, 234). The Levitts developed a 27-step method of mass-produced house construction that allowed them to produce homes quickly and economically, complete with appliances. Ultimately, Levittown consisted of over 17,000 homes and 82,000 residents. Government loan programs, affordable mortgages, and tax-deductible mortgage interest all made the housing attractive and accessible to the young families and returning veterans that would give birth to the postwar baby-boom generation. In the 1950s and 1960s, the Levitts built a second Levittown in Pennsylvania, and, in 1955, they started Levittown, New Jersey.

Sociologist Herbert Gans (1967), profiled below, spent two years living in and studying Levittown, New Jersey. Residents were relatively homogenous and mostly white, and had similar incomes. Gans concentrated on several concerns, including the quality of suburban life. He concluded that Levittown and suburbia fit the needs of the period. He argued that suburban families were close-knit and socially satisfied, rather than suffering a range of negative consequences (e.g., boredom and loneliness), as critics of these new areas had predicted.

To proponents, the suburbs are often hailed as an ideal in American way of life. They are considered models of the residential "good life." However, suburbs do have their own problems and critics. Suburbs experience racism and homelessness, as do cities (Dreier 1993). Suburban life is also the subject of satires and even negative attacks in movies (Muzzio and Halper 2002).

Suburbanization often led to urban decay. The poor remained in cities while the more affluent took flight to outlying areas. This left cities struggling with lower tax bases and numerous urban problems. In recent decades, the focus in many cities has turned to **urban renewal**—*government-funded programs that aim to rejuvenate cities.* These efforts support inner cities with new business, shopping, and residential projects that provide income. Another effort in bringing the middle-class or affluent back into central cities is **gentrification.** The *affluent buy run-down properties at low cost and fix them up as upscale residences.* This results in an increase in property values. Gentrification may be encouraged by government policy or private development (Beauregard 1990; Kerstein 1990).

Critics of these processes charge that they displace the poor by eliminating, without replacing, affordable housing. Sharon Zukin (1988) studied gentrification in an area of New York City in which artists turned previous Manhattan sweatshops into lofts where they lived and worked on their art. An artist community formed, attracting the attention of investors. Property values increased further, eventually even pushing some of the artists out of the area.

According to Joel Garreau (1991), recent years have also seen a growth in edge cities. These **edge cities** are *forms of self-sufficient suburbs that have extensive office and retail space, as well as plenty of entertainment and recreational facilities.* There are residences in these areas; however, there are more jobs than housing. This means edge-city populations are largest during the daytime, as people come into the area to work, and decrease in the evenings, when people return home. These edge cities grow up around major suburban highway interchanges in areas that were not cities even a few decades ago.

Garreau identified over 200 existing or planned edge cities around the United States, including over 20 each around Los Angeles; Washington, D.C.; and New York City. He summarizes the growth of these edge cities as a "third wave" of city dwelling occurring in the last half of the twentieth century. "First, we moved our homes past the traditional idea of what constituted a city. This was the suburbanization of America, especially after World War II. Then we wearied of returning downtown for the necessities of life, so we moved our marketplaces out to where we lived. This was the malling of America, especially in the 1960s and 1970s. Today, we have moved our means of creating wealth, the essence of urbanism—our jobs—out to where most of us have lived and shopped for two generations. That has led to the rise of the Edge City" (Garreau 1991, 4).

Nature of Urban Life and Community

Early sociological writing that compared the impact of rural and urban life was done by German sociologist Ferdinand Toennies (1855–1936), profiled below. Toennies (1963, orig. 1887) used the term *Gemeinschaft,* meaning "community," to describe *traditional social ties characterized by the importance of intimate relationships such as family, kin, and friendship; moral closeness/unity; and religion.* Toennies contrasted this with *Gesellschaft,* meaning "association," which describes *social ties characterized by a focus on self rather than community good, individuality, separation from others, and impersonality.* He characterized rural villages as exhibiting characteristics of community, whereas large cities led to a breakdown of these traditional ties. To Toennies, this was problematic rather than a positive trend.

Georg Simmel (1858–1918), another German sociologist writing around the same time as Toennies, was interested in the social implications of the size of groups. (Simmel is profiled and his work on group size is discussed in chapter 5.) Simmel also studied cities and the large collections of people interacting with each other. He said that people in cities develop certain responses to city life. They become emotionally reserved around others and respond intellectually rather than emotionally to situations. Additionally, because city dwellers cannot respond to every person they encounter, they develop what he called a *blasé attitude,* a sort of impersonality in which they weigh options and decisions before acting. For example, they may give directions to someone looking for a nearby address but ignore a panhandler's request for money. This sort of picking and choosing may appear selfish, but it allows them to cope with the multiple demands of urban life, plus it allows a type of personal freedom that traditional communities quash.

Another contemporary of Toennies and Simmel who gave attention to rural and urban ties was French sociologist Emile Durkheim (1858–1917), profiled in chapter 10. Durkheim's interest was solidarity—the bonds between people and what unites them. He felt that in traditional communities, social bonds were characterized by *mechanical solidarity.* Much like Toennies's concept of *Gemeinschaft,* **mechanical solidarity** *depends on commonality, shared values and beliefs, and little division of labor.* Personal differences are minimized. Durkheim contrasted this with **organic solidarity,** in which *social ties are based on differences.* Organic solidarity results from the division of labor characteristic of industrial societies and the new social bonds that form. Taking a more optimistic view of changing social ties than his contemporaries, Durkheim argued that individuals in cities become less tied to common concerns, but that an important, and positive, interdependence develops as people develop specialized roles.

More recent sociologists continue to give attention to the community and social bonds. For example, looking at the social networks that exist in communities, Barry Wellman (1999a), profiled below, argues that we have specialized community ties that provide us various resources. We may choose to live near our place of employment or near public transportation that we can use to travel to work. We may choose a particular area because our children will be assigned to a preferred school district.

Resources we can rely on are our social networks. (The importance of networks in our social lives was discussed in chapter 5.) According to Wellman, we have sparsely knit networks that change frequently. In this age of urbanization, many of our networks are dispersed. People know fewer neighbors and maintain most relationships with people outside of their neighborhoods. However, people still manage to maintain supportive networks even though they may be physically distant much of the time. Inviting a group of friends to one's home to play cards or hosting a club meeting are examples of how these networks are maintained and how important they are to our lives. In either of these examples, people may live, work, and regularly shop and pursue recreational activities in different neighborhoods, coming together for this event.

GLOBALIZATION AND THE INTERNET

Sociologists do not always agree on exactly what a community is. One study found over 95 different uses of the term *community* in sociological literature (Hillery 1955). Communities have been seen as geographic areas, social systems of interconnections, or personal relationships (Bell and Newby 1976). With the advent and widespread use on the Internet, sociologists have a potential new community to define and study.

Researchers have documented a wide array of community activities online including virtual sex, weddings, funerals, gift giving, hobby-sharing, friend seeking, and more (Hornsby 2001). David Bell examines the question of what types of communities are forming in cyberspace: he suggests that online communities are "imagined and held together by shared cultural practice (rather than just face-to-face interaction)" (2001, 95). Bell bases his discussion on the concepts of Benedict Anderson (1983) and Tim Edensor (2002), which challenge us to envision even nations as imagined communities. Because we can never personally know everyone in our nation, we draw our sense of shared identity from symbols we create (flags, national anthems, etc.) and cultural practices we create and share.

Bell (2001) summarizes several interrelated processes that are frequently perceived as threatening, or transforming, communities. He identifies these processes as *de-traditionalization* (a shift towards a post-traditional society), *globalization* (a growing interconnectedness of people around the globe), and *disembedding* (the uprooting and dispersal of cultural components from their traditional locations as globalization progresses). He ties these processes together with Giddens's (1991) concept that says we are in a period of history that encourages self-scrutiny and self-consciousness, concluding that "we can choose who we want to be (within certain structural limitations . . .) and to *imagine* new forms of community" (Bell 2001, 95–96).

The interrelationship between community, the Internet, and the issue of globalization also raises complex issues. Cyberspace supports globalized communities in that "globalization can be argued to open up the whole world as a potential source of community . . . the Internet gives us a vast reservoir of choices [of community] . . . and [the opportunity to] re-imagine the very notion of community. Cities have become too big, too fractured, too scary—and the Internet offers a safe space to build new communities in . . . a new way to belong" (Bell 2001, 96–97). Whether these processes have positive or negative implications for our ideals of community and whether the Internet is solution or problem is open to debate.

Even though the world's major cities are rife with population-related problems, they are also keys to globalization. Globalization, together with the importance of the Internet, has created *global cities*. These are cities across the world that serve as major financial centers tied together by the Internet and corporate entities that often transcend national boundaries, politics, and cultures. They are heavily influenced by global economic conditions in addition to national or regional conditions. They are more closely related to each other than to their own rural areas. They are also the cities with the greatest income inequality (Friedmann and Wolff 1982; Sassen 2001). They provide "infrastructure and expertise that enable corporations to co-ordinate and control their far-flung activities, serving as prime sites for incoming and outgoing foreign investment, and operating as central nodes for the international transmission of all kinds of information" (Hill and Fujita 2003, 207).

Even for cities that are not financial centers, globalization has had an impact. Hodos (2002) raises the question of whether there are other ways for cities to successful integrate globally rather than being financial centers. He uses Philadelphia, Pennsylvania, as a case study. City officials worked to reinvent Philadelphia during the 1990s in global terms, cultivating an image as an investment and tourism destination. This has been achieved through a focus on the history of the city, hotels, conventions, downtown cultural attractions, and selling foreign executives on the city's cultural assets and its location as an attractive business community.

BIOGRAPHIES

Herbert Gans

Herbert J. Gans (1927–) was born in Cologne, Germany. His Jewish family immigrated to Chicago in 1940, escaping the Nazi regime. A shy and unathletic child, Gans became an avid reader at an early age. He also became fascinated by American popular culture, writing essays for his high-school newspaper on the mass media, music, and sports (Gans 1990b).

Gans's undergraduate studies at the University of Chicago were interrupted when he was drafted in August 1945. GI Bill funds from his time in the military, however, helped him to be able to stay in school long enough to complete his master's degree when he returned to Chicago (Gans 1990b). Working in the area of city planning, Gans received an offer to work on a project applying social-science perspectives to planning while pursuing a Ph.D. in city planning at the University of Pennsylvania. Gans taught at the University of Pennsylvania and the Massachusetts Institute of Technology before taking a position at Columbia University in 1971.

Over the course of his career, Gans has authored over 170 articles published in academic journals and popular outlets. His works address issues including popular culture, urban planning, mass communications, urban poverty, social planning and policy, race, and ethnicity. He has also written over a dozen books, including *The Urban Villagers* (1982) and *The Levittowners* (1967). Two of his works, *Deciding What's News* (1979) and *The War against the Poor* (1995), received multiple awards from media, crime, and human rights organizations.

In addition to teaching and writing, Gans has been involved in civil rights and anti-poverty planning. During much of the 1970s, he was the film critic for *Social Policy*. Gans is also active in a number of professional organizations. He is a past president of the Eastern Sociological Society and the American Sociological Association (ASA). In 1999, he received the ASA Award for Contributions to the Public Understanding of Sociology (Gans, "Biography—Herbert J. Gans").

Mark Gottdiener

Mark Gottdiener is professor of sociology and adjunct professor of urban planning at the University at Buffalo. He has a varied background, having earned an undergraduate degree in mathematics, a master's degree in economics, and a doctorate in sociology. Gottdiener has worked as a transportation analyst and a consultant, as well as holding a number of academic positions. He has served as Chair of the National Task Force on Urban Governance of the National Association of State Universities and Land Grant Colleges in Washington, D.C. (Gottdiener, "Dr. Mark Gottdiener").

Gottdiener has served on the editorial boards of several journals, including the *American Journal Of Sociology, Consumption and Culture, Urban Studies, City, Social Thought and Research,* and *Consumption, Culture, and Markets.* He has authored, coauthored, or edited over a dozen books. His recent works include *Las Vegas: The Social Production of an All American City,* (1999), *New Forms of Consumption: Culture, Commodification, and the Media* (2000), and *The Theming of America: Dreams, Visions and Commercial Spaces* (2001) (Gottdiener, "Dr. Mark Gottdiener").

In another recent work, *Life in the Air: The New Culture of Air Travel* (2001), Gottdiener explores the social world of air travel. "Air travel," he says, "has become the major means by which people connect, not only on business trips, but for vacations and to see relatives" (quoted in Walker 2001). "In the end, we . . . will have to deal with our lives in the air in much the same way as we already deal with those lives on the ground-through effective environmental planning, psychological counseling, architectural design, political vision and smart corporate management" (quoted in Lewandowski 2001).

Thomas Robert Malthus

Thomas Robert Malthus (1766–1834) was born in Surrey, England. Various sources give his date of birth as February 13, 14, or 17, although he was likely born on the 13th (Peterson 1979, 21; Stapleton 1986, 20). He did not use the name "Thomas" in his formal writings. He signed his works and letters as "T. R. Malthus" or "T. Robt. Malthus" (Peterson 1979, 21).

Malthus attended Jesus College, where his main subject of study was mathematics. In 1805, he was appointed professor of history and political economy at the East India Company's newly established East India College. This was the first British professorship in political economy, and possibly the first in the world (Peterson 1979, 29). Malthus taught there for most of his life.

The work that made Malthus famous was an essay he first published anonymously with the lengthy title *An Essay on the Principle of Population, as It Affects the Future Improvement of Society, with Remarks on the Speculations of Mr. Godwin, M. Condorcet, and Other Writers* (Malthus 1926, orig. 1798). In his essay, Malthus responded to a utopian essay predicting a future without social or economic inequalities. His expanded 1803 version, retitled *An Essay on the Principle of Population; or, A View of Its Past and Present Effects on Human Happiness; with an Inquiry into Our Prospects Respecting the Future Removal or Mitigation of the Evils Which It Occasions,* would establish his scholarly reputation. There were seven editions of this work published in all, including one published posthumously.

Over the course of his career, Malthus argued against "poor laws" that he felt encouraged the poor to have large families (Digby 1986; Huzel 1986). As an economist, he also focused on the conspicuous consumption of the aristocracy (Cannadine 1986) and supported "corn laws" that he felt would economically protect Britain's grain producers (Vamplew 1986).

Although Malthus's views were often controversial, he held a number of prestigious positions. He was a member of the Political Economy Club, elected Fellow of the Royal Society, one of 10 royal associates of the Royal Academy of Literature, a member of the French Institute and Royal Academy in Berlin, and one of the first fellows of the Statistical Society when it was founded in 1834 (Peterson 1979, 33). Malthus died in Somerset, England, in 1834.

Robert Ezra Park

Born on Valentine's Day, Robert Ezra Park (1864–1944) was raised in rural Red Wing, Minnesota. As a college undergraduate, he played football and was so involved in extracurricular activities that his graduation was almost delayed (Martin, Mutchnick, and Austin 1990, 94). Park completed his master's and doctorate degrees in philosophy from Harvard and the University of Heidelberg, respectively.

Park's only formal study in sociology was taken under Georg Simmel. He was trained in philosophy, and was originally hired to teach one course in 1914 on "The Negro in America." However, Park taught at Chicago until retiring in 1936. As a testimony to the quality of his teaching, many of the students he trained would become well known in the field themselves. Several of Park's students, including Herbert Blumer and Louis Wirth, who are both profiled in this book, were elected president of the American Sociological Association (Coser 1977, 372).

Park specialized in race and city life, collective behavior, and human ecology. He felt that sociology was a science. Unlike many of his colleagues and students at Chicago, who were focused on implementing social reforms, Park did not want his students to think of sociology as "do-goodism" (Raushenbush 1979). Rather, he wanted them to be "super-reporters," using theory-driven concepts to objectively study and understand social life. Only then did he feel they could enact social reforms.

In addition to his teaching, which he loved so much that he regularly taught more courses than he was paid to teach, Park served as president of the American Sociological Association and the Chicago Urban League and was a delegate to the Institute of Pacific Relations. He was a member of the Social Science Research Council and edited numerous books and journals (Coser 1977, 370–71).

Park's academic influence and accomplishments are all the more notable in that he did not begin his academic career until he was 50 years old. Before teaching at Chicago, Park had spent 11 years as a newspaper reporter, working for newspapers in Minnesota, Detroit, Denver, New York, and Chicago (Coser 1977, 367). He had supplemented his income by writing magazine articles and through work as a publicist for a circus and later the Congo Reform Association (a group seeking reform in the African Congo). He also spent a number of years as a secretary and writer for Booker T. Washington and his Tuskegee Normal and Industrial Institute (now Tuskegee University). Park traveled through the Southern U.S. and Europe with Washington. He would continue his focus on issues of race for the rest of his life. After his retirement, Park taught at Fisk University until his death, one week before turning 80.

Ferdinand Toennies

German sociologist Ferdinand Toennies (1855–1936) attended several universities before receiving his doctorate in classical philology (historical and comparative linguistics) in 1877. His father's wealth enabled him to continue his studies at the University of Berlin and then London. He returned to Germany, where he joined the faculty at the University of Kiel as a *privatdozent* (an unpaid lecturer who depended on student fees).

Toennies was able to devote most of his time to writing for professional and political journals rather then teaching. However, he eventually became professor emeritus in sociology. Although "conservative by temperament," Toennies was active in socialist, trade union, and other progressive movements. He lost his university position in 1933 when he publicly denounced Nazism and anti-Semitism (Heberle 1968).

Famous for his concepts of *Gemeinschaft* and *Gesellschaft,* Toennies was also very interested in public opinion (Hardt and Splichal 2000) and what he called *special sociology,* a field he saw as divided into theoretical, applied, and empirical inquiries. Together with Georg Simmel (profiled in chapter 5) and Max Weber (profiled in chapter 2), Toennies was a founder of the German Sociological Society. He served as that organization's president from 1909 until 1933. He was also a member of the English and Japanese sociological societies as well as an honorary member of the American Sociological Society. His work was well known to several early American sociologists profiled in this book, including Albion Small (chapter 1), Robert E. Park (above), and Louis Wirth (below) (Cahnman and Heberle 1971).

Barry Wellman

Barry Wellman (1942–) developed the study of communities as social networks. In addition to teaching sociology at the University of Toronto, he directs the university's NetLab and conducts research with several outside labs and institutes, including the Centre for Urban and Community Studies. Much of Wellman's recent research analyzes computer networks as social networks. This covers a range of diverse topics, including the use of computers in our daily lives, virtual communities, the use of virtual workgroups, telecommuting, social support, social networks, and international comparisons of Internet use.

He has authored, coauthored, or edited over 200 articles and several books. Wellman has presented his work in almost 20 countries, and his work has been translated into numerous languages. His many awards and honors include the International Network for Personal Relationships' 1998 Mentoring Award and an Outstanding Lifetime Contribution Award by the Canadian Sociological and Anthropological Association bestowed in 2001. He was honored in 2001 by the University of Toronto, Department of Sociology "Barryfest" Conference entitled "Social Structure in a Changing World: Presentations in Honor of Barry Wellman." His sociology department's undergraduate research prize is designated the Barry Wellman Prize.

Wellman is founder of the International Network for Social Network Analysis and the sociology journal *City and Community.* His coedited book *Social Structures: A Network Approach* (1988) was named as a Book of the Century by the International Sociological Association. He also coined the phrases *network city, network of networks,* and *networked individualism,* which are widely used in network analyses. Wellman is Chair of the Communication and Information Section and Chair-Emeritus of the Community and Urban Sociology Section of the American Sociological Association (Wellman, "Barry Wellman").

Louis Wirth

Louis Wirth (1897–1952) was born in Gemunden, Germany. When he was 14, Wirth and a sister migrated to Omaha, Nebraska, to live with an uncle. Although Wirth was expected to work in the family dry-goods business after graduation, he won a scholarship to the University of Chicago. He began college as a pre-medical student but changed his major to sociology, becoming active in political, antiwar, and social causes (Salerno 1987). Wirth became a sociologist because "he believed that a science of human behavior was not only possible but indispensable to social betterment" (Sheldon 1968, 558).

After graduation, Wirth did not have the money to continue his education, so he took a position as a social worker. He was able to save enough money to visit his family in Germany and then to enter graduate school at the University of Chicago upon his return to America. To pay for his studies, Wirth taught introductory sociology courses. He continued to teach at Chicago after earning his doctorate in 1926. When he did not receive a full-time faculty position, he accepted a position at Tulane University. After traveling to Europe on a Social Science Research Council fellowship, he returned to Chicago as an assistant professor in 1931 (Salerno 1987).

Together with Edward Shils, Wirth translated German sociologist Karl Mannheim's work *Ideology and Utopia* into English. He incorporated German sociological literature into his courses and works, including his own application of Ferdinand Toennies's concepts of *Gemeinschaft* and *Gesellschaft.* Wirth's biographer Roger A. Salerno notes that Wirth's "study of urbanism . . . is the starting point for the construction of all modern urban sociological theory" (1987, vii).

Although Wirth is largely associated with urban sociology, he was influential in a number of areas. He was a president of the American Sociological Association and the first president of the International Sociological Association. In addition to his academic activities, Wirth was a government consultant and activist. He took an active role in an assortment of civic groups, hosted a radio show for NBC in conjunction with University of Chicago, served on the Urbanism Committee of the National Resources Planning Board, served as director of planning of the Illinois Post War Planning Commission, and was a founder and director of the American Council on Race Relations. Additionally, Wirth financed and housed the migration of 13 Jewish family members to the United States to escape Nazi Germany. By the time of his death, he was also deeply involved in civil rights, dying of a heart attack after delivering a keynote address on race relations (Salerno 1987, vii–49; Sheldon 1968).

CAREERS IN SOCIOLOGY

Those with an interest and training in demography and urban sociology have backgrounds that prepare them for careers including

- administrator
- city/town/county/parish manager
- communications director
- community developer
- community organizer/activist
- compliance coordinator
- demographer—forecasting for corporate/marketing/insurance
- demographer—government
- family-planning counselor
- fiscal analyst
- grant writer
- health planner
- housing-services-agency director/staff
- international-aid-agency staff
- journalist
- lobbyist
- market-research data analyst
- policy analyst
- politician
- population-studies researcher
- program evaluator
- program manager/director
- program/project coordinator
- public relations specialist
- relocation coordinator
- resource developer
- special-events coordinator
- strategic planner
- transportation analyst
- urban planner/research assistant

Additional Resources

Bureau of Labor Statistics. 2004. Urban and Regional Planners. In *Occupational Outlook Handbook, 2004–05 Edition.* U.S. Department of Labor. http://www.bls.gov/oco/ocos057.htm. The BLS provides an overview covering working conditions, requirements, employment outlook, data on earnings, and further information for anyone considering entering urban and regional planning.

Gans, Herbert. 1962. *The Urban Villagers: Group and Class in the Life of Italian-Americans.* New York: Free Press. Gans' study of the West End of Boston is a sociological classic dealing with ethnicity, race, class, and more.

Garreau, Joel. 1991. *Edge City: Life on the New Frontier.* New York: Doubleday. This book discusses the emergence of these large, self-sufficient suburbs and implications of this restructuring of urban life.

Gottdiener, Mark, Claudia C. Collins, and David R. Dickens. 1999. *Las Vegas: The Social Production of an All-American City.* Malden, Mass.: Blackwell. This book examines how Las Vegas grew into the fast-growing metropolitan area it is today, how it has concentrated on transforming its image, and the implications of these changes.

Kearl, Michael C. Demography. http://www.trinity.edu/~mkearl/demograp.html. This site provides an overview of demography as part of Michael C. Kearl's (Trinity University) Sociological Tour through Cyberspace.

Macionis, John J., and Vincent R. Parrillo. 2001. *Cities and Urban Life.* 2nd ed. Upper Saddle River, N.J.: Prentice Hall. This textbook covers classical and contemporary research on city life.

McFalls, Joseph A., Jr. 1998. Population: A Lively Introduction. In *Population Bulletin,* vol. 53, no. 3. Washington, D.C.: Population Reference Bureau. This readable introduction to covers demography basics as well as some population-related issues. It is also available online at http://www.prb.org/Template.cfm?Section=Population_Bulletin2&template=/ContentManagement/ContentDisplay.cfm&ContentID=9009.

Population Association of America. http://www.popassoc.org/. Members of this professional organization include sociologists, demographers, and a range of others interested in population issues.

Population Reference Bureau. http://www.prb.org/. This organization provides a wealth of information and analyses on U.S. and international population trends. Many of their resources are available online.

Sassen, Saskia. 2001. *The Global City: New York, London, Tokyo.* 2nd ed. Princeton, N.J.: Princeton University Press. This book looks at how New York, London, and Tokyo became key linked cities in the global economy.

United Nations Population Fund (UNFPA). http://www.unfpa.org/. This large international effort promotes funds and assists with various population programs, formulation of population policies, and raising awareness of population issues worldwide.

U.S. Census Bureau. http://www.census.gov/. As the largest statistical agency of the federal government, the U.S. Census Bureau provides an extensive amount of data.

CHAPTER 9
Social Change, Behavior, and Movements

Cultures and societies are dynamic. They constantly experience **social change,** meaning that *the structures of cultures and societies transform into new forms.* Changes may occur primarily within one society (e.g., a coup installs a new government) or encompass multiple societies (e.g., globalization brings a fast-food restaurant or department store to places previously without these entities).

Explaining social change has always been a major interest for sociologists. Sociologists who study social change focus their attention away from the routines of social life that are generally somewhat stable and predictable, as much as this book discusses. Instead, they examine **collective behaviors,** those *spontaneous activities that involve large numbers of people violating established norms.* Those behaviors occur when people react to something new or unfamiliar. The result may be minimal, unanticipated, or short-term changes. Those behaviors may also lead to **social movements,** *organized collective activities that deliberately seek to create or resist social change.* Social movements purposely result in long-term, sweeping changes. Such activities are increasingly referred to as **collective action** because of the *intent to bring about a lasting change* (Miller 2000, 5).

The study of collective action is subfield of sociology. Sociologists in the American Sociological Association have established their own interest group for this area. Collective action also overlaps with interests in a number of other disciplines, including public opinion studied in political-science courses, the movements studied in political and religious sociology, and mass behavior studied in popular-culture and mass-media courses (Shibutani 1988, 26).

COLLECTIVE BEHAVIOR

Social change is both unplanned and planned, and can brought about by spontaneous or institutionalized means (Macionis 1995, 638–39). This section on collective behaviors focuses on the spontaneous activities that lead to social change. The social-movement section below addresses more purposive efforts to effect change.

Forms of Collective Behavior

Collective behaviors take a variety of forms, all of great interest to sociologists. Several of those forms are discussed here.

Fashions and Fads

Fashion is *a social pattern of behavior or appearance embraced by large numbers of people for a long period of time.* Although clothing may be the first thing many people think of as fashion, fashion actually incorporates much more than what we wear. It characterizes automobiles, architectural and decorating styles, home furnishings, entertainment, medical practice, business management, politics, the arts, language, and even names. By definition, fashion changes. One preference replaces another, then that preference is replaced, and so on.

Herbert Blumer, profiled below, viewed fashion as a form of modern collective social life "scarcely to be found in settled societies, such as primitive tribes, peasant societies, or caste societies, which cling to what is established and has been sanctioned through long usage" (1968, 342). Many analyses of fashion have focused on the role commercial interests (such as product manufacturers and marketers) play in dictating fashion. Georg Simmel (1957), profiled in chapter 5, studied the sociology of fashion a century ago. He saw the wealthy as fashion trendsetters, with others following their example. Thorstein Veblen (1967), profiled below, suggested that some people buy expensive things to show that they could afford them. He called this *conspicuous consumption.* Pierre Bourdieu (1984) also looked at the selection of products as related to, and reinforcing, social position.

To find out more about how and why fashions change over time, Stanley Lieberson (profiled below) conducted an extensive study on our fashion tastes, focusing on children's first names. Unlike clothing and many of our material fashions, no commercial efforts are made to influence name choices. Therefore, names provide an opportunity to study what Lieberson calls *pure mechanisms of fashion.*

He found two major influences on our tastes: external social forces (such as commercialism) and our "internal taste mechanisms" (Lieberson 2000). These internal mechanisms work to generate fashion change because we simply find some things more appealing than others, and we get bored with the old. Lieberson applies his analyses to a variety of examples, including men's fedoras, the length of waists on women's garments, the use of nicknames by politicians and reporters, women's titles, and music. He finds these two factors at work regardless of what fashion he is examining. Lieberson also found that the speed of fashion change depends on price and durability. Fashions in inexpensive clothing that is easily worn out change quickly. Fashions in expensive products, such as furniture, change slowly.

Fashions are contrasted with fads. **Fads** are typically seen as *relatively novel behaviors that appear suddenly, spread rapidly, are enthusiastically embraced by a large number of people for a short period of time, and then mostly disappear.* Robert Park and Ernest Burgess wrote about fads as early as 1924.

Unlike fashions that modify or build on previous preferences, fads appear, spread quickly, and generally disappear. Examples of fads have included activities as diverse as flagpole sitting (attempts to set records for sitting atop a flagpole) during the 1920s, goldfish swallowing on college campuses a decade later, dance marathons, pet rocks, smiley-face logos, streaking (running naked through public events), the Rubik's cube puzzle, and toga parties (wearing togas to campus parties as in the 1978 movie "Animal House"). Not only do fashions last longer than fads, they also derive from something already there. For example, fashionable hemlines on skirts go up and down in different years, and the style changes from year to year. Skirts were not just suddenly all the rage at one point in history, only to relatively disappear a short time later, as did, say, the pet rock.

Rumors

Rumors are *unverified information spread through informal social interaction, and often derived from unknown sources.* Rumor thrives when the subject is important as well as when accurate and reliable information on the topic is lacking or ambiguous (Allport and Postman 1947).

Sociologists have a long-standing interest in rumors. Jane Addams, one of the earliest female sociologists in the United States (profiled in chapter 11), reported on a case of rumor running wildly through a Chicago neighborhood. The neighborhood was served by Hull House, a settlement house Addams ran that provided a range of services to immigrant residents of the area. She wrote that for a period extending over many weeks, Hull House experienced a stream of visitors insisting on seeing a mythical "devil-baby" allegedly housed there. Variations of the rumor told of a baby supposedly born to a religious mother and an atheist father who had commented that he would rather have the devil in his home than a certain holy picture. The result was allegedly the devil taking his baby's form and the fearful father delivering the child to Hull House. The number of visitors was so great that Addams (1914) reported that continuing the regular activities of Hull House became a challenge.

Although they can address any topic, most rumors involve some aspect of our everyday lives. That makes them seem relevant to many people. They may be either false or true, or at least have some aspect of correct information in them.

Miller (2000, 85–90) summarizes a wide variety of rumors that deal with products we use in our daily lives (e.g., the quality or content of food products), disasters (the presence of dangerous situations or outcomes), and atrocities (e.g., wartime acts). He notes that the Internet has provided an especially fertile place for conspiracy rumors to flourish and has also made the spread of rumors even faster.

A famous and well-studied case of a rumor involves the popular rock group the Beatles at the height of their popularity. According to the rumor, member Paul McCartney was dead and had been replaced by an imposter. As summarized by Rosnow and Fine (1976, 14–17), the rumor may have originated among a small group at Eastern Michigan University as early as 1967 without being picked up by the public. The rumor was aired publicly on October 12, 1969 by a caller to a Detroit radio station. The caller claimed that if the Beatles' song "Revolution 9" was played backwards, the words "number 9, number 9, number 9" were actually saying "Turn me on, dead man." Filtering out background noises at the end of their song "Strawberry Fields Forever" allowed listeners to hear a voice say, "I buried Paul."

On October 14, the University of Michigan newspaper carried the headline that Paul McCartney was dead, allegedly as the result of a 1966 automobile accident. The report, accompanied by a bloody photograph, stated that the singer had been decapitated in the accident and replaced by a look-alike. The article described the "clues" on the Beatles' album covers. The design on the *Sgt. Pepper* album cover reputedly showed grave flowers resembling Paul's guitar, or perhaps a letter *P.* The initials "O.P.D." on an armband worn by Paul could mean "Officially Pronounced Dead." Paul was the only Beatle not facing forward on the back cover. The photo on the cover of the *Abbey Road* album reputedly represented the group leaving a cemetery, with each member of the group representing a member of a funeral party. Paul was pictured barefoot and wearing a suit. He was interpreted to be, of course, the corpse. The license plate on a vehicle seen in the photograph read 28IF, interpreted to mean that Paul would have been age 28 if still alive.

Although the newspaper photograph and accident report would later be revealed as hoaxes, other "evidence" surfaced as the rumor swept across the country. Paul wore a black carnation while the other Beatles wore red carnations on the cover of the *Magical Mystery Tour* album. An apple insignia allegedly turned blood red on one album cover if immersed in water. Other clues were culled from the songs "I Am the Walrus" and "Glass Onion."

As Rosnow and Fine (1976, 16–17) explain, the evidence did not support the rumor that Paul died. Some of the "clues" were explained by additional rumors. For example, the O.P.D. armband was reportedly from the Ontario Police Department. The statement, "I buried Paul," may have actually been John Lennon commenting at the end of the recording session that some other element of the music had buried Paul's musical part in the arrangement. Speculation also arose that the Beatles themselves, nearing the group's break-up, had intentionally planted a number of clues. Both McCartney and Lennon denied this. Whatever the source of this rumor, it spread wildly, fueled by the intense interest in this very popular group, a lack of factual information, and possibly by intentionally placed "clues."

Many rumors die a natural death as the public tires of them or as associated tensions or events are eliminated. Most rumors die due to being disproved, becoming irrelevant, or by "wearing out" and dissipating (Rosnow and Fine 1976). Additionally, most reborn rumors run their course relatively quickly.

Some rumors do not die; rather, they become part of popular culture. An example is provided by the wealth of rumors that surround the assassination of President John F. Kennedy (Rosnow and Fine 1976). Rumors still abound about the number of shooters, those responsible, and possible involvement of other political figures.

Urban Legends

By definition, **urban legends** are *realistic but untrue stories that recount some alleged recent event.* They are typically entertaining tales of ironic and incredible things that have happened to some "friend of a friend." The sources of, or eyewitnesses to, these alleged events are difficult, if not impossible, to trace or verify. Urban legends, like rumor, thrive on ambiguity and the possibility that the alleged event occurred. They may even be a very persistent form of rumor.

Urban legends are a modern form of ancient folklore traditions, and some can even be traced back to these folktales (Brunvand 1993, 71–73). One well-known urban legend recounts the tale of someone waking up in a hotel room after a night spent having sexual intercourse with a stranger. The person wakes to find they have had a kidney stolen by an apparently skilled surgeon. Another familiar urban legend relates the story of someone who arrives home to find their Doberman choking on a human finger. The finger's owner turns out to be a burglar still hidden in the closet. Another urban legend, often told as a ghost story, tells the tale of a couple that finds the bloody hook of an insane, murderous escapee from a nearby institution hanging on the car-door handle after a tryst at Lover's Lane.

Just as ancient folktales taught moral lessons, urban legends also often provide cautionary warnings about modern society. The one-night-stand and hook tales imply that casual sexual relationships are dangerous and even deadly. To be safe, we should behave "morally." Yet there are inherent dangers of modern society incorporated that are outside of our control. There is evolving medical technology that makes human organs a valuable commodity. The Doberman tale warns us that there are bad people who will intrude into our own homes even when we have safeguards to keep out danger and are doing nothing wrong.

As society changes and people are faced with evolving and unfamiliar situations, urban legends arise as one response. As we rely more on virtual interactions and the Internet, urban legends find new and faster ways to spread.

Mass Hysteria

Mass hysteria occurs as a response to a real or imagined event. The event, or perceived event, triggers *a reaction in which people become excited to the point of losing their critical-thinking abilities and acting irrationally.* Theories of mass hysteria have suggested that a "circular reaction" occurs in which emotion and fear feed those emotions in others, spreading the "hysteria." However, this idea remains to be tested by researchers. Although sociologists are quite interested in the phenomenon, journalistic accounts provide most of the documentation on mass hysteria. Empirical scientific research on mass hysteria is sparse, numbering around only a dozen or so by David Miller's count (2000, 113–14).

A classic example of mass hysteria is the Halloween 1938 *War of the Worlds* radio-theater broadcast. A radio-theater group adapted an H. G. Wells novel about a Martian invasion, originally set in England, using the names of actual places in New York and New Jersey. Through a series of simulated news bulletins and reports interrupting a program of dance music, listeners heard announcers describe devastating Martian attacks in the New Jersey area and a nerve-gas attack on New York City. Many listeners had tuned in late and had not heard that the broadcast was staged. There were no commercials that would suggest the broadcast was not real. Although there were a few station breaks announcing that the program was staged, many listeners still believed they were hearing actual events. People panicked, fleeing the area. Listeners attempting to get more information flooded telephone lines for emergency services, hospitals, and media as well as calling friends and relatives. Ensuing media stories reported terrorized people stampeding out of theaters, having heart attacks, and even committing suicide. Although Miller notes that a number of these media stories were later shown to be unsubstantiated, some mass panic did occur, the event became part of American folklore, and new broadcast regulations were quickly put in place by the Federal Communications Commission (FCC) (2000, 114–15).

Crowds

The types of collective behavior discussed above involve activity by people dispersed across society. A sociological look at crowds draws attention to localized collective behavior. A **crowd** is *a temporary collection of people in physical proximity who interact and have a common focus.* People in the same place only become a crowd by definition when they find this focus.

Researchers have identified various types of crowds (Blumer 1969). One common type is a **casual crowd.** These are *people who just happen to be at the same place at the same time.* People gathering at the scene of a car accident or watching a crane place a steel beam on a high-rise building are all examples of a casual crowd. These types of crowds may be organized around **crowd crystals**—*those who draw attention to themselves in some manner* (Canetti 1962). A street-corner preacher or someone slipping on an icy curb might draw a casual crowd.

Stanley Milgram (profiled in chapter 10) and his associates studied casual crowds by having someone pause on a public sidewalk and look attentively towards the sixth floor of a nearby building. With this simple experiment, they were able to record the reaction of others passing by who, at least momentarily, joined the crowd by looking to see the object of interest. The researchers observed that almost all of the passersby looked up. The larger the crowd gathered at the scene, the more likely it was that passersby would actually stop long enough to stand with the crowd (Milgram, Bickman, and Berkowitz 1969).

Another type of crowd is a **conventional crowd.** These are *deliberate gatherings bound by norms of behavior.* Attendees at a wedding, fans at a rock concert, or the audience at a poetry reading are conventional crowds. Although the expected behavior differs greatly between these events, there are norms governing each of these settings that are generally observed by the crowd members. The members then disperse without incident when the event is concluded.

Some crowds function on emotion. These crowds may take different forms and may actually evolve from one form into another. An **expressive crowd** *forms specifically around events with emotional meaning for the members,* such as the championship game of a basketball tournament, a religious revival, or a political rally.

When emotions become intense, the result may be a crowd in action. As the crowd members interact, the emotional intensity builds into behavior that may be destructive or aggressive. The result may be a mob or even a riot. **Mobs** are *crowds that take action toward an emotionally driven goal.* Lynchings are well-known examples of mob behavior (Massey and Myers 1989).

Riots *involve public disorder that is less directed and may be of longer duration than mob behavior.* They may erupt as a result of an intensely emotional short-term event. For example, sports fans occasionally spill into the street after the conclusion of an important game, breaking windows, burning cars, and committing thefts or other destructive acts.

Riots sometimes occur as a response to some real or perceived social injustice. Urban riots have occurred over racial issues such as the death of Reverend Martin Luther King Jr. as well as the videotaped police beating of motorist Rodney King and the subsequent acquittal of the officers involved (e.g., Baldassare 1994; Carter 1992; Gale 1996). Riots have occurred as prisoners react to their surrounding conditions (e.g., Colvin 1982; Useem and Resig 1999). Riots that erupted in New York City after police raided a well-known gay establishment have become known as the Stonewall riots (taken from the name of the raided nightspot) and mark the beginning of the gay-rights movement (Teal 1971; Thorstad 1995). This is one of the few social movements for which the date the movement first took public action can be established.

Theories of Collective Behavior

Sociologists have developed several theories regarding why people in collectivities behave as they do. They are concerned with the spontaneity of the behavior and the social factors that influence this behavior.

Contagion Theory

An early theory on crowd behavior was developed by Gustave Le Bon (profiled below), who is sometimes referred to as the "father of collective behavior." His work was later refined by Herbert Blumer (1969). According to Le Bon's **contagion theory,** *being swept up in a crowd results in a hypnotic sort of influence on individuals.* Conscious personalities, personal will, discernment, and restraint disappear. They are replaced by unconscious and instinctual behaviors that draw power from the sentiment and anonymity of the crowd. In Le Bon's words, "in a crowd every sentiment and act is contagious, and contagious to such a degree that an individual readily sacrifices his personal interest to the collective interest. This is an aptitude very contrary to his nature, and of which a man is scarcely capable, except when he makes part of a crowd" (1960, 10). Thus, emotions pass through the crowd in a "contagious" manner, similar to the spread of a disease, culminating in some violent behavior.

Later researchers (e.g., McPhail 1991) have argued that Le Bon's assertions are, at the least, overly simplistic. Although crowds do have an impact on what people are willing to do, crowd members are not irrationally, unconsciously subsumed into some herd-type behavior. Contagion alone cannot explain all collective behavior, the cause of the behavior, and behavior that appears to be reasoned and rational.

Emergent-Norm Theory

Emergent-norm theory (Turner and Killian 1987) takes a social-interaction view of crowd behavior. According to this theory, *new norms develop (emerge) as events happen.* This norm development depends on communication and cues circulating among crowd members. It is guided by leaders that emerge as the situation progresses. Their behaviors serve as guides for action for other crowd members. Crowd participants interpret events, redefine the situation, follow the norms constructed by leaders, and establish "situational" behaviors.

Emergent-norm theory is often employed in studying disaster behaviors (Aguirre, Wenger, and Vigo 1998, 302). In the aftermath of the 1993 World Trade Center bombing, people largely evacuated in groups after some period spent milling around seeking information and advice from others. They discussed what might have happened and the danger level before leaving. This theory alone, however, cannot explain how and why leaders emerge or why people take different roles in such situations. Other factors not originally envisioned as central in emergent-norm theory may also be important. For example, in the World Trade Center study, the closer their preexisting social relationships with those around them, the more quickly the people evacuated. Surrounded by people they already knew and perceived to be helpful in determining a course of action made people more likely to quickly join in the collective behavior of evacuation (312).

Aguirre, Quarantelli, and Mendoza's (1988) study of streaking on college campuses shows that some behaviors that may take a bit of planning also fit into emergent-norm theory. Although streakers were often acting on impulse and emotion, they also understood the meaning and consequences of their actions.

Value-Added Theory

According to Neil Smelser (1962), there are six factors that contribute to collective behavior. Together, these *factors set the stage for collective action as people react to situations and events.* As the name **value-added theory** implies, each of the factors adds something of value to the collective action.

- The first factor, *structural conduciveness,* means the social structure is arranged such that collective behavior becomes possible (e.g., when authorities do not, or cannot, squelch activities).
- The second factor, *structural strain,* means that the fabric of the social structure is under tension. Deprivation, either real or perceived, can cause this (e.g., one group receiving, or being perceived as receiving, racial preference). Lack of good, accurate information can also add to strains, as rumors spread and people develop their own assessments of the "facts" as they believe them. (With this focus, this theory is sometimes called **structural-strain theory.**)
- The third factor is *generalized beliefs.* People come to focus on some specific person or thing as a source of difficulty and in need of change. This focus could target a person in power or a group in control. Additionally, people begin to feel that they can actually have an influence and make a desired change happen.
- The fourth factor, or the *precipitating factors,* identifies those events that confirm generalized beliefs and transform them into collective action. This might be a new governmental policy, enforcement of an existing law, or something else that focuses attention and energy.
- The fifth factor, *mobilization for action,* occurs when a leader or leaders take some initial action (e.g., the first stone is thrown).
- The sixth and final factor deals with the *breakdown of social control* by authorities. Due to inability, miscalculation, or lack of effort, existing social-control measures do not work. Protests and riots may occur, and disorder spreads. The result may even be a social movement.

Smelser's example illustrating these factors at work is the stock market crash of 1929. The U.S. capitalist market, the ability to transfer large amounts of money, and the ability to make immediate transactions combined to provide the *structural conduciveness* for the crash. A soaring market, dangerous speculations, and an economic downturn in many indicators produced *strain.* The lack of understanding about market mechanisms when prices fell, especially among inexperienced investors, was a *precipitating factor* that fed a *generalized belief* that it was time to get out of the market. This led to the *action,* a sell-off that the financial sector was *ineffectual in controlling.*

This theory explains collective behavior only in terms of reaction, rather than pro-action. It does not include the variety of motivations for involvement in social behaviors that may actually be behind behaviors. For example, some riot participants certainly believe that some slight has occurred that deserves protest. Others may join in for the primary goal of looting stores. Still others might be swept up in the crowd, unable to leave the area.

SOCIAL MOVEMENTS

Unlike the spontaneity of the collective behaviors discussed above, social movements intend to direct social change. These movements encompass a diversity of issues. Contemporary movements include efforts to draw attention to the rights of the disabled, animal rights, environmental activism, abortion (pro-choice and pro-life), AIDS activism, gay rights, civil rights, patients' rights, rights of those who choose to be childfree, gun control, the right to die (i.e., euthanasia), Mothers against Drunk Driving (MADD), the open-source software movement, and women's liberation, to name just a few. Sociologists are interested in how these movements form, why they arise, the forms they take and their life cycle, what change occurs, and the outcomes of that change.

Social movements work to accomplish their goals through actions that disrupt the established status quo, authority, and culture. Movement participants develop a sense of collective identity that bolsters their sense of having a shared cause and helps sustain their efforts, thereby sustaining the movement (Tarrow 1994). Some movements are fairly short-lived and either die out or accomplish their goals (e.g., local efforts to stop the construction of a nuclear power plant or prison). Other movements have long lives, some having adherents who participate for their entire lives (e.g., the NAACP) (Klandermans 2000, 246).

Formation of Social Movements

It is difficult to identify the beginning of most social movements as they are occurring. However, sociologists have suggested a number of factors that may be behind the birth of a social movement. These factors include the relative deprivation of one group to larger society, social unrest, dissatisfaction, a sense of injustice, ideology or beliefs, social stresses (such as a crisis or cultural lag), resources, organization, and an orientation toward change. Some factors seem to play a larger role in the formation of one social movement and less in others. However, social movements all involve collective action of people who work to enact some type of change they feel would be preferable in the social structure.

Freeman (1999, 19–20) studied four social movements of the 1960s and 1970s to better understand what is required for the formation of social movements. Her analyses of the civil rights, student protests, welfare rights, and women's liberation movements prominent during this period identify four elements that are essential for a social movement to form. She finds that there must be (1) a preexisting communications network that can be (2) co-opted to disseminate the ideas of the movement, along with (3) crises that spur involvement in the cause and (4) an effort to organize interested groups into a movement.

Freeman's analysis of the civil rights movement illustrates these elements. Churches and black colleges provided a communications network that predated the civil rights movement. Students and church members shared common experiences of racism and discrimination that led them to be receptive to the message of the movement when presented to them through these familiar and trusted networks. Emerging leaders, consisting of a number of church ministers, began to speak to these shared experiences and provide avenues for social action. Participation in social movements became, in Freeman's word, logical. In Montgomery, Alabama, when Rosa Parks refused to give up her seat on a bus to a white passenger, those hearing the civil rights message had the spark to ignite action. While Martin Luther King Jr. served as spokesperson, the ensuing Montgomery bus boycott was then largely organized by E. D. Nixon, a Pullman car porter and activist with the already established NAACP.

Social movements also use tactics designed to encourage a sense of community and belonging during difficult periods. Music, for example, can be utilized for this purpose. The civil rights movement's theme was the song "We Shall Overcome," a piece that traces its roots back to two gospel songs sung by slaves. The song also aided in recruitment and garnering support for the cause.

Types of Social Movements

Sociologists have no one single way to classify social movements. Some classifications consider movement goals or methods employed to achieve those goals. Herbert Blumer (1969) classified social movements as *general* or *specific.* General movements involve a change of values across society—for example, changes in the views and status of women brought about by the women's movement. These movements are not sharply focused on methods, which may actually be diffuse, with different branches of the movement supporting different activities (letter-writing campaigns, sit-ins, hiring a lobbyist, etc.). Specific movements have a more well-defined focus—for example, the antiabortion movement.

One commonly cited classification is provided by David Aberle (1966). He divides social movements into four types, broadly based on who they seek to change (individuals or society) and the extent of the change sought (small or sweeping). **Alternative social movements** *focus on partial change at the individual level.* Movements advocating birth control provide an example of this type of movement. **Redemptive social movements** *seek a total change of individuals.* Movements that aim to bring a state of grace to adherents are redemptive movements (e.g., born-again Christians). Like transformation movements, discussed below, they reject at least some features of the current society. **Reformative social movements** *seek a partial change of society.* Women's suffrage and child-labor laws fit this definition by seeking to reform voting laws and the status of women as well as the situation of children. **Transformative social movements** *support a total change of society.* Examples include millenarian and revolutionary movements.

Another type of social movement is the *reactionary social movement,* sometimes called a **countermovement.** Countermovements *organize in response to the changes brought about by other social movements.* Members perceive a threat from these changes and seek to protect their own established positions. For example, in response to the animal-rights movement, a countermovement has arisen defending targets of animal activism, such as factory farms and recreational hunting (Munro 1999).

Although there are many similarities between social movements and countermovements, their differences are important. As Johnson (1999) points out, since countermovements are protecting some already established economic and political interests, the resources are likely in place to facilitate their emergence and growth. Additionally, since they are responding to changes brought about by social movements, countermovements borrow the rhetoric of those movements but twist it to support their opposing goals.

Operation Rescue, an antiabortion movement that blockaded access to clinics that included abortion among their family-planning services, serves as an example of these tactics (Johnson 1999). Operation Rescue was devised as a part of a larger effort by right-wing Christian organizations to close abortion clinics nationwide. Beginning with a blockade at a New Jersey clinic in 1987, activists attempted to deny clinic access by surrounding clinic doors and windows. They prayed, sang religious and/or civil rights hymns, heard inspirational speeches, and utilized tactics including picketing, tying up clinic phone lines, and distributing "wanted posters" of clinic physicians. When arrested, activists went limp so that police had to carry them away.

Operation Rescue activists co-opted familiar rhetoric from progressive movements of the 1960s. They called themselves the "civil rights movement of the eighties," calling for "civil rights for the unborn" and "equal rights for unborn women." They sang freedom songs, held sit-ins, and cultivated media comparisons to the nonviolent tactics of the civil rights movement. As a result of a combination of injunctions, escalating violence attributed to their activists, and legislative and court action targeted to allowing clinic access, the countermovement was forced to refocus activities in new directions, such as picketing physicians' offices, homes, and other places they frequented. Although, as Johnson notes, the movement did focus attention on fetal rights and reduce the number of abortion facilities and physicians for a period of time, it did not achieve a recriminalization of abortion or significantly reduce public support for abortion.

Some groups also actively seek to avoid social change. The Amish generally hold to their traditions, but social forces such as farm economics and a growing need to find employment outside of the Amish community are pressuring them to modernize. While they see change as neither good nor evil, they do see it as potentially tempting young people and pulling them away from traditional sources of solidarity within the Amish community. However, the Amish have accommodated some planned changes through careful and deliberate selection (Savells 2001). For example, some dairy farmers have generators in their barns to keep commercially sold milk cool per health-department standards. Batteries that provide taillights at night on horse-drawn transportation are also allowed as a safety measure.

Decline of Social Movements

A number of factors, including world events, movement ideologies and chosen tactics/strategies, and movement organization, interact to influence the history of social movements. Frederick D. Miller (1999) identified four often-linked reasons why social movements decline: success, failure, co-optation, and repression.

The movement may achieve its goals. Such was the case for the women's suffrage movement. However, most movements have multifaceted agendas—for example, the civil rights movement. These movements may achieve some goals but find they must continue to work toward others. In an unusual case of a movement re-creating itself to address a different issue, the current March of Dimes organization began as a movement working to fight polio. After the development of the polio vaccine, the movement re-created itself to target birth defects, premature birth, and low birth weight.

The movement can end due to organizational failures. Strategies can be ineffectual, factional disputes can develop, or the movement may become so internally focused (*encapsulated* in Miller's terminology) that it loses touch and appeal with those outsiders it needs to survive and attract as new members. Stoper's study (1999) of the Student Nonviolent Coordinating Committee (SNCC), a 1960s movement founded to coordinate civil rights sit-ins, finds that the group moved on to organizing black voter registration and even seating black Mississippi delegates at the 1964 Democratic National Convention. However, after apparent successes, the group faced several crises and organizational problems that resulted in its demise.

Leaders may also be enticed with rewards that serve their own interests rather than those of the movement. This diverts the leader's attentions away from the goals of the movement. If leaders are rewarded for their position in the movement with more money or intangible benefits (e.g., status) than they could get from other occupations, their interest may become in maintaining their position rather than advancing the goals of the movement. Robert Michels (1962), profiled in chapter 5, argued that long-term political leaders' interests turn to maintaining their positions rather than advancing causes.

Powerful interests may repress a movement by using tactics such as bringing criminal sanctions against members and leaders; infiltrating the movement with spies; harassing, attacking, or threatening members or recruits; and spreading false information. Governments have attempted to repress anarchist movements in various countries, for example. Although efforts at repression may have the effect of strengthening the solidarity and resolve of the movement, it may also destroy the movement.

Theories of Social Movements

There are a number of theories about how and why social movements arise and the paths they take. In searching for explanations, sociologists have developed several theories. Two older perspectives are *deprivation theories* and *mass-society theory.* According to **deprivation theories,** *social movements arise when people feel deprived of something that others have or that they feel others have* (Merton 1968). Expectations, rather than absolute measures, are the key to whether or not people feel deprived. The slight (or perceived slight) may be a range of situations from poor working conditions to standard of living to racial preferences.

Social isolation is the key to **mass-society theory.** Proponents of this perspective argue that *modern society is alienating, immoral, apathetic, and discourages individuality, and that in this context, socially isolated people are attracted to social movements for personal reasons.* Joining gives them a sense of importance and intent. This makes them easily manipulated and easily influenced to join movements (Kornhauser 1959; Giner 1976; Melucci 1989). Both of these perspectives have received mixed support in the research, finding some support and much criticism. Newer theories focus on collective action and tying individual experience to the movement's goals.

Resource-Mobilization Theory

Sociologists have developed a different approach to understanding social movements that draws from our understanding of both collective action and organizations (see chapter 5). **Resource-mobilization theory** recognizes that *social movements need to generate adequate, and often substantial, resources to achieve their goals* (Zald and Ash 1966; see also McCarthy and Zald 2001). The resources they need to muster are extensive. They include money, membership, office facilities and equipment, communication processes, political influence, and a skill base with expertise in organization, leadership, and marketing the cause. Successes and limits are set by the resources a movement is able to mobilize.

These resources are mobilized through the efforts of **social-movement organizations (SMOs),** *formal organizations that seek social change by achieving a social movement's goals.* These SMOs can be studied just as sociologists study any formal organizational system (Gamson 1975; Jenkins 1983). Rather than being loose or chaotic confederations of people with similar interests, successful SMOs follow a bureaucratic structure in regard to leadership and administration. They are goal-oriented and see political participation as rational.

There may be more than one SMO in a social movement. The civil rights movement, for example, has included the NAACP, the SNCC, the Southern Christian Leadership Conference (SCLC), Students for a Democratic Society (SDS), the Black Panthers, and a number of other groups (Appelbaum and Chambliss 1995, 545–46). Because these SMOs are competing for limited resources and the same potential members and support bases, systems exist in which SMOs interact with each other and with other groups that have desired resources. Examining these interrelationships has provided an important step in the need for a theory that explains "panoplies and cascades of movements rather than single movements in isolation" (Collins 1999, 37). SMOs may find the need to cultivate **conscience constituents,** *people outside of the movement who provide resources but do not directly benefit from its goal accomplishment* (McCarthy and Zald 1973). Social movement "industries" may even arise to garner support for the cause.

Resource-mobilization theory points out the importance of resources to SMOs. However, critics question whether it adequately accounts for those who have only occasional involvement in movements and how much members and leaders are really willing to invest in personal costs to the organization. Randall Collins notes that sociologists need to have a much better understanding of two areas. In his view, one of these major areas of study still remains in regard to mobilization. "First, what causes interests to be mobilized in the first place? And second, what determines the extent to which the entire array of mobilized movements is fragments or consolidated? . . . [R]esource mobilization theory . . . [has been able] to offer a fair answer to the first question. The second remains on the agenda" (Collins 1999, 38).

New Social Movements

Since the 1960s, **new social movements** have arisen that focus on "*bringing about social change through the transformation of values, personal identities and symbols*" (Scott 1990, 18). The women's movement, the environmental movement, and the gay-rights movement all fit within this classification (Melucci 1980; McAdam, McCarthy, and Zald 1988). These new social movements are set apart from older movements by several features (Scott 1990). Unlike older movements, they are not primarily political. As such, they do not challenge the state and social structures directly. Rather, they are located in, and defend, civil society. Also unlike older movements, they do not rely on formal and hierarchical organizational structures. New movements utilize networking and grassroots mass-mobilization efforts to change cultural values and lifestyle alternatives. They emphasize personal autonomy and link personal experience to the ideology of the movement (Scott 1990, 21). For example, the women's movement encourages women to empower themselves and understand how their own daily lives are shaped, and can be improved, by the movement's concerns. Some observers, however, have argued that the differences between old and new social movements, especially their political efforts and organizational forms, are not as great as some theorists have suggested.

The activist organization AIDS Coalition to Unleash Power (ACT-UP) is a new social movement that formed in 1987 in response to federal policy and pharmaceutical companies that discriminated against people with HIV/AIDS. The organization's efforts have included some traditional tactics, such as demonstrations and sit-ins. However, it has also focused on changing cultural perceptions and attitudes. Education and attention-getting tactics, including throwing condoms in public, are some of the strategies used. Efforts have resulted in changes in public policy (e.g., an improved drug-testing and accelerated approval process, getting more women and minorities into clinical trials). Community activists now work with the National Institute of Health's AIDS Clinical Trials Group (NIH ACTG). Characteristic of new social movements, members themselves develop new skills, knowledge, and values. They become more educated on science and medicine, develop social skills, and become more assertive in dealing with their own health and health care professionals (Brashers et al. 2002).

GLOBALIZATION AND THE INTERNET

Social movements take place around the world. Many movements focus on issues within a specific nation and seek to address concerns within that nation. For example, two decades of a fish workers' movement in India has fought to protect the traditional fishing industry and the local marine environment (Chakraborty 1999). However, social movements may also embrace globalization in their causes. The environmental movement's "Think Global, Act Local" slogan provides an example (Held et al. 1999, 376–413).

Global culture is also carried by various social movements (Berger 2002), with some movements occurring in numerous countries, adjusting their tactics and goals to fit differing cultures. The women's movement, for example, has gone global, with supporters in each country working within their own cultural context and limitations. Arabic women have sought equal rights with men within the context of Islam (O'Kelly and Carney 1986).

Nongovernmental organizations (NGOs), which are *private organizations or groups of citizens that work against destructive government or large organizations,* engage in collective action on a large scale (Boli and Thomas 1997, 62). Many of these NGOs focus on human-rights issues. The women's movement has also learned to work with NGOs such as the United Nations (United Nations 2001). Among other movements teaming with NGOs are the environmental movement Greenpeace and campaigns to ban land mines (Roth 1998). This allows the movements to leverage the resources and influences of the NGOs. However, one review of the research concludes that social movements, with the possible exception of the environmental movement, have not been largely successful at transcending international borders (Klandermans 2000).

The Internet has provided a global and decentralized venue for the new social movements to operate and organize (Bell 2001, 173). For example, a Web-based attack on the sports-equipment company Nike focusing on the treatment of workers outside of the United States led to revised corporate policies (Hamon 1998). The Internet also provides extended opportunities to gain support and financial resources that did not previously exist. One aspect of Ron Eyerman's (2002) look at music and social movements concluded that the Internet has opened up a new and extremely lucrative source of revenue for white supremacist groups. As he explains, "through the Net, widely dispersed individuals can find one another, and movements can coordinate their meetings and other activities. For underground and illegal organizations, such as white power groups, the Net has permitted the sale and distribution of compact discs, newsletters and magazines, as well as identifying symbolic items such as T-shirts, buttons and so forth. This has become a multimillion-dollar industry in Sweden, which is a world leader in the distribution of white power compact discs, sold primarily through the Net" (Eyerman 2002, 449). The Internet provides extensive networking and communication opportunities conveniently and at minimal cost.

Another example of collective action online is the Robert S. Jervey Place, a low-income public-housing development in Wilmington, North Carolina. A task force turned to the Internet as part of a Jervey Place redevelopment project after the relationship between residents and the local housing authority became strained. Residents went online to learn about architecture and urban planning, and found architects and lawyers to assist in designing the housing community in ways that would best fit their needs. They even designed a Web site on the redevelopment project, complete with history, culture, and status reports (Mele 1999, 22–23).

A very effective use of the Internet for social action has been demonstrated by MoveOn.org. Billed on their Web page (http://www.moveon.org) as an organization "working to bring ordinary people back into politics," MoveOn.org builds electronic advocacy groups. One of their causes leading up to the March 2003 start of Operation Iraqi Freedom was an antiwar movement, "Win without War." MoveOn.org's "Win without War" campaign used the Internet to build a coalition of 32 organizations, including the NAACP, Sierra Club, National Organization for Women (NOW), and others representing millions of Americans who favored allowing the UN weapons inspectors in Iraq over waging war. They also organized an antiwar Virtual March on Washington on February 26, 2003. Over 400,000 people registered to participate in advance. By the close of business on that day, more than 1 million phone calls, faxes, and e-mails had been directed to representatives in Washington, D.C. Just a month before, another group known as Act Now to Stop War and End Racism (ANSWER) had primarily used the Internet, e-mail, and telephones to organize antiwar demonstrations in 25 countries, along with "transportation from more than 200 U.S. cities in 45 states for the rallies in Washington and San Francisco" (CNN 2003). MoveOn.org was also active in the 2004 US presidential campaign and has tackled issues as wide-ranging as Federal Comunications Commission rules on media control, working to save old growth forests, and overtime pay for American workers.

BIOGRAPHIES

Herbert Blumer

Herbert G. Blumer (1900–1987) was a member of the famous Chicago school of sociology, discussed in chapter 8. He was central to the development of symbolic interactionism, and even coined the term. Blumer kept alive George Herbert Mead's work when structural-functionalism arose as the dominant paradigm in American sociology during the 1950s (Shibutani 1988, 26). He was also influential in developing and proliferating ethnographic research (Prus 1996), a type of research discussed in more detail in chapter 10. Additionally, Blumer established collective behavior as a subfield of sociology.

However, Blumer was also a controversial figure. He was a critic of positivism in sociology, taking the position that humans could not be adequately studied using the same techniques applied to rats (Wellman 1988, 60). He also challenged some basic concepts, such as race relations, industrial relations, and public opinion, questioning whether they were adequate to describe what was being studied. Blumer's own work provoked sharp criticism, with Blumer himself even being called "the gravedigger of America Sociology" by an author whose work he critiqued (quoted in Becker 1988, 15).

Blumer's legacy, and American sociology, have endured. An entire issue of the journal *Symbolic Interaction* (vol. 11, no. 1, 1988) contained articles written in his honor, addressing both strengths and weaknesses of his work. In that issue, Blumer's former student Howard S. Becker, who is profiled in chapter 6, writes of his teacher, "Although he was an inspiring and effective teacher, an administrator of unequaled ability, and an outstanding labor arbitrator, his importance for us lies in his also being one of the most profound thinkers sociology has ever been fortunate enough to have . . . That profundity affected the entire field, so that most sociologists, even those who would not think of themselves as his disciples, rely on his conceptual contributions" (1988, 13).

Gustave Le Bon

Although he held a doctorate of medicine and would be remembered as a founder of social psychology, the career of Gustave Le Bon (1841–1931) reflects successive interests in other areas. Le Bon was born in Nogent-le-Rotrou, France. As a young adult, he traveled in Europe, North Africa, and Asia. He wrote several books on anthropology and archaeology after these trips. President Theodore Roosevelt reportedly kept Le Bon's *Psychological Laws of the Evolution of Peoples* (1894) in his room (Widener 1979, 23). Le Bon wrote an introduction to the 12th French edition of that work in 1927, when he was 86 years old.

After his travels, Le Bon turned his interests to the natural sciences. During this phase of his career, "he invented recording instruments . . . studied racial variations in cranial capacity, analyzed the composition of tobacco smoke, published a photographic method for making plans and maps . . . [published] the training of horses . . . and, finally, devoted more than ten years to research on black light, intra-atomic energy, and the equivalence of matter and energy" (Stoetzel 1968, 82).

In the third phase of his career, Le Bon finally turned his interests to social psychology. *The Crowd: A Study of the Popular Mind* (1960, orig. 1896) "laid the foundations for the study of mass human action" (Widener 1979, 13).

That work is still referenced in many sociology textbooks and courses today. Le Bon died at Marne-la-Coquette, France in 1931. He was 90 years old.

Stanley Lieberson

Stanley Lieberson (1933–) was born in Montreal, Canada, and raised in Brooklyn, New York. Lieberson began his college career at Brooklyn College where, as a freshman, he developed his initial interest in sociology. He had never heard of sociology until he took a survey social-science course taught by a sociologist. He was "turned on" by the course, finding that much of what he learned "rang true." After two years at Brooklyn College, he was accepted into the University of Chicago's graduate program where he earned his M.A. and Ph.D. in sociology. Lieberson took a Greyhound bus from New York City to Chicago and started graduate school there at age 19, largely because that school offered him financial support (Lieberson 1985). There, he earned his M.A. and Ph.D. in Sociology.

Several of Lieberson's notable books have won honors. *Ethnic Patterns in American Cities* (1963) was a revision of his prize-winning dissertation. *A Piece of the Pie: Blacks and White Immigrants Since 1880* (1980) received the Distinguished Contribution to Scholarship Award of the American Sociological Association. *A Matter of Taste: How Names, Fashions, and Culture Change* (2000) was a co-winner of the American Sociological Association's 2001 award for Best Book in the Sociology of Culture, Culture Section, as well as the winner of the Eastern Sociological Society's 2002 Mirra Komarovsky Book Award.

Lieberson has served as president of the American Sociological Association, the Sociological Research Association, and the Pacific Sociological Association. Other professional activities include being a Fellow of the American Academy of Arts and Sciences and a member of the National Academy of Sciences. He is currently Harvard University's Abbott Lawrence Professor of Sociology (Lieberson, "Stanley Lieberson").

Neil Smelser

Neil J. Smelser (1930–) was born in Kahoka, Missouri. He is University Professor Emeritus of Sociology at the University of California–Berkeley. Smelser is from an academic family. Both of his parents were teachers, and all three of their sons ended up in academics. Smelser began his college career at Harvard University. He initially considered following in his father's footsteps and getting a degree in philosophy. However, during his first year at Harvard, Smelser discovered the Department of Social Relations. After graduation, he went to Oxford, where he earned his master's degree. There he decided that he wanted to focus on sociology (Smelser 1984). He earned his doctorate from Harvard in 1958.

Smelser joined the faculty at the University of California–Berkeley that same year. Over the course of his career, his research interests have included sociological theory, economic sociology, collective behavior, the sociology of education, social change, and comparative methods. The numerous books and articles he has authored or coauthored include the text *Sociology,* which has been translated into Italian and Russian; *Social Change in the Industrial Revolution* (1959); *Theory of Collective Behavior* (1962); *Problematics of Sociology: The Georg Simmel Lectures* (1995); and *The Social Edges of Psychoanalysis* (1999).

Smelser received a Rhodes Scholarship to Oxford University and a Guggenheim fellowship. His honors and awards include election to the American Academy of Arts and Sciences, the American Philosophical Society, and the National Academy of Sciences. He also served as the 88th president of the American Sociological Association ("Smelser, Neil" 1983; Smelser, "Neil J. Smelser").

Pitirim A. Sorokin

Pitirim A. Sorokin (1889–1968) was born in Russia. During the Russian Revolution, he participated in a number of anti-Communist activities, opposing leaders including Lenin and Trotsky. His efforts led to his imprisonment and even a death sentence imposed by the Communist government in his province.

After his release, Sorokin founded the first Department of Sociology at the University of St. Petersburg. He was also the department's first professor and departmental chair. In 1922, he was finally banished by the Soviet government for his political activities (Sorokin 1963b).

Sorokin came to the United States first as visiting lecturer on the Russian Revolution, then as a faculty member at the University of Minnesota. In 1930, he became a naturalized American citizen, and the first professor and chair of Harvard University's Department of Sociology. Sorokin remained at Harvard until his retirement in 1959.

Over the course of his career, Sorokin published 200 journal articles, even more editorials and essays, and 35 books, many of which were translated into other languages. His topics included philosophic thought, rural sociology, stratification, social mobility, social change, sexuality, personality, law, revolution, social organization, and the Russian-American relationship. Sorokin's work influenced the theorizing of Harvard colleague Talcott Parsons and his well-known students including Jessie Bernard, Robert K. Merton, and George Homans (who are profiled in this book). Sorokin called his *Fads and Foibles in Modern Sociology and Related Sciences* (1956) "a serious criticism of some of the fashionable currents of thought and research in recent American sociology" and credited it with influencing C. Wright Mills's *Sociological Imagination* (1963a, 296).

Thorstein Veblen

Thorstein Veblen (1857–1929) was born on a Wisconsin farm. He was the 6th of 12 children. His parents were Norwegian immigrants, and Veblen later studied Scandinavian cultures and interests (Edgell 2001). Veblen's father sent him to Carleton College, a conservative Christian school, without consulting his son as to whether he desired to attend. Veblen graduated from Carleton but never fit in. He was out of place as a Norwegian, an agnostic, and an irreverent student (Coser 1977, 277). Not fitting in was a pattern that followed Veblen throughout his subsequent studies at Johns Hopkins University and Yale, where he earned a doctorate in 1884. Veblen could not get a job after earning his doctorate, so he returned to the family farm. In 1891, after marrying, Veblen, "wearing a coonskin cap," went to Cornell University to study economics (Davis 1968, 303).

Over the course of his professional career, he taught at the University of Chicago, Stanford University, the University of Missouri, and the New School for Social Research. He also held a government position. Veblen's problems with fitting in followed him throughout these positions. His writings were radical and his teaching methods unorthodox. His affairs with women led to further employment problems.

Veblen "developed an economic sociology of capitalism that criticized the acquisitiveness and predatory competition of American society and the power of the corporation" (Abercrombie, Hill, and Turner 2000, 373). His most famous work was *The Theory of the Leisure Class* (1967, orig. 1899), which he wrote while at Chicago, analyzing patterns of "conspicuous consumption" and "conspicuous waste." Veblen also used the concept of culture lag (see chapter 3) to analyze social processes (Davis 1968, 304). He also edited the *Journal of Political Economy.*

In 1918, Veblen became editor of the *Dial,* founded by Ralph Waldo Emerson. That led to his widespread popularity. Lewis Coser quotes one observer who noted that there were "Veblenists, Veblen clubs, Veblen remedies for the sorrows of the world . . . even . . . Veblen girls" (1977, 287). However, Veblen's popularity eventually waned as he continued to publish controversial viewpoints and be at odds with professional colleagues. He became increasingly reclusive, thinking he had been forgotten, and died of heart disease in 1929. Ironically, Veblen's work was rediscovered during the Great Depression that started the year of his death. His work was incorporated into sociology courses and sales of his books increased rapidly (Coser 1977, 289).

CAREERS IN SOCIOLOGY

Those with an interest and training in social change and collective action have backgrounds that prepare them for careers including

- activist
- advocate for special-interest groups
- communications director
- community developer
- development officer

- disaster-relief-organization director/staff
- evaluation researcher
- fiscal analyst
- foreign-service worker
- fund-raiser
- grant writer
- human-resources-organization director/staff
- international-aid-agency staff
- journalist
- lobbying researcher
- lobbyist
- military-affairs analyst
- nonprofit-organization director/staff
- outreach coordinator
- planning director
- policy analyst
- political staff
- political strategist
- politician
- program evaluator
- program manager/director
- program/project coordinator
- public archivist
- public relations specialist
- relocation coordinator
- resource developer
- social activist
- social historian
- special-vents coordinator
- strategic planner

Additional Resources

American Sociological Association, Collective Behavior and Social Movements. http://www.asanet.org/sectioncbsm/. This section of the American Sociological Association focuses on the study of people in action in wide-ranging situations, from crowds to disasters to social movements.

Best, Joel, ed. 2001. *How Claims Spread: Cross-National Diffusion of Social Problems.* Hawthorne, N.Y.: Aldine de Gruyter. This collection of research articles on diverse issues examines how social problems are constructed and spread across time and culture.

Freeman, Jo, and Victoria Johnson, eds. 1999. *Waves of Protest: Social Movements since the Sixties.* Lanham, Md.: Rowman and Littlefield. This series of essays draws from research on a variety of different social movements to discuss social movement mobilization, organization, consciousness, strategy and tactics, and decline.

Lieberson, Stanley. 2000. *A Matter of Taste: How Names, Fashions, and Culture Change.* New Haven, Conn.: Yale University Press. The author uses first names as a starting point to understand the mechanism behind how fashions, taste, and culture change.

McAdam, Doug, and David A. Snow, eds. 1997. *Social Movements: Readings on their Emergence, Mobilization, and Dynamic.* Los Angeles: Roxbury. The dynamics of social movements are addressed by drawing from a wide range of movements around the world and a focus on cultural and gender issues.

Miller, David L. 2000. *Introduction to Collective Behavior and Collective Action.* 2nd. ed. Prospect Heights, Ill.: Waveland Press. This textbook covers a range of issues and research studies that illustrate the concepts in the title.

MoveOn.org. http://www.moveon.org/. Visit this site to see how it leverages the power of the Internet to encourage grassroots involvement in politics and build electronic advocacy groups.

Piven, Frances Fox, and Richard A. Cloward. 1977. *Poor People's Movements.* New York: Vintage. This book assesses the successes and failures of four twentieth-century U.S. social movements associated with the poor.

Public Agenda Online. http://www.publicagenda.org/. This organization provides a wealth of information regarding public opinion on topics largely of political and policy interest.

Public Knowledge Project. http://www.pkp.ubc.ca/about/index.html. This site is part of an effort to explore the ability and role of new technologies in making scholarly research more accessible and usable. This project is discussed in John Willinsky's book *If Only We Knew* (see below).

Willinsky, John. 2000. *If Only We Knew: Increasing the Public Value of Social Science Research.* New York: Routledge. This book explores how the Internet can be used to make social-science research a public resource, generating support and understanding, and helping citizens better engage in public issues. Visit the Public Knowledge Project, cited above, in conjunction with the first chapter.

CHAPTER 10

Research Methods

Understanding what sociologists do and how they do it requires an introduction to the basics of sociological investigation. In conducting research, sociologists follow scientific guidelines incorporating an assortment of theories and methods that provide for accuracy in gathering, processing, and making sense of information. Conducting scientific research provides a way for sociologists to accomplish one of the central tasks of sociology, "gather[ing] factual information about the work of social life" (Sherman 1985, 23). Research methodology is one of most important subfields in sociology (Simon and Scherer 1999).

Emile Durkheim (1858–1917), profiled below, conducted early research demonstrating that sociology can be used to scientifically expose the impact of social factors on our lives. His topic was suicide, an event that may initially appear to be entirely dependent on internal factors such as depression. Rather than looking at the circumstances surrounding individual cases of suicide, Durkheim (1966) looked at rates of suicides. Using data drawn from government sources, he was able to demonstrate that there are social forces at work.

By looking for social factors that increase the likelihood of suicide, Durkheim showed that suicide is related to **social integration,** or *the strength of social ties connecting individuals to society.* He found suicide rates were higher among men and the wealthy. Rates were also higher among Protestants rather than Catholics, the unmarried rather than the married, and the childless rather than parents. Suicide rates were lower in rural areas. Each of these factors, he argued, was related to how integrated these groups are into the social fabric.

Durkheim even found that suicide rates were lower during times of political crisis. He explained that "great social disturbances and great popular wars rouse collective sentiments, stimulate partisan spirit and patriotism and, concentrating activity towards a single end, at least temporarily, cause a stronger integration of society" (1966, 12). Later research looking at suicide rates among

Australian women during World War II supported Durkheim's findings (O'Malley 1975). Suicide rates for women fell when Australia entered the war, when the war went badly in North Africa, and when Singapore fell, threatening Australian security.

CONDUCTING SOCIOLOGICAL RESEARCH

Sociologists use theories (see chapter 2) as the basis for expressing "their assumptions or hypotheses very systematically and discuss[ing] in a very comprehensive way how far their theories explain social life . . . they provide new insights into behavior and the workings of societies" (Wallace and Wolf 1991, 3). **Hypotheses** are *theory-based statements about the relationship between two or more factors that can be tested through research.* Sociologists call these factors *variables.* **Variables** are *factors whose value changes (or varies) from case to case.* Age, sex, and income are all examples of variables. The hypothesis should state how changes in one variable will impact the other variable. The statement "As level of education increases, income will also increase" is an example of a hypothesis that can be tested by research that compares the two variables.

Sociologists try to determine whether there is a causal relationship between variables. Having a **causal relationship** means that *one variable produces a change in another variable.* "The amount of alcohol consumed by a driver increases the likelihood that the driver will have an accident" provides an illustration of a causal relationship. A causal relationship between two variables is not the same as a *correlation.* A **correlation** means that *two variables change together in some predictable way.* When one variable changes, the other variable also changes, but not because one variable actually causes the other to change. The actual cause of the change is some other factor outside of the two variables. Finding that outside factor often requires additional research.

A well-used example that illustrates the difference between causation and correlation is provided by a study that found a correlation between the number of storks in an area of northwestern Europe and the number of babies born in that area. Where there were more storks, there were also more babies. However, contrary to the old tale that storks bring babies, there is no causal relationship between these two variables. This is an example of a **spurious relationship.** There was *an apparent connection between variables that was actually false, or the result of something else.* In this case, the correlation is due to a third variable—urbanization. Larger concentrations of people meant more babies and more housing with chimneys, which provided more nesting places for storks (cited in Singleton et al. 1993).

It is important that sociologists know the accuracy and limits of their research. To this end, they need to know the validity of their data. **Validity** refers to *whether the research actually measures what the researcher intends to measure.* For example, researchers who want to measure self-esteem need to ensure that they are not actually measuring something else that might be related to self-esteem, such as the person's unusually bad or good experience at work or in class that particular day that might impact how they respond to questions about their abilities (Sullivan 2001, 132). Sociologists also need to know the reliability of their data. **Reliability** refers to *whether research results would be the same if the research were repeated at different times or if the same thing were studied in different ways.* Researchers have various procedures to assess and establish validity and reliability (Campbell and Stanley 1963; Zeller and Carmines 1980).

Sociologists also try to practice **objectivity** when conducting research, *not allowing personal opinions or biases to influence the research, outcomes, or interpretation of the data.* Max Weber (1946) advocated a value-free sociology. He thought that sociologists should be objective and sociology should be detached or disinterested from any personal or political interests. Many sociologists feel that abandoning Weber's position could lead to inaccurate research findings (Gordon 1988).

Objectivity can be a challenge to researchers, partly because sociologists are humans who do bring their own perspectives and biases with them to the research arena. They also sometimes conduct research in areas they find personally difficult or offensive. For example, James Carey (1972) sometimes felt in danger when studying amphetamine users, because his research subjects were erratic and could be violent. Diana Scully (1990) conducted a series of face-to-face interviews with convicted rapists to study the question of why men rape. In her research, she found that rape was frequently used as punishment, revenge, an antecedent to another crime such as burglary, and a means to access sexually unavailable women. Overwhelmingly, the interviews revealed objectification and contempt of women by men who expressed pleasure in the act. Scully reports finding some of these interviews to be difficult for her, particularly those in which the rapist took obvious glee in the details of his crime.

Rebecca Campbell (2002) also studied rape and examined the impact of the research on the researcher. She argued that emotions can be useful in research, actually enhancing the researcher's understanding of the issue. To sociologist Dorothy Smith, profiled below, research should reflect the perspective of those who are the subjects of the research, not the researcher. Feminist researchers such as Smith also emphasize the idea that research subjects should benefit from research rather than just be used for the researcher's benefit.

SOCIOLOGICAL RESEARCH METHODS

To conduct research, sociologists must gather data. **Data** are *"any pieces or assemblages of information gathered for the purpose of research"* (Sherman and Straus 2002, 45, emphasis mine). Data can take a variety of forms, and includes "any information gathered by a researcher in order to develop insights. A list of companies polluting the groundwater in a county, the titles of books persons remember enjoying reading when they were children, physicians' explanations of how they select drugs for people with AIDS, and descriptions of the body language used by U.S. senators when questioning a potential Supreme

Court justice are all examples of information that could be used as data by sociologists" (Sherman and Straus 2002, 45).

Sherman and Straus (2002) organize data gathering into four different methods: methods of questioning, methods of noticing, methods of analysis, and methods of explanation. The following sections will highlight some of the ways sociologists might tackle these methods. Keep in mind that an entire book (indeed, many books) could be written addressing each of these methods. The information here merely provides an introductory foray into sociological research.

Questioning

One of the most widely used tools that sociologists rely on to address questions about the social world is the survey. A **survey** is *research in which people are asked questions by an interviewer or provided in a questionnaire to determine their attitudes, opinions, and behaviors.* Surveys try to represent the views or attitudes of a **population universe,** *all the people in the group to which the results will be applied.* To accomplish this, researchers have to generate a sample of people that represent this larger population. A **sample** is *a subset of the larger population that will serve as the data source.*

Samples may be selected based on specific characteristics. These types of samples are called **nonprobability samples.** A researcher interested in the experiences of college students might be particularly interested in what transfer students or returning students have to say. She might go to the transfer student office and survey the first ten students that walk into the office every day for a month. This technique will provide opinions of some transfer students, but there is no way to be sure that these students' perspectives represent all transfer students. They may be unique in some way (e.g., the "early-birds" might be older or part-time students who stop in at the office on their way to full-time jobs and have very different attitudes than younger or unemployed students). A probability sample would overcome this problem.

In **probability samples,** various techniques are used *to ensure that every individual person in the population universe has an equal chance of being selected.* This type of sample is also called a **random sample** because probability samples are rooted in probability theory, researchers can estimate how well their sample really does represent the population they want it to represent. In reality, however, certain people are regularly eliminated from that population universe because they are difficult to contact. This generally includes people living in institutions (e.g., prisons, long-term care facilities), people living in temporary residences, and military personnel.

Surveys can take the form of questionnaires or interviews. **Questionnaires** provide *a series of written questions to which participants are asked to respond.* The survey might be designed so that respondents must choose from a series of pre-selected responses (in a format much like a multiple-choice examination) or they might allow the person to respond freely with longer, more in-depth or descriptive responses. The questionnaire may also combine these formats depending on the research design.

Interviews provide *a series of questions administered by a person.* Interviews may be conducted face-to-face, by telephone, or even video-teleconferencing. The structure of interviews varies depending on the purposes of the research. The interview may be very structured following a specific question order to a more free-flowing type of interview that allows the person being interviewed to elaborate on answers, with follow-up questions arising out of those responses (Sherman and Straus, 2002, 46–53).

Researchers must be careful when using surveys to be sure that their results are accurate. They must be sure their sample population actually does represent the population universe. They must consider issues of validity and reliability as discussed above. They must also pay close attention to what percentage of people they select for their sample actually participate in the research (Melevin 1997).

However, accurate survey results depend on good sampling techniques, not surveying large numbers of people. Although the U.S. population numbers over 200 million people, typical public-opinion polls (an example of surveys) only use 1,000 to 1,500 respondents. An example of the importance of good sampling rather than large numbers of respondents is provided by two major polls that were conducted to predict the outcome of the 1936 U.S. presidential election (Bryson 1976). The race was between Republican Alfred E. Landon and Democrat Franklin Delano Roosevelt. *Literary Digest* sent out 10 million ballot surveys asking people which candidate they supported in the upcoming presidential election. They used telephone directories, club membership lists, and car registrations to develop their mailing list. The result was a largely upper-class, and traditionally Republican, sample of people who could afford cars and telephones in 1936. On the basis of the more than 2 million responses they received, *Literary Digest* predicted a 57 percent to 43 percent Landon victory. However, 61 percent of the vote, and the presidency, went to Roosevelt.

George Gallup and the American Institute of Public Opinion (now the Gallup Organization, an internationally known polling organization) accurately predicted Roosevelt's win. They did so by using scientific sampling techniques and polling only 300,000 people. Although that would be a huge number of people to poll today, it is a significantly smaller sample than the *Literary Digest* poll.

Many people in the United States are also familiar with a variety of **pseudo-polls,** *nonscientific and nonrepresentative polling efforts* (ESOMAR/WAPOR 1998). These include **self-selection polls,** in which *the participants themselves choose whether to participate rather than being selected through some scientific sampling method.* Self-selection polls take a variety of forms including convenience polls and televoting. **Convenience polls**—*querying those who are at hand*—include such nonscientific surveys as person-on-the-street interviews (e.g., journalists stopping members of the public and asking their opinion on some topic), mail-in coupons, and questionnaires in popular magazines. **Televoting**—*callers recording their opinions by telephoning a particular phone number*—is another misleading polling technique. The popular television show *American Idol,* where contestants compete for a music-recording contract, uses this technique, with the audience voting on their preferred singer among a weekly field of contestants. Self-selection polls are also popular on the Internet.

Other pseudo-polls are actually intended to disseminate, rather than gather, information. Telemarketers, special-interest groups, and political campaigns sometimes use **push polls** to communicate biased information. In these so-called polls, *questions are often worded as statements that support, or "push," a particular position.* This may be done during a political campaign to produce inaccurate poll results that support a particular position. Another practice, **fund-raising under the guise of polling (frugging),** involves *telephone calls or mailings that are actually intended to solicit donations but are disguised as opinion polls.* Since these practices are formulated to present a position, generate a particular response, or get funding, they are of no value in determining public opinion. Scientific polls, unlike pseudo-polls, use good sampling methodology and gather, rather than impart, information (ESOMAR/WAPOR 1998).

Sociologists also sometime use focus groups in their research. **Focus groups** are *in-depth, qualitative interviews with a specifically selected small number of people.* The focus group technique originated in work by Robert K. Merton (profiled in chapter 2). Focus groups are routinely used in marketing to represent consumer populations. Through moderated discussions, focus-group participants respond to open-ended questions designed to elicit their perceptions and responses on a range of issues and ideas. They are used for such efforts as soliciting general reactions and feedbacks to products, movies, or even political issues. Focus groups also provide new ideas and assist researchers in developing more refined questionnaires (Edmunds 1999).

Noticing

Sociologists think of the world as a social laboratory. This requires that they often go out into society, or *the field,* to conduct research, or *fieldwork.* This often involves **ethnographic research (ethnography),** a *"social science method that involves the observation of the interactions of everyday life"* (Warren 2000, 852). Ethnography is observational research that seeks to understand the social organization of people's daily lives and their natural worlds.

There are various types of observational research (Adler and Adler 1984). In some studies, the researcher becomes an active participant in the social situations they are researching. William Foote Whyte, profiled in chapter 11, spent several years participating in the life of "Cornerville," a run-down section of Boston. Whyte befriended a member of the neighborhood, who introduced him to other residents and familiarized him with the subculture of the community. Whyte was able to study the area in more richness and detail than he could have otherwise, even living there after marrying (Whyte 1943).

Ethnographic research contributes to **verstehen,** *Max Weber's concept that sociologists should develop subjective understanding by taking someone else's position mentally to understand their social world, lives, and perspectives.* Because ethnography takes this micro focus, it is often associated with symbolic-interactionist theory (described in chapter 2) and can be traced back to the early sociologists studying city life at the University of Chicago (discussed in chapter 8). Other research discussed throughout this book is also ethnographic, including Goffman's (1959) dramaturgical study of how we present ourselves to others, in chapter 4, and Becker's (1963) studies of deviance, discussed in chapter 6. Some researchers, such as William Foote Whyte, have built their careers by conducting well-done ethnographic research.

Sociologists also *conduct research using data that was collected by other people for a purpose other than the research for which it is being used.* This type of data is known as **secondary data.** Data from the U.S. Census, crime statistics, and government documents are all examples of secondary data. Some secondary data regularly used by sociologists consists of large national studies. For example, the National Survey of Families and Households (NSFH) was conducted by the Center for Demography, University of Wisconsin, and funded by government grants (National Survey of Families and Households, home page). It contains a variety of quantitative information from thousands of participants about family life. The data set was made available to researchers who have questions they want to study that can be addressed by using the information that study collected. Using this extensive data set, researchers have been able to examine areas as wide-ranging as divorce, stepfamilies, caring for children and the elderly, cohabitation, childbearing decisions, contraceptive sterilization, and aging, to name a few (NSFH homepage).

Analyzing

The range of data-analysis techniques sociologists employ is well beyond the scope of this book. However, there are some basics to data analysis that are important in understanding the overall social-science research process. Sociologist Paul Lazarsfeld, profiled below, developed several methods of analysis that are important research tools, or the basis of many of the tools, used by sociologists today.

Much sociological research is **quantitative,** meaning that it is *based on numerical analysis of data.* The U.S. Census and the NSFH are examples of quantitative research. Sociological research can also be **qualitative,** meaning that it is *based on the interpretation of nonnumerical data.* Goffman's dramaturgical analyses and Garfinkel's ethnomethodological studies, discussed in chapter 4, are examples of qualitative research. Sociologists select the best type of research strategy to answer their question. They may even mix and match quantitative and qualitative methods to get a more complex picture of their topic.

Sociologists must also consider whether routine means of gathering data are appropriate or provide the best approaches. For example, the homeless live in places such as subway tunnels and may change location depending on time of day. This means the usual ways of gathering data (e.g., telephone surveys, mailing surveys, even going door to door) are not useful in conducting research on the homeless and researchers must devise appropriate strategies for data gathering (Dept of HUD 2004; Jencks 1994; Simpson and Middleton 1997). Geographic information systems, generally considered tools for geographers, surveyors, or outdoor enthusiasts, also provide new ways for sociologists to analyze urban crime patterns (Carrozza and Seufert 1997). Sociologist Andrew Greeley, profiled below, has even developed interactive data-analysis techniques that he works into the novels he writes.

In studying public opinion, Stanley Milgram (1977), profiled below, devised a novel method he felt would eliminate several common problems, such as participant's providing politically correct replies to interviewers. He used a "lost-letter technique" in which he placed stamped, addressed letters at strategic places around a city, such as telephone booths. The idea was to give the appearance that the letter owner had lost the letter before mailing it. The letters were addressed to various fictitious organizations. Some were addressed to communist or Nazi organizations, some to a medical-research group, and others to a private person. Milgram noted how many letters were returned to each organization, as a rough measure of community orientations toward political institutions. He saw mailing the letter as providing tacit support of the addressee. Over 70% of the letters addressed to the medical-research group and the private person were returned. Only a quarter of those to the communists or Nazi parties were returned. Additionally, few of the letters in the former group had been opened before being returned; almost one-half of the letters in the latter group had been opened. This unobtrusive approach provided an inventive way to find gross differences of opinion where there is strong public sentiment and polarization on an issue.

Before analyzing their research results, sociologists must have the data in a format that allows them to examine and manipulate it. Some data, such as quantitative data from public opinion polls or consumer surveys, is put into computerized databases. This format allows the researchers to write computer programs to perform their analyses. Qualitative data might be in the form of interview transcripts or handwritten notes of research observations. Sociologists' data might also be in some other format. Some sociologists, for example, use visual imagery in their analyses, so they have collections of photographs or videos to analyze. Additionally, they should be sure to **clean the data.** This does not mean that they change it; rather, it means they *perform some procedure to double-check its accuracy.*

Sociologists use a variety of methods to analyze data and decide what it means. They might use basic **descriptive statistics,** *procedures that assist in organizing, analyzing, and interpreting data.* These procedures provide summaries that are familiar to many people. They may be as basic as determining the **average** (*arithmetic mean*), **median** (*the center number, where exactly half the numbers are higher in value and half are lower*), or the **mode** (*the most frequently occurring value*). They may also employ **inferential statistics** that *make general-*

izations from sample data to larger population. These techniques are based on **probability theories** used by statisticians that *estimate the likelihood that something will occur*—for example, the likelihood of winning a raffle when buying one ticket (Sullivan 2001, 421–49). As noted above, these are the same theories behind probability samples. These analyses can involve special sophisticated statistical techniques. Sociologists must be aware that, if not conducted carefully and presented appropriately, statistics can be misleading or give a completely wrong picture of the situation (Best 2001; Campbell 1999). The implications can be serious, especially when the statistics are used to formulate policies on social issues.

In analyzing qualitative data, sociologists use techniques that allow researchers to see patterns. Rather than trying to support preconceived theories, they often let patterns emerge from the data (Sullivan 2001, 450–74). They look at attitudes, beliefs, and behaviors just as quantitative researchers do; they simply approach their processes of investigation, discovery, and analysis in a different way.

Explaining

In an **experiment,** the researchers set up *a controlled situation in which they can manipulate at least one independent variable.* They pay particular attention to trying to determine whether any causal relationship exists between variables as discussed above. Milgram's research on obedience (1963, 1974) and Zimbardo's Stanford Prison Experiment (Zimbardo 1972, 2000; Haney, Banks, and Zimbardo 1973), discussed in chapter 5, are examples of this type of research. Experiments are not as widely used in sociology as other research methods. They are more commonly used by psychologists or social psychologists, like Milgram and Zimbardo. Experiments can test causality, but they are sometimes criticized for not being realistic, and the findings are hard to generalize to other populations (Kish 1987).

When conducting experiments and other research, researchers must be careful to guard against influencing the results of their research. They must design their research to avoid the **Hawthorne Effect,** which refers to *results achieved because research subjects know they are being studied.* The term comes from studies conducted at Western Electric's Hawthorne plant in the 1920s and 1930s (Roethlisberger and Dickson 1939; Mayo 1933). To study how various working conditions impacted productivity, the researchers made a number of changes around the plant, such as lighting, work schedules, and break periods. They found that any change increased productivity, even those changes that they thought were not helpful to workers (e.g., decreasing the lighting). Productivity also stayed higher even when they changed the conditions back to what they had been originally. The increases in productivity were actually due to the workers knowing that they were participating in a research study. They were working harder because of the attention they were receiving and the interest generated by the research, not because the physical changes necessarily improved their ability to do their jobs.

Sociologists may also combine their research tools and skills to conduct evaluation research. The focus of **evaluation research** is to *plan or assess the efficiency and effectiveness of various interventions and programs.* Sociologists follow several basic steps to conduct evaluations (Koppel 2001; Steele 1996). This type of research provides a way to scientifically examine whether an organization's goal are being met, to determine any impact programs are having, and to design new policies and approaches to address social issues (Rossi, Freeman, and Lipsey 1999; Peterson et al. 1994; Weiss 1998). Because evaluation research is examining programs and policies, researchers need to be especially prepared to deal with the political issues that may be involved.

RESEARCH ETHICS

Research ethics have been a concern for sociologists since the discipline was founded (Bellah 1983). Sociologists must be concerned that their research does not harm or mislead research participants. Concerns about research ethics involving human subjects came to public attention during the post–World War II Nuremburg Trials of Nazi physicians (Bower and deGusparis 1978). During the Vietnam era, suspicions grew as to how the government might use research findings. The National Research Act was passed in 1974 that mandated institutional review boards (IRBs) that approve research projects to ensure they are ethical. Additional guidance was later provided by the Code of Federal Regulations Governing Research on Human Subjects (45 CFR 46) (Iutcovich and Hoppe 2001).

The American Sociological Association (ASA) and other professional sociological organizations consider ethical behavior so important that they have developed a code of ethics focusing on research that provides guidelines to be followed by members. The first ASA Code of Ethics became effective in 1971 (ASA Code of Ethics). It has been updated several times. Many principles shared by ethical professional codes that have been identified by Iutcovich and Hoppe (2001, 57–58) include

- the competence of professionals doing the work
- honesty and fairness, including an awareness of potential conflicts of interest and no inclusion of harmful activities
- upholding scientific standards, objectivity, and responsibility for actions
- respect for others
- social responsibility—a requirement to consider the potential impact of research

Several sociological studies have involved serious ethical concerns. The experiments by Milgram (1963, 1974) and Zimbardo (Zimbardo 1972, 2000; Haney, Banks, and Zimbardo 1973) presented serious ethical questions regarding whether or not the participants experienced psychological harm. Additionally, research conducted by Laud Humphreys (1970) is often cited in introductory textbooks as an example of unethical research and the types of concerns of which sociologists should be aware.

Humphreys studied male casual and anonymous homosexual behavior in "tearooms" which are places such as public restrooms. He offered to be a "watch queen," acting as a lookout for male participants of sex acts who would warn them of others approaching the restroom. This allowed him to be present while the activity occurred. Unknown to the participants in those acts, Humphreys took notes on the behavior he observed.

To find out more about those men's lives, he recorded the license plate numbers of over 100 men. He was able to obtain their names and addresses through public motor-vehicle records. A year later, Humphreys went to their homes in disguise, where he interviewed them on the pretense of conducting a social-health survey. Humphreys found from this research that most of these men led conventional lives. They had families, held jobs, and were respected community members.

Humphreys has been criticized for deception, not providing informed consent to his research subjects, and violating their privacy. In response, he argued that there was no other way to gain the information he had obtained. He also argued that no one was harmed and participants' confidentiality was maintained throughout the research. Humphreys did receive an award for his book, *The Tearoom Trade,* as well as support for showing that these sexual preferences were more common than previously believed (Warwick 1973). However, his research is still ethically controversial.

RESEARCH ON THE INTERNET

The Internet clearly provides sociologists and social researchers both new research opportunities and challenges. Harris Interactive, an organization that has conducted polls for several decades, has developed a technique of online research that they argue is very close in validity to older methods of conducting surveys by telephone or mail. Their approach involves registering willing online participants and sometimes offering incentives to participate in research. Advantages of Internet surveys over traditional methods may include better accuracy of results, faster data collection, and less cost (Bayer 2003).

The Internet is also a rich research venue for conducting qualitative studies. Focus-group research, for example, can be conducted online and even "transformed" to include people in different locations and those who would not have been able to participate in face-to-face discussions. The use of specially designed software tools to record group interaction documents and reveals patterns of decision making by participants (Mann and Stewart 2000).

E-mail has been utilized as a research tool, for example, in assessing adolescent risk behavior. Using e-mail journals, researchers were able to study teen behaviors and spend a great deal of time "listening" to what the teens had to say. The teens liked having that amount of attention paid to their inputs. E-mail is cheap, fast, and reliable. It allowed large amounts of text to be transmitted quickly and accurately to the researchers and provided them a regular inflow of fresh data (Hessler et al. 2003). E-mail has even been used by researchers who applied Milgram's lost-letter technique to study cyberspace (Castelli, Zogmaister, and Arcuri 2001).

Using the Internet and other information and collaborative technologies in research raises a host of issues. The Internet provides a plethora of readily accessible information that is potentially of value to researchers. Research participants are also readily available online for researchers interested in that user population. However, conducting research online provides new challenges in determining the usefulness of materials, including the quality of information, the level of available information (e.g., introductory or more advanced), and the expertise of the author (Bell 2001). Ethical guidelines require that researchers be aware of technical issues involving anonymity and privacy (Cho and LaRose 1999). Additionally, in the virtual world of the Internet where identities are easily constructed and reconstructed (e.g., Bell 2001; Kendall 2002) and where hackers and unauthorized users are rampant, researchers are faced with finding ways to establish that their research participants are really who they say they are. David Bell (2001, 186–204) covers a number of other non-method-specific considerations that arise when conducting online research.

The existence of the Internet itself also provides research issues that did not previously exist. As David Bell says, "we need to consider issues that arise when (i) researching cyberspace, (ii) researching *in* cyberspace, and (iii) researching *cyberspace in cyberspace*" (2001, 187). Even the very organization of Web sites and the included links is, in itself, worthy of research (Bell 2001).

THE RESEARCH PROCESS

Sociologists use the tools they have to design research that best fits the circumstances, issues, and questions they are investigating. There is no exact process that they follow in conducting their inquiries. There are, however, certain steps that all sociological research involves in some form and at some stage in the research process.

Select and define a question. Sociologists can study anything in the social world that catches their interest. Obviously, there is no end to the topics they might address. One of the first challenges sociologists face in conducting research is to refine their interest into a specific research question. These questions may arise from some long-standing personal interest. The questions may be assigned by someone the sociologist works for, such as the head of a government agency. They may develop out of the sociologists' conversations with professional colleagues, clients, students, or others even in nonacademic social situations. Stanley Milgram, for example, developed research based on discussions with his family (Takooshian 2000).

Learn what any existing research says. Like other scientific research, sociological investigation builds on what others have already learned about the topic at hand. An early step in the research process is to read the existing literature on the topic. Finding the work that has already been done on the topic involves a number of approaches, including visiting libraries, searching databases, and contacting other researchers interested in the topic.

By doing this background work, sociologists can discover what theories and methods have been applied in previous research. They can also look for any problems that other researchers have encountered and any suggestions for further research offered in these studies. They may discover that their question has already been answered to their satisfaction. In that case, they might determine that there is no need to replicate something that has already been done. Or they might determine that there is a new way to examine the issue, so they refine their research question and address it a bit differently than originally envisioned.

Design a research methodology that incorporates ethical considerations. Sociologists select research strategies to fit the question they are asking. They may use a variety of skills and incorporate both qualitative and quantitative methods. For example, Aaron Young (2000) combined three approaches to study the implications of a juvenile-curfew law that a city council was considering overturning. He used telephone surveys, self-administered questionnaires, and secondary analysis of data on citations issued for curfew violations to develop a more complex picture of the situation than would have been available using just one technique. He was able to reveal information about who supported the curfew and whether it was disproportionately impacting minority youth. He was even able to suggest ways to curb youth deviance beyond relying on curfews.

Research strategies should also take into consideration such issues as how much the research will cost, how it will be funded, and who will work on the project. Some research can be conducted with no financial costs using resources readily available to the researcher (e.g., data from government publications or freely available public databases). Some research may be paid for by grants from government sources or other organizations.

The research design must also incorporate ethical considerations. It should be legal and meet the ethical standards set forth by professional organizations. Many universities and other institutions also require that all research designs be approved by ethics review boards before research begins. These boards ensure that any potential harm to participants and issues such as privacy have been properly considered.

Conduct the research. Gathering data is generally the lengthiest part of the research process. Some types of research may be concluded in a few days or weeks. For example, researchers that conduct quantitative analyses using data previously generated from national surveys may be able to complete this part of their research within a short time frame. Researchers that go into the field and conduct ethnographic research may take years to complete this phase of the research process. In this phase, sociologists should try to be objective. They should also use care to record their data accurately and in ways they can understand later.

Analyze the data. Researchers must analyze their data and determine what it means. In this stage of the process, they decide what they have learned from their research. By analyzing and studying the data, sociologists are able to determine what their research tells them about their question. If the research was based on a hypothesis, they can decide whether that hypothesis is supported, or whether it should be rejected or modified in some way. This step in the process may require expertise in certain research strategies or statistical procedures.

Researchers also have several other things to consider in this stage of their research. They should think about whether there were any problems with their research (e.g., problems encountered during the research that may have made a difference in the research results). This may allow them to suggest different or better research methods for future research. They should consider the limits of their research (e.g., to which groups it applies and does not apply).

Report the results. Sociologists share and communicate what they find in a variety of ways. The most common methods of sharing their findings are to present them at a professional meeting of sociologists or by publishing the findings in a professional sociology journal. Both of these venues are designed to allow other sociologists and students to learn more about the topic and the theories and methods used to conduct the research. They also allow researchers to receive feedback from other researchers on their work. Some sociologists present their research to corporate or business clients, in books, or in articles for the popular press. They may also be interviewed by journalists about their work. Sometimes, they are even asked to speak to Congress as experts on their topic (Herring 2002).

These presentations should all be customized to suit the audience. When writing for a professional journal primarily read by colleagues or students, sociologists often use technical terminology and go into detail about their research methods. These articles often include detailed tables of analyses that help colleagues evaluate the quality of the research and the results. When presenting research to a corporate client, or other non-sociologist group, sociologists might use a series of computer-generated slides with short statements and bullet points. If reporting their research to a corporate or general audience, they typically try to avoid technical terms unfamiliar to nonsociologists, focusing on the results and what the results mean for individuals. When directing their research findings to politicians, they might focus on putting the research into larger social context by discussing what previous research found, their own results, and the larger social implications of their results.

BIOGRAPHIES

Emile Durkheim

Emile Durkheim (1858–1917) was the first French academic sociologist and one of the "founding fathers" of the discipline. Durkheim "stands out as sociology's most successful founder, not only because he established the field in the elite university system in France, but also because he gave it enough of method and intellectual content so that it could be built upon elsewhere . . .

Durkheim is the archetypical sociologist because institutionally he had to be most conscious of what would make sociology a distinctive science in its own right" (Collins 1994, 45–46).

Durkheim was born in the French province of Lorraine. His father was a rabbi, descended from a long line of rabbis (Coser 1977, 143). Durkheim planned to become a rabbi himself, and attended a rabbinical school to prepare. As a young man, he became interested in Catholicism and then turned away from anything other than a scholarly interest in religion. However, he incorporated religion into his sociological works. Durkheim's last major work, *The Elementary Forms of Religious Life* (1912), remains an important work on the sociology of religion.

Durkheim was devoted to academics. He worked throughout his life to establish sociology as an academic discipline and held the first full professorship in social science in France. As one biographer says, Durkheim "did more to inculcate a sociological perspective across the spectrum of academic disciplines than any other figure, with the possible exception of Marx" (Thompson 1982, 17).

He also devoted his career to "construct[ing] a scientific sociological system, not as an end in itself, but as a means for the moral direction of society. From this purpose Durkheim never departed" (Coser 1977, 145). He traveled to Germany, where he was impressed by the scientific research he observed. In 1889, Durkheim established and became the editor of the scholarly sociology journal *L'Annee Sociologique,* emphasizing the importance of methodological research (Coser 1977, 147). "He was convinced that the journal, by its scope and scholarship, could do more for the establishment of sociology than any single work" (Thompson 1982, 27). In the decade immediately following the establishment of his journal, Durkheim produced three of his most famous works: *The Division of Labor in Society* (1964a, orig. 1893), *The Rules of Sociological Method* (1964b, orig. 1895), and *Suicide* (1966, orig. 1897).

Andrew M. Greeley

Andrew M. Greeley (1928–) has a unique background among his sociologist colleagues. In addition to being a sociologist, Greeley also fills varied roles, including priest, professor, researcher, columnist, and novelist.

Greeley was ordained a Catholic priest in 1954, a vocation he had sought since the second grade. He found the largely Irish population in his parish different, specifically more affluent and educated, than immigrants he had learned about in seminary. This was particularly true for the youth. As a result, Greeley began to study sociology to learn more about issues such as social class (Greeley 1990, 134). In 1959, he published his first book, *The Church in the Suburbs,* which addressed changes this upward mobility of the laity would have on the church.

Greeley's interests eventually led to his enrollment at the University of Chicago, where he obtained his doctorate in 20 months. As part of his dissertation, he began working with the National Opinion Research Center (NORC), an independent, nonprofit research center that is affiliated with the university. Greeley still continues that affiliation.

Over the course of his career, his three main sociological interests have been studies of Catholic education, empirical studies on ethnic subcultures in the United States, and reformulating questions in the sociology of religion as a cultural system. He has empirically documented changes within the Catholic Church and Catholic opinions. Greeley's work devotes a great deal of attention to looking at the variety of ways religion can be treated as a variable in sociological analyses and how sociologists measure subjective concepts such as religiosity, religious behavior, or religious imagination (e.g., how people view God). He has conducted research on such varied topics as the sociology of the country club, the paranormal, and papal elections. Greeley's numerous publications include *The Mary Myth* (1977), a look at the Catholic devotion to Mary, the mother of Jesus, from a sociological perspective (Greely 1986, 1990, 1999).

Applying his interests in new directions, Greeley began to write novels about his sociological research topics. He has now authored over 30 best-selling novels and two autobiographies. In his novels, Greeley employs interactive data-analysis techniques, utilizing data analysis to tell a story about his subject. He has also conducted research on the readers of his novels to see whether the reading impacts the readers' religious imagination. Greeley even works research into his autobiographies (1986, 1999). As he says of the connection between his research and writing, "fiction and data analysis are both modes of storytelling, with a beginning, a middle, and an end, with plot, conflict, and resolution. Analyzing data prepared me to write fiction; writing fiction made me a more skilled data analyst" (1990, 146).

Greeley often faced opposition from the Church for his writing and research activities. Although he does hold university appointments, he had difficulty obtaining a university position because, he feels, of his priesthood. Greeley summarizes his career like this: "I started out life wanting to be a priest. I continued my life in the priesthood wanting to be a sociologist to serve the church. I discovered the church did not need or want a sociologist and became a professional sociologist who was also a priest. Then my sociology persuaded me that the best way I could be a priest was by writing theological novels set in the same context and about the same subjects as my sociological research" (1990, 147).

Paul Lazarsfeld

Paul Felix Lazarsfeld (1901–76) has been called "the founder of modern empirical sociology" (Jerabek 2001). He was born in Vienna, Austria, and studied mathematics at the University of Vienna. Lazarsfeld received his doctorate in applied mathematics in 1925.

He traveled to the United States in the early 1930s as a Rockefeller fellow. After visiting several research universities, Lazarsfeld was offered a position at Columbia University. Shortly afterward, he founded and became director of the

Newark University Research Center in New Jersey. There, as in later positions, Lazarsfeld provided many refugee social scientists their first U.S. jobs (Sills 1979, 413). He also became research director of the Princeton Radio Project—a famous project that studied the influence of radio broadcasting on listeners.

Over the course of his career, Lazarsfeld founded four research institutes, published 600 scholarly articles and studies, and organized more than a dozen symposia and anthologies. He was president of the American Sociological Association and the American Association for Public Opinion Research and a member of the National Academy of Sciences and the National Academy of Education. He received honorary degrees from Yeshiva, Chicago, Columbia, and the University of Vienna. Lazarsfeld was the first American to receive an honorary degree from the Sorbonne in Paris. He was also awarded the Golden Cross of Merit, the national decoration of Austria (Jerabek 2001, 241; Sills 1979, 421).

Lazarsfeld is a cofounder of mathematical sociology. His methodological innovations include reason analysis (looking at the causes and motives leading to an individual decision or behavior), latent structure analysis (a multidimensional analysis developed before computers were used in sociology), groundbreaking work in statistical analyses of surveys, and the program analyzer (a tool that recorded listeners reactions to radio programs). The latter contribution served as an inspiration to Robert K. Merton (profiled in chapter 2) in his eventual development of the focus group. He also had a long and fruitful collaboration with Merton. Among the research Lazarsfeld published was work on unemployment, public opinion, market research, mass media, communications, political sociology, the history of empirical social research, and applied sociology (Jerabek 2001).

Lazarsfeld retired from Columbia University in 1971, teaching afterwards as Distinguished Professor at the University of Pittsburgh. Lazarsfeld died in New York City in 1976. In 1997, Columbia University renamed his former research center the Paul Lazarsfeld Center of the Social Sciences.

Stanley Milgram

Social psychologist Stanley Milgram (1933–84) conducted a series of experiments (discussed in more detail in chapter 5) in which he demonstrated that ordinary people would conform to orders by authority figures even when the outcome could be potentially dangerous, if not lethal. These studies remain some of the most important research on social conformity, providing "one of the most singular, most penetrating, and most disturbing inquiries into human conduct that modern psychology has produced in this century" (Blass 1999, 457).

Milgram conducted his obedience studies during the early 1960s while a professor at Yale University. Although he conducted a variety of other innovative experiments on topics such as community attitudes and urban maps, he remains largely known for the obedience research that he conducted very early in his career. When Milgram died 20 years later, he was still being asked to discuss his work in that area (Blass, 2000).

Milgram was also an innovative teacher, leaving teaching materials that fill 106 boxes in the Yale University archives (Takooshian 1999, 10). He used his courses to examine his past research, and ideas gleaned from students and family became new research projects. He also designed class experiences that emphasized to students how similar they were to the subjects in his obedience studies. One former student, for example, recalls spending an entire class period rearranging tables at Milgram's direction, which they did without question (Takooshian 2000, 19).

Milgram also produced several educational films. *The City and the Self* was awarded the silver medal of the International Film and Television Festival of New York. Together with the producers of the 1970s drama *Medical Center,* Milgram created show segments to study the relationship between violence on television and viewer aggression. This makes Milgram "the first and only researcher who was able to get a major TV network to create segments of an ongoing popular prime-time program tailored to meet the needs of an experiment" (Blass 1999, 456). Stanley Milgram died of his fifth heart attack at age 51 after chairing a dissertation defense earlier in the day.

Dorothy Smith

Born in Great Britain, Dorothy Smith (1926–) was a clerical worker who enjoyed reading about sociology. That early interest in the field eventually became a Ph.D. from the University of California–Berkeley, where her thesis supervisor was Erving Goffman (profiled in chapter 4). Today, Smith has earned the position of professor emerita at the University of Toronto (Campbell, 2003).

Smith's influences include a course on George Herbert Mead, the writings of Karl Marx, and ethnomethodology. (Both of these sociologists and the area of ethnomethodology are discussed in this book.) Smith was also heavily influenced by phenomenology, a type of sociology that looks at everyday life and how we understand and create everyday situations (Campbell, 2003).

Her books include *The Everyday World as Problematic: A Feminist Sociology* (1987); *The Conceptual Practices of Power: A Feminist Sociology of Knowledge* (1990); *Text, Facts, and Femininity: Exploring the Relations of Ruling* (1990); and *Writing the Social: Critique, Theory, and Investigations* (1998). Although her writing has been described as "dense" (Campbell 2003, 6), Smith has become widely known for her work in feminist sociological theory. She has also soundly critiqued sociological practices and what she argues is an absence of women or distortion of their experiences in traditional sociology (Laslett and Thorne 1992, 60).

Smith's feminist analyses have been central to her "rethinking of the methods of social analysis that were available in the 1970s" (Campbell 2003, 13). She has developed an "institutional ethnography," that, rather than taking an objective stance, "construct[s] accounts from the standpoint of those with whom or for whom the researcher chooses to work" (17). As noted by one observer,

Dorothy Smith developed a "a *sociology for women* . . . that has become a *sociology for people*" (3).

CAREERS IN SOCIOLOGY

Those with an interest and training in sociological research methods have backgrounds that prepare them for careers including

- business analyst
- consultant
- data analyst
- data quality coordinator
- demographer
- evaluation researcher
- fiscal analyst
- health analyst
- health-care researcher
- insurance analyst
- interviewer
- marketing/consumer researcher
- policy analyst
- private-research-firm analyst
- professional sociologist
- program evaluator
- project director/analyst
- public-opinion pollster
- research analyst
- research assistant/associate
- research-institute director/staff
- statistician
- survey researcher
- writer

Additional Resources

American Sociological Association. American Sociological Association Code of Ethics. http://www.asanet.org/members/ecoderev.html. The ASA has established these principles and ethical standards to guide sociologists throughout their professional responsibilities and conduct.

American Sociological Association. Methodology Section. http://www.qmp.isr. umich. edu/asam/. This section focuses on encouraging the development and application of research methodologies in sociology.

Babbie, Earl R. 2003. *The Practice of Social Research.* 10th ed. Belmont, Calif.: Wadsworth. A popular textbook, this work covers basic and advanced techniques for social research including a focus on qualitative methods.

Best, Joel. 2001. *Damned Lies and Statistics: Untangling Numbers from the Media, Politicians, and Activists.* Berkeley: University of California Press. This book helps the reader to develop a critical-thinking approach to statistics with discussions on bad statistics, "mangled numbers," inappropriate comparisons, and implications when bad statistics are applied to matters such as policy.

Campbell, Steve. 1999. *Statistics You Can't Trust.* Parker, Colo.: Think Twice Publishing. This book provides easy to understand examples that help nonstatisticians to be more critical evaluators of statistics and understand the ways data can be misrepresented, intentionally and unintentionally.

The Gallup Organization. http://www.gallup.com/. Founded by pioneering pollster Dr. George Gallup, this organization has been conducting polls since the 1930s.

Harris Interactive. http://www.harrisinteractive.com/. Long known for conducting the Harris Poll, this organization is now pioneering Internet-based surveys.

Mann, Chris, and Fiona Stewart. 2000. *Internet Communication and Qualitative Research: A Handbook for Researching Online.* Thousand Oaks, Ca: Sage. This book covers a range of practical information on developing and applying Internet-based qualitative methods, including ethical and power issues as well as conducting interviews, focus groups, and participant observation online.

Miller, Arthur G. 1986. *The Obedience Experiment: A Case Study of Controversy in Social Science.* New York: Praeger. The ethical controversies of Milgram's classic experiment are revisited, as are other experiments.

Reinharz, Shulamit. 1992. *Feminist Methods in Sociological Research.* New York: Oxford University. A wide variety of feminist research methodologies and variety of feminist perspective are covered in this book.

Sullivan, Thomas J. 1992. *Applied Sociology: Research and Critical Thinking.* New York: Macmillian. This book focuses on the application of sociological and social science research to addressing social problems and developing critical thinking skills.

Trochim, William M. Center for Social Research Methods. http://www.socialresearch methods.net. William Trochim's Center for Social Research Methods is a comprehensive resource center on the Web, including an online social-research-methods textbook.

Whyte, William Foote. 1984. *Learning from the Field: A Guide from Experience.* Beverly Hills, Calif.: Sage. This book provides a look at field research from one of the most well-known participant-observers in the discipline.

CHAPTER 11

Preparing to Be a Sociologist and Career Opportunities

As the earlier chapters in this book show, sociology is an excellent field for people who are interested in other people and a wide range of topics within and across cultures and societies. Sociologists use their training in theory and research, and their unique perspectives, in a variety of occupations. They also have a number of educational options that allow them to study sociology and specific topics within the discipline in as much depth as they desire.

ACADEMIC TRAINING FOR SOCIOLOGISTS

Sociology is taught in some high schools. These classes provide an important opportunity to share a sociological perspective, because they may be the only sociology training that many students receive. However, sociology courses at this level do not receive a great deal of attention from the discipline and have been cited for problems including inadequate training of teachers and in-course objectives, content, and materials (DeCesare 2002; Lashbrook 2001). Quality high-school programs could help produce better college sociology majors as well as a better public image for the discipline as a whole (Seperson 1994). An advanced-placement (AP) test in sociology that would provide college credit in sociology is currently being developed and may be available by the time you read this book (Persell 2001).

People interested in studying sociology in college have several options. They can earn a degree at both the undergraduate and graduate levels. Additionally, Anne Arundel Community College in Arnold, Maryland, offers a "Letter of Recognition" in sociology. That is believed to be the only such program at the community college level at this writing. Students take courses including an introductory course, a course on social and behavioral research tools and methods, and an elective covering a target area of interest (gerontology, religion, etc.).

The baccalaureate degree in sociology can be either a bachelor of arts (BA) or a bachelor of science (BS) degree. These courses of study provide training in the core areas of the discipline. Students take courses covering the sociological imagination, research, and theory. They also typically study several interest areas such as the family, health and illness, or religion to which these core concepts are applied.

At the graduate level, students can earn a master's degree (a master of arts [MA] or master of sciences [MS]) or doctorate (doctor of philosophy [Ph.D.]). Courses in these advanced degrees are generally taught as seminars that involve much classroom discussion between students and their professors. Assignments are often papers that require students to apply theoretical perspectives and to design or conduct research on some topic of interest.

At the doctoral level, students will choose a specific area of specialization. In addition to required courses in theory and research, students will take a number of courses concentrating on that selected area (health and illness, the family, race/ethnicity, collective behavior, etc.). After graduation, they will be considered an expert and a specialist in that aspect of sociology. Some schools require that the student also specialize in theory, research, or both.

In addition to completing their course work, students obtaining advanced degrees in sociology also often have to take comprehensive examinations. These examinations require students to demonstrate their knowledge in specific areas such as theory, research, and their special interest area. Depending on university requirements, these examinations may be written, oral, or require both written and oral parts. They may take several hours to complete or several days depending on the program requirements.

Graduate students also typically have to demonstrate their abilities by producing a thesis or dissertation. These are lengthy manuscripts (often book length) that report the details of original research the students conduct under the supervision of their professors. The thesis or dissertation then must be presented to a committee of professors and "defended" to their satisfaction. This process usually involves a number of rewrites of the document that polish it to get ready for the committee members to read. The students then generally meet with the committee and describe key points about why the research was conducted, how it was conducted, and what it contributes to our sociological knowledge. The committee members then have an opportunity to ask questions about the research and findings. Writing a thesis or dissertation is a huge project and may take anywhere from several months to several years.

The Popularity of Studying Sociology

Just as for other academic subjects, the popularity of studying sociology varies over time. A look back over the past three decades shows that sociology as an academic major increased in the United States in popularity during the early 1970s. However, that popularity waned during the mid-1970s through the mid-1980s. During the late 1980s, the number of sociology degrees awarded

Table 11.1
Number of Sociology Degrees Awarded by Degree Level, Selected Years 1970–2000

Year	Bachelor's	Master's	Doctorate
1970	30,848	1,816	505
1975	31,858	2,135	680
1980	19,181	1,372	600
1985	12,165	1,045	486
1990	15,993	1,213	448
1995	22,974	1,790	555
2000	25,598	1,996	634

Source: American Sociological Association (2002b).

began to increase, indicating a renewed growth in the discipline that continued through 2000. Over the 1990s, the number of people receiving bachelor degrees in sociology increased by 60 percent. At the graduate level, the number of master's degrees increased by 67 percent, and the number of doctorates awarded increased by almost 42 percent. In 2000, 25,598 bachelor's degrees, 1,996 master's, and 634 doctorates in sociology were conferred by American universities (see table 11.1).

Enrollments in graduate sociology programs also grew during the early 1990s. However, the late 1990s saw a decline in the number of students enrolled in graduate programs. This is typical of graduate-school enrollments overall when the economy is strong. Enrollments decline as people choose to enter the workforce and have an easier time findings jobs than they do in harder economic times. Enrollments in undergraduate sociology programs also declined during that same period (Merola 2002).

Characteristics of Sociology Students

Many of the recognized founders of sociology and acknowledged theorists in the discipline were men. With the influences of feminist perspectives and the increasing attention to the contributions of women throughout the history of the discipline, women have now outpaced men in receiving sociology degrees at every level. Women have long received the majority of undergraduate degrees awarded in sociology, while the majority of graduate degrees were awarded to men. However, during the mid-1980s, women in graduate programs made great gains on their male counterparts. By 2000, at the bachelor's, master's, and doctorate levels, more women than men received degrees in sociology (see table 11.2).

Table 11.2
Percentage of Sociology Degrees Awarded at Each Degree Level by Gender,
Selected Years 1970–2000

	Bachelor's		Master's		Doctorate	
Year	Men	Women	Men	Women	Men	Women
1970	40.3%	59.7%	62.7%	37.3%	81.6%	18.4%
1975	41.9%	58.1%	61.8%	38.2%	69.1%	30.9%
1980	33.3%	66.7%	49.8%	50.2%	61.5%	38.5%
1985	31.0%	69.0%	45.0%	55.5%	50.0%	50.0%
1990	31.6%	68.4%	41.3%	58.7%	51.3%	48.7%
1995	32.4%	67.6%	37.9%	62.1%	47.0%	53.0%
2000	29.8%	70.2%	31.9%	68.1%	41.2%	58.8%

Source: American Sociological Association (2002c).

Over the last four decades, women have increased the share of doctoral degrees earned in the sciences. In 2001, over half of all Ph.D.s in psychology and sociology were earned by women. The average percentage of doctorate degrees earned by women studying sociology was greater than that earned by women in economics, political science, and the physical or biological sciences (see table 11.3).

Many great contributions to the discipline have been made by sociologists of color. However, just as for women, the contributions of many of these sociologists were discounted or not recognized until recent years. The percentage of doctorates in sociology awarded to persons of color has increased over the past quarter century. In 2000, just over 25 percent of new Ph.D. recipients were members of a racial/ethnic minority group (see table 11.4). Over one-third of all recipients of master's and bachelor's degrees in sociology were also persons of color (ASA 2004a, data not shown).

Persons of color are also increasingly holding full-time faculty positions. However, whites still hold disproportionately more of the highest-ranking positions in graduate sociology departments (ASA 2002a). Data tabulated by the ASA suggest some increases in the numbers and promotion of persons of color in faculty positions in the coming decade (ASA 2002a). Larger numbers of minority students and faculty help to prevent the isolation or "token" status that can occur when there are very limited numbers of a group and provide larger and more diverse scholar networks (American Sociological Association 2002a;

Table 11.3
Average Percentage of Doctorate Degrees Earned by Women in Selected Disciplines, 2001

Discipline	Percentage
Psychology	66.9%
Sociology	58.4%
Biological Sciences	44.9%
Political Science	33.5%
Economics	28.3%
Physical Sciences	24.6%

Source: American Sociological Association (2004b).

Table 11.4
Racial/Ethnic Identity of Sociology Ph.D. Recipients, 1980, 1990, 2000*

	White	Black	Asian or Pacific Islander	Hispanic	Native American or Alaskan Native	Other or Unknown Races and Ethnicity
1980	85.6% (452)	4.4% (23)	2.7% (14)	3.0% (16)	0.4% (2)	4.0% (21)
1990	78.4% (258)	7.0% (23)	4.6% (15)	8.2% (27)	0.3% (1)	1.5 (5)
2000	74.3% (382)	11.1% (57)	6.2% (32)	5.1% (26)	1.2% (6)	2.1% (11)

Source: American Sociological Association (2004a). *Numbers in parentheses show numbers of PhDs earned in each category.

Levine 1993). They also provide a more diverse perspective and voice to the discipline.

SOCIOLOGISTS IN THE WORKPLACE (ACADEMICS AND BEYOND)

Sociological training provides a broad range of job skills sought by employers. Armed with this training, their sociological perspectives, and diverse interests, sociologists are employed throughout society.

Job Skills

Sociology graduates have special skills that interest a range of employers. The Society for Applied Sociology ("Hiring a Person") identifies three skill areas in particular that are of great interest to employers. First, since the sociological perspective focuses on social systems and situations, sociology students have been trained to look at the "big picture." Rather than focusing on an issue as an isolated problem or condition, sociologists put issues in social context. They look for how issues are interrelated to other parts of society, what factors are influencing the situation, and what factors are influenced by various issues. This is a skill that interests, among other employers, those who need strategic and policy planners, organizational development, and project management expertise.

Second, sociology graduates have also been trained in problem identification and problem solving. They have been taught to apply research skills and strategies, focus their questions, support their arguments with data, and critically evaluate published analyses. These types of critical-thinking skills are particularly valuable in market research and data collection and analyses.

Third, sociology graduates also have valuable training to better understand and interact in our multicultural world. Sociology courses focus on understanding the importance of history and culture in our lives, the interrelationships of different aspects of the social world, and respecting the range and form those cultures, values, and belief systems take. By studying both cross-cultural similarities and differences, sociology students are exposed to the depth and complexity of human relationships. They build skills employers are interested in for human relations, criminal justice, and positions requiring multicultural interaction among others.

Sociology students interested in academic positions will need to focus on developing skills in reviewing research literature, conducting statistical analyses, grant writing, and understanding and applying theoretical perspectives. The most important skills for those who want to work outside of academics are report writing, basic statistical analysis and research design, and oral presentation. Sociologists should also develop good data-presentation skills and computer skills (Hawdon and Mobley 2001).

Career Preparation

Most jobs for which the bachelor's degree prepares students will not have the title of "sociologist." However, a bachelor's in sociology provides an excellent background for a variety of career choices. Sociology students gain a strong liberal-arts education that touches on a range of areas from the arts and sciences to skills in writing and research.

Career preparation for undergraduate sociology students can be even further enhanced by adding another major or minor. The American Sociological Association (ASA) recommends that undergraduate sociology majors take a multidisciplinary approach to their degree by planning double majors in criminal justice, economics, English, anthropology, a second language, political science, or education. Recommended minors or concentration areas include computer science, business management, marketing, human services, law and society, or pre-law (American Sociological Association 1999a, 7).

Another ASA recommendation is that students take advantage of the internship opportunities provided by many colleges. Whether the position is paid or unpaid, internships provide a number of advantages to undergraduate sociology students. They allow students to try out various careers, provide experience that can be used on a résumé, help students acquire new skills, and provide a means to apply skills learned in the classroom. They also provide networking opportunities and may give participants an edge in the job market (American Sociological Association 1999a, 7–8).

Sociologists at Work

When sociologists go to work, they could be going almost anywhere! They are in the classroom and throughout the community, nation, and world using their skills.

Sociological Practice

Most sociologists with bachelor's degrees and most with master's degrees hold positions in applied or clinical sociology. Applied and clinical sociology are considered **sociological practice,** *a sociological focus in which sociological theory, methods, and findings are utilized to bring about positive social changes.* Although these positions may involve teaching and research, the emphasis in sociological practice is not on teaching or conducting research for the sake of knowledge. Rather, it is the practical application of sociological skills to make a difference in the world (e.g., Rebach and Bruhn 2001). Over a quarter of all American sociology departments have applied specialties that emphasize ways to put sociological knowledge and skills to work to improve society (American Sociological Association 1999b).

Overall, 27 percent of sociologists work in applied settings (Billson 1996, 54). Many of those working in sociological practice hold more than one position. For example, they might hold an academic position teaching sociology and also work as a consultant (Bruhn 2001).

Sociologists who hold master's and doctorate degrees can apply for **certification** in the area of clinical sociology. This means that *their knowledge and skills are evaluated by other sociologists and meet certain professional standards.* Becoming certified means that a sociologist has demonstrated that they know how to use sociology satisfactorily to their professional colleagues. A certification is not a license to practice sociology. Because no such license exists and anyone can claim to practice sociology, certification is a way to demonstrate to employers, colleagues, and others that the sociologist's abilities meet the standards deemed critical to the field (Kallen 2001).

The Sociological Practice Association (SPA) offers a certified-clinical-sociologist program for practicing sociologists. Started in 1984, this certification program requires a graduate degree in sociology and 1,500 hours of supervised experience in sociological practice or one year of full-time practice work. Applicants must present a portfolio that further documents their training, experience, skills, references, and adherence to professional ethics. The applicant must also demonstrate their abilities in a workshop or conference.

Sociologists with undergraduate degrees are not eligible for certification. However, undergraduate programs that emphasize sociological practice can be accredited by the Commission on Applied and Clinical Sociology. Graduates of these programs can note this accreditation as evidence that their course of study met with rigorous standards.

Where Sociologists Work

Sociology provides a solid background for people interested in pursuing further education in any number of fields. Sociology is a good undergraduate degree for anyone interested in continuing their studies at the graduate level in social work, law, or policy. Obtaining an undergraduate degree in sociology can also be a good basis for those interested in teaching. Those with more advanced training in sociology at the master's or doctorate level may pursue careers in research organizations, urban planning, program management, theology, or policymaking.

Social advocacy is an area that appeals to many sociologists. Sociologists apply their training and understanding of social institutions in advocacy positions throughout the community. This might take the form of work in nonprofit organizations or various social causes (e.g., domestic-violence shelters, environmental groups). They might work with children, the elderly, or the disabled, and community-development, housing, or foster-care agencies. Sociologists participate in school boards, advocate for students with special needs, and apply their expertise in administrative positions (Strand 2002).

Sociologists also contribute to public policy. They participate in panels that brief members of Congress on research on social issues. By briefing Congress, sociologists have the opportunity to "bring findings from research studies to the attention of the policy community in ways that both promote knowledge and make it accessible to relevant publics" (Herring 2002). The legislative topics that these panels have addressed include terrorism, responses to disasters, welfare reform, marriage incentives, and health insurance for children. Sociologists have even developed a scale of risk for drivers, addressing the public-safety questions of when high-risk drivers should be allowed back on the road (Weinrath 1997).

In the corporate world, sociology students may find positions in human-resource management and industrial relations. Some pursue positions that involve health services or counseling, such as family planning or rehabilitation counseling. Sociology students may apply their training to advertising, sales, or public relations. Their training may also be used in the area of journalism. Those interested in the areas of conformity and deviance may choose to enter the criminal-justice field as police officers, probation officers, correctional officers, and so on, or they might even use their skills as jury consultants (Lindner 1997) or as mediators in dispute resolution (Diaz 2001). Those primarily interested in demography may find employment in marketing, planning, or consulting.

Sociologists are also working in technology industries. For example, the author of this book works in the information-technology sector of a major corporation applying sociological tools in the growing field of collaborative technologies. These technologies focus on looking for new ways that people can better communicate and share information and ideas. This work involves applying what sociologists know about group dynamics and organizations to help high-level decision makers focus and achieve their organizational strategies more effectively and efficiently. Many sociologists in high-tech fields conduct research and make technology recommendations (Guice 1999). Salaries for sociologists working in high-tech industries tend to be higher than salaries in many other areas, including academics. However, the career ladder may be limited, in that sociologists are often passed over for promotions to generalist management positions in these industries (Guice 1999).

Of course, sociologists also teach sociology. The majority of sociologists with doctorate degrees work in academics. They hold positions that emphasize teaching and/or research at colleges or universities. According to the ASA, sociology is taught in over 3,000 colleges and universities in the United States alone. Teaching at the high-school level typically requires a graduate degree or a certain number of graduate-level course credits in sociology. Schools may also require that the person teach other courses in addition to sociology.

Some sociologists teach in adjunct positions. That means they do not hold full-time faculty positions at the college or university for which they teach. Rather, they are paid to teach one or more courses on an as-needed basis. The majority of sociology departments that grant graduate degrees (8 out of 10) employ adjunct faculty. Approximately one-quarter of the faculty employed in these departments are adjuncts. Some adjuncts are seeking full-time teaching positions. Other adjuncts are employed elsewhere and teach to supplement their income and because they enjoy teaching and interacting with students (American Sociological Association 2002d).

Salaries for Sociologists

In 2002, the median annual earnings for sociologists was $53,160 (Bureau of Labor Statistics 2004b). The median means that income distribution is divided into two equal groups. One half the group has incomes above the median. The other half has incomes below the median. Compared with other social scientists, the median income for sociologists is lower than the median annual earnings political scientists. However, it is higher than the median annual earnings for anthropologists and archaeologists, and historians, and is very close to that of geographers (see table 11.5).

Table 11.5
Median Annual Earnings for Selected Social-Science Fields, 2002

Field	Median Annual Earnings, 2002
Anthropologists and Archaeologists	$38,620
Geographers	$53,420
Historians	$42,030
Political scientists	$80,560
Sociologists	$53,160
Median all *(Does not include economists, market and survey researchers, psychologists, and urban and regional planners)*	$52,280

Source: Bureau of Labor Statistics (2004b).

Table 11.6
Average Sociology Faculty Salaries in 2003/04 and Percentage of Salary Change, 1982/83–2003/04

Rank	2003/04 Average Salary	1982/83-2003/04 *(% change)*
Full Professor	$76,200	+20.5%
Associate Professor	$56,212	+15.1%
Assistant Professor	$46,409	+18.8%
New Assistant Professor	$45,722	+26.7%
Instructor/Lecturer	$36,855	+15.0%
All Faculty Ranks	$59,686	+21.4%

Source: American Sociological Association (2004d).

The average salary for sociology faculty in 2003/04 was $59,686. On the low end of the salary scale, sociology instructors who generally do not have a doctorate earned an average of $36,855. Full professors earned an average of $76,200. Overall, for all faculty ranks, salaries increased by 21.4 percent during the past two decades (in constant 2003 dollars). Full professors saw the greatest salary increases (20.5 percent) (see table 11.6).

Overall employment for sociologists is expected to grow about as fast as the average for all occupations through 2010. That means employment is projected to increase 10 to 20 percent. The Bureau of Labor Statistics (BLS) rates prospects best for those with advanced degrees and who desire work outside of academic settings. The BLS also rates job prospects as good in areas outside traditional social science that require research, communication, and quantitative skills.

PROFESSIONAL ORGANIZATIONS

Sociology students, as well as longtime professionals, can benefit from networking within the discipline. Sociologists can join international organizations, such as the International Sociological Association (ISA), or national organizations, such as the American Sociological Association (ASA). Many of these organizations are large. At this writing, the ISA claims over 3,300 members from 91 countries. The ASA has almost 14,000 members. Members of these professional organizations often include nonsociologists who are interested in social issues as well as people employed in government, business, or nonprofit organizations outside of academics. Most sociology organizations welcome students as members, and many provide special activities such as newsletters or mentoring programs especially for student members. Student discounts are also common.

Some sociological associations or organizations take a regional focus drawing members from specific geographic areas of the United States. Other types of groups that students may benefit from joining are organized around a specific area of interest. The Association of Black Sociologists (ABS) and Sociologists for Women in Society (SWS) are two such organizations, focusing on issues that will serve African American people and issues of gender, respectively. The Sociological Practice Association (SPA) and Society for Applied Sociology (SAS) focus on applications of sociological expertise outside of the academic setting. (As of this writing, these two organizations are considering merging together.)

The larger sociology organizations, such as ISA and ASA, also have subsections that focus on areas of interest. Joining one of these subsections provides members (including students) an opportunity to network with sociologists sharing interests in the same aspects of society. Often, these sections provide newsletters, announcements, and other information specific to the topic area. As of 2004, the ASA had over 40 of these special-interest sections. Some of the largest sections are those focusing on sex and gender, medical sociology, culture, and organizations, occupations, and work (see table 11.7).

Sociologists can also increase their knowledge, networking, and professional reputations by joining associations or organizations associated with other disciplines that share areas of interest. For example, some sociologists interested in family issues are members of the National Council on Family Relations (NCFR). Sociologists with interests in health and illness might consider organizations such as the American Public Health Association (APHA). Those interested in political sociology might also join an organization such as the American Political Science Association (APSA).

Table 11.7
Sections of the American Sociological Association

Aging and the Life Course	Marxist Sociology
Alcohol, Drugs, and Tobacco	Mathematical Sociology
Animals and Society	Medical Sociology
Asia and Asian America	Mental Health
Children and Youth	Methodology
Collective Behavior and Social Movements	Organizations, Occupations, and Work
Communication and Information Technologies	Peace, War, and Social Conflict
Community and Urban Sociology	Political Sociology
Comparative and Historical Sociology	Political Economy of the World Systems
Crime, Law, and Deviance	Population
Culture	Race, Gender, and Class
Economic Sociology	Racial and Ethnic Minorities
Education	Rationality and Society
Emotions	Religion
Ethnomethodology and Conversation Analysis *	Science, Knowledge, and Technology
Evolution and Sociology *	Sex and Gender
Family	Sexualities
History Of Sociology	Social Psychology
International Migration	Sociological Practice
Labor and Labor Movements	Teaching and Learning
Latino/a Sociology	Theory
Law	* Section in Formation

Source: American Sociological Association (2004c).

Sociology organizations hold meetings and other professional activities in which members gather to share their research, teaching, and professional expertise; network; and further enhance their professional skills. Conference agendas and formats vary as widely as interest areas. Many conferences focus on presentations of new research and include seminars focused on developing skills such as teaching and research.

Presentations at professional meetings are made in several different formats and range in the formality of the presentation. These may be formal lecture-type presentations, often followed by a question-and-answer period, or they may be discussions between interested colleagues seated around a table or conference room. Informal poster sessions are often included as well. In this format, researchers set up static displays of their research findings on a wall or table. Meeting attendees can browse the displays and ask further questions of the authors informally as it suits their interest. Many people are familiar with this type of format from other events such as school science fairs or trade shows.

Other conference activities often include workshops on teaching, research methods, techniques for statistical analysis or other skill development led by recognized experts in the area, information on available research funding opportunities or grant-writing workshops, book and software exhibits, awards ceremonies, employment services, events specially organized for student attendees, and various business meetings to address organizational governance. Social events such as alumni events, receptions, or welcome seminars for new members and students are also often on the agenda.

BIOGRAPHIES

Jane Addams

Jane Addams (1860–1935) was a sociologist whose work helped shape the famous Chicago school of sociology (see chapter 8). Addams contributed important work in the area of applied sociology. She lectured around the country, authored 11 books and hundreds of articles that often referred to her sociological perspective, and "coordinated and led a massive network of women sociologists" at the University of Chicago (Deegan 1988, 3). However, due to the segregation and discrimination rampant in sociology during her lifetime, Addams was never granted full recognition for her contributions to sociology or a full-time faculty position in the department. All women sociologists at the University of Chicago were eventually transferred into the Social Work Department. As a result, Addams became primarily identified with that field, and her early influence in sociology was discounted (Deegan 1988).

Addams is perhaps best known for founding Chicago's Hull House in 1889. Fashioned after a settlement house Addams had observed in London's East End, Hull House provided a wide range of services for its poor, largely immigrant neighborhood. These services grew to include a kindergarten, day care, classes for adults, a public kitchen, a coffee house, a library, a book bindery, an employment bureau, and a labor museum. Hull House also provided recreational facilities, such as a gymnasium and swimming pool, as well as outlets for the arts, including an art gallery and studio, a music school, and a little theater group. Addams lived and worked at Hull House until her death.

Whereas men controlled the University of Chicago Sociology Department, Hull House became the "institutional center for research and social thought" for Chicago's women sociologists (Deegan 1988, 33; see also Lengermann and Niebrugge-Brantley 1998, 65–89). *Hull House Maps and Papers* (1895) focused on the characteristics of urban populations, mapping these populations, and issues of immigration and poverty. Hull House strongly influenced the direction of Chicago sociology and many of the areas of urban sociology pursued by the department for several decades.

Addams supported the women's suffrage movement and the peace movement during World War I. Her efforts in her local community led to positions as a Chicago garbage inspector and a member of the Chicago Board of Education. She held founding or leadership roles in many organizations, including the American Sociological Society (later the American Sociological Association), the Campfire Girls, the National Conference of Charities and Corrections (later the National Conference of Social Work), the Women's International League for Peace and Freedom, the American Civil Liberties Union (ACLU), and the National Association for the Advancement of Colored People (NAACP).

Addams received a number of honors over her career. In 1910, she received the first honorary degree bestowed on a woman by Yale University. She was awarded the Nobel Peace Prize in 1931 for her peace efforts during World War I, the first American woman so honored. After her death, Addams was commemorated on a 1940 U.S. postage stamp.

Arthur B. Shostak

Applied sociologist Arthur B. Shostak (1937–) earned an undergraduate degree in industrial and labor relations from Cornell University. He received his Ph.D. from Princeton University in 1961. After six years at the Wharton School of Finance and Commerce, Shostak joined the faculty at Drexel University in 1967, until his recent retirement.

An expert of futurism, Shostak was appointed director of the Drexel University Center for Employment Futures (DCEF) in 1967. He has worked as a futurist consultant for various corporations and government entities. Shostak is author of well over 100 articles and more than 20 books. His works have addressed various issues including computerization of the labor movement, men and abortion, and first-person accounts by grassroots activists and "studies of that which we hesitate to tell," such as childhood sexual victimization and having a sibling murdered (Shostak, Vita). He also edited *Utopian Thinking in Sociology: Creating the Good Society,* a teaching resource from the American Sociological Association.

Sociologists should study utopian thought, according to Shostak, because the "study of utopian thought uncovers hidden assumptions about possibilities . . . about 'human nature', the workings of history, and the ability of humankind to craft a society and life that honors us all" (2001). Utopian thought can help sociology "usefully reconnect with neglected aspects of its origins, as such early contributors as Comte, Saint-Simon, Simmel, Weber, and others, including Harriet Martineau and the forgotten very early 'Mothers of Sociology' at the University of Chicago. All had something of value to say about utopian matters (ideals, vision, etc.), albeit not always of a flattering vein" (Shostak 2001). Among the other benefits Shostak sees are sociologists learning to explore new possibilities and develop new cultural insights by studying how different cultures envision utopia (Drexel University, "Arthur B. Shostak, Ph.D."; Shostak, "Arthur B. Shostak," 2001).

Stephen F. Steele

Applied sociologist Stephen F. Steele is professor of sociology at Anne Arundel Community College (AACC) in Arnold, Maryland, near Annapolis. Steele also teaches graduate courses at the School of Professional Studies in Business and Education at Johns Hopkins University. He is an "advocate for understanding the practical value of the application of social science" (Steele, Home Page), with much of his focus on developing courses and teaching materials for applied courses as well as working with sociology departments and faculty in developing their own applied emphases.

Steele directed the Center for the Study of Local Issues (CSLI) at AACC, working with the American Sociological Association (ASA) to draw attention to local research centers and the applied practice of social science. Currently, he is active in developing the Institute for the Future at AACC that "provides a more humane tomorrow by encouraging dialogue about the future today" (Institute for the Future, "IF@AACC"). Steele is a member of the World Future Society and organizer of the Chesapeake Chapter of the World Future Society. He is also a consultant on research, evaluation, and planning.

Steele has served as both president and executive officer for the Society for Applied Sociology. In 1998, he received the Alex Boros Award from that organization for his contributions to the field of applied sociology. Steele has also been active in the ASA. He is a past chair of the Committee on Membership and has been awarded by the Section on Undergraduate Education. Steele has also served as chair of the Sociological Practice Section of the ASA and, in 2001, received the William Foote Whyte Award from that section in recognition of his many contributions to sociological practice (Steele "Home Page").

Roger A. Straus

Clinical sociologist Roger Austin Straus (1948–) was born in New York. He received his doctorate from the University of California–Davis in 1977. Over the course of his career, Straus has worked for various organizations. He currently provides marketing research and consulting to pharmaceutical companies.

Straus is a cofounder of the Clinical Sociology Association, the organization that is now the Sociological Practice Association. He was also editor of the organization's newsletter. His publications include works on self-hypnosis, marriage and family therapy, and his well-known text *Using Sociology: An Introduction from the Applied and Clinical Perspectives* (2002), currently in its third edition ("Straus, Roger Austin" 2003).

One focus of Straus's work has been to "help people and peer groups attain greater self-directed control over the conditions and circumstances of their lives." As he continues, "humans are active, striving, creative, and competent beings—not merely passive responders to internal or external pressures and forces" ("Straus, Roger Austin" 1983, 459).

Lester Ward

Lester Frank Ward (1841–1913) was born in Joliet, Illinois. He was the youngest of 10 children of a laborer who moved the family frequently looking for new work. They traveled by covered wagon to Iowa in 1855. The children worked and hunted to help feed the family. Ward had only intermittent formal schooling and was largely self-educated. He taught himself biology, physiology, Greek, German, Latin, and French (Pfautz 1968, 473; Healy 1972, 35).

He was able to save enough money to attend one semester at his first real school, the Susquehanna Collegiate Institute of Towanda, Pennsylvania, in 1861. Before he was able to save enough for another semester, the Civil War began, and Ward enlisted as a private in the Union army. He served for 27 months and was shot three times during the Battle of Chancellorsville. As a result of his war experiences, Ward became a "liberal mind free of all partisanship and politics, and dedicated to the emancipation of humanity on all fronts" (Chugerman 1965, 31).

After the war, Ward obtained a government position and again started to save for college. He was finally able to enter Columbian University (now George Washington University) in 1867 as a sophomore. He was 26 years old. By 1872, he had earned his undergraduate degree, a master of arts, after studying botany, qualitative chemistry, and practical anatomy; a bachelor of laws (plus his admittance to the bar); and a diploma in medicine (Chugerman 1965, 33).

Ward worked for the Treasury Department, the Bureau of Statistics, and the Smithsonian Institute. He became chief of the Division of Navigation and Immigration, chief paleontologist at the United States Geological Survey, and Honorary Curator of Botany and Paleontology in the National Museum in Washington. He was a fellow of the American Association for the Advancement of Science, a member of the National Academy of Sciences, and the first president of the American Sociological Society (now the American Sociological Association). Ward sold his home to subsidize the publication of a book *Dynamic Sociology* (1883), which he had worked on for 14 years, and lectured at several universities. Although offered positions at the Sorbonne and other well-known European universities, in 1906 he finally accepted a newly created position as chair of sociology at Brown University. He taught at Brown for the remaining seven years of his life (Chugerman 1965, 35–36; Pfautz 1968, 473–75; Healy 1972, 35–38).

When Lester Ward died at the age of 72, the flag was flown at half-mast in Washington. Obituaries called him a "scientist who will unquestionably rank as one of the half dozen greatest thinkers in his field that the world has produced," a "true genius," and the "last of the great sociological giants of the Nineteenth Century." They also said he had lived a life "given to humanity; he longed to show the way of nobler living" (quoted in Chugerman 1965, 37, 39).

William Foote Whyte

William Foote Whyte (1914–2000), born in Springfield, Massachusetts, was the son of a college professor. Although he had hoped to become a novelist or playwright, he became well known for his writings on the extensive fieldwork he conducted throughout his career as a sociologist. Whyte's first book, *Street Corner Society* (1943), is considered a classic work of sociology. It was a participant-observation of life in a slum area in Boston. Whyte conducted the research as a junior fellow at Harvard before completing his doctorate at the University of Chicago. He considered *Street Corner Society* to be among his favorite books and his best (Whyte 1969). In recognition of the book's enduring value to the field, the Eastern Sociological Society held a special session featuring Whyte in 1993 on the 50th anniversary of its publication.

Whyte emphasized the importance of applied research throughout his career. He wrote that "it seems to me likely that our field would progress more rapidly if more people were willing to do applied research. If a man has an obligation to try to apply his research findings, the effort he must make to come to terms with the realities of the field situation is likely to prevent him from indulging in ivory tower theorizing, which sounds impressive but leads nowhere. In short, I regard application as a necessary testing ground for the knowledge we think we have acquired" (1969, 42).

Over the course of his career, Whyte conducted fieldwork in the United States, Canada, and Latin America. He was involved in a wide range of organizations, including the Industrial Relations Research Association, the Center for the Study of Metropolitan Problems for the National Institute for Mental Health (NIMH), and the Subcommittee on Research of the National Manpower Commission of the Department of Labor. He was also involved with Congress on several issues. Whyte was active in the Society for Applied Anthropology, including a period as editor of *Human Organization*. After his retirement, he became president of the American Sociological Association, taking the opportunity of his presidential address to emphasize applied sociology. He became actively involved in the Consortium of Social Science Associations, an effort to strengthen relationships between social scientists and government. Whyte also continued to engage in research as professor emeritus, authoring or coauthoring 8 of his 21 books after his retirement (Whyte 1994).

Additional Resources

American Sociological Association. 1999. *Careers in Sociology.* 5th ed. Washington, D.C.: American Sociological Association. This publication answers the question "What can I do with a degree in sociology?" It also provides school and job-hunting advice and several career profiles of sociologists. It is also available online at http://www.asanet.org/student/career/homepage.html.

———. 2003. *Careers in Clinical Sociology.* Washington, D.C.: American Sociological Association. This book explains what clinical sociology is and how to prepare for a career in the field and offers other professional advice. It is also available online at http://www. asanet.org/student/career/clinsoc_45575v2.pdf.

Billson, Janet Mancini. 1996. *Mastering the Job Market with a Graduate Degree in Sociology.* Washington, D.C.: American Sociological Association. This publication provides the practical advice promised in the title.

Rebach, Howard M., and John G. Bruhn, eds. 2001. *Handbook of Clinical Sociology.* New York: Kluwer/Plenum. This book covers what clinical sociology is, how it is used, and ethical concerns, as well as highlighting a variety of careers chosen by clinical sociologists.

Society for Applied Sociology. http://www.appliedsoc.org/. A focus for members of this organization is applying sociological knowledge and tools in society.

Sociological Practice Association. http://www.socpractice.org/. This professional organization of clinical and applied sociologists provides resources for sociological practice, including certification.

Steele, Stephen F., Jammie Price. 2004. *Applied Sociology: Terms, Topics, Tools, and Tasks.* Nelson, Canada: Wadsworth. Although designed as an ancillary to introductory sociology texts, this book contains two informative chapters on job-seeking and careers specifically for those with a bachelor's degree in sociology.

Stephens, W. Richard, Jr. 1998. *Careers in Sociology.* 2nd ed. Boston: Allyn and Bacon. This series of biographies demonstrates the range of careers available to sociologists. Online at http://www.abacon.com/socsite/careers.html.

Straus, Roger, ed. 2002. *Using Sociology: An Introduction from the Applied and Clinical Perspectives.* 3rd ed. Rowman and Littlefield. This text provides an introduction to sociological practice and explains how sociology can be put to work to enact positive social change.

Glossary

Ableism Prejudice against the disabled that justifies unequal treatment of the group on the basis of their assumed characteristics.

Absolute definition of poverty A definition set by the Federal Office of Management and Budget: those people living in families with an income below a poverty threshold are considered "poor" by the government.

Achieved status A position acquired through personal effort.

Ageism Prejudice against the elderly that justifies unequal treatment of the group on the basis of their assumed characteristics.

Age-sex pyramid A graph that shows the population not only by age but also by the relative proportion of men and women in each age group.

Age-specific fertility rate The number of births to women by age group in a population.

Age-specific mortality rate The number of deaths per age group in a population.

Aggregate People who just happen to be in the same place at the same time.

Alternative social movement Collective action focusing on partial change at the individual level, such as movements advocating birth control.

Anomie An uncomfortable and unfamiliar state of normlessness that results when shared norms or guidelines break down.

Anticipatory socialization Learning and adopting the behavior and attitudes of a group someone desires or expects to join.

Apartheid Laws that formalized strict racial segregation.

Apportionment A process of determining how many of the 435 seats in the U.S. House of Representatives are allotted to each state.

Ascribed status A position involuntarily acquired through birth.

Assimilation The process of a cultural group losing its identity and being absorbed into the dominant culture.

Average The arithmetic mean.

Back-stage behavior The term from dramaturgical analysis for actions that occur out of sight of any audience.

Glossary

Bourgeoisie   Capitalists who own the factories, industrial machinery, and banks.

Bureaucracy   A formal organization controlled by explicit written rules, regulations, and specified responsibilities for actions.

Caste society   A society in which a person's location in the social strata is ascribed by birth rather than based on individual accomplishments.

Casual crowd   A collection of people who just happen to be gathered in the same place at the same time.

Category   People who share some common characteristic or status.

Causal relationship   One variable producing a change in another variable.

Certification   A formal acknowledgement earned by clinical sociologists demonstrating that their knowledge and skills have been evaluated by other sociologists and meet certain professional standards.

City   A type of incorporated place with defined geographic boundaries.

Class   A continuum of economic positions that leads to differences in lifestyle or life chances.

Class consciousness   Workers' recognition of themselves as a social class with interests opposed to the bourgeoisie.

Classless society   A society that has no economic strata.

Class society   A society in which social stratification is based on a combination of ascribed and achieved statuses.

Cleaning data   Performing some procedure to double-check the data's accuracy.

Coercive formal organization   An organization that people join involuntarily, such as a prison.

Cognitive development   The process through which children develop the ability to learn, understand, and engage in logical thought.

Collective action   Activity intended to bring about a lasting change.

Collective behavior   Spontaneous activities that involve large numbers of people violating established norms.

Concentric-zone model   An urban-development model that sees city growth as a series of five widening circles, or zones.

Conformity   Sharing certain norms, values, behaviors, and sometimes even opinions.

Conscience constituents   People outside of a social movement who provide resources but do not directly benefit from its goal accomplishment.

Contagion theory   The perspective that being swept up in a crowd results in a hypnotic sort of influence on individuals.

Convenience poll   A polling technique that queries those who are at hand.

Conventional crowd   A deliberate gathering bound by norms of behavior.

Conversation analysis   An offshoot of ethnomethodology that focuses on the importance of conversation in creating social order.

Core country   In world-systems theory, a powerful industrial country that dominates the global capitalist system.

Correlation   Two variables changing together in some predictable way.

Counterculture   A culture that opposes patterns of the dominant culture.

Countermovement   Collective action organized in response to the changes brought about by other social movements (also known as a reactionary movement).

Cracker   Someone who gains unauthorized access to computers, often for criminal or malicious purposes.

Crime   An act defined as so unacceptable that it has been prohibited by a code of laws.

Criminologist   A sociologist or other social scientist who studies the criminal-justice system, criminal law, and social order.

Crowd   A temporary collection of people in physical proximity who interact and have a common focus.

Crowd crystal   One who draws attention to him or herself in some manner.

Crude birthrate   The number of live births in a year per 1,000 people in a population.

Crude death rate   The number of deaths in a year per 1,000 people in a population.

Cultural lag   A gap occurring when different aspects of culture change at different rates.

Cultural relativism   Judging other cultures by those cultures' own standards.

Cultural-transmission theory   The perspective that deviance is learned and shared through interaction with others.

Culture   All of the ideas, beliefs, behaviors, and products common to, and defining, a group's way of life.

Culture shock   Confusion that occurs when encountering unfamiliar situations and ways of life.

Cyberpunk   Those involved in writing that envisions a future of ever-present and ever-powerful computer technology.

Data   Any pieces or assemblages of information gathered for the purpose of research.

Demographer   A person who practices demography.

Demographic-transition theory   The theory that industrialization brings about specific patterns of population change.

Demography   The study of human populations involving statistical description and analyses of population size and structure.

Dependency theory   A perspective that focuses on the reliance of poor nations on the wealthy.

Deprivation theory   A theoretical perspective that says social movements arise when people feel deprived of something that others have or that they feel others have.

Descriptive statistics   Procedures that assist in organizing, analyzing, and interpreting data.

Deviance   The violation of some cultural norm or value.

Differential association   The idea that deviance results from interacting with deviant associates.

Digital divide   The gap between those who have access to, and can effectively use, information and collaborative technologies such as the Internet and those who are unable to do so.

Discrimination   Unequal treatment of people based on their group membership.

Dramaturgical analysis   A micro-theoretical perspective comparing our everyday social interactions to theatrical performances.

Dyad   A group of two.

Dysfunction   An undesirable function.

Edge city   A form of self-sufficient suburb that has extensive office and retail space, as well as plenty of entertainment and recreational facilities.

Ego   Freud's term for our "self," our personality, which balances the urges of the id with the requirements of a civil society.

Emergent-norm theory   A theoretical perspective on crowd behavior that argues that new norms develop (emerge) as events happen.

Emigration   The movement of people out of an area.

Endogamous marriages   Cultural rules requiring that people marry only within their own group.

Ethnocentrism   Judging other cultures by the standards of one's own culture.

Ethnographic research (ethnography)   A qualitative research method that involves the observation of the interactions of everyday life.

Ethnomethodology   Literally "people making sense of their everyday social activities," this perspective examines our patterns of everyday life and how people construct their social worlds.

Evaluation research   Research that plans or assesses the efficiency and effectiveness of various interventions and programs.

Exchange theory   A theoretical perspective that assumes people interact and trade the resources (money, affections, etc.) that they bring to interactions in ways that maximize benefits and reduce costs to themselves.

Experiment   A controlled situation in which the researcher can manipulate at least one independent variable.

Expressive crowd   A collection of people that forms specifically around events with emotional meaning for the members.

Expressive leader   A leader who concerns him or herself with the emotional well-being of the group.

Fad   A relatively novel behavior that appears suddenly, spreads rapidly, is enthusiastically embraced by a large number of people for a short period of time, and then mostly disappears.

Fashion   A social pattern of behavior or appearance embraced by large numbers of people for a long period of time.

Feminist theory   A woman-centered theoretical perspective arguing that social systems oppress women and that this oppression can and should be eliminated.

Feminization of poverty   An increase in the proportion of the poor who are women.

Fertility   Reproductive performance indicated by the incidence of childbearing in a population.

Focus groups   In-depth, qualitative interviews with a specifically selected small number of people.

Folkways   Weak norms that are often informally passed down from previous generations.

Formal organization   A large, secondary social collectivity that is organized and regulated for purposes of efficiency by structured procedures.

Front-stage behavior   The term from dramaturgical analysis for actions that occur for an audience.

Functionalism (also structural-functionalism)   The theoretical perspective that views society as a complex system of interrelated parts working together to maintain stability.

Fund-raising under the guise of polling (frugging)   Telephone calls or mailings that are actually intended to solicit donations but are disguised as opinion polls.

Gemeinschaft   Toennies's term, meaning "community," that describes traditional social ties characterized by the importance of intimate relationships such as family, kin, and friendship; moral closeness/unity; and religion.

Gender-role socialization   The process of learning to take on socially approved roles for males and females.

Gentrification   A process in which the affluent buy run-down properties at low cost and fix them up as upscale residences.

Gerontologist   A sociologist or other scientist who studies aging and ageism.

Gesellschaft   Toennies's term, meaning "association," that describes social ties characterized by a focus on self rather than community good, individuality, separation from others, and impersonality.

Globalization   A social process in which geographical constraints on social and cultural patterns diminish, and in which people become increasingly aware of those changes.

Grand theory   An abstract level of theorizing that tries to explain the entire social structure at once and is difficult, if not impossible, to test through research.

Group   A collection of people who interact regularly based on some shared interest and who develop some sense of belonging that sets them apart from other gatherings of people.

Group dynamics   The scientific study of groups and group processes.

Groupthink   The phenomenon in which group members faced with making a decision focus so much on getting along, being seen as a "good" group member, and agreeing that they may not adequately evaluate the option they are considering.

Hacker   Programmer who engages in activities of breaching computer security systems or writing viruses.

Hate crime   A crime that is committed based on the victims' characteristics such as race, ethnicity, gender, sexual orientation, disability, or religion.

Hawthorne Effect   Research results achieved because research subjects know they are being studied.

Heterosexism   Prejudice toward homosexuals that justifies unequal treatment of the group on the basis of their assumed characteristics.

Hidden curriculum   Schools' imparting conformity to the norms, values, and beliefs held by wider society in addition to academic subjects.

High culture   Things that are generally associated with the social elite.

Hypothesis   A theory-based statement about the relationship between two or more factors that can be tested through research.

Id   Freud's term for our basic biological drives and needs.

Ideal culture   The values and norms claimed by a society.

Immigration   The movement of people into an area.

Impression management   Consciously attempting to direct and control how others see us through the impressions we make in their minds.

Inequality   The degree of disparity of valued-resource distribution within society.

Inferential statistics   Techniques that make generalizations from sample data to larger population.

Informal organization   An organization that does not involve formalized or rigorous rules, roles, and responsibilities.

Information and collaborative technologies   Technologies that make information sharing easier, more convenient, faster, and often real-time.

In-group   A group with which we identify and feel a sense of belonging and loyalty.

Institutional discrimination   Discrimination that is part of the operation of social systems.

Instrumental leader   A leader who focuses on getting specific jobs done.

Intergenerational mobility   Movement within the social strata that occurs from generation to generation.

Interview   A series of questions administered by a person.

Intragenerational mobility   Movement within the social strata that occurs within the lifetime of an individual.

Iron Law of Oligarchy   Michels's concept that every bureaucracy would invariably turn into an organization ruled by a few elite individuals (i.e., rule by a few).

Labeling theory   The perspective that the response of others to behavior, rather than the behavior itself, defines (labels) the behavior as deviant and impacts further deviance.

Language   A system of symbols that allows communication among members of a culture.

Latent functions   Functions that are unintended and less recognized than manifest functions.

Leader   Someone who is able to influence others toward some future direction, event, goal, or purpose.

Liberal feminism   A woman-centered perspective that locates inequality in a lack of opportunity and education for women as well as traditional views of gender that limit women's roles.

Linguistic-relativity hypothesis   The idea that language reflects cultural perceptions.

Looking-glass self   Cooley's concept that society provides a sort of mirror that reflects to us who we are and on the basis of which we form our self-image.

Macro perspective   A perspective that looks at social processes throughout society.

Manifest functions   Obvious and intended functions.

Marxist feminism   A woman-centered perspective that argues that the capitalist economic structure favors men.

Mass hysteria   A reaction to a real or imagined event in which people become excited to the point of losing their critical-thinking abilities and acting irrationally.

Mass media   Impersonal communications that are directed in a one-way flow to a large audience.

Mass-society theory   A theoretical perspective arguing that modern society is alienating, immoral, apathetic, and discourages individuality, and that in this context, socially isolated people are attracted to social movements for personal reasons.

Master status   A status that becomes more socially important than all other statuses.

Material culture   All the tangible products created by human interaction.

McDonaldization   The process in which principles used in fast-food restaurants to achieve maximum efficiency spread and become dominant in other sectors of society or the world.

Mechanical solidarity   Social relationships based on commonality, shared values and beliefs, and little division of labor.

Median   The center number, where exactly half the numbers are higher in value and half are lower.

Medicalization of deviance   Issues that were formerly defined in moral or legal terms becoming redefined as medical issues.

Micro perspective   A perspective that focuses on patterns of individual interactions.

Middle-range theory   A theory that is more limited than a grand theory and can be tested through research.

Migration   The movement of people into and out of a specific area.

Migration rate   The change per 1,000 people in the population of an area in a given year.

Mob   A crowd that takes action toward an emotionally driven goal.

Mode   The most frequently occurring value.

Modernization theory   A perspective that argues that breaking with tradition and embracing capitalist industrialization would lead to economic, social, cultural, political, and technological development in poor countries.

Moral boundaries   A shared sense of acceptable behavior that establishes right and wrong and sanctions for behaviors that fall outside permissible bounds.

Moral development   How people progress from the self-centeredness of a small child, through learning, to understand others' standpoints and develop an abstract sense of fairness.

Mores   Strongly held norms.

Mortality   Incidence of deaths in a population.

Multicultural global feminism   A woman-centered perspective that recognizes the need to include the diversity of women's voices by other characteristics such as race, ethnicity, class, age, sexual orientation, and able-bodiedness.

Multiculturalism   A recognition of and respect for cultural differences.

Multiple-nuclei model   A theory of urban development that sees city development as occurring in irregular patterns.

Multiuser domain (MUD)   Online social worlds where the participants are able to interact and control various aspects of the program.

Neofunctionalism   An expansion of traditional structural-functionalism that tries to respond to critics in such ways as incorporating some of the ideas of conflict theorists and recognizing the importance of the micro perspective.

Networks   The patterned relationships that connect us with those outside of our established groups.

New social movement   A movement that focuses on bringing about social change through the transformation of values, personal identities, and symbols.

Nongovernmental organization (NGO)   A private organization or group of citizens that works against destructive governments or large organizations.

Nonmaterial culture   The intangible creations of human interaction.

Nonprobability sample   A sample selected on the basis of specific characteristics.

Normative organization   An organization that people join voluntarily and without financial compensation because they believe the cause is worthy.

Norms   Shared rules or expectations specifying appropriate behaviors in various situations.

Objectivity   Not allowing personal opinions or biases to influence the research, outcomes, or interpretation of the data.

Organic solidarity   Social ties based on differences.

Organization   An identifiable group that has a specific purpose.

Out-group   A group with which we do not identify or toward which we may even feel animosity.

Paradigm   A broad assumption about how the world works.

Peer group   Those of similar age, social class, and interests.

Peripheral country   In world-systems theory, a poor country that is exploited for its raw materials and inexpensive labor by core countries.

Personality   Our unique sense of who we are.

Political economy   A perspective that focuses on the interrelationships between political and economic forces and the way they propel urban events.

Popular culture   Activities that are widespread in a culture, with mass accessibility and appeal, and pursued by large numbers of people across all social classes.

Population pyramid   A graphic depiction of a country's population composition.

Population universe   All the people in a group to which research results will be applied.

Positional mobility   Movement within the social strata that occurs due to individual effort.

Positive check   An event that would limit population growth by increasing the death rate.

Positivism   A way to understand the social world based on scientific facts.

Power   The ability to influence others, even if those others resist.

Prejudice   A preconceived and irrational attitude toward people based on their group membership.

Preventative check   An event that would limit population growth by reducing the birthrate.

Primary deviance   Violation of a social norm that goes undiscovered or is considered excusable by others.

Primary group   A small group in which all the members have enduring, intimate face-to-face interaction and cooperation.

Probability sample   A sample in which every individual person in the population universe has an equal chance of being selected (also called a random sample).

Probability theory   A theory used by statisticians that estimates the likelihood that something will occur.

Proletariat   Factory workers who work for the bourgeoisie to produce products.

Pseudo-poll   A nonscientific and nonrepresentative polling effort.

Psychophysiology   The science that deals with the interplay between psychological and physiological processes.

Push poll   A pseudo-poll in which questions are worded as statements that support, or "push," a particular position.

Qualitative research   Research based on the interpretation of nonnumerical data.

Quantitative research   Research based on numerical analysis of data.

Questionnaire   A series of written questions to which participants are asked to respond.

Racism   The belief that one racial or ethnic group is naturally inferior or superior, thus justifying unequal treatment of the group on the basis of their assumed characteristics.

Radical feminism   A woman-centered perspective that argues that, regardless of all other inequalities women face in their lives, male domination is the most fundamental oppression and violence is one key method of controlling women.

Random sample   A sample in which every individual person in the population universe has an equal chance of being selected (also called a probability sample).

Rational-choice theory   A theoretical perspective arguing that people make choices purposely, based on their preferences and evaluation of options and opportunities.

Rationalization   An ongoing search for increasing efficiency, or looking for the most efficient means for doing things.

Real culture   The values and norms that are actually practiced in a culture.

Redemptive social movement   Collective action that seeks a total change of individuals, such as with born-again Christianity.

Redistricting   A process of redrawing political districts after apportionment.

Reference group   Those with which we compare ourselves.

Reformative social movement   Collective action that seeks a partial change of society, such as women's suffrage and child-labor laws.

Relative definition of poverty   Defining poverty on the basis of whether basic needs and wants are met.

Reliability   Whether research results would be the same if the research were repeated at different times of if the same thing were studied in different ways.

Resocialization   A process of altering aspects of a person's personality by controlling the environment.

Resource-mobilization theory   A perspective that recognizes that social movements need to generate adequate, and often substantial, resources to achieve their goals.

Riot   Collective behavior involving public disorder that is less directed and may be of longer duration than mob behavior.

Role   The behavior expected of someone in a particular status.

Role conflict   A situation that occurs when roles for the different statuses a person holds conflict with each other.

Role set   All of the roles that go with a single status.

Role strain   Tension that occurs when two or more roles associated with a single status are in conflict.

Role taking   The ability to take the role of others in social interaction, enabling us to see ourselves as we perceive society sees us.

Rumor   Unverified information spread through informal social interaction, and often derived from unknown sources.

Rural area   An area with a sparse population density that does not fit the definition of urban.

Sample   A subset of the larger population that will serve as a data source.

Scapegoating   Focusing blame on another person or category of people for one's own problems.

Secondary data   Data that was collected by other people or for a purpose other than the research for which it is being used.

Secondary deviance   Deviance committed as a result of the reactions of others to previous deviant behavior.

Secondary group   A group in which all members do not interact directly and have relationships that are not permanent.

Sector model   A theory of urban development that sees cities as growing in wedge-shaped areas extending outward from the central business district of the city.

Self-fulfilling prophecy   Behavior based on a self-concept that has been formed on the basis of a label.

Self-selection poll   A poll in which the participants themselves choose whether to participate rather than being selected through some scientific sampling method.

Semiperipheral country   In world-systems theory, a country that is somewhat industrialized and is able to exploit peripheral countries but is, in turn, exploited by core countries.

Sexism   The belief that one sex is naturally inferior or superior, thus justifying unequal treatment of the group on the basis of their assumed characteristics.

Social change   Structures of cultures and societies transforming into new forms.

Social class   A position based on the unequal location of people within economic groups.

Social-conflict theory   A macro-theoretical perspective that focuses on competition between groups in society.

Social construction of reality   The process by which people interact and shape reality.

Social-control theory   A theoretical perspective on deviance that asks not why people deviate, but rather why they conform.

Social facts   The system of laws, morals, values, religious beliefs, customs, fashions, rituals, and the myriad cultural and social rules governing social life.

Social institution   A major social organization formed to meet our human needs.

Social integration   The strength of social ties connecting individuals to society.

Socialization   A lifelong social process of learning cultural patterns, behaviors, and expectations.

Social mobility   Movement within the stratification system from one position, or strata, to another.

Social movement   An organized collective activity that deliberately seeks to create or resist social change.

Social-movement organization (SMO)   A formal organization that seeks social change by achieving a social movement's goals.

Social processes   The way society operates.

Social stratification   The structured hierarchy, or social strata, that exists in a society.

Social structures   The way society is organized around the regulated ways people interrelate and organize social life.

Society   People who interact and share a common culture.

Sociobiology   A perspective that ties together culture and biology, arguing that there are biological bases for some human behaviors.

Socioeconomic status (SES)   A ranking derived from combining multiple dimensions of stratification.

Sociological imagination   Mills's concept of the connection between biography and history that is central to learning to understand and then change society.

Sociological practice   A sociological focus in which sociological theory, methods, and findings are utilized to bring about positive social changes.

Sociologist   A person who practices sociology.

Sociology   The scientific study of the development, structure, interaction, and collective behavior of social relationships.

Sociospatial model   A model of city development that views local areas as being comprised of various, often competing, growth networks rather than a single coalition.

Speciesism   A belief in the superiority of humans over other species of animals.

Spurious relationship   An apparent connection between variables that is false, or the result of something else.

Status   An established social position.

Status set   All the statuses a person holds at once.

Stereotype   A belief that generalizes certain exaggerated traits to an entire category of people.

Stigma   A powerful negative label that changes a person's social identity and how that person sees him or herself.

Structural-functionalism (also functionalism)   The theoretical perspective that views society as a complex system of interrelated parts working together to maintain stability.

Structural mobility   Mobility that occurs as a result of changes in the occupational structure of a society.

Structural-strain theory   The theory that anomie results from inconsistencies between the culturally approved means to achieve goals and those actual goals.

Subculture   A smaller culture within a dominant culture that has a way of life distinguished in some important way from that dominant culture.

Suburb   An urban area outside of city boundaries.

Suburbanization   The process of population moving out of central cities to surrounding areas.

Superego   Freud's term for our internalized social controls, culture, values, and norms.

Survey   Research in which people are asked questions by an interviewer or provided in a questionnaire to determine their attitudes, opinions, and behaviors.

Symbol   Something that stands for, represents, or signifies something else in a particular culture.

Symbolic interactionism   A micro-theoretical perspective that focuses on patterns of individual interactions.

Taboo   A norm that is so objectionable that it is strictly forbidden.

Tautological   Making a circular argument.

Televoting   A poll in which callers record their opinions by telephoning a particular phone number.

Theory   The analysis and statement of how and why a set of facts relates to each other.

Thomas Theorem   The understanding that if we define situations as real, they are real in their consequences.

Total institution   A place where a large number of people live and work, cut off from wider society for an appreciable period of time, leading an enclosed, formally administered life.

Transactional leader   A leader who is task-oriented and focuses on getting group members to achieve goals.

Transformational leader   A leader who encourages others to go beyond the routine by building a different type of organization that focuses on future possibilities.

Transformative social movement   Collective action that supports a total change of society, such as millenarian and revolutionary movements.

Triad   A three-person group.

Urban ecology   The interaction between human population and the environment, including both material and nonmaterial aspects of human culture.

Urbanized area   A densely settled central place and adjacent territories with residential populations of 50,000 or more people.

Urban legend   A realistic but untrue story that recounts some alleged recent event.

Urban renewal   Government-funded programs that aim to rejuvenate cities.

Urbanization   The increasing percentage of a population living in urbanized areas.

Utilitarian organization   An organization that people join to gain some material benefit.

Validity   Whether research actually measures what the researcher intends to measure.

Glossary

Value A culturally defined idea about what is important.

Value-added theory The theory that a set of factors jointly set the stage for collective action as people react to situations and events.

Variable A factor whose value changes (or varies) from case to case.

V*erstehen* Weber's concept of subjective understanding through which we take someone else's position mentally to understand their actions.

Virtual team A work group that allows members to work on a project from more than one location.

World-systems theory A perspective that focuses on the capitalist world economy in which countries are linked by economic and political ties.

References

Abbate, J. 1999. *Inventing the Internet.* Cambridge: MIT Press.

Abercrombie, Nicholas, Stephen Hill, and Bryan S. Turner. 2000. *The Penguin Dictionary of Sociology.* 4th ed. London: Penguin Books.

Aberle, David F. 1966. *The Peyote Religion among the Navajo.* Chicago: Aldine.

Ackerman, Diane. 1994. *A Natural History of Love.* New York: Random House.

Ackroyd, Judith, and Andrew Pilkington. 1999. "Childhood and the Construction of Ethnic Identities in a Global Age: A Dramatic Encounter." *Childhood* 6, no. 4:443–54.

Ackroyd, S., and P. Thompson. 1999. *Organizational Misbehavior.* Thousand Oaks, Calif.: Sage.

Addams, Jane. 1914. "A Modern Devil-Baby." *American Journal of Sociology* 20:117–18.

Adler, P. A., and P. Adler. 1994. "Observational Techniques." In *Handbook of Qualitative Research,* ed. N. K. Denzin and Y. S. Lincoln. Thousand Oaks, Calif.: Sage.

Agnew, R. 1991. "A Longitudinal Test of Social Control Theory and Delinquency." *Journal of Research in Crime and Delinquency* 28:126–56.

Aguirre, A., Jr., and D. V. Baker, eds. 2000. *Structured Inequality in the United States: Discussions on the Continuing Significance of Race, Ethnicity, and Gender.* Upper Saddle River, N.J.: Prentice Hall.

Aguirre, B. E., E. L. Quarantelli, and Jorge L. Mendoza. 1988. "The Collective Behavior of Fads: The Characteristics, Effects, and Career of Streaking." *American Sociological Review* 53:569–84.

Aguirre, B. E., Dennis Wenger, and Gabriela Vigo. 1998. "A Test of the Emergent Norm Theory of Collective Behavior." *Sociological Forum* 13, no. 2:301–20.

Ahmed, Akbar. 2002. "Ibn Khaldun's Understanding of Civilizations and the Dilemmas of Islam and the West Today." *Middle East Journal* 56, no. 1:20–45.

Akers, Ronald L., Marvin D. Krohn, Lonn Lanza-Kaduce, and Marcia Radosevich. 1979. "Social Learning and Deviant Behavior." *American Sociological Review* 44:636–55.

References

Alcock, John. 2001. *The Triumph of Sociobiology*. Oxford: Oxford University Press.

Aldrich, Howard E., and Peter V. Marsden. 1988. "Environments and Organization." In *Handbook of Sociology*, ed. Neil J. Smelser. Newbury Park, Calif.: Sage.

Alexander, Jeffrey C. 1998. *Neofunctionalism and After*. Malden, Mass: Blackwell.

Alger, Janet M., and Steven F. Alger. 2003. *Cat Culture: The Social World of a Cat Shelter*. Philadelphia: Temple University Press.

Allport, G. W., and L. J. Postman. 1947. *The Psychology of Rumor*. New York: Holt, Rinehart, and Winston.

American Sociological Association. 1999. "American Sociological Association Code of Ethics." http://www.asanet.org/members/ecoderev.html (accessed January 10, 2005).

———. 1999a. *Careers in Sociology*. 5th ed. Washington, D.C.: American Sociological Association.

———. 1999b. *Guide to Graduate Departments in Sociology*. Washington, D.C.: American Sociological Association.

———. 2002a. "The Pipeline for Faculty of Color in Sociology." 27 October. http://www.asanet.org/research/pipeline/text.html (accessed June 4, 2003).

———. 2002b. "Sociology Degrees Awarded by Degree Level, 1970–2000." 27 October. http://www.asanet.org/research/numsocbylev.html (accessed June 2, 2003).

———. 2002c. "Sociology Degrees Awarded by Level of Degree and Gender, 1966–2000." 27 October. http://www.asanet.org/research/socdeglevgen.html (accessed June 2, 2003).

———. 2002d. "Use of Adjunct and Part-Time Faculty in Sociology." 27 October. http://www.asanet.org/research/adjunct/text.html (accessed June 4, 2003).

———. 2004a. "Doctorate Recipients in Selected Social Science Disciplines, US Citizens and permanent Residents, by Race and Ethnicity, 1980, 1990, 2000, 2001." 8 September. http://www.asanet.org/research/docsocscirac.html (accessed December 2, 2004).

———. 2004b. "Percentage of Doctorate Degrees Earned by Women in Select Disciplines: 1966–2001.: 8 Sept. http://www.asanet.org/research/docsocscigen.html (accessed November 28, 2004).

———. 2004c. "Sections of the American Sociological Association." 13 Sept. http//www.asanet.org/sections/general.html (accessed December 2, 2004).

———. 2004d. "Sociology Faculty Salaries by Rank, Academic Years 1982/83 to 2003/04 (in Constant 2003 Dollars)." http://www.asanet.org/research/adjfacsal.html (accessed December 2, 2004).

Andersen, Margaret L. 1993. *Thinking about Women: Sociological Perspectives on Sex and Gender*. 3rd ed. New York: Macmillan.

Andersen, Margaret L., and Patricia Hill Collins. 2003. *Race, Class, and Gender: An Anthology*. 5th ed. Belmont, Calif.: Wadsworth.

Anderson, Benedict. 1983. *Imagined Communities: Reflections on the Origin and Spread of Nationalism*. London: Verso.

Angell, Robert Cooley. 1968. "Cooley, Charles Horton." In *The International Encyclopedia of the Social Sciences*, ed. David Sills. New York: Macmillan and Free Press.

Appelbaum, Richard P. 1988. *Karl Marx*. Newbury Park, Calif.: Sage.

Appelbaum, Richard P., and William J. Chambliss. 1995. *Sociology*. New York: Harper Collins College Publishers.

Aries, P. 1962. *Centuries of Childhood*. Trans. R. Baldick. New York: Random House.

Arluke, Arnold, and Clinton R. Sanders. 1996. *Regarding Animals.* Philadelphia: Temple University Press.

Asch, Solomon E. 1952. *Social Psychology.* Englewood Cliffs, N.J.: Prentice Hall.

———. 1955. "Opinions and Social Pressures." *Scientific American* 193, no. 5: 31–35.

Atchley, R. C. 2000. *Social Forces and Aging: An Introduction to Social Gerontology.* 9th ed. Belmont, Calif.: Wadsworth.

Baali, Fuad. 1988. *Society, State, and Urbanism: Ibn Khaldun's Sociological Thought.* Albany, N.Y.: SUNY Press.

Babbie, Earl. 1994. *The Sociological Spirit.* 2nd ed. Belmont, Calif.: Wadsworth/ITP.

———. 1996. "Sociology: Under Fire or Firing Up?" *Social Insight: Knowledge at Work* 1: 31–34.

Baldassare, Mark. 1994. *The Los Angeles Riots: Lessons for the Urban Future.* Boulder, Colo.: Westview Press.

Baldwin, James D. 1986. *George Herbert Mead: A Unifying Theory for Sociology.* Newbury Park, Calif.: Sage.

Bales, Robert F., and Fred L. Strodtbeck. 1951. "Phases in Group Problem-Solving." *Journal of Abnormal and Social Psychology* 46:484–94.

Bannister, Robert C. 1987. *Sociology and Scientism: The American Quest for Objectivity, 1880–1940.* Chapel Hill: University of North Carolina Press.

———. 1991. *Jessie Bernard: The Making of a Feminist.* New Brunswick, N.J.: Rutgers University Press.

Barber, Benjamin R. 1996. *Jihad vs. McWorld.* New York: Ballantine.

Bayer, Leonard. 2003. "An Interview with Our Methodology Expert." Harris Interactive, August. http://www.harrisinteractive.com/tech/HI_Methodology_Overview.pdf (accessed August 30, 2003).

Bazzini, D. G., W. D. McIntosh, S. M. Smith, S. Cook, and C. Harris. 1997. "The Aging Woman in Popular Film: Underrepresented, Unattractive, Unfriendly, and Unintelligent." *Sex Roles* 36:531–43.

Beauregard, R. A. 1990. "Trajectories of Neighborhood Change: The Case of Gentrification." *Environment and Planning* 22:855–74.

Bechmann, Gotthard, and Nico Stehr. 2002. "The Legacy of Niklas Luhmann." *Society* 39 (Jan./Feb.):67–75.

Becker, Ernest. 1971. *The Lost Science of Man.* New York: George Braziller.

Becker, Howard S. 1963. *The Outsiders: Studies in the Sociology of Deviance.* Glencoe, Ill.: Free Press.

———. 1988. "Herbert Blumer's Conceptual Impact." *Symbolic Interaction* 11, no. 1:13–21.

"Becker, Howard Saul." 1992. In *Contemporary Authors,* vol. 134, ed. Susan M. Trosky. Detroit: Gale Research.

Belasco, Warren, and Philip Scranton, eds. 2002. *Food Nations: Selling Taste in Consumer Societies.* New York: Routledge.

Bell, C., and H. Newby. 1976. "Communion, Communalism, Class, and Community Action: The Sources of the New Urban Politics." In *Social Areas in Cities,* vol. 2., ed. D. Herbert and R. Johnston. Chichester, N.Y.: Wiley.

Bell, Daniel. 1973. *The Coming Crisis of Postindustrial Society: A Venture in Social Forecasting.* New York: Basic Books.

———. 1989. "The Third Technological Revolution and Its Possible Economic Consequences." *Dissent* (spring): 164–76.

References

Bell, David. 2001. *An Introduction to Cybercultures.* London: Routledge.

Bell, Wendell. 1997. *Foundations of Futures Studies: Human Science for a New Era.* New Brunswick, N.J.: Transaction.

Bellah, Robert N. 1983. "The Ethical Aims of Sociological Inquiry." In *Social Science as Moral Inquiry,* ed. N. Haan, R. N. Bellah, P. Rabinow, and E. M. Sullivan. New York: Columbia University Press.

Bellah, Robert N., Richard Madsen, William M. Sullivan, Ann Swindler, and Steven M. Tipton. 1985. *Habits of the Heart: Individualism and Commitment in American Life.* New York: Harper and Row.

Bellamy, Carol. 2002. *The State of the World's Children: 2003.* New York: United Nations Children's Fund (UNICEF).

Bendix, Reinhard. 1968. "Weber, Max." In *The International Encyclopedia of the Social Sciences,* ed. David Sills. New York: Macmillan and Free Press.

Berger, Peter L. "Peter Berger." Biography, Boston University. http://www.bu.edu/religion/faculty/individualfaculty/berger.htm (accessed July 29, 2003).

———. 1963. *Invitation to Sociology: A Humanistic Perspective.* Woodstock, N.Y.: Overlook Press.

———. 2002. "Introduction: The Cultural Dynamics of Globalization." In *Many Globalizations: Cultural Diversity in the Contemporary World,* ed. Peter L. Berger and Samuel P. Huntington. New York: Oxford University Press.

Berger, Peter, and Thomas Luckmann. 1966. *The Social Construction of Reality.* New York: Doubleday.

"Berger, Peter Ludwig." 1981. In *Contemporary Authors, New Revision Series,* vol. 1, ed. Ann Evory. Detroit: Gale Research.

Bernstein, Jared, Lawrence Mishel, and Chauna Brocht. "Any Way You Cut It: Income Inequality on the Rise Regardless of How It's Measured." Washington, D.C.: Economic Policy Institute. http://www.epinet.org/briefingpapers/inequality/ineq_bp.pdf (accessed August 31, 2003).

Best, Amy L. 2000. *Prom Night: Youth, Schools, and Popular Culture.* New York: Routledge.

Best, Joel. 2001. *Damned Lies and Statistics: Untangling Numbers from the Media, Politicians, and Activists.* Berkeley: University of California Press.

Best, Raphaela. 1983. *We've All Got Scars: What Boys and Girls Learn in Elementary School.* Bloomington: Indiana University Press.

Biggart, Nicole Woolsey. 1987. "Book Review: Writing for Social Scientists: How to Start and Finish Your Thesis, Book, or Article, by Howard S. Becker with a chapter by Pamela Richards." *American Journal of Sociology* :92:1548–1550.

Billson, Janet Mancini. 1996. *Mastering the Job Market with a Graduate Degree in Sociology.* Washington, D.C.: American Sociological Association.

Birke, Lynda, and Mike Michael. 1998. "The Heart of the Matter: Animal Bodies, Ethics, and Species Boundaries." *Society and Animals* 6:245–61.

Blass, Thomas. 1999. "Stanley Milgram." In *American National Biography,* ed. J. A. Garraty. Cary, N.C.: Oxford University Press and American Council of Learned Societies.

———. 2000. "The Milgram Paradigm after 35 Years: Some Things We Now Know About Obedience to Authority." In *Obedience to Authority: Current Perspectives on the Milgram Paradigm.* Ed. Thomas Blass. Mahwah, NJ: Lawrence Erlbaum.

———. 2002. "Perpetrator Behavior as Destructive Obedience: An Evaluation of Stanley Milgram's Perspective, the Most Influential Social-Psychological Approach to the Holocaust." In *Understanding Genocide: The Social Psychology of the Holocaust,* ed. L. Newman and R. Erber. New York: Oxford University Press.

Blau, Peter M. 1964. *Exchange and Power in Social Life.* New York: Wiley.

———. 1977. *Inequality and Heterogeneity: A Primitive Theory of Social Structure.* New York: Free Press.

———. 1995. "A Circuitous Path to Macrostructural Theory." In *Annual Review of Sociology,* ed. John Hagan, Karen S. Cook. vol. 21. Palo Alto, Calif.: Annual Reviews.

Blau, Peter M., and Otis Dudley Duncan. 1967. *The American Occupational Structure.* New York: Wiley.

"Blau, Peter Michael." 1981. In *Contemporary Authors, New Revision Series,* vol. 1, ed. Ann Evory. Detroit: Gale Research.

Blau, Reva. 2002. "Michael Peter Blau." In *Footnotes* 30, #4 (April). Washington, D.C.: American Sociological Association.

Block, Jean H. 1983. "Differential Premises Arising from Differential Socialization of the Sexes: Some Conjectures." *Child Development* 54:1335–54.

Bloom, Samuel W. 2002. *The Word as Scalpel: A History of Medical Sociology.* New York: Oxford University Press.

Blumer, Herbert. 1968. "Fashion." In *The International Encyclopedia of the Social Sciences,* ed. David Sills. New York: Macmillan and Free Press.

———. 1969. "Collective Behavior." In *Principles of Sociology,* 3rd ed., ed. Alfred McClung Lee. New York: Barnes and Noble Books.

Boas, Frank. 1911. *Handbook of American Indian Languages.* Washington, D.C.: Government Printing Office.

Bogler, Ronit, and Anit Somech. 2002. "Motives to Study and Socialization Tactics among University Students." *Journal of Social Psychology* 142, no. 2:233–48.

Boli, J., and G. M. Thomas. 1997. "World Culture in the World Polity: A Century of International Non-governmental Organization." *American Sociological Review* 37:547–59.

Bortnick, Barry. 1999. "Amazon Jungle to Ivory Tower." *Santa Barabara News-Press,* 19 April. http://www.anth.ucsb.edu/images/Aj2it.pdf (accessed August 15, 2003).

Bott, Elizabeth. 1971. *Family and Social Network.* New York: Free Press.

Bottomore, T. B. 1965. *Classes in Modern Society.* London: Allen and Unwin.

Bourdieu, P. 1984. *Distinction: A Social Critique of the Judgement of Taste.* Routledge: London.

Bower, R. T., and P. deGusparis. 1978. *Ethics and Social Research.* New York: Praeger.

Bradshaw, York, and Michael Wallace. 1996. *Global Inequalities.* Thousand Oaks, Calif.: Pine Forge.

Brashers, Dale E., Stephen M. Haas, Judith L. Neidig, and Lance S. Rintamaki. 2002. "Social Activism, Self-Advocacy, and Coping with HIV Illness." *Journal of Social and Personal Relationships* 19, no. 1:113–33.

Breyer, Michelle R. 1996. "Making a Dogged Appeal: Rent-to-Own Industry Seeks to Brush Up on Image." *Austin American Statesman,* 6 November.

References

Brown, L. R., W. V. Chandler, C. Flavin, J. Jacobson, C. Pollock, S. Postel, L. Starke, and E. C. Wolf. 1987. "Analyzing the Demographic Gap." In *State of the World, 1987: A Worldwatch Institute Report on Progress Toward a Sustainable Society,* ed. L. R. Brown et al. New York: W. W. Norton.

Brown, S. E., F. Esbensen, and G. Geis. 1991. *Criminology: Explaining Crime and Its Context.* Cincinnati, Ohio: Anderson.

Brownstein, Henry. 2000. *The Social Reality of Violence and Violent Crime.* Boston: Little, Brown.

Bruhn, John G. 2001. "On Becoming a Clinical Sociologist." In *Handbook of Clinical Sociology,* ed. Howard M. Rebach and John G. Bruhn. New York: Kluwer/Plenum.

Brunvand, Jan Harold. 1993. *The Baby Train and Other Lusty Urban Legends.* New York: W. W. Norton.

Bryson, M. C. 1976. "The Literary Digest Poll: Making of a Statistical Myth." *American Statistician* 30 (November): 184.

Bureau of Labor Statistics. 2004a. "Highlights of Women's Earnings in 2003." Report 978. September. http://www.bls.gov.cps/cpswom2003.pdf (accessed December 2, 2004).

Bureau of Labor Statistics. 2004b. "Social Scientists, Other." In *Occupational Outlook Handbook, 2004–05 Edition.* U.S. Department of Labor. http://www.bls.gov/oco/ocos054.htm (accessed December 2, 2004).

Burgess, Ernest W. 1925. "The Growth of the City: An Introduction to a Research Project." In *The City,* ed. Robert E. Park, Ernest W. Burgess, and Roderick D. McKenzie. Chicago: University of Chicago Press.

Burns, Tom. 1992. *Erving Goffman.* London: Routledge.

Butler, R. N. 1975. *Why Survive? Being Old in America.* New York. Harper and Row.

Cahnman, Werner J., and Rudolf Heberle, eds. 1971. *Ferdinand Toennies on Sociology: Pure, Applied, and Empirical.* Chicago: University of Chicago.

Calhoun, Craig. 2003. "Robert K. Merton Remembered." *Footnotes* 31, no. 3:1, 8. http://www.asanet.org/footnotes/mar03/indextwo.html (accessed August 8, 2003).

Campbell, Donald T., and Julian C. Stanley. 1963. *Experimental and Quasi-Experimental Designs for Research.* Chicago: Rand McNally.

Campbell, Marie. 2003. "Dorothy Smith and Knowing the World We Live In." *Journal of Sociology and Social Welfare* 30, no. 1:3–22.

Campbell, Rebecca. 2002. *Emotionally Involved: The Impact of Researching Rape.* New York: Routledge.

Campbell, Steve. 1999. *Statistics You Can't Trust.* Parker, Colo.: Think Twice Publishing.

Canetti, E. 1962. *Crowds and Power.* London: Gollancz.

Cannadine, David. 1986. "Conspicuous Consumption by the Landed Classes, 1790–1830." In *Malthus and His Time,* ed. Michael Turner. New York: St. Martin's Press.

Cantor, Muriel G. 1988. "Jessie Bernard: An Appreciation." *Gender and Society* 3:264–70.

Capizzano, Jeffrey, Kathryn Tout, and Gina Adams. 2000. "Child Care Patterns of School-Age Children with Employed Mothers." Occasional Paper no. 41. Washington, D.C.: Urban Institute. http://www.urban.org/url.cfm?ID=310283 (accessed June 20, 2003).

Caplow, Theodore. 1984. "Rule Enforcement without Visible Means: Christmas Gift-Giving in Middletown." *American Journal of Sociology* 89:6.

Carey, James. 1972. "Problems of Access and Risk in Observing Drug Scenes." In *Research on Deviance,* ed. J. Douglas. New York: Random House.

Carley, Kathleen. 1991. "A Theory of Group Stability." *American Sociological Review* 56:331–54.

Carneiro, Robert L. 1968. "Spencer, Herbert" In *The International Encyclopedia of the Social Sciences,* 15 ed. David Sills. New York: Macmillan and Free Press.

Carroll, John B., ed. 1956. *Language, Thought, and Reality: Selected Writings of Benjamin Lee Whorf.* Cambridge: MIT Press.

Carrozza, Mark A., and Robert L. Seufert. 1997. "One Picture Is Worth a Thousand Calculations. GIS: A New Tool for Data Analysts." *Social Insight: Knowledge at Work* 2, no. 1:16–21.

Carter, Gregg Lee. 1992. "Hispanic Rioting During the Civil Rights Era." *Sociological Forum* 7, no. 2:301–22.

Castelli, Luigi, Cristina Zogmaister, and Luciano Arcuri. 2001. "Exemplar Activation and Interpersonal Behavior." *Current Research in Social Psychology* 6, no. 3. http://www.uiowa.edu/~grpproc/crisp/crisp.6.3.htm (accessed December 2, 2004).

Castells, M. 2001. *Internet Galaxy: Reflections on the Internet, Business, and Society.* New York: Oxford University Press.

Castles, Stephen. 2003. "Towards a Sociology of Forced Migration and Social Transformation." *Sociology* 37, no. 1:13–34.

Cavender, Grey. 1990. "Alternative Criminological Theory: The Labelling Perspective and Critical Criminology." In *Handbook of Contemporary Criminology.* ed. Joseph Sheley. Belmont Ca: Wadsworth, pp. 315–32.

———. 1991. "Alternative Theory: Labeling and Critical Perspectives." In *Criminology: A Contemporary Handbook.* Belmont, Calif.: Wadsworth.

Chafetz, Janet Saltzman. 2001. "Theoretical Understandings of Gender: A Third of a Century of Feminist Thought in Sociology." In *Handbook of Sociological Theory,* ed. Jonathan H. Turner. New York: Kluwer Academic/Plenum.

Chagnon, Napoleon. 1997. *Yanomamo.* 5th ed. Fort Worth, Tex.: Harcourt Brace.

"Chagnon, Napoleon A." 1990. In *Contemporary Authors,* vol. 130, ed. Susan M. Trosky. Detroit: Gale Research.

Chagnon, Napoleon. "Napoleon Chagnon responds to Darkness in El Dorado" http://www.anth.ucsb.edu/chagnon.html (accessed November 28, 2004).

Chakraborty, Somen. 1999. *A Critique of Social Movements in India.* New Delhi: India Social Institute.

Chambliss, William J. "William Chambliss." Sociology Faculty and Staff, George Washington University. http://www.gwu.edu/~soc/w_chambliss.html (accessed July 29, 2003).

———. 1964. "A Sociological Analysis of the Law of Vagrancy." *Social Problems* 12:67–77.

———. 1973. "The Saints and the Roughnecks." *Society* 11, 1 (Nov.–Dec.): 24–31.

———. 1975. "Toward a Political Economy of Crime." *Theory and Society* 2:149–70.

———. 1987. "I Wish I Didn't Know Now What I Didn't Know Then." *Criminologist* 12:1, 5–7, 9.

———. 1988. *On the Take: From Petty Crooks to Presidents.* Bloomington: Indiana University Press.

References

———. 1989. "State-Organized Crime." *Criminology* 27:183–208.

———. 1994. "Policing the Ghetto Underclass: The Politics of Law and Law Enforcement." *Social Problems* 41, no. 2:177–94.

Chambliss, William J., and Robert B. Seidman. 1982. *Law, Order, and Power.* Rev. ed. Reading, Mass.: Addison-Wesley.

Chambliss, William J., and Marjorie Zatz. 1994. *Making Law: Law, State, and Structural Contradiction.* Bloomington: Indiana University Press.

Chase-Dunn, Christopher. 2001. "World-Systems Theory." In *Handbook of Sociological Theory,* ed. Jonathan H. Turner. New York: Kluwer Academic/Plenum.

Chase-Dunn, Christopher, and Peter Grimes. 1995. "World-System Analysis." *Annual Review of Sociology* 21, eds. John Hagan, Karen S. Cook. Palo Alto, Ca: Annual Reviews.

Chayko, Mary. 2002. *Connecting: How We Form Social Bonds and Community in the Internet Age.* New York: SUNY Press.

Chesler, Ellen. 1992. *Woman of Valor: Margaret Sanger and the Birth Control Movement in America.* New York: Simon and Schuster.

Chesney-Lind, Meda, and Karlene Faith. 2001. "What about Feminism? Engendering Theory-Making in Criminology." In *Explaining Criminals and Crime,* ed. Raymond Paternoster and Ronet Bachman. Los Angeles: Roxbury.

Ching, F. 1994. "Talking Sense on Population." *Far Eastern Economic Review.* October 6.

Cho, H., and R. LaRose. 1999. "Privacy Issues in Internet Surveys." *Social Science Computer Review* 17:421–34.

Christiansen, Karl. 1977. "A Preliminary Study of Criminality Among Twins." In *Biosocial Bases of Criminal Behavior,* ed. Samuel Mednick. New York: Gardner.

Christie, Nils. 1993. *Crime Control as Industry.* London: Routledge.

Chugerman, Samuel. 1965. *Lester Ward: The American Aristotle.* New York: Octagon Books.

Clark, Jon. 1990. "Anthony Giddens, Sociology, and Modern Social Theory." In *Anthony Giddens: Conflict and Controversy,* ed. Jon Clark, Celia Modgil, and Sohan Modgil. London: Falmer Press.

Clark, Ronald W. 1980. *Freud: The Man and the Cause.* New York: Random House.

Cloward, Richard A., and Lloyd E. Ohlin. 1960. *Delinquency and Opportunity: A Theory of Delinquent Gangs.* New York: Free Press.

CNN. 2003. "Activists Hold 'Virtual March' on Washington." CNN.com, 28 February. http://www.cnn.com/2003/TECH/ptech/02/26/virtual.protest/ (accessed March 1, 2003).

Coale, Ansley J. 1999. "Kingsley Davis." *Proceedings of the American Philosophical Society* 143, no. 3:453–54.

Cohen, Albert K. 1971. *Delinquent Boys: The Culture of the Gang.* New York: Free Press.

Coleman, James. 1990. "Robert K. Merton as Teacher." In *Robert K. Merton: Consensus and Controversy,* ed. Jon Clark, Celia Modgil, and Sohan Modgil. London: Falmer Press.

Coleman, J. S., and T. J. Fararo. 1992. *Rational Choice Theory: Advocacy and Critique.* Newbury Park, Calif.: Sage.

"Collins, Patricia Hill." 1997. In *Contemporary Authors,* vol. 154, ed. Terrie M. Rooney. Detroit: Gale.

Collins, Patricia Hill. 2000. *Black Feminist Thought: Knowledge, Consciousness, and the Politics of Empowerment.* Rev. ed. Boston: Unwin Hyman.

Collins, Randall. 1986. "The Passing of Intellectual Generations: Reflections on the Death of Erving Goffman." *Sociological Theory* 4:106–13.

———. 1988. *Theoretical Sociology.* New York: Harcourt Brace Jovanovich.

———. 1989. "Toward a Neo-Meadian Sociology of Mind." *Symbolic Interaction* 12:1–32.

———. 1994. *Four Sociological Traditions.* New York: Oxford University Press.

———. 1999. "The European Sociological Tradition and Twenty-First-Century World Sociology." In *Sociology for the Twenty-First Century,* ed. Janet L. Abu-Lughod. Chicago: University of Chicago Press.

Colvin, Mark. 1982. "The 1980 New Mexico Prison Riot." *Social Problems* 29, no. 5:449–63.

Comte, Auguste. 1896. *The Positive Philosophy of Auguste Comte.* 1838. Reprint, London: Bell.

"Conrad, Peter." 2000. In *Contemporary Authors, New Revision Series,* vol. 88, ed. Scot Peacock. Detroit: Gale Group.

Conrad, Peter. "Peter Conrad." Sociology Department Faculty, Brandeis University. http://www.brandeis.edu/departments/sociology/conrad.html (accessed August 9, 2003).

Conrad, Peter, and Joseph W. Schneider. 1980. *Deviance and Medicalization: From Badness to Sickness.* St. Louis, Mo.: C. V. Mosby.

Cook, Gary A. 1993. *George Herbert Mead: The Making of a Social Pragmatist.* Urbana: University of Illinois Press.

Cook, Karen S. 1987. *Social Exchange Theory.* London: Sage.

———. 2002. "Colleagues Remember Peter Blau." *Footnotes* 30, 4 (April). Washington, D.C.: American Sociological Association. http://www.asanet.org/footnotes/apr02/fn4.html (accessed August 8, 2003).

Cooley, Charles Horton. 1964. *Human Nature and the Social Order.* 1902. Reprint, New York: Schocken.

Cooper, C. R., and J. Denner. 1994. "Theories Linking Culture and Psychology: Universal and Community-Specific Processes." *Annual Review of Psychology* 49:559–84.

Cose, Ellis. 1993. *The Rage of a Privileged Class.* New York: HarperCollins.

Coser, Lewis A. 1956. *The Functions of Social Conflict.* Glencoe, Ill.: Free Press.

———. 1977. *Masters of Sociological Thought: Ideas in Historical and Social Context.* 2nd ed. New York: Harcourt Brace Jovanovich.

Crawford, Robert. 1986. "Individual Responsibility and Health Politics." In *The Sociology of Health and Illness,* 2nd ed., ed. P. Conrad and R. Kern. New York: St. Martin's Press.

Cressey, Donald Ray. 1953. *Other People's Money: A Study in the Social Psychology of Embezzlement.* Glencoe, Ill.: Free Press.

Cross, R., S. P. Borgatti, and A. Parker. 2001. "Beyond Answers: Dimensions of the Advice Network." *Social Networks* 23, no. 3:215–35.

Cross, S. E., and H. R. Markus. 1999. "The Cultural Constitution of Personality." In *Handbook of Personality,* 2nd ed., ed. L. A. Pervin and O. P. Johns. New York: Guilford.

Crowley, Joan E. 1985. "Longitudinal Effects of Retirement on Men's Psychological and Physical Well-Being." In *Retirement among American Men,* ed. Herbert S. Parnes. Lexington, Mass.: Heath.

References

Crozier, M. 1964. *The Bureaucratic Phenomenon.* London: Tavistock.

Curtis, Bruce. 1981. *William Graham Sumner.* Boston: Twayne.

Curtiss, Susan R. 1977. *Genie: A Psycholinguistic Study of a Modern-Day "Wild Child."* New York: Academic.

Dahrendorf, R. 1959. *Class and Class Conflict in Industrial Society.* Stanford, Calif.: Stanford University Press.

Daly, Kathleen, and Meda Chesney-Lind. 1988. "Feminism and Criminology." *Justice Quarterly* 5:497–538.

Darwin, Charles R. 1981. *The Descent of Man.* 1871. Reprint, Princeton, N.J.: Princeton University Press.

———. 1996. *On the Origin of Species,* ed. G. Beer. 1859. Reprint, New York: Oxford University Press.

Davies, Mark, and Denise B. Kandel. 1981. "Parental and Peer Influences on Adolescents' Educational Plans: Some Further Evidence." *American Journal of Sociology* 87:363–87.

Davis, A. J. 1984. "Sex-differentiated Behaviors in Non-Sexist Picture Books." *Sex Roles.* 11:1-16.

Davis, Arthur K. 1968. "Veblen, Thorstein." In *The International Encyclopedia of the Social Sciences,* ed. David Sills. New York: Macmillan and Free Press.

Davis, Kingsley. 1940. "Extreme Social Isolation of a Child." *American Journal of Sociology* 45:554–65.

———. 1947. "Final Note on a Case of Extreme Isolation." *American Journal of Sociology* 52:432–47.

Davis, Kingsley, and Wilbert Moore. 1945. "Some Principles of Stratification." *American Sociological Review* 10:242–49.

DeCesare, Michael A. 2002. "The Lesson to be Learned: The Past Troubles and Future Promise of Teaching High School Sociology." *Teaching Sociology* 30: 302–16.

Deegan, Mary Jo. 1988. *Jane Addams and the Men of the Chicago School, 1892–1918.* New Brunswick, N.J.: Transaction Books.

Demetriou, Christina, and Andrew Silke. 2003. "A Criminological Internet Sting: Experimental Evidence of Illegal and Deviant Visits to a Website Trap." *British Journal of Criminology* 43, no. 1:213–22.

Department of Housing and Urban Development. 2004. "A Guide to Counting Unsheltered Homeless People." US Department of Housing and Urban Development, November 4. http://www.hud.gov/offices/cpd/homeless/library/counting homeless/index.cfm (accessed December 2, 2004).

Deva, Janadas. 2003. "Words That Linger after Bombs Fall Silent." *Straits Times Interactive,* 27 April. http://straitstimes.asia1.com.sg/columnist/0,1886,145–185610,00.html (accessed August 10, 2003).

Devers, Gail. 2004. "A Glance Back at the Starting Line." http://www.gaildevers. com/biography.htm (accessed December 2, 2004).

Diaz, Mary Kirby. 2001. "What Is a Sociologist-Mediator?" *Social Insight: Knowledge at Work* 6:26–28.

Dibbell, Julian. 1999. "A Rape in Cyberspace; Or How an Evil Clown, a Haitian Trickster Spirit, Two Wizards, and a Cast of Dozens Turned a Database into a Society." In *High Noon on the Electronic Frontier: Conceptual Issues in Cyberspace,* ed. Peter Ludlow. Cambridge: MIT Press.

Diener, E., S. Fraser, A. Beaman, and R. Kelem. 1976. "Effects of Deindividuation Variables on Stealing among Halloween Trick-or-Treaters." *Journal of Personality and Social Psychology* 33:178–83.

Digby, Anne. 1986. "Malthus and Reform of the English Poor Laws." In *Malthus and His Time,* ed. Michael Turner. New York: St. Martin's Press.

DiMaggio, Paul. 1982. "Cultural Capital and School Success." *American Sociological Review* 47:189–201.

DiMaggio, Paul, Eszter Hargittai, W. Russell Neuman, and John P. Robinson. 2001. "Social Implications of the Internet." *Annual Review of Sociology* 27. ed. John Hagan, Karen S. Cook. Palo Alto, Ca.: Annual Reviews.

Dion, K., E. Berscheid, and E. Walster. 1972. "What Is Beautiful Is Good." *Journal of Personality and Social Psychology* 24:285–90.

Dogan, Mattei. 2000. "The Moving Frontier of the Social Sciences." In *The International Handbook of Sociology,* ed. Stella R. Quah and Arnaud Sales. London: Sage.

Domhoff, G. William. 1974. *The Bohemian Grove and Other Retreats.* New York: Harper and Row.

Dowie, Mark. 1977. "Pinto Madness." *Mother Jones* 2 (Sep./Oct.): 18–32.

Dreier, Peter. 1993. "America's Urban Crisis: Symptoms, Causes, Solutions." *North Carolina Law Review* 71:5.

———. 2001. "How Will You Spend the 21st Century?" *Footnotes* 29, 6 (July/August): 11–12. http://www.asanet.org/footnotes/julyaugust01/fn12.html (accessed May 1 2003).

Drexel University. "Arthur B. Shostak, Ph.D." Expert File. http://www.futureshaping.com/shostak/pages/expertfile.html (accessed August 20, 2003).

Du Bois, W.E.B. 1996. *The Philadelphia Negro: A Social Study.* 1899. Reprint, Philadelphia: University of Pennsylvania Press.

Du Bois, William. 2001. "Design and Human Behavior: The Sociology of Architecture." In *Applying Sociology: Making a Better World.* eds. William DuBois and R. Dean Wright. Boston: Allyn and Bacon.

Dunbar, Leslie W. 1988. *The Common Interest: How Our Social-Welfare Policies Don't Work, and What We Can Do about Them.* New York: Pantheon.

Durkheim, Emile. 1956. *Sociology and Education.* New York: Free Press.

———. 1964a. *The Division of Labor in Society.* 1893. Reprint, New York: Free Press.

———. 1964b. *The Rules of Sociological Method.* 1895. Reprint, New York: Free Press.

———. 1966. *Suicide: A Study in Sociology.* 1897. Reprint, New York: Free Press.

Edensor, Tim. 2002. *National Identity, Popular Culture, and Everyday Life.* Oxford: Berg.

Eder, Donna. 1995. *School Talk: Gender and Adolescent Culture.* New Brunswick, N.J.: Rutgers University.

Edgell, Stephen. 2001. *Veblen in Perspective.* Armonk, N.Y.: M. E. Sharpe.

Edmunds, H. 1999. *The Focus Group Research Handbook.* Chicago: NTC Business Books.

Eitle, David J. 2002. "Exploring a Source of Deviance-Producing Strain for Females: Perceived Discrimination and General Strain Theory." *Journal of Criminal Justice* 30, no. 5:429–42.

Elliott, James R. and Ryan A. Smith, 2004. "Race, Gender, and Workplace Power." *American Sociological Review.* 69:365–86.

References

Ellison, P., J. Govern, H. Petri, and M. Figler. 1995. "Anonymity and Aggressive Driving Behavior: A Field Study." *Journal of Social Behavior and Personality* 10:265–72.

Elwell, Frank W. "The Sociology of C. Wright Mills." http://www.faculty.rsu.edu/~felwell/Theorists/Mills/index.htm (accessed December 31, 2002).

———. 1999. *Industrializing America: Understanding Contemporary Society through Classical Sociological Analysis.* Westport, Conn.: Praeger.

———. 2001. *A Commentary on Malthus' 1798 Essay on Population as Social Theory.* Lewiston, N.Y.: Edwin Mellen Press.

Engels, Friedrich. 1964. "Outlines of a Critique of Political Economy." In *The Economic and Philosophic Manuscripts of 1844,* ed. D. Struik. 1844. Reprint, New York: International.

———. 1981. "Demoralisation of the English Working Class." In *Crime and Capitalism,* ed. D. Greenberg. Palo Alto, Calif.: Mayfield.

Enos, Sandra. 2001. *Mothering from the Inside.* New York: State University of New York Press.

Erikson, Erik H. 1985. *The Life Cycle Completed: A Review.* New York: W. W. Norton.

Erikson, Kai. 1966. *Wayward Puritans: A Study in the Sociology of Deviance.* New York: Wiley.

———. 1978. *Everything in Its Path.* New York: Touchstone Books.

———. 1986. "Book Review: Writing for Social Scientists: How to Start and Finish Your Thesis, Book, or Article, by Howard S. Becker with a chapter by Pamela Richards." *Contemporary Sociology* 15:808–10.

Erikson, Robert S., Norman R. Luttbeg, and Kent L. Tedin. 2000. *American Public Opinion: Its Origins, Content, and Impact.* New York: Longman.

ESOMAR/WAPOR. 1998. "ESOMAR/WAPOR Guide to Opinion Polls Including the ESOMAR International Code of Practice for the Publication of Public Opinion Poll Results." European Society for Opinion and Marketing Research (ESOMAR) and the World Association for Public Opinion Research (WAPOR). http://www.esomar.org/main.php?a=2&p=76 (accessed July 20, 2003).

Etzioni, Amitai. 1975. *A Comparative Analysis of Complex Organization: On Power, Involvement, and Their Correlates.* New York: Free Press.

Eyerman, Ron. 2002. "Music in Movement: Cultural Politics and Old and New Social Movements." *Qualitative Sociology.* 25, no. 3:443–58.

Feagin, J. R., and M. P. Sikes. 1994. *Living with Racism: The Black Middle-Class Experience.* Boston: Beacon Press.

Featherman, David L., and Robert M. Hauser. 1978. *Opportunity and Change.* New York: Academic Press.

Federal Bureau of Investigation. 2004. *Hate Crime Statistics, 2003.* Washington, D.C.: Federal Bureau of Investigation, U.S. Department of Justice. http://www.fbi.gov/ucr/01hate.pdf (accessed November 27, 2004).

Federman, Mark. "Marshall McLuhan." McLuhan Program in Culture and Technology. http://mcluhan.utoronto.ca/marshal.htm#MM (accessed August 10, 2003).

———. "On Reading McLuhan." McLuhan Program in Culture and Technology. http://mcluhan.utoronto.ca/OnReadingMcLuhan.pdf (accessed August 10, 2003).

Feinberg, Barbara Silberdick. 1985. *Marx and Marxism.* New York: Franklin Watts.

Fenstermaker Berk, Sarah. 1985. *The Gender Factory: The Apportionment of Work in American Households.* New York: Plenum.

Ferree, M. M., and E. J. Hall. 1990. "Visual Images of American Society: Gender and Race in Introductory College Textbooks." *Gender and Society* 4:500–33.

Figart, D. M., and J. Lapidus. 1998. "Will Comparative Worth Reduce Race-Based Wage Discrimination?" *Review of Radical Political Economics* 30, no. 3: 14–24.

Fine, Gary Alan. 2001. "Enacting Norms: Mushrooming and the Culture of Expectations and Explanations." In *Social Norms,* ed. Michael Hechter and Karl-Dieter Opp. New York: Russell Sage Foundation.

Finnegan, W. 1998. *Cold New World: Growing Up in a Harder Country.* New York: Random House.

Fischer, C. 1992. *America Calling: A Social History of the Telephone to 1940.* Berkeley: University of California Press.

Fishman, R. 1987. *Bourgeois Utopias: The Rise and Fall of Suburbia.* New York: Basic Books.

Forbes. 2004. "Forbes 400 Richest in America 2004." Forbes.com. http://www.forbes.com/richlist (accessed December 2, 2004).

Forsyth, Donelson R. 1990. *Group Dynamics.* 2nd ed. Pacific Grove, Calif.: Brooks/Cole.

Foster, Janet. 1990. *Villains: Crime and Community in the Inner City.* London: Routledge.

Frank, Nancy, and Michael J. Lynch. 1992. *Corporate Crime, Corporate Violence.* Albany, N.Y.: Harrow and Heston.

Frank, Robert, and Phillip Cook. 1995. *The Winner Take All Society: Why the Few at the Top Get So Much More than the Rest of Us.* New York: Penguin.

Freeman, Jo. 1999. "On the Origins of Social Movements." In *Waves of Protest: Social Movements Since the Sixties,* ed. Jo Freeman and Victoria Johnson. Lanham, Md.: Rowman and Littlefield.

French, J. R. P., Jr., and B. Raven. 1959. "The Bases of Social Power." In *Studies in Social Power,* ed. D. Cartwright. Ann Arbor, Mich.: Institute for Social Research.

Freud, Sigmund. 1950. *The Ego and the Id.* Trans. Joan Riviere. 1923. Reprint, London: Hogarth Press and the Institute of Psycho-analysis.

———. 1950. *The Interpretation of Dreams.* Trans. A. A. Brill. 1900. Reprint, New York: Modern Library.

Friedman, Samuel R. 1999. *Social Networks, Drug Injectors' Lives, and HIV/AIDS.* New York: Kluwer Academic.

Friedmann, John, and Goetz Wolff. 1982. "World City Formation: An Agenda for Research and Action." *International Journal of Urban and Regional Research* 6:309–44.

Frisby, David. 1984. *Georg Simmel.* Ed. Peter Hamilton. N.Y.: Tavistock.

Fuchs, Stephan. 1999. "Niklas Luhmann." *Sociological Theory* 17, no. 1:117–19.

Gailey, C. W. 1987. "Evolutionary Perspectives on Gender Hierarchy." In *Analyzing Gender: A Handbook of Social Science Research.* Eds. B. B. Hess, M. M. Ferree. Newbury Park, NJ: Sage.

Gale, Dennis E. 1996. *Understanding Urban Unrest: From Reverend King to Rodney King.* Thousand Oaks, Calif.: Sage.

Gamson, William. 1975. *The Strategy of Social Protest.* Homewood, Ill.: Dorsey.

Gans, Herbert J. "Biography—Herbert J. Gans." http://www.sociology.columbia.edu/downloads/curriculum_vitae/hjg1.pdf (accessed April 11, 2003).

References

———. 1967. *The Levittowners: Life and Politics in a New Suburban Community.* New York: Pantheon Books.

———. 1990a. "Deconstructing the Underclass: The Term's Danger as a Planning Concept." *Journal of the American Planning Association* 56:271–77.

———. 1990b. "Relativism, Equality, and Popular Culture." In *Authors of Their Own Lives,* ed. Bennett M. Berger. Berkeley: University of California Press.

———. 1995. *The War against the Poor: The Underclass and Antipoverty Policy.* New York: Basic Books.

———. 2001. "The Uses of Poverty: The Poor Pay All." In *Down to Earth Sociology: Introductory Readings,* 11th ed., ed. James M. Henslin. New York: Free Press.

Garfinkel, Harold. 1967. *Studies in Ethnomethodology.* Englewood Cliffs, N.J.: Prentice Hall.

———. 1988. "Evidence for Locally Produced, Naturally Accountable Phenomena of Order, Reason, Meaning, Method, Etc. in and as of the Essential Quiddity of Immortal Ordinary Science (I of IV): An Announcement of Studies." *Sociological Theory* 6, no. 1:103–9.

———. 1996. "Ethnomethodology's Program." *Social Psychology Quarterly* 59, no. 1:5–21.

———. 2002. *Ethnomethodology's Program: Working Out Durkheim's Approach,.* ed. Anne Warfield Rawls. Lanham, Md.: Rowman and Littlefield.

Garreau, Joel. 1991. *Edge City: Life on the New Frontier.* New York: Doubleday.

Gastil, J. 1990. "Generic Pronouns and Sexist Language: The Oxymoronic Character of Masculine Generics." *Sex Roles* 23:629–43.

Gaylord, Mark S., and John F. Galliher. 1988. *The Criminology of Edwin Sutherland.* New Brunswick, N.J.: Transaction Books.

Gecas, Viktor. 2000. "Socialization." In *Encyclopedia of Sociology,* 2nd ed., ed. Edgar F. Borgatta and Rhonda J. V. Montgomery. New York: Macmillan.

Gellner, Ernest. 1975. "Cohesion and Identity: The Maghreb From Ibn Khaldun to Emile Durkheim." *Government and Opposition* 10, no. 2:203–18.

Gibson, Campbell. 1998. "Population of the 100 Largest Cities and Other Urban Places in the United States: 1790 to 1990." Population Division Working Paper no. 27. Washington, D.C.: U.S. Bureau of the Census. http://www.census.gov/population/www/documentation/twps0027.html (accessed April 20, 2003).

Giddens, Anthony. "An Interview with Anthony Giddens." Polity. http://www.polity.co.uk/giddens/interview.htm (accessed April 5, 2003).

———. 1991. *Modernity and Self-Identity: Self and Society in the Late Modern Age.* Cambridge, UK: Polity Press.

———. 2000. *Runaway World: How Globalization Is Reshaping Our Lives.* New York: Routledge.

Gilligan, Carol. 1982. *In a Different Voice: Psychological Theory and Women's Development.* Cambridge: Harvard University Press.

Gilligan, Carol, Janie V. Ward, and Jill M. Taylor, eds. 1989. *Mapping the Moral Domain: A Contribution of Women's Thinking to Psychological Theory and Education.* Cambridge: Harvard University Press.

Giner, S. 1976. *Mass Society.* London: Martin Robertson.

Glass Ceiling Commission. 1995. *Good for Business: Making Full Use of the Nation's Human Capital: A Fact-Finding Report of the Federal Glass Ceiling Commission.* Washington, D.C.: U.S. Government Printing Office.

Glueck, Sheldon, and Eleanor Glueck. 1950. *Unravelling Juvenile Delinquency.* New York: Commonwealth Fund.

———. 1956. *Physique and Delinquency.* New York: Harper and Row.

Goffman, Erving. 1959. *Presentation of Self in Everyday Life.* Garden City, N.Y.: Anchor.

———. 1961. *Asylums.* New York: Doubleday.

———. 1963a. *Behavior in Public Places.* New York: Free Press.

———. 1963b. *Stigma: Notes on the Social Organization of Spoiled Identity.* New York: Free Press.

———. 1967. *Interaction Ritual: Essays on Face to Face Behavior.* Garden City, N.Y.: Anchor.

Gordon, M. M. 1988. *The Scope of Sociology.* New York: Oxford University Press.

Goring, Charles. 1972. *The English Convict: A Statistical Study.* 1913. Reprint, Montclair, N.J.: Patterson Smith.

Gottdiener, Mark. "Dr. Mark Gottdiener." Vita. http://sociology.buffalo.edu/vita gottdiener.htm (accessed August 15, 2003).

———. 1985. *The Social Production of Urban Space.* Austin: University of Texas Press.

Gottdiener, Mark, Claudia C. Collins, and David R. Dickens. 1999. *Las Vegas: The Social Production of an All-American City.* Malden, Mass.: Blackwell.

Gottfredson, Michael R., and Travis Hirschi. 1990. *A General Theory of Crime.* Stanford, Calif.: Stanford University Press.

Gracey, Harry L. 2001. "Learning the Student Role: Kindergarten as Academic Boot Camp." In *Down to Earth Sociology: Introductory Readings,* 11th ed., ed. James M. Henslin. New York: Free Press.

Granovetter, Mark. 1973. "The Strength of Weak Ties." *American Journal of Sociology* 78:1360–80.

———. 1982. "The Strength of Weak Ties: A Network Theory Revisited." In *Social Structure and Network Analysis,* ed. Peter Marsden and Nan Lin. Beverly Hills, Calif.: Sage.

Greeley, Andrew M. 1986. *Confessions of a Parish Priest: An Autobiography.* New York: Simon and Schuster.

———. 1990. "The Crooked Lines of God." *Authors of Their Own Lives,* ed. Bennett M. Berger. Berkeley: University of California Press.

———. 1999. *Furthermore! Memories of a Parish Priest.* New York: Tom Doherty Associates.

Grier, Lee W. 1971. "The History of the Teaching of Sociology in the Secondary School." Ed.D. diss., Duke University.

Griffin, E. 1997. *A First Look at Communication Theory.* New York: McGraw-Hill.

Gros, Jean-Germain. 2003. "Trouble in Paradise: Crime and Collapsed States in the Age of Globalization." *British Journal of Criminology* 43, no. 1:63–80.

Guice, Jon. 1999. "Sociologists Go to Work in High Technology." *Footnotes* (November). http://www.asanet.org/footnotes/nov99/fn13.html (accessed May 1, 2003).

Guillen, Mauro F. 2001. "Is Globalization Civilizing, Destructive, or Feeble? A Critique of Five Key Debates in the Social Science Literature." In *Annual Review of Sociology,* 27, ed. Karen S. Cook and John Hagan. Palo Alto, Calif.: Annual Reviews.

Gusfield, Joseph R. 1980. Foreword to *Deviance and Medicalization: From Badness to Sickness,* by Peter Conrad and Joseph W. Schneider. St. Louis, Mo.: C. V. Mosby.

References

Hagen, Edward H., Michael E. Price, John Tooby. 2001. "Prelimininary Report." University of Ca–Santa Barbara. http://www.anth.ucsb.edu/ucsbpreliminaryreport.pdf (accessed November 28, 2004).

Hall, W. 1986. "Social Class and Survival on the S.S. Titanic." In *Social Science and Medicine.* 22: 687–90.

Hambrick, D. C. 1995. "Fragmentation and Other Problems CEOs Have with Their Top Management Teams." *California Management Review* 37, 3 (spring): 110–27.

Hamilton, Peter. 1983. *Talcott Parsons.* New York: Tavistock.

———. 1984. Editor's foreword to *Georg Simmel.* NY: Taristock.

Hamon, Amy. 1998. " 'Hacktivists' of All Persuasions Take Their Struggle to the Web." *New York Times,* 31 October.

Haney, Craig, Curtis Banks, and Philip Zimbardo. 1973. "Interpersonal Dynamics in a Simulated Prison." *International Journal of Criminology and Penology* 1:69–97.

Hardt, Hanno, and Slavko Splichal, eds. and trans. 2000. *Ferdinand Toennies on Public Opinion: Selections and Analyses.* Lanham, Md.: Rowman and Littlefield.

Harris, Chauncey D., and Edward D. Ullman. 1945. "The Nature of Cities." *Annals* 242 (November): 7–17.

Harris, Marvin. 1974. *Cows, Pigs, Wars, and Witches.* New York: Random House.

———. 2001. "Marvin Harris: Explains the Unexplainable." Interview by Barbara Spronk. *Aurora Online.* http://aurora.icaap.org/archive/harris.html (accessed August 10, 2003).

Hartley, Eugene. 1946. *Problems in Prejudice.* New York: King's Crown Press.

Harvey, David. 1985a. *Consciousness and the Urban Experience.* Oxford: Blackwell.

———. 1985b. *The Urbanisation of Capital.* Oxford: Blackwell.

Hasson, Judi. 2002. "Sometimes a Great Notion." *Federal Computer Week,* 11 March. http://www.fcw.com/fcw/articles/2002/0311/tec-csc-03–11–02.asp (accessed August 2, 2003).

Hawdon, James, and Catherine Mobley. 2001. "Applied Sociology: What Skills Are Important?" *Social Insight: Knowledge at Work* 6:12–20.

Hawley, Amos. 1950. *Human Ecology: A Theory of Community Structure.* New York: Ronald Press.

Hayes, Edward Cary. 1927. "Albion Woodbury Small." In *American Masters of Social Science,* ed. Howard W. Odum. New York: Henry Holt.

Headley, B. D. 1991. "Race, Class, and Powerlessness in World Economy." *Black Scholar* 21:14–21.

Healy, Mary Edward. 1972. *Society and Social Change in the Writings of St. Thomas, Ward, Sumner, and Cooley.* Westport, Conn.: Greenwood Press.

Heberle, Rudolf. 1968. "Toennies, Ferdinand." In *The International Encyclopedia of the Social Sciences,* ed. David Sills. New York: Macmillan and Free Press.

Hechter, Michael, and Karl-Dieter Opp. 2001. Introduction to *Social Norms,* ed. Michael Hechter and Karl-Dieter Opp. New York: Russell Sage Foundation.

Heimer, K., and R. L. Matsueda. 1994. "Role-Taking, Role Commitment, and Delinquency: A Theory of Differential Social Control." *American Sociological Review* 59:365–90.

Held, D., A. McGrew, D. Goldblatt, and J. Perraton. 1999. *Global Transformations.* Stanford, Calif.: Stanford University Press.

Hellriegel, Don, John W. Slocum Jr., and Richard W. Woodman. 2001. *Organizational Behavior.* 9th ed. Cincinnati, Ohio: South-Western College Publishing.

Henslin, James M., ed. 2001a. *Down to Earth Sociology: Introductory Readings.* 11th ed. New York: Free Press.

———. 2001b. "The Survivors of the F-227." In *Down to Earth Sociology: Introductory Readings,* 11th ed., ed. James M. Henslin. New York: Free Press.

———. 2001c. "What Is Sociology? Comparing Sociology and the Social Sciences." In *Down to Earth Sociology: Introductory Readings,* 11th ed., ed. James M. Henslin. New York: Free Press.

Herman, Nancy J. 1993. "Return to Sender Reintregrative Stigma-Management Sratigies of Ex-Psychiatric Patients." In *Journal of Contemporary Ethnography.* 22: 29–30.

Herring, Lee. 2002. "Sociological Work Enhances Recent Congressional Briefings." *Footnotes* 30, 6 (July/August). http://www.asanet.org/footnotes/julyaugust02/fn1.html (accessed August 8, 2003).

Hessler, Richard M., Jane Downing, Cathleen Beltz, Angela Pelliccio, Mark Powell, and Whitley Yale. 2003. "Qualitative Research on Adolescent Risk Using E-Mail: A Methodological Assessment." *Qualitative Sociology* 26, no. 1:111–24.

Heymann, Jody. 2000. *The Widening Gap: Why America's Working Families Are in Jeopardy and What Can Be Done about It.* New York: Basic Books.

Hill, Richard Child, and Kuniko Fujita. 2003. "The Nested City: Introduction." *Urban Studies* 40, no. 2:207–17.

Hiller, E. T. 1933. *Principles of Sociology.* N.Y.: Harper and Row.

Hillery, C. A. 1955. "Definitions of Community: Areas of Agreement." *Rural Sociology* 20:93–118.

"Hirschi, Travis." 1984. In *Contemporary Authors, New Revision Series,* vol. 13, ed. Linda Metzger. Detroit: Gale Research.

Hirschi, Travis. 1969. *Causes of Delinquency.* Berkeley: University of California Press.

Hochschild, Arlie. 1983. *The Managed Heart: Commercialization of Human Feeling.* Berkeley: University of California Press.

Hochstetler, Andy, Heith Copes, and Matt DeLisi. 2002. "Differential Association in Group and Solo Offending." *Journal of Criminal Justice* 30, no. 6:559–66.

Hodos, Jerome I. 2002. "Globalization, Regionalism, and Urban Restructuring: The Case of Philadelphia." *Urban Affairs Review* 37, no. 3:358–79.

Homans, George Caspar. 1964. "Bringing Men Back In." *American Sociological Review* 29:809–18.

———. 1969. "A Life of Synthesis." In *Sociological Self-Images: A Collective Portrait,* ed. Irving Louis Horowitz. Beverly Hills, Calif.: Sage.

———. 1974. *Social Behavior: Its Elementary Forms.* Rev. ed. New York: Harcourt Brace Jovanovich.

———. 1984. *Coming to My Senses: The Autobiography of a Sociologist.* New Brunswick, N.J.: Transaction Books.

Hooton, Earnest. 1939a. *The American Criminal: An Anthropological Study.* Cambridge: Harvard University Press.

———. 1939b. *Crime and the Man.* Cambridge: Harvard University Press.

Hornsby, Ann M. 2001. "Surfing the Net for Community: A Durkheimian Analysis of Electronic Gatherings." In *Illuminating Social Life.* 2nd ed., ed. Peter Kivisto. Thousand Oaks, Calif.: Pine Forge Press.

Horne, Christine. 2001. "Sociological Perspectives on the Emergence of Social Norms." In *Social Norms,* ed. Michael Hechter and Karl-Dieter Opp. New York: Russell Sage Foundation.

References

Horowitz, Irving Louis. 1983. *C. Wright Mills: An American Utopian.* New York: Free Press.

Hoyt, Homer. 1939. *The Structure and Growth of Residential Neighborhoods in American Cities.* Chicago: University of Chicago Press.

Hudson, Michael. 1993. "How the Poor Pay More: Big Premiums on Big Ticket Items." *Business and Society Review* 85:43–46.

Human Rights Watch. 1999. "Broken People: Caste Violence Against India's 'Untouchables.'" Human Right Watch. http://www.hrw.org/reports/1999/india/ (accessed May 1, 2003).

Humphreys, Laud. 1970. *Tearoom Trade: Impersonal Sex in Public Places.* Chicago: Aldine-Atherton.

Hunley, J. D. 1991. *The Life and Thought of Friedrich Engels.* New Haven, Conn.: Yale University Press.

Hunter, James D., and Stephen C. Ainley, Eds. 1986. *Making Sense of Modern Times: Peter L. Berger and the Vision of Interpretive Sociology.* London: Routledge and Kegan Paul.

Huzel, J. P. 1986. "The Demographic Impact of the Old Poor Law: More Reflections on Malthus." In *Malthus and His Time,* ed. Michael Turner. New York: St. Martin's Press.

Hyman, Herbert H. 1942. "The Psychology of Status." *Archives of Psychology* 38:15.

Hyman, Herbert H., and Eleanor Singer. 1968. *Readings in Reference Group Theory and Research.* New York: Free Press.

Illich, Ivan. 1976. *Medical Nemesis.* New York: Bantam Books.

Independent Commissions on International Humanitarian Issues. 1985. *Famine: A Man-Made Disaster?* New York: Random House.

Ingraham, Chrys. 1999. *White Weddings: Romancing Heterosexuality in Popular Culture.* New York: Routledge.

Inkeles, Alex. 1979. "Continuity and Change in the American National Character." In *The Third Century: America as a Post-Industrial Society,* ed. Seymour Martin Lipset. Stanford, Calif.: Hoover Institution Press.

Institute for the Future. "Institute for the Future@ AACC (IF@AACC)." http://www.aacc.edu/future (accessed November 30, 2004).

Irvine, Leslie. 2004. *If You Tame Me: Understanding Our Connection With Animals.* Philadelphia: Temple University Press.

Iutcovich, Joyce Miller, and Sue Hoppe. 2001. "Ethics and Sociological Practice." In *Handbook of Clinical Sociology,* 2nd ed., ed. Howard M. Rebach and John G. Bruhn. New York: Kluwer/Plenum.

Jackson, Kenneth. 1985. *Crabgrass Frontier: The Suburbanization of the United States.* New York: Oxford University Press.

Janis, Irving L. 1983. *Groupthink: Psychological Studies of Policy Decisions and Fiascoes.* 2nd ed. Boston: Houghton Mifflin.

———. 1989. *Crucial Decisions: Leadership in Policymaking and Crisis Management.* New York: Free Press.

———. 1991. "Groupthink." *The Organizational Behavior Reader.* 5th ed., ed. David A. Kolb, Irwin M. Rubin, and Joyce S. Osland. Englewood Cliffs, N.J.: Prentice Hall.

Jankowski, Martin Sanchez. 1991. *Islands in the Street: Gangs and American Urban Society.* Berkeley: University of California Press.

Jencks, Christopher. 1994. *The Homeless.* Cambridge: Harvard University Press.

Jenkins, Craig J. 1983. "Resource Mobilization Theory and the Study of Social Movements." *Annual Review of Sociology* eds. John Hagan, Karen S. Cook. vol. 9. Palo Alto, Calif.: Annual Reviews.

Jerabek, Hynek. 2001. "Paul Lazarsfeld—The Founder of Modern Empirical Sociology: A Research Biography." *International Journal of Public Opinion Research* 13, no. 3:229–44.

Johnson, David, and Frank P. Johnson. 2000. *Joining Together: Group Therapy and Group Skills.* Boston: Allyn and Bacon.

Johnson, Victoria. 1999. "The Strategic Determinants of a Countermovement: The Emergence and Impact of Operation Rescue Blockades." In *Waves of Protest: Social Movements since the Sixties,* ed. Jo Freeman and Victoria Johnson. Lanham, Md.: Rowman and Littlefield.

Joinson, A. 1998. "Causes and Implications of Disinhibited Behavior on the Internet." In *Psychology and the Internet,* ed. J. Gackenbach. London: Academic Press.

Jones, David A. 1986. *History of Criminology: A Philosophical Perspective.* New York: Greenwood Press.

Jung, D. I., and B. J. Avolio. 1999. "Effects of Leadership Style and Followers' Cultural Orientation on Performance in Group and Individual Task Conditions." *Academy of Management Journal* 42:208–18.

Kallen, David J. 1995. "Some History of Clinical Sociology and Sociological Practice, Part I." *Clinical Sociology Review* 13:1–23.

Kallen, David. 2001. "Clinical Sociology." Interview by Kathy S. Stolley. *About.com.* 24 March. http://sociology.about.com/library/weekly/aa032401a.htm (accessed April 1, 2001).

Kandal, Terry R. 2001. "Robert Michels' Sexual Ethics." *Society* 38, 3 (Mar./Apr.): 60–66.

"Kanter, Rosabeth Moss." 2002. In *Contemporary Authors, New Revision Series,* vol. 106. Detroit: Thompson/Gale.

Kanter, Rosabeth Moss. "Rosabeth Moss Kanter." Faculty and Research, Harvard Business School. http://dor.hbs.edu/fi_redirect.jhtml?facInfo=bio&facEmId=rkanter&loc=extn (accessed August 15, 2003).

———. 1977. *Men and Women of the Corporation.* New York: Basic Books.

———. 1983. *The Change Masters: Innovation for Productivity in the American Corporation.* New York: Simon and Schuster.

———. 1995a. "Corporate Communities." Interview by David Gergen. PBS, 1 November. MacNeil/Lehrer Productions. http://www.pbs.org/newshour/gergen/kanter.html (accessed September 15, 2003).

———. 1995b. *World Class: Thriving Locally in the Global Economy.* New York: Simon and Schuster.

———. 2001. *Evolve! Succeeding in the Digital Culture of Tomorrow.* Boston, Mass.: Harvard Business School Press.

Kates, R. W. 1993. "Ending Deaths from the Famine: The Opportunity in Somalia." *New England Journal of Medicine* 328:1055–57.

Katz, Sidney. 2001. "The Importance of Being Beautiful." In *Down to Earth Sociology: Introductory Readings,* 11th ed., ed. James M. Henslin. New York: Free Press.

Kelly, Jonathan. 1981. *Revolution and the Rebirth of Inequality.* Berkeley: University of California Press.

References

Kelman, Herbert C., and V. Lee Hamilton. 1989. *Crimes of Obedience: Toward a Social Psychology of Authority and Responsibility.* New Haven, Conn.: Yale University Press.

Kendall, Lori. 2002. *Hanging Out in the Virtual Pub.* Berkeley: University of California Press.

Kenen, Regina. 1982. "Soapsuds, Space and Sociability: A Participant Observation of the Laundromat." *Urban Life* 11 no. 2, 163–83.

Kennedy, L. W. 1990. *On the Borders of Crime: Conflict Management and Criminology.* New York: Longman.

Kerstein, R. 1990. "Stage Models of Gentrification: An Examination." *Urban Affairs Quarterly* 25:620–39.

Kilbourne, Jean. 2000. *Killing Us Softly 3: Advertising's Image of Women.* Northampton, Mass.: Media Education Foundation. Video.

Kilpatrick, Dean G., Patricia A. Resick, and Linda M. Williams. 2001. "Fostering Collaborations between Violence against Women Researchers and Practitioners." *Social Insight: Knowledge at Work* 6:29–35.

Kimmel, Chad. 1998. "On Being a Sociologist." *Social Insight: Knowledge at Work* 3:7–8.

Kimmel, M. S. 2000. *The Gendered Society.* N.Y.: Oxford University Press.

King, Harry, and William J. Chambliss. 1984. *Harry King: A Professional Thief's Journey.* New York: Wiley.

King, Karen N. 2002. "The Art of Impression Management: Self-Presentation in Local-Level Campaign Literature." *Social Science Journal* 39, no. 1:31–41.

Kish, Leslie. 1987. *Statistical Design for Research.* New York: Wiley.

Klandermans, Bert. 2000. "Social Movements: Trends and Turns." In *The International Handbook of Sociology,* ed. Stella R. Quah and Arnaud Sales. London: Sage.

Knox, E. G., and E. A. Gilman. 1997. "Hazard Proximities of Childhood Cancer in Great Britain from 1953–1980." *Journal of Epidemiology and Community Health* 51:151–59.

Kohlberg, Lawrence. 1984. *The Psychology of Moral Development.* Vol. 2. New York: Harper and Row.

Kohn, Melvin L. 1977. *Class and Conformity.* 2nd ed. Chicago: University of Chicago Press.

Konicki, Steve. 2002. "Groupthink Gets Smart." *Information Week,* 14 January. http://www.informationweek.com/story/showArticle.jhtml?articleID=6500684 (accessed August 2, 2003).

Koppel, Ross. 2001. "Evaluation" In *Handbook of Clinical Sociology.* 2nd ed., ed. Howard M. Rebach and John G. Bruhn. N.Y.: Kluwer/Plenum.

Kornhauser, William. 1959. *The Politics of Mass Society.* New York: Free Press.

Kozol, Jonathan. 1991. *Savage Inequalities.* New York: Crown.

Krackow, A., and T. Blass. 1995. "When Nurses Obey or Defy Inappropriate Physician Orders: Attributional Differences." *Journal of Social Behavior and Personality* 10:585–94.

Kubler-Ross, Elizabeth. 1969. *On Death and Dying.* New York: Macmillan.

Kuhn, Thomas. 1970. *The Structure of Scientific Revolutions.* 2nd ed. Chicago: University of Chicago Press.

Lai, G. 2001. "Social Support Networks in Urban Shanghai." *Social Networks* 23, no. 1:73–85.

Lashbrook, Jeff. 2001. "Sociology in High Schools: A Profile of New York State." *Teaching Sociology* 29:354–59.

Laslett, Barbara, and Barrie Thorne. 1992. "Considering Dorothy Smith's Social Theory: Introduction." *Sociological Theory* 10, no. 1:60–62.

Lawson, Helene M. 2000. *Ladies on the Lot: Women, Car Sales, and the Pursuit of the American Dream.* Lanham, Md.: Rowman and Littlefield.

Le Bon, Gustave. 1960. *The Crowd: A Study of the Popular Mind.* 1896. Reprint, New York: Viking.

Lee, Daniel. 2000. "The Society of Society: The Grand Finale of Niklas Luhmann." *Sociological Theory* 18, no. 2:320–30.

Lemert, Charles. 2001. "Mysterious Powers of Social Structures." In *Understanding Inequality: The Intersection of Race/Ethnicity, Class, and Gender,* ed. Barbara A. Arrighi. Lanham, Md.: Rowman and Littlefield.

Lemert, Edwin. 1951. *Social Pathology.* New York: McGraw-Hill.

Lengermann, Patricia Madoo, and Jill Niebrugge-Brantley. 1998. *The Women Founders: Sociology and Social Theory, 1830–1930.* Boston: McGraw-Hill.

Lenski, Gerhard. 1984. *Power and Privilege: A Theory of Social Stratification.* Chapel Hill: University of North Carolina Press.

———. 1992. "New Light on Old Issues: The Relevance of 'Really Existing Socialist Societies' for Stratification Theory." In *Social Stratification: Class, Race, and Gender in Sociological Perspective,* ed. David B. Grusky. Boulder, Colo.: Westview Press.

Lenski, Gerhard, Jean Lenski, and Patrick Nolan. 1991. *Human Societies: An Introduction to Macrosociology.* 6th ed. New York: McGraw-Hill.

Levine, Felice. 1993. "MOST: A Pipeline to Diversity in Sociology." *Footnotes* 21:4.

Lewandowski, Jennifer. 2001. "Gottdiener Explores 'Life in the Air.'" *University of Buffalo Reporter,* 26 April. http://www.buffalo.edu/reporter/vol32/vol32n29/n3.html (accessed September 15, 2003).

Lewin, Kurt. 1948. *Resolving Social Conflicts: Selected Papers on Group Dynamics.* New York: Harper.

Lewis, David Levering. 2000. *W.E.B. Du Bois.* New York: Henry Holt.

Lieberson, Stanley. "Stanley Lieberson." Sociology Department Faculty, Harvard University. http://www.wjh.harvard.edu/soc/faculty/lieberson/ (accessed August 15, 2003).

———. 1985. "Stanley Lieberson." Interview by John Talbot, Jared Epstein, and Dean Hunsaker. *Berkeley Faculty, Live!* October. http://sociology.berkeley.edu/faculty_live/faculty.asp#lieberson (accessed August 9, 2003).

———. 2000. *A Matter of Taste: How Names, Fashions, and Culture Change.* New Haven, Conn.: Yale University Press.

Lin, Nan, Walter M. Ensel, and John C. Vaughn. 1981. "Social Resources and Strength of Ties: Structural Factors in Occupational Status Attainment." *American Sociological Review* 46:393–405.

Lindesmith, Alfred. 1968. *Addiction and Opiates.* Chicago: Aldine.

Lindner, Rosalyn. 1997. "Jury Consultants: You Be the Judge." *Social Insight: Knowledge at Work* 2, 7–12.

Link, Bruce G., and Jo C. Phelan. 2001. "Conceptualizing Stigma." *Annual Review of Sociology* 27, ed. John Hagan, Karen S. Cook. vol. 9. Palo Alto, Calif.: Annual Reviews.

References

Lipman-Blumen, Jean. 1979. "Bernard, Jessie." In *The International Encyclopedia of the Social Sciences, Biographical Supplement,* ed. David Sills. New York: Macmillan and Free Press.

Lipnack, J., and J. Stamps. 1997. *Virtual Teams: Reaching across Space, Time, and Organizations.* Somerset, N.J.: Wiley.

Lisle, Laurie. 1999. *Without Child: Challenging the Stigma of Childlessness.* New York: Routledge.

Livernash, Robert, and Eric Rodenburg. 1998. "Population Change, Resources, and the Environment." *Population Bulletin* 53, no. 1 Washington, D.C.: Population Reference Bureau.

Logan, John R., and Harvey L. Molotch. 1987. *Urban Fortunes: The Political Economy of Place.* Berkeley: University of California Press.

Lombroso, Cesare. 1876. *The Criminal Man.* Milan: Hoepli.

———. 1968. *Crime: Its Causes and Remedies.* 1911. Reprint, Montclair, N.J.: Patterson Smith.

Lombroso, Cesare, William Ferrero. 1980. *The Female Offender.* 1909. Reprint, William S. Hein.

London, Bruce. 1987. "Structural Determinants of Third World Urban Change: An Ecological and Political Economic Analysis." *American Sociological Review* 52:28–43.

Lorber, Judith. 1998. *Gender Inequality: Feminist Theories and Politics.* Los Angeles: Roxbury.

Luhmann, Niklas. 1982. *The Differentiation of Society.* New York: Columbia University Press.

Lurie, Elinore E. 1981. "Nurse Practitioners: Issues in Professional Socialization." *Journal of Health and Social Behavior* 22 (March): 31–48.

Lynch, Michael J., and Paul B. Stretesky. 2001. "Radical Criminology." In *Explaining Criminals and Crime,* ed. Raymond Paternoster and Ronet Bachman. Los Angeles: Roxbury.

MacAndrew, Craig, and Robert B. Edgerton. 1969. *Drunken Comportment: A Social Explanation.* New York: Aldine de Gruyter.

Macionis, John J. 1995. *Sociology.* 5th ed. Englewood Cliffs, N.J.: Prentice Hall.

MacLeod, Jay. 1995. *Ain't No Makin' It: Aspirations and Attainment in a Low-Income Neighborhood.* Boulder, Colo.: Westview Press.

Malthus, Thomas. 1926. *First Essay on Population.* 1798. Reprint, London: Macmillan.

Mann, Barry. 1993. *Sigmund Freud.* Vero Beach, Fla.: Rourke Publications.

Mann, Chris, and Fiona Stewart. 2000. *Internet Communication and Qualitative Research: A Handbook for Researching Online.* Thousand Oaks, Calif.: Sage.

Mann, Coramae Richey. "Coramae Richey Mann." People, Department of Criminal Justice, Indiana University–Bloomington. http://www.indiana.edu/~crimjust/faculty/Mann.htm (accessed August 9, 2003).

———. 1987. "Racism in the Criminal Justice System: Two Sides of a Controversy—The Reality of a Racist Criminal Justice System." *Criminal Justice Research Bulletin* 3:1–5.

———. 1993. *Unequal Justice: A Question of Color.* Bloomington: Indiana University Press.

———. 1995. "Seventeen White Men and Me." In *Individual Voices, Collective Visions: Fifty Years of Women in Sociology,* ed. Ann Goetting and Sarah Fenstermaker. Philadelphia: Temple University Press.

Mann, D., and M. Sutton. 1998. "Netcrime: More Change in the Organisation of Thieving." *British Journal of Criminology* 38, no. 2:201–28.

Mann, S. A., M. D. Grimes, A. A. Kemp, and P. J. Jenkins. 1997. "Paradigm Shifts in Family Sociology? Evidence from Three Decades of Family Textbooks." *Journal of Family Issues* 18 (May): 315–49.

Margolis, Maxine L. 2002. "Marvin Harris, 1927–2002." *Department of Anthropology Newsletter,* University of Florida (spring): 9. http://web.anthro.ufl.edu/ newsletter/newsletter2002.pdf (accessed August 3, 2003).

Marrow, Alfred Jay. 1969. *The Practical Theorist: The Life and Work of Kurt Lewin.* New York: Basic Books.

Martel, Martin U. 1979. "Parsons, Talcott." In *The International Encyclopedia of the Social Sciences, Biographical Supplement,* ed. David Sills. New York: Macmillan and Free Press.

Martin, Douglas. 2001. "Marvin Harris." *New York Times,* 28 October.

Martin, Randy, Robert J. Mutchnick, and W. Timothy Austin. 1990. *Criminological Thought: Pioneers Past and Present.* New York: Macmillan.

Marvin, F. S. 1965. *Comte: The Founder of Sociology.* New York: Russell and Russell.

Marx, Karl. 1977a. *Capital: A Critique of Political Economy.* 3 vols. 1867. Reprint, New York: Random House.

———. 1983. "Manifesto of the Communist Party." In *The Portable Karl Marx,* ed. Eugene Kamenka. 1848. Reprint, N.Y.: Penguin.

Marx, Karl, and Friedrich Engels. 1956. *The Holy Family.* 1846. Reprint, Moscow: Foreign Language Publishing House.

Masini, Eleonora Barbieri. 2000. "Futures Research and Sociological Analysis." In *The International Handbook of Sociology,* ed. Stella R. Quah and Arnaud Sales. London: Sage.

Massey, James L., and Martha A. Myers. 1989. "Patterns of Repressive Social Control in Post-Reconstruction Georgia, 1882–1935." *Social Forces* 68:458–88.

Maynard, Douglas W. 1996. "Introduction of Harold Garfinkel for the Cooley-Mead Award." *Social Psychology Quarterly* 59, no. 1:1–4.

Mayo, E. 1933. *The Human Problems of an Industrial Civilization.* New York: Macmillan.

McAdam, Doug, John D. McCarthy, and Mayer N. Zald. 1988. "Social Movements." In *Handbook of Sociology,* ed. Neil J. Smelser. Newbury Park, Calif.: Sage.

McCarthy, E. D. 1989. "Emotions Are Social Things: An Essay in the Sociology of Emotions." In *The Sociology of Emotions: Original Essays and Research Papers,* ed. E. D. McCarthy and D. D. Franks. Greenwich, Conn.: JAI Press.

McCarthy, John D., and Mayer N. Zald. 1973. *The Trend of Social Movements in America: Professionalization and Resource Mobilization.* Morristown, N.J.: General Learning.

———. 2001. "The Enduring Vitality of the Resource Mobilization Theory of Social Movements." In *Handbook of Sociological Theory,* ed. Jonathan H. Turner. New York: Kluwer Academic/Plenum.

McFalls, Joseph A., Jr. 1998. "Population: A Lively Introduction." vol. 53, no. 3. Washington, D.C.: Population Reference Bureau.

McLanahan, Sara S., and G. Sandefur. 1994. *Growing Up with a Single Parent.* Cambridge: Harvard University Press.

McLuhan, M. 1964. *Understanding Media.* London: Routledge.

McLuhan, M., and Q. Fiore. 1967. *The Medium Is the Message.* London: Allen Lane.

References

McLuhan Program in Culture and Technology. "History and Mandate." http://mcluhan.
utoronto.ca/about_history.htm (accessed August 10, 2003).

McPhail. Clark. 1991. *The Myth of the Madding Crowd.* New York: Aldine.

Mead, George Herbert. 1934. *Mind, Self, and Society.* Chicago: University of Chicago
Press.

Mele, Christopher. 1999. "Cyberspace and Disadvantaged Communities: The Internet
as a Tool for Collective Action." In *Communities in Cyberspace,* ed. Marc A.
Smith and Peter Kollock. London: Routledge.

Melevin, Paul T. 1997. "Harder than It Looks: Four Sources of Error Common to Survey Research." *Social Insight: Knowledge at Work* 2, no. 1:38–43.

Melkote, Srinivas R., and D. J. Liu. "The Role of the Internet in Forging a Pluralistic Integration: A Study of Chinese Intellectuals in the United States." *Gazette* 62, no.
6:495–504.

Melucci, Alberto. 1980. "The New Social Movements: A Theoretical Approach." *Social
Science Information* 19, no. 2:199–226.

———. 1989. *Nomads of the Present: Social Movements and Individual Needs in Contemporary Society.* Philadelphia: Temple University Press.

Merola, Stacey S. 2002. "A Ten-Year Perspective on the Status of Sociology." *Footnotes*
30, #8 (November). http://www.asanet.org/footnotes/nov02/fn24.html (accessed
May 28, 2003).

Merton, Robert K. 1968. *Social Theory and Social Structure.* 2nd ed. New York: Free
Press.

———. 1976. "Discrimination and the American Creed." In *Sociological Ambivalence
and Other Essays.* New York: Free Press.

———. 1990. "Epistolary Notes on the Making of a Sociological Dissertation Classis:
'The Dynamics of Bureaucracy.'" In *Structures of Power and Constraint: Papers
in Honor of Peter M. Blau,* ed. Craig Calhoun, Marshall W. Meyer, and W.
Richard Scott. Cambridge: Cambridge University Press.

Michels, Robert. 1962. *Political Parties: A Sociological Study of the Oligarchical Tendencies of Modern Democracy.* 1911. Reprint, New York: Free Press.

Milanovic, Branko. 2002. "True World Income Distribution, 1988 and 1993: First Calculation Based on Household Surveys Alone." *Economic Journal* 112, 476:
51–92.

Milanovic, Branko, and Shlomo Yitzhaki. 2002. "Decomposing World Income Distribution: Does the World Have a Middle Class?" *Review of Income and Wealth* 48,
no. 2:155–75.

Milgram, Stanley. 1963. "Behavioral Study of Obedience." *Journal of Abnormal and Social Psychology* 67:371–78.

———. 1967. "The Small World Problem." *Psychology Today* 1:62–67.

———. 1974. *Obedience to Authority.* New York: Harper and Row.

———. 1977. "The Lost Letter Technique." *The Individual in a Social World: Essays
and Experiments.* Reading, Mass.: Addison-Wesley.

Milgram, Stanley, L. Bickman, and L. Berkowitz. 1969. "Note on the Drawing Power of
Crowds of Different Size." *Journal of Personality and Social Psychology*
13:79–82.

Miller, David L. 2000. *Introduction to Collective Behavior and Collective Action.* 2nd.
ed. Prospect Heights, Ill.: Waveland Press.

Miller, Frederick D. 1999. "The End of SDS and the Emergence of Weatherman: Demise through Success." In *Waves of Protest: Social Movements since the Sixties,* ed. Jo Freeman and Victoria Johnson. Lanham, Md.: Rowman and Littlefield.

Miller, J. G. 1999. "Cultural Psychology: Implications for Basic Psychological Theory." *Psychological Science* 10:85–91.

Mills, C. Wright. 1959. *The Sociological Imagination.* New York: Oxford University Press.

Moghadam, Valentine M. 1999. "Gender and Globalization: Female Labor and Women's Mobilization." *Journal of World-Systems Research* 5, no. 2:367–88.

Montgomery, M., R. Stren, B. Cohen, and H. Reed, eds. 2003. *Cities Transformed: Demographic Change and Its Implications in the Developing World.* Washington, D.C.: National Academy Press.

Moreland, Richard L., and John M. Levine. 2002. "Socialization and Trust in Work Groups." *Group Processes and Intergroup Relations* 5, no. 3:185–201.

Moyer, Imogene L. 2001. *Criminological Theories: Traditional and Nontraditional Voices and Themes.* Thousand Oaks, Calif.: Sage.

Munro, Lyle. 1999. "Contesting Moral Capital in Campaigns against Animal Liberation." *Society and Animals* 7:35–53.

Muzzio, Douglas, and Thomas Halper. 2002. "Pleasantville? The Suburb and Its Representation in American Movies." *Urban Affairs Review* 37, no. 4:543–74.

Myrdal, Gunnar. 1944. *An American Dilemma: The Negro Problem and Modern Democracy.* New York: Harper and Brothers.

National Survey of Families and Households (NSFH). Home page. Center for Demography, University of Wisconsin. http://www.ssc.wisc.edu/nsfh/home.htm (accessed August 1, 2003).

National White Collar Crime Center and the Federal Bureau of Investigation. 2003. *IFCC 2002 Internet Fraud Report.* National White Collar Crime Center. http://www1.ifccfbi.gov/strategy/2002_IFCCReport.pdf (accessed August 10, 2003).

Navarro, Vicente. 1993. *Dangerous to Your Health: Capitalism in Health Care.* New York: Monthly Review Press.

———, ed. 2000. *The Political Economy of Social Inequalities: Consequences for Health and Quality of Life.* Amityville, N.Y.: Baywood.

Newman, Katherine S., and Margaret M. Chin. 2003. "High Stakes: Time Poverty, Testing, and the Children of the Working Poor." *Qualitative Sociology* 26, no. 1:3–34.

Oakley, Ann. 1984. *The Captured Womb: A History of the Medical Care of Pregnant Women.* New York: Blackwell.

Ogburn, William F. 1964. *On Culture and Social Change.* Chicago: University of Chicago Press.

O'Kelly, C. G., and L. S. Carney. 1986. *Women and Men in Society: Cross Cultural Perspectives in Gender Inequality.* 2nd ed. Belmont, Calif.: Wadsworth.

O'Malley, P. 1975. "War and Suicide." *British Journal of Criminology* 15.

O'Rand, Angela M. 1992. "Social Inequality." In *Social Issues,* ed. Robert D. Benford. New York: Macmillan Library Reference USA.

Orenstein, Peggy. 2000. *Flux: Women on Sex, Work, Kids, Love, and Life in a Half-Changed World.* New York: Doubleday.

References

Ostrander, Susan A. 1984. *Women of the Upper Class.* Philadelphia: Temple University Press.

Page, Clarence. 2003. "Another War, Another Euphemism to Disguise the Horror of War." *Salt Lake Tribune,* 29 March. http://www.sltrib.com/2003/Mar/03292003/commenta/42944.asp (accessed August 10, 2003).

Palen, John J. 1986. *The Urban World.* 3rd ed. New York: McGraw-Hill.

Palmore, Erdman B., Bruce M. Burchett, Gerda G. Fillenbaum, Linda K. George, and Laurence M. Wallman. 1985. *Retirement: Causes and Consequences.* New York: Springer.

Park, Kristin. 2002. "Stigma Management among the Voluntarily Childless." *Sociological Perspectives* 45, no. 1:21–45.

Park, Robert, and Ernest Burgess. 1924. *Introduction to the Science of Sociology.* Chicago: University of Chicago Press.

Parsons, Talcott. 1951. *The Social System.* New York: Free Press.

Paternoster, Raymond, and Ronet Bachman, eds. 2001. *Explaining Criminals and Crime.* Los Angeles: Roxbury.

Payer, Lynn. 1988. *Medicine and Culture.* New York: Penguin.

Pearlin, Leonard I. 1989. "The Sociological Study of Stress." *Journal of Health and Social Behavior* 30:241–56.

Peel, J. D. Y. 1971. *Herbert Spencer.* New York: Basic Books.

Perlow, Victor. 1988. *Super Profits and Crises.* New York: International.

Perry, Barbara. 2001. *In the Name of Hate.* New York: Routledge.

Perry, Marc J., and Paul J. Mackun. 2001. "Population Change and Distribution." Washington, D.C.: U.S. Bureau of the Census. http://www.census.gov/prod/2001pubs/c2kbr01–2.pdf (accessed April 20, 2003).

Persell, Caroline H. 2001. "ASA Task Force on AP Course in Sociology Gets Down to Work." *Footnotes* 29, no. 9, December:4 http://www.asanet.org/footnotes/dec01/ (accessed August 8, 2003).

Petersen, William. 1979. "Davis, Kingsley." In *The International Encyclopedia of the Social Sciences, Biographical Supplement,* ed. David Sills. New York: Macmillan and Free Press.

Peterson, J. L., J. J. Card, M. B. Eisen, and B. Sherman-Williams. 1994. "Evaluating Teenage Pregnancy Prevention and Other Social Programs: Ten Stages of Program Assessment." *Family Planning Perspectives* 26 (May): 116–20, 131.

Peterson, S. B., and M. A. Lach. 1990. "Gender Stereotypes in Children's Books: Their Prevalence and Influence on Cognitive and Affective Development." *Gender and Education* 2, no. 2:185–97.

Peterson, William. 1979. *Malthus.* Cambridge: Harvard University Press.

Pfautz, Harold W. 1968. "Ward, Lester F." In *The International Encyclopedia of the Social Sciences,* ed. David Sills. New York: Macmillan and Free Press.

Piaget, Jean. 1926. *The Language and Thought of the Child.* New York: Harcourt Brace.

———. 1928. *Judgement and Reasoning in the Child.* New York: Harcourt Brace.

———. 1930. *The Child's Conception of Physical Causality.* New York: Harcourt Brace.

———. 1932. *The Moral Judgement of the Child.* New York: Harcourt Brace.

Piccinino, Linda J., and William D. Mosher. 1998. "Trends in Contraceptive Use in the United States: 1982–1995." *Family Planning Perspectives* 30, no. 1:4–10, 46.

Pichanick, Valerie Kossew. 1980. *Harriet Martineau.* Ann Arbor: University of Michigan Press.

Planned Parenthood Federation of America (PPFA). "Planned Parenthood Health Centers." Planned Parenthood Federation of America. http://www.planned parenthood.org/Zip.htm(accessed December 2, 2004).

Poggi, Gianfranco. 1990. "Anthony Giddens and 'The Classics.'" In *Anthony Giddens: Conflict and Controversy,* ed. Jon Clark, Celia Modgil, and Sohan Modgil. London: Falmer Press.

Porter, Elias. 1962. "The Parable of the Spindle." *Harvard Business Review* 40, 3 (May/June): 58–66.

Prus, Robert. 1996. *Symbolic Interaction and Ethnographic Research.* Albany: State University of New York Press.

Quattrone, George A. 1986. "On the Perception of a Groups' Variability." In *Psychology of Intergroup Relations. 2nd ed.,* eds. Stephen Worchel and William G. Austin Chicago: Nelson-Hall.

Quinney, Richard. "Richard Quinney." Vita. http://www.sociology.niu.edu/rqvita.html (accessed August 20, 2003).

———. 1970. *The Social Reality of Crime.* Boston: Little, Brown.

———. 1974. *Critique of Legal Order: Crime Control in Capitalist Society.* Boston: Little, Brown.

———. 1980. *Class, State, and Crime.* 2nd ed. New York: Longman.

Raine, Adrain. 1993. *The Psychopathology of Crime: Criminal Behavior as a Clinical Disorder.* San Diego, Calif.: Academic.

Ramm, Thilo. 1968. "Engels, Friedrich." In *The International Encyclopedia of the Social Sciences,* ed. David Sills. New York: Macmillan and Free Press.

Rapoport, Robert N. 1997. "Families as Educators for Global Citizenship: Five Conundrums of Intentional Socialization." *International Journal of Early Years Education* 5, no. 1:67–77.

Raushenbush, Winifred. 1979. *Robert E. Park: Biography of a Sociologist.* Durham, N.C.: Duke University Press.

Rawls, Anne Warfield. 2002. "Editor's Introduction" In *Ethnomethodology's Program: Working Out Durkheim's Approach,* ed. Harold Garfinkel with Anne Warfield Rawls. Lanham, Md.: Rowman and Littlefield.

Read, Piers Paul. 1975. *Alive: The Story of the Andes Survivors.* New York: HarperCollins.

Rebach, Howard M. 2001. "Mediation and Alternative Dispute Resolution." In *Handbook of Clinical Sociology,* ed. Howard M. Rebach and John G. Bruhn. New York: Kluwer/Plenum.

Rebach, Howard M., and John G. Bruhn. 2001. "Theory, Practice, and Sociology." In *Handbook of Clinical Sociology,* ed. Howard M. Rebach and John G. Bruhn. New York: Kluwer/Plenum.

Reiman, Jeffrey. 1998. *The Rich Get Richer and the Poor Get Prison.* Boston: Allyn and Bacon.

Restivo, Sal. 1991. *The Sociological Worldview.* Cambridge, Mass.: Blackwell.

Rhoades, Lawrence J. 1981. *A History of the American Sociological Association: 1905–1980.* Washington, D.C.: American Sociological Association.

Rhode, D. L. 2001. *The Unfinished Agenda: Women and the Legal Profession.* Chicago: American Bar Association.

Riain, Sean O., and Peter B. Evans. 2000. "Social Mobility." In *Encyclopedia of Sociology,* 2nd ed. New York: Macmillan Reference USA.

References

"Ritzer, George." 1987. In *Contemporary Authors, New Revisions Series.* vol. 20, ed. Linda Metzger and Deborah A. Straub. Detroit: Gale Research.

Ritzer, George. "George Ritzer." Department of Sociology, University of Maryland. http://www.bsos.umd.edu/socy/ritzer/ritzer_cv.html# (accessed December 2, 2004).

———. 1988. *Contemporary Sociological Theory.* 2nd ed. New York: Knopf.

———, ed. 2000a. *The Blackwell Companion to Major Social Theorists.* London: Blackwell.

———. 2000b. *The McDonaldization of Society.* Rev. ed. Thousand Oaks, Calif.: Pine Forge Press.

Roethlisberger, F. J., and W. J. Dickson. 1939. *Management and the Worker.* New York: Wiley.

"Rosabeth Moss Kanter." Business: The Ultimate Resource. http://www.ultimatebusinessresource.com/downloads/uk/mosskanter.pdf (accessed September 15, 2003).

Rosenhan, D. L. 1973. "On Being Sane in Insane Places." *Science,* 19 January, 250–58.

Rosnow, Ralph L., and Gary Alan Fine. 1976. *Rumor and Gossip: The Social Psychology of Hearsay.* New York: Elsevier.

Ross, Catherine E., and Chia-ling Wu. 1995. "The Links between Education and Health." *American Sociological Review* 60:719–45.

Rossi, P. H., H. E. Freeman, and M. W. Lipsey. 1999. *Evaluation: A Systematic Approach.* 6th ed. Thousand Oaks, Calif.: Sage.

Rostow, W. W. 1960. *The Stages of Economic Growth: A Non-Communist Manifesto.* Cambridge: Cambridge University Press.

Roth, K. 1998. "New Minefields for N.G.O.s." *Nation,* 13 April, 22–24.

Rowe, Kathleen. 2001. "The Unruly Woman: Gender and the Genres of Laughter." In *Understanding Inequality: The Intersection of Race/Ethnicity, Class, and Gender,* ed. Barbara A. Arrighi. Lanham, Md.: Rowman and Littlefield.

Russell, Glenn. 2000. "School Education in the Age of the Ubiquitous Networked Computer." In *Technology Today.* 22:389–400.

Rymer, Russ. 1993. *Genie: An Abused Child's Flight from Silence.* New York: HarperCollins.

Sacks, Harvey. 1984. "On Doing 'Being Ordinary.'" In *Structures of Social Action,* ed. J. Maxwell Atkinson and John Heritage. Cambridge: Cambridge University Press.

Salerno, Roger A. 1987. *Louis Wirth: A Bio-Bibliography.* New York: Greenwood Press.

Saltzman, Ann L. 2000. "The Role of the Obedience Experiments in Holocaust Studies: The Case for Renewed Visibility." In *Obedience to Authority: Current Perspectives on the Milgram Paradigm,* ed. Thomas Blass. Mahwah, N.J: Lawrence Erlbaum.

Sasaki, Masamichi. 2000. "Japanese Sociology." In *Encyclopedia of Sociology,* 2nd ed., ed. Edgar F. Borgatta and Rhonda J. V. Montgomery. New York: Macmillan.

Sassen, Saskia. 2001. *The Global City: New York, London, Tokyo.* 2nd ed. Princeton, N.J.: Princeton University Press.

Savage, M., and A. Warde. 1993. *Urban Sociology, Capitalized Modernity.* London: Macmillan.

Savells, Jerry. 2001. "Social Change among the Amish." In *Down to Earth Sociology: Introductory Readings,* 11th ed., ed. James M. Henslin. New York: Free Press.

Scheff, Thomas. 1994. *Bloody Revenge: Emotions, Nationalism, and War.* San Francisco: Westview Press.

Scheuch, Erwin K. 2000. "German Sociology." In *Encyclopedia of Sociology,* 2nd ed., ed. Edgar F. Borgatta and Rhonda V. J. Montgomery. New York: Macmillan.

Schultz, Emily A. 1990. *Dialogue at the Margins: Whorf, Bakhtin, and Linguistic Relativity.* Madison: University of Wisconsin Press.

Schwartz, John, and Matthew Wald. 2003. "Is 'Groupthink' Part of the Problem with NASA Again?" *New York Times,* 23 March.

Scott, Alan. 1990. *Ideology and the New Social Movements.* London: Unwin Hyman.

Scully, Diana. 1990. *Understanding Sexual Violence: A Study of Convicted Rapists.* Boston: Unwin Hyman.

Segalman, Robert. 1998. "Speech to Speech: Extending Phone Service for the Speech Disabled." *Social Insight: Knowledge at Work* 3:33–37.

Sen, A. K. 1981. *Poverty and Famine: An Essay on Entitlement and Depravation.* Oxford, England: Clarendon Press.

Seperson, Susanne B. 1994. "What's Wrong with Sociology? Its Public Image." *Sociological Forum* 10:309–12.

Sernau, Scott. 2001. *Worlds Apart: Social Inequalities in a New Century.* Thousand Oaks, CA: Pine Forge Press.

Shah, Vimal P. 2000. "Indian Sociology." In *Encyclopedia of Sociology,* 2nd ed., ed. Edgar F. Borgatta and Rhonda J. V. Montgomery. New York: Macmillan.

Sheldon, Eleanor Bernert. 1968. "Wirth, Louis." In *The International Encyclopedia of the Social Sciences,* ed. David Sills. New York: Macmillan and Free Press.

Sheldon, William. 1949. *Varieties of Delinquent Youth.* New York: Harper and Row.

Sherif, Muzafer. 1966. *In Common Predicament: Social Psychology of Intergroup Conflict and Cooperation.* Boston: Houghton Mifflin.

Sherif, Muzafer, and Carolyn W. Sherif. 1953. *Groups in Harmony and Tension.* New York: Harper and Row.

Sherman, Brian. 1985. "Doing Sociological Research That Counts." In *Using Sociology: An Introduction from the Clinical Perspective,* ed. Roger A. Straws. Bayside, N.Y.: General Hall.

Sherman, Brian S. and Roger A. Straus. 2002. "Noticing, Questioning, Explaining: Research Methods." In *Using Sociology: An Introduction from the Clinical Perspective.* 3rd ed., ed. Roger A. Straws. Lanham, M.D.: Rowman and Littlefield.

Shibutani, Tamotsu. 1988. "Herbert Blumer's Contributions to Twentieth-Century Sociology." *Symbolic Interaction* 11, no. 1:23–31.

Shilling, Chris. 2002. "Culture, the 'Sick Role,' and the Consumption of Health." *British Journal of Sociology* 53, no. 4:621–38.

Shivley, J. 1992. "Cowboys and Indians: Perceptions of Western Films among American Indians and Anglos." *American Sociological Review* 57:725–34.

Shostak, Arthur B. "Arthur B. Shostak." Vita. http://www.futureshaping.com/shostak/pages/resume.html (accessed August 20, 2003).

———. 2001. "Utopian Thinking in Sociology." Interview by Meghan Rich. In *Footnotes.* Washington, D.C.: American Sociological Association. 29, 9 (Dec.) http://www.utopianideas.net/interviews/AShostak.htm (accessed August 8, 2003).

References

———. 2003. *Viable Utopian Ideas: Shaping a Better World.* Armonk, N.Y.: M. E. Sharpe.

Siegel, Jerrold. 1978. *Marx's Fate: The Shape of a Life.* University Park: Pennsylvania State University Press.

Sills, David. 1979. "Lazarsfeld, Paul F." In *The International Encyclopedia of the Social Sciences, Biographical Supplement,* ed. David Sills. New York: Macmillan and Free Press.

Simmel, Georg. 1957. "Fashion." *American Journal of Sociology* 62:541–58.

Simon, Julian. 1996. *The Ultimate Resource 2.* Princeton, N.J.: Princeton University Press.

Simon, Rita J., and Jennifer Scherer. 1999. "What Matters in Sociology?" *Sociological Inquiry* 69:296–302.

Simons, R. L., and P. A. Gray. 1989. "Perceived Blocked Opportunity as an Explanation of Delinquency among Lower-Class Black Males: A Research Note." *Journal of Research in Crime and Delinquency* 26, no. 1:90–101.

Simpson, Ludi, and Elizabeth Middleton. 1997. "Who Is Missed by a National Census? A Review of Empirical Results from Australia, Britain, Canada, and the USA." Centre for Census and Survey Research, University of Manchester, June. http://www.ccsr.ac.uk/publications/working/missed.htm (accessed March 2, 2003).

Simpson, Sally S., and Lori Elis. 1996. "Theoretical Perspectives on Corporate Victimization of Women." In *Corporate Victimization of Women,* ed. Elizabeth Szockyj and James Fox. Boston: Northeastern University Press.

Singer, Eleanor. 1981. "Reference Groups and Social Evaluations." In *Social Psychology: Sociological Perspectives.* eds. Morris Rosenberg and Ralph H. Turner. NY: Basic Books.

Singleton, Royce, Bruce C. Straits, Margaret M. Straits, and Ronald J. McAllister. 1993. *Approaches to Social Research.* New York: Oxford.

Small, Mario Luis, and Katherine Newman. 2001. "Urban Poverty after 'The Truly Disadvantaged': The Rediscovery of the Family, the Neighborhood, and Culture." In *Annual Review of Sociology,* ed. John Hagan, Karen S. Cook. vol. 27. Palo Alto, Calif.: Annual Reviews.

"Smelser, Neil." 1983. In *Contemporary Authors, New Revision Series,* vol. 8, ed. Ann Evory and Linda Metzger. Detroit: Gale Research.

Smelser, Neil J. "Neil J. Smelser." University of California–Berkeley. http://sociology.berkeley.edu/faculty/smelser/index.html (accessed August 8, 2003).

———. 1962. *Theory of Collective Behavior.* New York: Free Press.

———. 1984. "Neil Smelser." Interview by Scott Busby and Alan Stein. *Berkeley Faculty, Live!* October. http://sociology.berkeley.edu/faculty_live/faculty.asp#smelser (accessed August 9, 2003).

———. 1985. "Evaluating the Model of Structural Differentiation in Relation to Educational Change in the Nineteenth Century." In *Neofunctionalism,* ed. Jeffery C. Alexander. Beverly Hills, Calif.: Sage.

Smith, A. D. 1990. "Towards a Global Culture?" *Theory of Culture and Society* 7:171–91.

Smith, Charles U., and Lewis M. Killian. 1990. "Sociological Foundations of the Civil Rights Movement." In *Sociology in America,* ed. Herbert J. Gans. Newbury Park, Calif.: Sage.

Snow, Loudell F. 1993. *Walkin' Over Medicine.* Boulder, CO.: Westview.

Society for Applied Sociology. "Hiring a Person with a Bachelor's Degree in Sociology." Waco, Tex.: Society for Applied Sociology. http://www.aacc.cc.md.us/soc/ AppliedCourse/socbrochure.rtf (accessed February 8, 2003).

Solomon, K., and P. A. Szwabo. 1994. "The Work-Oriented Culture: Success and Power in Elderly Men." In *Older Men's Lives,* ed. E. Thompson Jr. Thousand Oaks, Calif.: Sage.

Solorzano, D. G. 1991. "Mobility Aspirations among Racial Minorities, Controlling for SES." *Sociology and Social Research* 75:182–88.

Sorokin, Pitirim A. 1963a. *A Long Journey: The Autobiography of Pitirim A. Sorokin.* New Haven, Conn.: College and University Press.

———. 1963b. "Sociology of My Mental Life." In *Pitirim A. Sorokin in Review,* ed. Philip J. Allen. Durham, N.C.: Duke University Press.

———. 1898. *The Principles of Sociology.* New York: Appleton.

Spates, James L. 1976. "Countercultural and Dominant Cultural Values: A Cross-National Analysis of the Underground Press and Dominant Cultural Magazines." *American Sociological Review* 41:868–83.

Spirou, Costas, and Larry Bennett. 2002. "Revamped Stadium . . . New Neighborhood?" *Urban Affairs Review* 37, no. 5:675–702.

Spitzer, Steven. 1980. "Toward a Marxian Theory of Deviance." In *Criminal Behavior: Readings in Criminology,* ed. Delos H. Kelly. New York: St. Martin's Press.

Sprecher, S., and K. McKinney. 1993. *Sexuality.* Thousand Oaks, Calif.: Sage.

Sproull, L. S., and S. B. Kiesler. 1991. *Connections: New Ways of Working in the Networked Organization.* Boston: MIT Press.

St. Jean, Yanick, and Joe R. Feagin. 1998. *Double Burden: Black Women and Everyday Racism.* Armonk, N.Y.: M. E. Sharpe.

Stanley, Thomas J. 1996. *The Millionaire Next Door: The Surprising Secrets of America's Wealthy.* Atlanta: Longstreet Press.

Stapleton, B. 1986. "Malthus: The Origins of the Principle of Population?" In *Malthus and His Time,* ed. Michael Turner. New York: St. Martin's Pres.

Starr, Harris E. 1925. *William Graham Sumner.* New York: Henry Holt.

Steele, Stephen F. Home Page. http://mywebpages.comcast.net/sf.steele.HomePage SSteele.htm (as accessed November 24, 2004).

Steele, Stephen F. 1996. "Five Steps to an Evaluation: The Five D's." *Social Insight: Knowledge at Work* 1:52.

Stoetzel, Jean. 1968. "Le Bon, Gustave." In *The International Encyclopedia of the Social Sciences,* ed. David Sills. New York: Macmillan and Free Press.

Stolley, Kathy Shepherd, and Archie E. Hill. 1996. "Presentations of the Elderly in Marriage and Family Textbooks." *Teaching Sociology* 24, no. 1:34–45.

Stoper, Emily. 1999. "The Student Nonviolent Coordinating Committee: Rise and Fall of a Redemptive Organization." In *Waves of Protest: Social Movements since the Sixties,* ed. Jo Freeman and Victoria Johnson. Lanham, Md.: Rowman and Littlefield.

Strand, Kerry J. 2002. "Sociologists Involved in Local School (Systems)." *Footnotes* 30, 8 (November). http://www.asanet.org/footnotes/nov02/fn22.html (accessed August 8, 2003).

Straus, Roger, ed. 1994. *Using Sociology: An Introduction from the Applied and Clinical Perspectives.* Dix Hills, N.Y.: General Hall.

"Straus, Roger Austin." 1983. In *Contemporary Authors,* vol. 109, ed. Hal May. Detroit: Gale Research.

References

"Straus, Roger Austin." 2003. In *Who's Who in America,* 57th ed., vol. 2, ed. Danielle Netta. New Providence, N.J.: Marquis Who's Who.

Stretesky, Paul, and Michael J. Lynch. 1999. "Environmental Justice and the Predictions of Distance to Accidental Chemical Releases in Hillsborough County, Florida." *Social Science Quarterly* 80:840–43.

Sullivan, Thomas J. 2001. *Methods of Social Research.* Fort Worth, Tex.: Harcourt College Publishers.

———. 2003. *Introduction to Social Problems.* 6th ed. Boston: Allyn and Bacon.

Sumner, William Graham. 1906. *Folkways: A Study of the Sociological Importance of Usages, Manners, Customs, Mores, and Morals.* Boston: Ginn.

Sutherland, Edwin H. 1947. *Principles of Criminology.* 4th ed. Philadelphia: Lippincott.

———. 1985. *White Collar Crime: The Uncut Version.* New Haven, Conn.: Yale University Press.

Sutherland, Edwin H., and Donald R. Cressey. 1978. *Criminology.* 10th ed. Philadelphia: Lippincott.

Sutherland, Edwin H., Donald R. Cressey, and David Luckenbill. 1992. *Principles of Criminology.* Philadelphia: Lippincott.

Switzer, J. Y. 1990. "The Impact of Generic Word Choices: An Empirical Investigation of Age- and Sex-related Differences." *Sex Roles* 22:69–82.

Szasz, Thomas. 1970. *The Myth of Mental Illness: Foundations of a Theory of Personal Conduct.* New York: Harper and Row.

Szockyj, Elizabeth, and Gilbert Geis. 2002. "Insider Trading Patterns and Analysis." *Journal of Criminal Justice* 30:273–86.

Sztompka, Piotr. 1986. *Robert K. Merton: An Intellectual Profile.* New York: St. Martin's Press.

Takooshian, Harold. 2000. "How Stanley Milgram Taught about Obedience and Social Influence." In *Obedience to Authority: Current Perspectives on the Milgram Paradigm,* ed. Thomas Blass. Mahwah, N.J.: Lawrence Erlbaum.

Tarnow, Eugen. 2000. "Self-Destructive Obedience in the Airplane Cockpit and the Concept of Obedience Optimization." In *Obedience to Authority: Current Perspectives on the Milgram Paradigm,* ed. Thomas Blass. Mahwah, N.J.: Lawrence Erlbaum.

Tarrow, Sidney. 1994. *Power in Movement: Social Movements, Collective Action, and Mass Politics in the Modern State.* Cambridge: Cambridge University Press.

Teal, D. 1971. *The Gay Militants.* New York: Stein and Day.

Tewksbury, Richard, and Deanna McGaughey. 1997. "Stigmatization of Persons with HIV Disease: Perceptions, Management, and Consequences of AIDS." *Sociological Spectrum* 17, no. 1:49–70.

Thomas, William I., and Dorothy S. Thomas. 1928. *The Child in America: Behavior Problems and Programs.* New York: Knopf.

Thomas, William I., and Florian Znaniecki. 1918–1920. *The Polish Peasant in Europe and America.* 5 vols. Chicago: University of Chicago Press.

Thompson, Kenneth. 1982. *Emile Durkheim.* N.Y.: Tavistock.

Thompson, T. L. and E. Zerbinos. 1995. "Gender Roles in Animated Cartoons: Has the Picture Changed in 20 Years?" *Sex Roles.* 32:651–73.

Thomson, D. S. 2000. "The Sapir-Whort Hypothesis: Worlds Shaped by Words." In *Conformity and Conflict,* ed. J. Spradley and D. W. McCurdy. Boston: Allyn and Bacon.

Thorne, Barrie, and Zella Luria. 1986. "Sexuality and Gender in Children's Daily Worlds." *Social Problems* 33, no. 3:176–90.

Thorstad, David. 1995. "Homosexuality and the American Left: The Impact of Stonewall." *Journal of Homosexuality* 29, no. 4:319–49.

Tierney, Patrick. 2000. *Darkness in El Dorado: How Scientists and Journalists Devastated the Amazon.* New York: W. W. Norton.

Tilman, Rick. 1984. *C. Wright Mills: A Native Radical and His American Intellectual Roots.* University Park: Pennsylvania State University Press.

Toennies, Ferdinand. 1963. *Community and Society (Gemeinschaft and Gesellschaft).* 1887. Reprint, New York: Harper and Row.

Townsend, D. M., S. M. DeMarie, and A. R. Hendrickson. 1998. "Virtual Teams: Technology and the Workplace of the Future." In *The Academy of Management Executive* 12, no. 3 (Aug.): 17–29.

Trager, George L. 1968. "Whorf, Benjamin L." In *International Encyclopedia of the Social Sciences,* vol. 16, ed. David L. Sills. New York: Macmillan and Free Press.

Treiman, Donald J. 1977. *Occupational Prestige in Comparative Perspective.* New York: Academic.

Trevino, A. Javier. 2001. "Introduction: The Theory and Legacy of Talcott Parsons." In *Talcott Parsons Today: His Theory and Legacy in Contemporary Sociology,* ed. A. Javier Trevino. Lanham, Md.: Rowman and Littlefield.

Tuckman, Bruce W. 1965. "Developmental Sequences in Small Groups." *Psychological Bulletin* 63:384–99.

Tumin, Melvin M. 1953. "Some Principles of Stratification: A Critical Analysis." *American Sociological Review* 18:387–93.

———. 1985. *Social Stratification: The Forms and Functions of Inequality.* 2nd ed. Englewood Cliffs, N.J.: Prentice Hall.

Turner, Jonathan H. 1998. "Must Sociological Theory and Sociological Practice Be So Far Apart? A Polemic Answer." *Sociological Perspectives* 41:243–58.

———. 2001. "Can Functionalism Be Saved?" In *Talcott Parsons Today: His Theory and Legacy in Contemporary Sociology,* ed. A. Javier Trevino. Lanham, Md.: Rowman and Littlefield.

Turner, Jonathan H., and Alexandra Maryanski. 1979. *Functionalism.* Menlo Park, Calif.: Benjamin/Cumings.

Turner, Ralph, and Lewis Killian. 1987. *Collective Behavior.* Englewood Cliffs, N.J.: Prentice Hall.

United Nations. 2001. *Human Development Report: 2000.* New York: Oxford University Press.

———. 2003. *Human Development Report: 2003.* New York: Oxford University Press.

United Nations Population Division. 2002. "World Urbanization Prospects: The 2001 Revision." New York: United Nations. http://www.un.org/esa/population/publications/wup2001/WUP2001_CH1.pdf (accessed July 5, 2003).

———. 2003. "World Population Prospects: The 2002 Revision Highlights." New York: United Nations. http://www.un.org/esa/population/publications/wpp2002/WPP2002-HIGHLIGHTSrev1.PDF (accessed July 5, 2003).

U.S. Census Bureau. "Population and Housing Unit Counts: Table 4." *1990 Census of Population and Housing.* U.S. Department of Commerce, U.S. Census Bureau. http://www.census.gov/population/censusdata/table-4.pdf (accessed May 15, 2003).

References

U.S. Census Bureau. 2001a. "Population Change and Distribution: 1990 to 2000." U.S. Department of Commerce, U.S. Census Bureau. http://www.census.gov/prod/2001pubs/c2kbrØ1-2.pdf

U.S. Census Bureau. 2001b. "PrevliminaryEstimates Show Improvement in Census 2000 Coverage." U.S. Department of Commerce; U.S. Census Bureau. http://www.census.gov/Press-Release/www/2001/cbØ1cnØ3.html (accessed December 31, 2002).

————. 1999. "How People Use the Census." U.S. Department of Commerce, U.S. Census Bureau. http://www.census.gov/dmd/www/dropin4.htm (accessed December 31, 2002).

————. 2003. International Data Base. 17 July release. http://www.census.gov/ipc/www/idbnew.html. (accessed May 1, 2003).

U.S. Census Bureau. 2004a. "Table 4: Poverty Status of Families, by Type of Family, Presence of Related Children, Race, and Hispanic Origin: 1959 to 2003." U.S. Department of Commerce, U.S. Census Bureau, 26 August. http://www.census.goc/hhes/poverty/histpov/hstpov4.html (accessed December 5, 2004).

————. 2004b. "People and Families in Poverty by Selected Characteristics: 2000 and 2001." U.S. Department of Commerce, U.S. Census Bureau, 26 August. http://www.census.gov/hhes/poverty/poverty03/table3.pdf (accessed November 28, 2004).

————. 2004c. "Race and Hispanic Origin of Householder—Households by Median and Mean Income: 1967 to 2003." U.S. Department of Commerce, U.S. Census Bureau, 27 August. http://www.census.gov/hhes/income/histinc/h05.html (accessed November 28, 2004).

————. 2004d. "Table H-2. Share of Aggregate Income Received by Each Fifth and Top 5 Percent of Households (All Races): 1967 to 2003." U.S. Department of Commerce, U.S. Census Bureau, 27 August. http://www.census.gov/hhes/income/histinc/hØ2ar.html (accessed November 28, 2004).

————. 2004e. "Poverty Thresholds for 2003 by Size of Family and Number of Related Children under 18 Years (Dollars)." U.S. Department of Commerce, U.S. Census Bureau, 26 August. http://www.census.gov/hhes/poverty/threshld/thresh03.html (accessed November 28, 2004).

Useem, Bert, and Michael D. Resig. 1999. "Collective Action in Prisons: Protests, Disturbances, and Riots." *Criminology* 37:735–59.

Vamplew, Wray. 1986. "Malthus and the Corn Laws." In *Malthus and His Times,* ed. Michael Turner. New York: St. Martin's Press.

van de Kaa, D. J. 1987. "Europe's Second Demographic Transition." *Population Bulletin* 42, no. 1. Washington DC: Population Refernce Bureau.

Veblen, Thorstein. 1967. *The Theory of the Leisure Class.* 1899. Reprint, New York: Viking.

Volkart, E. H. 1968. "Thomas, W. I." In *The International Encyclopedia of the Social Sciences,* ed. David Sills. New York: Macmillan and Free Press.

Volti, R. 2001. *Society and Technological Change.* 4th ed. New York: Worth.

Voss, Thomas, and Martin Abraham. 2000. "Rational Choice Theory in Sociology: A Survey." In *The International Handbook of Sociology,* ed. Stella R. Quah and Arnaud Sales. London: Sage.

Walker, Ruth. 2001. "Meet the New Airport: Temple, Mall, Design Hub." *Christian Science Monitor,* 23 August. http://www.csmonitor.com/2001/0823/p18s1-altr.html (accessed September 10, 2003).

Wallace, Ruth A., and Alison Wolf. 1999. *Contemporary Sociological Theory: Continuing the Classical Tradition.* 5th ed. Upper Saddle River, N.J.: Prentice Hall.

Wallerstein, Immanuel. "Immanuel Wallerstein Curriculum Vita." Yale University Faculty. http://www.yale.edu/socdept/faculty/cvs/cvwallerstein.pdf (accessed August 15, 2003).

———. 1974. *The Modern World System.* New York: Academic Press.

———. 2000. *The Essential Wallerstein.* New York: New Press.

Walton, John. 2000. "Urban Sociology." In *The International Handbook of Sociology,* ed. Stella R. Quah and Arnaud Sales. London: Sage.

Warr, Mark. 2001. "The Social Origins of Crime: Edwin Sutherland and the Theory of Differential Association." In *Explaining Criminals and Crime,* ed. Raymond Paternoster and Ronet Bachman. Los Angeles: Roxbury.

Warren, Carol A. B. 2000. "Ethnography." In *Encyclopedia of Sociology,* 2nd ed., ed. Edgar F. Borgatta and Rhonda J. V. Montgomery. New York: Macmillan Reference.

Warwick, D. P. 1973. "*Tearoom Trade:* Ends and Means in Social Research." *Hastings Center Studies* 1:27–38.

Waters, Malcolm. 2001. *Globalization.* London: Routledge.

Waters, Tony. 2001. *Bureaucratizing the Good Samaritan: The Limitations of Humanitarian Relief Operations.* Boulder, Colo.: Westview Press.

Weber, Marianne. 1975. *Max Weber: A Biography.* Ed. and trans. Harry Zohn. New York: Wiley.

Weber, Max. 1946. *From Max Weber: Essays in Sociology,* ed. and trans. Hans Gerth and C. Wright Mills. London: Routledge and Keegan Paul.

———. 1947. *The Theory of Social and Economic Organization.* New York: Oxford.

Weinrath, Michael. 1997. "When Should We Put High Risk Drivers Back on the Road? Development of the Scale of Risk for Drivers." *Social Insight: Knowledge at Work* 2:25–28.

Weiss, C. H. 1998. *Evaluation: Method for Studying Programs and Policies.* 2nd ed. Upper Saddle River, N.J.: Prentice Hall.

Weiss, Gregory L., and Lynne E. Lonnquist. 1994. *The Sociology of Health, Healing, and Illness.* Englewood Cliffs, N.J.: Prentice Hall.

Weitzman, Lenore J. 1985. *The Divorce Revolution: The Unexpected Social and Economic Consequences for Women and Children in America.* New York: Free Press.

———. 1996. "The Economic Consequences of Divorce Are Still Unequal: Comment on Peterson." *American Sociological Review* 61:537–38.

———. 1999a. "From Little Boxes to Loosely Bounded Networks: The Privatization and Domestication of Community." In *Sociology for the Twenty-First Century,* ed. Janet L. Abu-Lughod. Chicago: University of Chicago Press.

———. 1999b. *Networks in the Global Village.* Boulder, Colo.: Westview Press.

Wellman, Barry. "Barry Wellman Homepage." Department of Sociology, University of Toronto. http://www.chass.utoronto.ca/~wellman/

Wellman, B., J. Salaff, D. Dimitrova, L. Garton, M. Gulia, and C. Haythornwaite. 1996. "Computer Networks as Social Networks: Collaborative Work, Telework, and Virtual Community." *Annual Review of Sociology.* 22. Eds. John Hagan and Karen S. Cook. Palo Alto, Ca: Annual Reviews.

Wellman, David. 1988. "The Politics of Herbert Blumer's Sociological Method." *Symbolic Interaction* 11, no. 1:59–68.

References

Wells-Barnett, Ida B. 1970. *Crusade for Justice: The Autobiography of Ida B. Wells.* Ed. Alfreda M. Duster. Chicago: University of Chicago Press.

White, Harrison. 1970. "Search Parameters for the Small World Problem." *Social Forces* 49:259–64.

Whyte, William Foote. 1969. "Reflections on My Work." In *Sociological Self-Images: A Collective Portrait,* ed. Irving Louis Horowitz. Beverly Hills, Calif.: Sage.

———. 1943. *Street Corner Society.* Chicago: University of Chicago Press.

———. 1994. *Participant Observer: An Autobiography.* Ithaca, N.Y.: ILR Press.

Widener, Alice. 1979. *Gustave Le Bon.* Indianapolis, Ind.: Liberty Press.

Williams, J. A., Jr., J. A. Vernon, M. C. Williams, and K. Malecha. 1987. "Sex Role Socialization in Picture Books: An Update." *Social Science Quarterly* 68: 148–56.

Williams, Phil. 2001. "Organized Crime and Cybercrime: Synergies, Trends, and Responses." *Cipherwar,* 15 August. http://www.cipherwar.com/news/01/cyber-mafias.htm (accessed July 10, 2003).

Williams, Robin M., Jr. 1970. *American Society: A Sociological Interpretation.* 3rd ed. New York: Knopf.

Williams, Terry. 1989. *The Cocaine Kids: The Inside Story of a Teenage Drug Ring.* Reading, Mass.: Addison-Wesley.

Wilson, Edward O. 1975. *Sociobiology: The New Synthesis.* Cambridge: Harvard University Press.

———. 1978. *On Human Nature.* Cambridge: Harvard University Press.

———. 1994. *Naturalist.* Washington, D.C.: Island Press/Shearwater Books.

Wilson, James Q., and Richard J. Herrnstein. 1985. *Crime and Human Nature.* New York: Simon and Schuster.

"Wilson, William J." 1981. In *Contemporary Authors, New Revision Series,* vol. 1, ed. Ann Evory. Detroit: Gale Research.

Wilson, William Julius. "William Julius Wilson Biography." Harvard University. http://ksghome.harvard.edu/~.WWilson/FullBio.html (accessed November 29, 2004).

———. 1987. *The Truly Disadvantaged: The Inner City, the Underclass, and Public Policy.* Chicago: University of Chicago Press.

———. 1996. *When Work Disappears: The World of the New Urban Poor.* New York: Knopf.

———. 1997. "Interview with William Julius Wilson." Interview by Henry Louis Gates Jr. PBS and WGBH/Frontline. http://www.pbs.org/wgbh/pages/frontline/shows/race/interviews/wilson.html (accessed September 9, 2003).

———. 2000. "Ray Suarez Talks with W. J. Wilson on his Book *The Bridge Over the Racial Divide: Rising Inequality and Coalition Politics.*" Interview by Ray Suarez. PBS, 5 January. http://www.pbs.org/newshour/gergen/jan-june00/wilson_1–5.html (accessed September 9, 2003).

Wirth, Louis. 1938. "Urbanism as a Way of Life." *American Journal of Sociology* 44:1–24.

Wolff, Edward N. 1995. *Top Heavy: A Study of the Increasing Inequality of Wealth in America.* New York: Twentieth Century Fund Press.

Wolff, Kurt. 1964. "Introduction" In *The Sociology of Georg Simmel,* ed. and trans. Kurt Wolff. 1902. Reprint, New York: Free Press.

Wolfgang, Marvin E. 1973. "Cesare Lombroso." In *Pioneers in Criminology,* ed. Hermann Mannheim. Montclair, N.J.: Patterson Smith.

Wood, Eileen, Charlene Y. Senn, Serge Desmarias, Laura Park, and Norine Verberg. 2002. "Sources of Information About Dating and Their Perceived Influence on Adolescents." *Journal of Adolescent Research* 17, no. 4:401–17.

Woods, Tania. 1998. "Have a Heart: Xenotransplantation, Nonhuman Death, and Human Distress." *Society and Animals* 6:47–65.

Wright, Richard A. "Sample Entry: Sutherland, Edwin H." *Encyclopedia of Criminology.* http://www.fitzroydearborn.com/chicago/criminology/sample-sutherland-edwin.php3 (accessed May 19, 2003).

Wrong, Dennis. 1959. "The Functional Theory of Stratification: Some Neglected Considerations." *American Sociological Review* 24:772–82.

———. 1977. *Population and Society.* New York: Random House.

Yaralian, Pauline S. and Adrian Raine. 2001. "Biological Approaches to Crime: Psychophysiology and Brain Dysfunction." In *Explaining Criminals and Crime,* ed. Raymond Paternoster and Ronet Bachman. Los Angeles: Roxbury.

Young, Aaron R. 2000. "Overcoming Sociological Illiteracy: A Public Policy Challenge for Applied Sociology." *Social Insight: Knowledge at Work* 5:17–21.

Young, Alford A., Jr., and Donald R. Deskins Jr. 2001. "Early Traditions of African-American Sociological Thought." In *Annual Review of Sociology,* vol. 27, ed. Karen S. Cook and John Hagan. Palo Alto, Calif.: Annual Reviews.

Zald, Mayer, and Roberta Ash. 1966. "Social Movement Organization: Growth, Decay, and Change." *Social Forces* 44:327–41.

Zeller, R. A., and E. G. Carmines. 1980. *Measurement in the Social Sciences: The Link between Theory and Data.* Cambridge: Cambridge University Press.

Zimbardo, Philip G. Home page. http://www.zimbardo.com/zimbardo.html (accessed August 1, 2003).

———. 1972. "Pathology of Imprisonment." *Society* 9, no. 3 (April): 4–8.

———. 1973. "A Field Experiment in Auto Shaping." In *Vandalism,* ed. C. Ward. New York: Van Nostrand Reinhold.

———. 2000. "Reflections on the Stanford Prison Experiment: Genesis, Transformations, Consequences." In *Obedience to Authority: Current Perspectives on the Milgram Paradigm,* ed. Thomas Blass. Mahwah, N.J.: Lawrence Erlbaum.

Zola, Irving Kenneth. 1982. *Missing Pieces: A Chronicle of Living with a Disability.* Philadelphia: Temple University Press.

Zukin, Sharon. 1980. "A Decade of the New Urban Research." *Theory and Society* 9:575–601.

———. 1988. *Loft Living: Culture and Capital in Urban Change.* London: Radius.

Zurcher, Louis A. 1967. "Navy Boot Camp: Role Assimilation in a Total Institution." *Sociological Inquiry* 37, no. 1.

Index

Index

Index

Human nature, 57, 61–62, 236
Humphreys, Laud, 212–13
Hussein, Saddam, 141
Hypotheses, 204, 216

I, Mead's theory of, 63–64
Ibn Khaldun, Abu Zaid Abdal Rahman, 4,
  14–15
Id, 65, 75
Ideal culture, 46
Imagination, sociological, 8–9, 16
Immigration, 122, 145, 154, 235
Impression management, 70, 77
Income, 132, 133, 144, 168, 204; global,
  145–46; and stratification in the U.S.,
  134–37
India: castes, 132; sociology in, 10; and
  Hindu cow veneration, 50–51, 54;
  Malthus and, 173; and social movements,
  194
Industrial Revolution, 6, 26, 159
Inequality, 131, 134, 139, 140, 150, 166,
  173; and deviance, 114, 116, 117, 126;
  and feminist theory, 26–27; and global-
  ization, 145–47, 171; and health care,
  30–31; and social conflict theory, 25–26.
  See also Stratification
Inferential statistics, 210–11
Informal organizations, 93
Information technologies. *See* Communica-
  tion and information technologies;
  Internet
In-groups, 84
Innovation, deviance and, 114
Institutional discrimination, 142
Institutional Review Boards (IRBs), 212
Institutions. *See* Social Institutions
Instrumental approach to leadership, 88
Intergenerational mobility, 143
International Sociological Association
  (ISA), 10–11, 150, 175, 176, 233
Internet, 2, 12, 86, 97, 144, 170, 175–76; and
  collective behavior, 182, 184; and com-
  munity, 170–71; and deviance, 122–23;
  and the digital divide, 145; and globaliza-
  tion, 12–13, 98–99; and norms, 52–53;
  and research, 208, 213–14; and sharing
  culture, 52–53; and social change, 12–13,
  194–95; and socialization, 73; and social
  movements, 194–95; and stratification,
  145; and subcultures, 53
Interpretive theory, 15, 28, 69, 74. *See also*
  Symbolic interactionism

Interviews, 36, 70–71, 207, 208
Intragenerational mobility, 143
"Iron cage" of McDonaldization, 97
Iron Law of Oligarchy, 96, 102
Isolation, social, 61, 192

Jackson, Rev. Jesse, 8
Janis, Irving, 91–92
Japan, 159, 175; business etiquette of, 52;
  sociology in, 10

Kanter, Rosabeth Moss, 7, 98, 101–2, 144
Kenen, Regina, 70
Kennedy, John F., 92, 100, 146, 183
King, Martin Luther, Jr., 8, 148, 185, 189
King, Rodney, 185
Kohlberg, Lawrence, 65
Korean War, 124
Kozol, Jonathan, 144
Kuhn, Thomas, 21

Labeling theory, 27, 118–19, 123
Language, 27, 42, 48–49, 56, 64, 65, 66; and
  gender, 46–47, and globalization, 52;
  military use of, 47
Latent functions, 24, 25, 35
Latinos/Latinas. *See* Hispanics
Lawson, Helene, 66
Lazarsfeld, Paul Felix, 209, 218–19
Leadership, 88, 96, 144, 186, 191, 192;
  types of, 88
Le Bon, Gustave, 186, 196–97
Legitimate power, 89, 101
Lemert, Charles, 118, 131
"Letter of Recognition" in sociology, 223
Levittown, 167–68
Lewin, Kurt, 87, 102
Lieberson, Stanley, 180–81, 197
Life-history analysis, 78, 128
Linguistic-relativity hypothesis, 48
Literary Digest, The, 207
Lombroso, Cesare, 111–12, 117, 125–26
Looking-glass self, 62–63, 74
Lost letter technique, 210, 214
Luhmann, Niklas, 25, 33–34
Lynching, 6, 18, 185

MacAndrew, Craig, 62
Macro-level paradigms, 22, 137, 143. *See
  also* Structural-functionalism; Social-
  conflict perspective
Malthus, Thomas Robert, 10, 158–59, 173
Manifest functions, 24, 25, 35

Index

Index

Socialization, 61, 141; of adults, 67–69; anticipatory, 36, 38; and deviance, 121; families and, 66; and gender roles, 66, 67; and globalization, 72–73; and the Internet, 73; and mass media, 67; process of, 66–68; re-socialization, 68–69; in schools, 66–67, 73; total institutions and 68, 69; theories of, 61–66; and workplace, 67–68;

Social mobility, 133, 143–45, 198, 217; types of, 143–44

Social movement industries, 193

Social movement organizations, 192

Social movements, 179, 185, 188–94; decline of, 191; formation of, 188–89; and globalization, 194; and the Internet, 194–95; new, 193–94; theories of, 192–94; types of, 189–91

Social networks. *See* Networks

Social processes, 2, 3, 199

Social sciences: focus of sociology compared with other, 11; sociology as, 3; sociology salaries compared with other, 231–33; women in sociology compared with other, 226–27

Social stratification. *See* Stratification

Social structure, 2, 6, 9, 11, 25, 44, 120, 131, 142, 143–45

Society, 3, 41, 43, 138–39, 204; and globalization, 43; and social change, 179; types of, 132–34

Society for Applied Sociology (SAS), 228, 233

Sociobiology, 51, 57, 112

Socioeconomic status (SES), 141

Sociological imagination, 8–9, 16, 198, 224

Sociological practice, 229. *See also* Applied sociology; Clinical sociology

Sociological Practice Association (SPA), 230, 233

Sociologists, 2; and academic training, 223–24, 225; famous, 8; job skills, 228; Nobel Prize winning, 8, 236; salaries of, 231–33; status of, 140. *See also* Careers in sociology

Sociologists for Women in Society (SWS), 233

Sociology, 1; as academic discipline, 9–11, 217; benefits of perspective, 2–4, 14; careers in, 7–8; college and university programs, 223–24; and common sense, 4; compared with other social sciences, 11;

in high schools, 10, 223, 231; history of, 4–7, 162, 164–65; minorities in, 7, 226–27; popularity of studying, 224–25; and professional organizations, 10–11, 233–35; and student characteristics, 225–27; and textbook content, 44, 142; women in, 7, 225–26, 227. *See also* Applied sociology; Clinical sociology; Sociological Practice

Socio-spatial model, 167

Solidarity: mechanical, 169; organic, 169

Sorokin, Pitirim A., 37, 100, 198

Southern Christian Leadership Conference (SCLC), 192

Space shuttle, 92

Speciesism, 143

Spencer, Herbert, 11, 23, 37

Spurious relationships, 204

Stages of group development, 87

Stages of socialization, Mead's, 64

Stanford Prison Experiment, 92–93, 104, 211

Statistics: descriptive, 210; inferential, 210–11

Status, 44, 119, 139, 140, 141, 144, 191; types of, 44–45

Status set, 44

Steele, Stephen F., 237

Stereotypes, 4, 62, 67, 117, 126, 142

Stigmas, 119

Sting, The, 128

Stonewall Riots, 185

Storming stage of group development, 87

Stratification, 131, 198; forms of, 132–34; and gender, 137, 138, 142, 147; and globalization, 145–47; and the Internet, 145; maintenance of, 141–43; and multidimensional perspective, 140–41; and poverty, 134–38; and social-conflict perspective, 139–40; and social mobility, 143–45; sources of, 137–41; structural-functionalist perspective, 137–39, 147; in the U.S., 134–37, 138

Straus, Roger Austin, 237

Street Corner Society, William Foote Whyte, 208, 239

Structural functionalism, 23–25, 29, 100–101, 196; and deviance, 112–16, and health care, 30; and stratification, 137–39

Structural mobility, 143–44

Structural strain theory, 114, 115, 187

Structuration, 14

Index

About the Author

KATHY S. STOLLEY is an applied sociologist, managing an electronic meeting facility, providing advisory, consulting, and facilitation services on organizational processes and issues in a multinational organization. In addition, she is an online Adjunct Professor for Anne Arundel Community College. She is also the editor of the journal *Social Insight: Knowledge at Work.*